M000031468

Hellenic Studies 48

THE MASTER OF SIGNS

Recent Titles in the
Hellenic Studies Series

Archilochos Heros: The Cult of Poets in the Greek Polis
Master of the Game: Competition and Performance in Greek Poetry
Yearning for the Infinite: Desire and Possession in Three Platonic Dialogues
Black Doves Speak: Herodotus and the Languages of Barbarians
Amphoteroglōssia: A Poetics of the Twelfth-Century Medieval Greek Novel
Victim of the Muses: Poet as Scapegoat, Warrior and Hero
Pointing at the Past: From Formula to Performance in Homeric Poetics
The Life and Miracles of Thekla: A Literary Study
Homeric Conversation
The Culture of Kitharoidia
The Power of Thetis and Selected Essays
Comparative Anthropology of Ancient Greece
Poetic and Performative Memory in Ancient Greece
Weaving Truth: Essays on Language and the Female in Greek Thought
Ritual and Performativity: The Chorus in Old Comedy
The Epic City: Urbanism, Utopia, and the Garden in Ancient Greece and Rome
Plato's Symposium: Issues in Interpretation and Reception
Paradise Earned: The Bacchic-Orphic Gold Lamellae of Crete
Concordia Discors: Eros and Dialogue in Classical Athenian Literature
King of Sacrifice: Ritual and Royal Authority in the Iliad
The Feast of Poetry: Sacrifice and Performance in Aristophanic Comedy
C. P. Cavafy, *The Canon: The Original One Hundred and Fifty-Four Poems*
Sappho in the Making: The Early Reception
The Oral Palimpsest: Exploring Intertextuality in the Homeric Epics
Practitioners of the Divine: Greek Priests and Religious Officials from Homer to Heliodorus
Zeus in the Odyssey
The Politics of Ethnicity and the Crisis of the Peloponnesian League
Genos Dikanikon: Amateur and Professional Speech in the Courtrooms of Classical Athens
Fragments of Sappho: A Commentary
Recapturing a Homeric Legacy: Images and Insights from the Venetus A Manuscript of the Iliad
Homer the Classic
Hippota Nestor
The New Sappho on Old Age: Textual And Philosophical Issues
Pindar's Verbal Art: An Ethnographic Study of Epinician Style

THE MASTER OF SIGNS

Signs and the Interpretation of Signs in Herodotus' Histories

Alexander Hollmann

CENTER FOR HELLENIC STUDIES
Trustees for Harvard University
Washington, DC
Distributed by Harvard University Press
Cambridge, Massachusetts, and London, England
2011

The Master of Signs: Signs and the Interpretation of Signs in Herodotus' *Histories*
By Alexander Hollman
Copyright © 2011 Center for Hellenic Studies, Trustees for Harvard University
All Rights Reserved.
Published by Center for Hellenic Studies, Trustees for Harvard University, Washington, D.C.
Distributed by Harvard University Press, Cambridge, Massachusetts and London, England

EDITORIAL TEAM
Senior Advisers: W. Robert Connor, Gloria Ferrari Pinney, Albert Henrichs, James O'Donnell, Bernd Seidensticker
Editorial Board: Gregory Nagy (Editor-in-Chief), Christopher Blackwell, Casey Dué (Executive Editor), Mary Ebbott (Executive Editor), Scott Johnson, Olga Levaniouk, Anne Mahoney, Leonard Muellner
Production Manager for Publications: Jill Curry Robbins
Web Producer: Mark Tomasko
Cover Design: Joni Godlove
Production: Kerri Cox Sullivan

Chapter 3.1 was originally published as "The Manipulation of Signs in Herodotos' *Histories*," *Transactions of the American Philological Association* 135:2 (2005), pp. 279–327.
Copyright © 2005 American Philological Association. Reprinted with permission by The Johns Hopkins University Press.

LIBRARY OF CONGRESS CATALOGING-IN-PUBLICATION DATA

Hollmann, Alexander.
The master of signs : signs and the interpretation of signs in Herodotus' Histories / by Alexander Hollmann.
p. cm. — (Hellenic studies ; 48)
Includes bibliographical references and indexes.
ISBN 978-0-674-05588-9 (alk. paper)
1. Herodotus. History. 2. Symbolism in literature. I. Title.
PA4004.H56 2010
938'.03—dc22 2010045794

D · M
MUHAE
OPTIMAE · FELIVM

Contents

Acknowledgments

THIS BOOK STARTED LIFE AS A PH.D. DISSERTATION, the writing of which I completed largely while seated on a couch with an implacably immobile cat on my lap. These lengthy periods of enforced motionlessness greatly helped concentrate my mind on the text of Herodotus, and I have dedicated this book to her *manes* in gratitude for her good humor and company during those years.

A dissertation completion fellowship from the Whiting Foundation made the couch-sitting possible in the first place and greatly accelerated the dissertation's progress.

I thank my readers, Albert Henrichs, Greg Nagy, and Christopher Jones, for their regular and generous feedback during the process of writing. Now, as a supervisor of students myself, I am in a position to appreciate just how much attention and time they gave to me.

Albert Henrichs' infectious enthusiasm, his encyclopedic knowledge of the Greeks and their religion, and his ability to find interest and excitement in even the smallest scrap of Greek text were a constant inspiration to me and it was somehow fitting that I chose to write on an equally charming and wide-ranging ancient author.

As will be clear from my footnotes, Greg Nagy's teaching and writing were fundamental in drawing my attention to the language of signs in Greek literature, and it is quite true to say that my book (and indeed its title) would have been unthinkable without his work. I thank him also for his support and encouragement over many years and through difficult times.

Sumi Furiya, Judson Herrman, Andrew Nicolaysen, and Fred Porta, fellow members of Albert Henrichs' *eranos* of dissertators, formed the first audience for some of my ideas and their reactions and questions helped me to formulate them more clearly.

Kathleen Coleman read an early draft of the manuscript with great attention and saved me from numerous imprecise expressions and infelicities of style. Those that remain are my responsibility alone.

My time at the Center for Hellenic Studies (2004–2005), though spent largely on a different project, provided me with a wonderful library and an idyllic setting to work further on this book, and the opportunity to interact with other scholars.

At the University of Washington a term's leave for Junior Faculty Development gave me valuable time for updating and completion of the manuscript. I am grateful to my senior colleagues in the Department of Classics and to chairs Jim Clauss and Alain Gowing for their encouragement and for helping me balance teaching and research while protecting me from excessive administrative responsibility.

I benefited greatly from the comments of Rosaria Munson, who read an earlier version of my manuscript and whose work on Herodotus has influenced mine.

The editorial and production staff at the Center of Hellenic Studies made the process of formatting the manuscript and transforming it into print much more painless than it otherwise might have been. I am particularly thankful to Jill Curry Robbins for her efficiency and helpfulness in this regard and Joni Godlove for her vibrant cover design using my pen-and-ink drawing.

Chapter 3.1 was previously published as "The Manipulation of Signs in Herodotus' *Histories*" in *Transactions of the American Philological Association* 135.2 (2005) and appears here with permission from Johns Hopkins University Press.

Finally, I would like to express my deep gratitude to my fellow scholar, colleague, and wife, Olga Levaniouk, for her advice on points both small and big and most of all for her love and support at every stage of this journey.

Introduction

THIS WORK IS AN INVESTIGATION OF SIGNS, their interpretation, and the use to which they are put in the *Histories* of Herodotus. The collocation 'signs' and 'Herodotus' is most likely to suggest the bizarre portents, riddling oracles, and striking dreams which make an impression on every reader of the *Histories*. Yet there are other types of signs and sign systems at play in the work to which Herodotus draws our attention: human speech as a coded system able to manipulate and be manipulated; visual signs in the form of objects, gifts, artifacts, writing, markings, even the human body, all capable of being invested with meaning; human actions, gestures, and ritual also form a system of signs that, as Herodotus shows, need decoding and whose meaning is conventionally and culturally determined.

Some of these sign systems have received scholarly attention *separatim*. Herodotean dreams and oracles each have a monograph devoted to them. Recent works on religion in the *Histories* (Harrison 2000, Mikalson 2003) have again spurred interest in these areas.[1] Lateiner's article on non-verbal communication in the *Histories* has made a fundamental contribution to the field and already proceeds on a theoretical model in which the function of the sign is recognized and instances of non-verbal communication are seen in terms of a signifier residing in an action, gesture, non-verbal sound, or object which corresponds to a signified.[2] Dewald's study of significant objects in Herodotus is likewise an important contribution, and is also based on an appreciation of the semiotic role that such objects play in the *Histories* as a means of communication both between figures in the work and between author and audience.[3] More recently, the work of Munson has drawn attention to the ainetic mode in Herodotus (Munson 2001a) and also to Herodotus as interpreter and provider of glosses (Munson 2005). Other scholars have played a no-less-

1 Dreams: Frisch 1968. Oracles: Crahay 1956, Kirchberg 1965.

2 Lateiner 1987.

3 Dewald 1993.

important role in drawing attention in a more general fashion to the semiotic in Herodotus. Benardete, writing in the late sixties, when semiotics as a discipline was coming into its own, was perhaps the first to apply terms drawn from this field to the work of Herodotus and to pose questions using this framework.[4] Hartog and Nagy have been sensitive to this approach, calling attention, for example, to Herodotus as transmitter and decoder of signs.[5] Nagy's picture of Herodotus as a "master of speech," corresponding to his vision of Pindar as "master of song," one who perpetuates the *kleos* of the figures in his work while also dispensing praise and blame, has had the most profound effect on my work here, together with his exploration of *sêma* and *noêsis* (1990a), and its influence is seen on many of the following pages. Lastly, Thomas' (2000) treatment of Herodotus in the context of fifth-century scientific, medical, and philosophical writing has explored such terms as *marturion* and *tekmêrion* as well as the use of proofs and reasoning by signs.

There still exists, however, no overall examination of signs and the process of signification and interpretation in the *Histories* as well as the use to which sign interpreters (including Herodotus) put their interpretations. It is therefore part of the aim of this project to consider both together and separately the various sign systems present in the *Histories*. I also investigate the terminology used by Herodotus to describe the transmission, reception, and decoding of signs, and argue that he had at his disposal an array of terms with which to describe the semiotic activities of the figures in his work and his own activities as transmitter and interpreter of signs. This is not to make of Herodotus a semiotician *avant la lettre*: one cannot speak of him as a theoretician, or point to a passage where he elaborates on the nature and function of the sign. He is, however, what I would call a master of signs, asserting his control over the transmission of them and calling attention to his skill (σοφίη) at interpreting them, which he demonstrates in his own right and at the hand of those figures in his work who distinguish themselves in this respect. It is in the identification of this persona and the demonstration of its connection with the realm of signs that the other aim of this book lies.

Before I sketch an outline of my investigation, a few words about the methodological approach I have followed. It goes without saying that a book on signs and signification must make use of the terminology of semiotics. I have, however, drawn only on those basic distinctions and terms which I have found useful, and will explain them here. Firstly, the concept of the sign.

4 Benardete 1969.

5 Hartog 1988; Nagy 1990b.

The model of the sign I have used is a triadic one, made up of *signifier* or *sign vehicle* (e.g. a word, object, gesture), *signified* (the meaning or sense conveyed by this word, object, or gesture), and *referent* (what the signifier ultimately refers to).[6] The signifier and signified make up a unit together, which may be termed the sign, but by common convention "sign" is also used of the signifier or sign vehicle alone. What constitutes a sign? The definition I have used is a broad one: anything, whether object, sound, action, or event, which is capable of standing for something in some respect.[7] Signs (that is to say, signifiers), provided they are recognized as such, may be drawn from any quarter, as is demonstrated by the agreement of the seven Persian conspirators that a horse's whinny will act as a sign indicating which of them is to be king (3.84.3).[8] Anything can be a sign; however, as Peirce puts it, "Nothing is a sign unless it is interpreted as a sign."[9]

Such signs are conventional signs, signs whose meanings are determined according to a code agreed upon explicitly or implicitly. There exists a further group of signs, the category of so-called natural signs. These are signs that are not produced for the purpose of communication but that are nevertheless interpreted as having meaning by the interpreter. Such signs are used as proof or evidence of something, a μαρτύριον or τεκμήριον, to employ the terms used by Herodotus himself. Thus a piece of land given by the people of Kroton to Kallias the *mantis* and the *absence* of land given to Dorieus, the exiled Spartan king, act as μαρτύρια for the Crotoniates that the only foreign help they received in their war against Sybaris was from Kallias (5.45.2).[10]

6 Thus, for example, in one oracle given to the Athenians, they are told to call upon their brother-in-law for help (7.189.1). The *signifier* here is the word 'brother-in-law', what is *signified* by this arrangement of phonemes is 'brother of one's sister', but the task faced by the Athenians is to find out the *referent*, namely which brother-in-law is meant. The terms *signifier* and *signified* go back to Saussure's distinction between *signifiant* and *signifié* (Saussure 1983), which resembles the Stoic distinction between τὸ σημαῖνον and τὸ σημαινόμενον (Sextus Empiricus *Adversus Mathematicos* 8.11–12); on ancient theories of the sign, see Manetti 1993. The notion of the triad is not Saussure's however: on this, see Nöth 1990:89–91. Artayktes and the οἶκος of Protesilaos (9.116.3) are discussed in ch. 3.1.2.6 below.

7 Nöth 1990:81, following Peirce and Morris: "Every object, event, or behavior is thus a potential sign. Even silence can have the semiotic function of a zero sign. . . . Everything can thus be perceived as a natural sign of something else, and by prior agreement between a sender and a receiver, every object can also serve as a conventional sign. This does not mean that every phenomenon of the world is semiotic. It only means that under conditions of semiosis every object can become a sign to a given interpreter."

8 See ch. 2.1.4 and 3.1.3.3.

9 As quoted in Nöth 1990:42.

10 An example of the *modus tollens* (If *p*, then *q*, but if not-*q*, then not-*p*). See Manetti 1993:41. The Stoics also referred to such signs as σημεῖα, but as will be seen in ch. 1.1, Herodotus never uses σημήιον in this sense, only τεκμήριον and μαρτύριον.

So much for the sign itself. Next let us consider the process of communication using signs. Here we will make use of the terms "encode," "decode," "message," and "code" following the model suggested by Jakobson, as shown in Figure 1:[11]

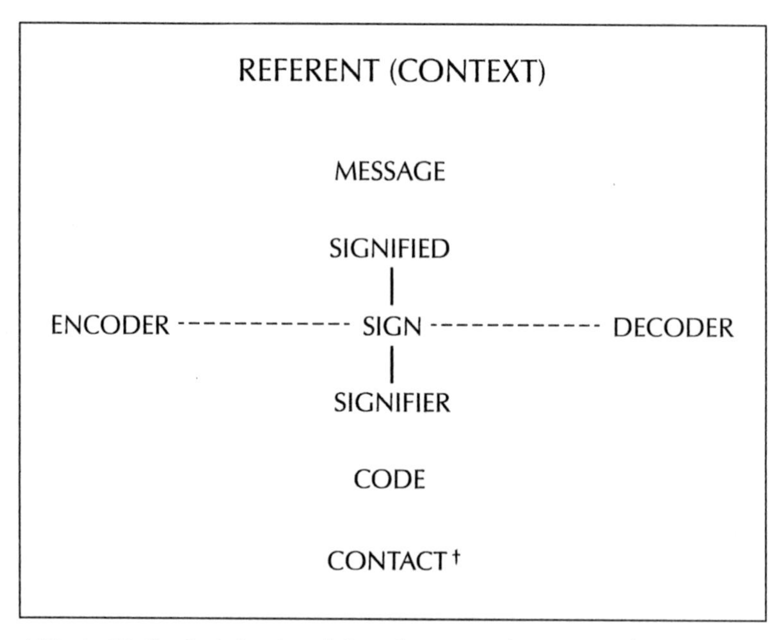

† "Contact" is the physical and psychological connection between encoder and decoder along which information about the channel of communication and keeping it open can be passed ("phatic function").

Figure 1. Process of Communication Using Signs

According to this model, the sender encodes the message he wishes to send in terms of a code, which he then transmits. The recipient receives the coded communication, consisting of a sign or signs, and decodes them in terms of the code used to encode them, so that each signifier receives a signified and the total message emerges. As will be shown in this book, there is potential for confusion at every stage of this process: in particular, much depends on firstly recognizing that a communication is in a coded form, and then determining the nature of this code.

Let us turn from questions of method to the structure of the book, which is divided into three parts. Part I examines the vocabulary used by Herodotus

11 Jakobson 1962.

in connection with signs and the process of signification outlined above, and shows that it is more extensive than has perhaps been previously realized. Part II is an investigation into the various sign systems found in the *Histories*: portents, dreams, oracles, *mantikê* in general, the *ainos*, names and naming, action, gesture, and ritual objects as signs. Here too it has been my concern to show Herodotus' use of the vocabulary discussed in Part I and to demonstrate more clearly the semiotic aspects involved in these categories. Part III looks at the people who decode and manipulate signs, beginning with the manipulators. I suggest Herodotus' affinity to these figures and demonstrate his personal involvement in the processes he describes. In conclusion I show that he projects a clearly observable narrative persona, which I have labeled the "master of signs," and that the features of this persona overlap substantially with what are considered to be the distinctive features of his work. While clothed in language found in fifth-century scientific and medical writing, at the core of this figure is the archaic *sophos*, who through his mastery of signs investigates, interprets, praises, blames, and warns.

Part 1

The Vocabulary of Signs, Their Transmission, Reception, and Interpretation

1.1 The Sign

HERODOTUS HAS FEW WORDS TO CONVEY THE GENERAL CONCEPT OF A SIGN.[1] These do not occur as frequently as verbal forms based on some of the same stems. Thus there are only nine instances of the noun σημήιον ('sign, device on shield'), for example, but some seventy instances of the verbal form of the same stem, σημαίνω ('send or convey a sign, indicate'), or two instances of σύμβολον ('token'), as compared to twenty-seven of the verb συμβάλλεσθαι in the sense of 'interpret a sign'.

1.1.1 σημήιον

To begin with the stem σημ-, the source of our terms 'semiotics' and 'semantics', the noun σημήιον comes perhaps closest to our general term 'sign'. Herodotus uses it of signs that the gods send mortals, portents (6.27.1, 3: see ch. 2.1 below), but it may also refer to the design on a shield (1.171.4) or on a ship (8.92.2), particular markings on an animal (the Apis bull: 2.38.2, 3.28.3), or something used as a marker (horn of cattle as gravemarker: 2.41.4), as well as signs in the sense of signals used in a military context (7.128.2, 9.59.2).[2] It is never, however, used of the linguistic sign.

The term σῆμα, familiar to audiences of Homer in all the senses of σημήιον just listed, and, additionally, in the important sense of 'tomb' or 'tomb-marker', is found in Herodotus, but only in this latter sense of a grave. In the fifth-century prose of Herodotus all its other meanings are subsumed by

1 There are of course other words in Herodotus' work which refer to particular types of sign or sign systems. Thus the vocabulary of portents includes τέρας, ὄρνις, and οἰωνός, that of dreams ὄνειρος, ὄψις, ἐνύπνιον, that of oracular signs μαντήιον, χρησμός, and χρηστήριον: see chapters 2.1, 2.2, and 2.3 below. For the moment, however, we are only concerned with general words for the concept of a sign.

2 Also used in the meaning of a device or design is ἐπίσημον: 1.195.2 (on top of a staff); 8.88.2 (on a ship); 9.74.2 (on a shield).

the form σημήιον. The play between the general sense of 'sign' and the more specific one of 'tomb', which Nagy, for example, has pointed out in the Homeric poems, is thus mostly absent from Herodotus' work, although Benardete has argued for its presence in Herodotus' description of the Nasamones, a Libyan tribe (4.172.3) who obtain oracles (μαντεύονται) by sleeping on the tombs (σήματα) of their ancestors, that is to say, the tombs become the source of σήματα, signs.[3]

Herodotus never uses σημήιον in the sense of a proof in an argument, a meaning found, for example, in Thucydides.[4] This meaning is, however, to be found in the terms τεκμήριον and μαρτύριον, which are discussed below in this chapter (ch. 1.1.3, 1.1.4).

1.1.2 σύμβολον, συμβόλαιον

Another productive root for the vocabulary of signs in Herodotus is a deverbative of συμβάλλω, which yields both σύμβολον and συμβόλαιον, familiar to us in English as 'symbol'.[5] But the instances of these nouns are even fewer in number than those of σημήιον: σύμβολον occurs twice in the same passage, while συμβόλαιον appears only once. At 6.86.α.5 and β.1, σύμβολα (a *plurale tantum* in Herodotus) are quite literally things put together, a token consisting of a set of objects, the combination of which produces a sign indicating that the bearers stand in a certain relationship to each other with certain rights and duties.[6] The name of the sign can also be connected with the process that

3 For the double meaning of σῆμα in Homer, see Nagy 1990a:202–222, who sees a tomb/sign connection in the portent of the preserved fish that come to life in the presence of Artayktes: cf. discussion below and references in ch. 3.1.3.3. On the Nasamones and their σήματα, see Benardete 1969:126. The passage is discussed in ch. 2.4 below.

4 Thucydides 1.6.2; 1.10.1; 1.21.1; 1.132.1; 2.41.4; 2.42.1; 4.120.3. Cf. Thomas 2000:191–192: "Another common word for evidence, or signs from which you can infer, is *semeion*, which takes on the technical meaning of 'symptom' in medical works. But Herodotus retains its primary meaning of 'mark, sign'." According to Fowler 1996, σημεῖον appears only once in the authors he lists as contemporaries or predecessors of Herodotus (62–69), in a fragment of Herodoros (FGH 31 F 22a). Further discussion in ch. 3.2.2 below.

5 See Struck 2004 and Müri 1976 for the history and evolution of this term.

6 On the *sumbolon* as token marking the bearer as subject to the duties and privileges of guest-friendship, cf. Müri 1976:2–7. On the plural form, see Müri 1976:15, who explains it as referring to the agreement itself resulting from the creation of the markers, and compares the plural usage in the terms σπονδαί, ὅρκια, ὅρκοι, δεξιαί. See Struck 2004; Steiner 1994:30–31; and Müri 1976 on the general concept and for literary examples. Struck (77–110), following Müri, argues that in the fifth and fourth centuries BCE *sumbolon* is confined to this narrower meaning of 'contract marker', with additional specialized senses in Pythagoreanism, the mysteries, and divination, and only takes on broader and more expanded meanings beginning in the third century.

interprets it: the physical putting together of the pieces produces a mental 'putting together' in the minds of those holding the pieces, as well as reflecting the actual coming together or agreement of the two parties.[7] In the passage cited above, the Spartan Glaukos is entrusted with a deposit by a wealthy Milesian and a set of σύμβολα created to control access to this money. He is to present the money to any man who can show the other half of these σύμβολα, but when the sons of the man eventually do so, Glaukos claims that he has no memory (οὔτε μέμνημαι τὸ πρῆγμα, 6.86.β.2) of having accepted the money, and, consequently, that he does not know what they are talking about.[8]

The related term συμβόλαιον is used once, at 5.92.η.3, in a context involving the transmission of signs, or, more accurately, the refusal to transmit signs.[9] Unlike the *sumbola* of Glaukos, the *sumbolaion* in this passage is not a physical token, but rather consists of a coded utterance. Periandros consults his dead wife Melissa at the Thesprotian *nekuomantêion* in order to find the location of some hidden money (παρακαταθήκης πέρι).[10] Melissa refuses to make an oracular pronouncement (note Herodotus' use of the verb σημαίνω, for which see below, ch. 1.2.1). She does however give an indication (μαρτύριον) that it really is her ghost and that the message is authentic by means of a sign, which Herodotus refers to later as a συμβόλαιον:

> μαρτύριον δέ οἱ εἶναι ὡς ἀληθέα ταῦτα λέγει, ὅτι ἐπὶ ψυχρὸν τὸν ἰπνὸν Περίανδρος τοὺς ἄρτους ἐπέβαλε. ταῦτα δὲ ὡς ὀπίσω ἀπηγγέλθη τῷ Περιάνδρῳ (πιστὸν γάρ οἱ ἦν τὸ συμβόλαιον, ὃς νεκρῷ ἐούσῃ Μελίσσῃ ἐμίγη), ἰθέως δὴ μετὰ τὴν ἀγγελίην κήρυγμα ἐποιήσατο ἐς τὸ Ἥραιον ἐξιέναι πάσας τὰς Κορινθίων γυναῖκας.
>
> (5.92.η.2–3)

7 See Müri 1976:14, who shows that the neuter form is a *nomen rei qua agitur*: "Sumbolon muss dann sein: das konkrete Ding, an dem die Vereinbarung sich auswirkt und sichtbar wird. In ihm stellt sich das Vertagsverhältnis dar." See also Struck 2004:90–94 for the idea that *sumbolon* is also connected with *sumballein* in the sense of meeting, bumping into someone or something. He cites for example [Aeschylus] *Prometheus Bound* 487, Aeschylus *Suppliants* 502, *Homeric Hymn to Hermes* 30, where *sumbolos* and *sumbolon* have the sense of 'ominous chance meeting'.

8 The link between understanding, or the ability to decode, a sign and memory may be seen in 3.51.1, discussed below in ch. 1.3.2.

9 The word chiefly occurs in the meaning of 'an arrangement, transaction' (e.g. Hesychius s.v. and see Müri 1976:14 n.11: "Für den kaufmännischen Verkehr ist in Attika *sumballein* terminus technicus, das Substanstiv dazu heisst *to sumbolaion*"), but here as at Euripides *Ion* 411 seems to have the meaning of a 'sign or token'.

10 The set-up of this story is thus similar to the Glaukos episode, where a deposit of money (παραθήκη, 6.86.β.1) is also at issue. Both stories are told by narrators other than Herodotus, and in both contexts the speaker is attempting to persuade his audience of a particular point: here Sokles the Corinthian tries to convince the Spartans of the evils of tyranny.

> As a *marturion* for him that this was true, she said that Periandros had put his loaves into the oven when it was cold. When this was reported back to Periandros (the token [*sumbolaion*] was a trustworthy one to him, since he had had intercourse with Melissa when she was dead), he put out a proclamation immediately after this message that all the wives of the Corinthians should go to the temple of Hera.

Melissa's reply that Periandros put his loaves into the oven when it was cold is a coded message, directed solely to the recipient, who is the only one in a position to decode it, thus making it absolutely genuine, πιστόν.[11] He fits together signifier and signified, the words of Melissa and the real message they carry, just as one fits together the two halves of a material token (σύμβολον).[12] Herodotus tells us only that Periandros finds the συμβόλαιον true or reliable, "since he slept with her when she was dead." He makes us follow the same process of decoding and reading that Periandros has gone through: the cold oven is the dead body of Melissa, the loaves the seed of Periandros.[13] Since Melissa and the oven are cold, neither the seed nor the loaves will grow or rise. The interpretation of this sign lies in seeing the metaphorical relationship between the sign elements which make up the συμβόλαιον and the events of the past.[14] It is one of several examples in the *Histories* where the audience is left to complete an interpretation suggested by Herodotus.[15]

[11] The self-concealing and self-directing nature of the cryptic utterance is thus like the *ainos*, for which see below, ch. 2.5. It also functions like the *sumbolon* in the sense of the mystic password among initiates which identifies them to each other but which also represents special knowledge gained through initiation into the mysteries. On this sense of the *sumbolon*, see Müri 1976:37–44; Struck 2004:104–107; and Levaniouk 2007.

[12] As an example of a σύμβολον which consists of the signs of language rather than signs residing in a physical object, Steiner 1994:31 cites Plato *Epistles* 13 (to Dionysios of Syracuse), which begins with what he says will be a σύμβολον of the fact the letter is from him, an anecdote which is known both to himself and Dionysios (360a).

[13] For a different kind of oven also used metaphorically in an oracular context, see the oracle given to Arkesilaos at 4.163.3, discussed in ch. 2.3 below. Cf. Pellizer 1993 for an analysis of the narrative structure of the story using the approach of Greimas.

[14] For metaphorical relationships between signifier and signified, cf. e.g. 1.78.1–3 (discussed in ch. 2.1.6), 4.163.3 (discussed in ch. 2.3.3), 4.132.2–3 (discussed in ch. 2.8.2).

[15] Cf., for example, 4.79.1–2 and 7.57.2 as discussed in ch. 2.1.6 on portents; 3.58.2 as discussed in ch. 2.3.3 on oracles.

1.1.3 τεκμήριον

This is glossed by Powell in his lexicon as 'piece of evidence', and while it is the case that Herodotus does use the word to refer to something that serves to establish an argument, or make an assertion more persuasive, there is often an additional dimension to the word, which is better captured by LSJ, where it is defined as 'a sure sign or token'.[16] All instances of the noun (and three out of the five instances of the denominative τεκμαίρομαι) are used exclusively by Herodotus himself in the first person, and for this reason are of special interest for what they reveal of his cognitive process and use of signs.[17] Especially interesting is the connection between τεκμήρια and signs: as mentioned above, the words τεκμήριον and μαρτύριον in Herodotus often appear in the sense of the earlier σῆμα and later σημεῖον in the meaning of a proof residing in a sign.[18]

To take an example from the last book of the work, Herodotus speaks of the role of the divine (τὰ θεῖα) at the Battle of Mykale (9.100.2).[19] On the basis of many τεκμήρια, but two in particular, he infers that the divine played a role: δῆλα δὴ πολλοῖσι τεκμηρίοισί ἐστι τὰ θεῖα τῶν πραγμάτων.[20] The first

16 LSJ s.v. τεκμήριον (I.1), citing Herodotus 2.13 and 9.100. Cf. Thomas 2000:191: "*Tekmeria* ... one may wish to translate as 'proof' in the sense of decisive evidence which, given the limits of the evidence, can lead to a conclusion. For Aristotle later, it denoted conclusive proof that is formally valid, a philosophically rigorous formulation which would be inappropriate and anachronistic at this earlier stage. Sometimes in Herodotus (as well as other fifth-century writers) we would prefer to translate it as 'evidence'—and a similar blurring is visible in English usage, when one says 'I have evidence' in such as way as to mean 'I have proof, I have evidence which is decisive'. But it usually implies in the *Histories* more than simply evidence, something closer to probative evidence (or even 'argument')."

17 Characteristically construed with the first person singular of the personal pronoun in the dative: τεκμήριον δέ μοι τόδε. Instances: 2.13.1; 2.43.2; 2.58; 2.104.4; 3.38.2 (here without μοι); 7.238.2; 9.100.2 (without μοι).

18 The two stems *sêm-* and *tekmr-*, while of course quite distinct in origin, do overlap in meaning in the sense that both refer to a mark of some kind (cf. Herodotus' parallel use of the adjectives ἄσημος and ἀτέκμαρτος, discussed below). σῆμα in the Homeric corpus can be used in the sense that Herodotus uses τεκμήριον, namely of a proof in the form of a sign, e.g. when Odysseus proves his identity to Eumaios and a herdsman by revealing his scar to them as a σῆμα ἀριφραδές (*Odyssey* 21.217–220). On this meaning of σῆμα in Homer, see Nagy 1990a:203–207. In later authors, σημεῖον can bear this meaning: see note above under σημήιον, 1.1.1. For τεκμήριον and other forms of this root in Herodotus' predecessors and contemporaries, see ch. 3.2.2 below and Thomas 2000 and Fowler 1996.

19 On portents and the divine, see ch. 2.1 below.

20 Herodotus uses the expression "many *tekmêria*" in several other places in the work (2.43.2, 3.38.2, 7.238.2) invariably in a self-confident and even polemical tone. The expression τεκμήριον καὶ τόδε (2.13.1, 2.104.4) also implies the existence of further *tekmêria* that the author could mention. As Thomas points out (2000:192, 199), one sometimes wonders what these many other *tekmêria* on which he never chooses to elaborate are. For the polemical tone and a comparison with other writers, see ch. 3.2.2 below.

is a φήμη, a mysterious report that seems to "fly in" from nowhere (ἐσέπτατο, 9.100.1; on the same phenomenon cf. ἡ κληδὼν αὕτη ἐσέπτατο, 9.101.3), to the effect that the Greek allies have been victorious that day at Plataiai (9.101.2).[21] This immediately heartens the soldiers, so that they fight more keenly. The second is the appearance of a herald's staff (κηρυκήιον, 9.100.1), found lying on the beach, which Herodotus never elaborates on, but which he obviously takes to be an indication of supernatural activity.[22] Both of these phenomena are signs, the one auditory, the other visual, a sign-bearing object: thus here Herodotus' τεκμήρια are precisely indicatory signs interpreted and marshaled as evidence.

Consider also the famous anthropological experiment of Dareios at 3.38, by which he determines that the Greeks, who burn their dead, are just as disgusted at the idea of eating them as the Indians, who eat their dead fathers, are at the idea of burning their bodies. The different readings of human behavior and ritual act as a τεκμήριον for Herodotus' proposition that νόμος is relative and that each man prefers his own νόμοι:

> ὡς δὲ οὕτω νενομίκασι τὰ περὶ τοὺς νόμους οἱ πάντες ἄνθρωποι, πολλοῖσί τε καὶ ἄλλοισι τεκμηρίοισι πάρεστι σταθμῶσθαι, ἐν δὲ δὴ καὶ τόδε . . .
>
> 3.38.1
>
> That all men have this custom concerning their practices may be measured by many *tekmêria*, and in particular by the following . . .

Human behavior and ritual, νόμοι, are signs with accompanying codes that may be read and interpreted, and nowhere is this made clearer than here.[23]

[21] Other instances of κληδών at 5.72.4 (priestess of Athene on the Athenian akropolis tells Kleomenes to leave the sanctuary because he is a Dorian) and 9.91.1. *Nomen est omen*: the name of a Samian envoy, Hegesistratos, is accepted by the Spartan commander Leotykhides as a good omen for the forthcoming battle at Mykale. See further ch. 2.1 on portents and ch. 2.6 on names and naming.

[22] See ch. 2.8.3 on objects as signs and the metonymic relationship between deity and objects associated with the deity.

[23] Cf. Munson 2005:76–78: "This dialogue includes three sets of participants, each using three different types of cultural codes: a linguistic code, a code of communication (how things are said, including expressions and gestures), and a code of customs, the last representing the substance of the discourse." Cf. also Thomas 2000:193–194, who likewise characterizes this passage, together with the others mentioned here, as an inference from custom. See ch. 2.7 below for further on behavior as sign system. Note the linking in this passage of τεκμήρια with a verb of inference, σταθμῶμαι, and cf. the collocation συμβάλλομαι τεκμαιρόμενος (2.33), discussed below, ch. 1.3.1.

Similarly, relying on his knowledge of Persian behavior and custom, Herodotus reads the behavior of Xerxes, when the latter has the corpse of Leonidas mutilated, as a sign of the great wrath he must have had for the man when he was alive:

> δῆλά μοι πολλοῖσι μὲν καὶ ἄλλοισι τεκμηρίοισι, ἐν δὲ καὶ τῷδε οὐκ ἥκιστα γέγονε, ὅτι βασιλεὺς Ξέρξης πάντων δὴ μάλιστα ἀνδρῶν ἐθυμώθη ζῶντι Λεωνίδῃ· οὐ γὰρ ἄν κοτε ἐς τὸν νεκρὸν ταῦτα παρενόμησε, ἐπεὶ τιμᾶν μαλίστα νομίζουσι τῶν ἐγὼ οἶδα ἀνθρώπων Πέρσαι ἄνδρας ἀγαθοὺς τὰ πολέμια.[24]
>
> 7.238.2
>
> It is clear to me from many other *tekmêria* and in particular the following one that Xerxes was angered above all others by Leonidas when he was alive: otherwise he would never have committed these outrages against his corpse, since Persians most of all the peoples I know have the custom of honoring men who have proved themselves brave in battle.

The mutilated body then acts as a sign, which Herodotus reads against his knowledge of Persian νόμοι, which in themselves constitute another set of signs.[25] At 2.104.4 mutilation of the body is also read as a sign (μέγα ... τεκμήριον) and used as proof: Herodotus relies on the fact that Phoenicians who have become assimilated to Greek culture no longer practice circumcision to prove his point that circumcision among the Phoenicians is not a native practice, but one copied (μιμέονται) from the Egyptians.

1.1.4 μαρτύριον

Parallel in use to τεκμήριον is the noun μαρτύριον, a piece of evidence used as a proof.[26] As Thomas puts it: "What is clear is that when Herodotus speaks

24 For an evaluation of three instances of Persian behavior as described by Herodotus (the attempted immolation of Kroisos by Kyros; the lashing of the Hellespont by Xerxes; Xerxes' branding of the Thebans after Thermopylai), see Keaveney 1996. Strangely enough, Keaveney sees Xerxes' mutilation of Leonidas as, "in a perverted fashion," a paying of tribute to him (46n120).

25 See ch. 2.8.6 and ch. 3.1.2.4 below for the body used as sign-bearer and for mutilation of the body as a semiotic act.

26 According to Fowler 1996:74 the word does not occur in any of the extant fragments of Herodotus' predecessors or contemporaries. If, however, the search is broadened to include writers on subjects beyond the field of history, one finds numerous instances in the Hippocratic

of *marturia*, he means evidence to back up his statement, and the root sense of 'witness' is in play; they tend to be the kinds of evidence that are tangible, visible or the kind of evidence that might be presented in law-courts."[27] As with τεκμήριον, the evidence may consist of a sign and its interpretation. The difference between *tekmêrion* and *marturion* as signs in the *Histories* seems to lie in the use to which they may be put: a *tekmêrion* can be used as an indication allowing one to make an inference and which can be used to support an argument, while the *marturion* acts itself as a proof to show that something is or is not so.

By my reckoning, four of the nine instances of the noun *marturion* and the two of the four instances of verb μαρτυρέω in the *Histories* involve signs.[28] At 5.45, μαρτύρια form the basis of proof behind conflicting accounts given by the Sybarites and the Crotoniates of the fall of Sybaris. The Sybarites claim that the Crotoniates took their city with the help of the self-exiled heir to the Spartan throne, Dorieus, while the Crotoniates maintain that they received no help from foreigners except for Kallias, a seer and refugee from Sybaris. Both cities back up their claims by pointing to various objects and facts as μαρτύρια: μαρτύρια δὲ τούτων ἑκάτεροι ἀποδεικνύουσι τάδε (5.45.1).[29] Among those that the Sybarites point to are the sanctuary and temple to Athene Krathia. These objects, through the Sybarites' action of pointing and the story attached to them (Dorieus dedicated them, and so, presumably, must have been active in

corpus, along with τεκμήριον, and the verbal form is found in a fragment of Alkmaion of Kroton (FGH 24 B 1): see ch. 3.2.2 below.

27 Thomas 2000:191.

28 Powell counts 10 instances of the noun, if μαρτύριον instead of τεκμήριον is read at 2.104.4, a fact which underlines the occasionally overlapping nature of the words (cf. Thomas 2000:191n5 on this "blurredness"). Instances of μαρτύριον (* marks usage by Herodotus himself): 2.22.2* (direction of winds provide μέγιστον μαρτύριον that the origin of Nile flooding cannot be melted snow); 4.118.4 (μέγα μαρτύριον that the Persians are out to conquer Scythia rather than just take revenge for their previous enslavement); 5.45.1 (bis) and 5.45.2 (μαρτύρια provided by Sybarites and Crotoniates in form of objects and sanctuaries); 5.92.η.2 (Melissa provides Periandros with a μαρτύριον that it really is her talking); 7.221* (dismissal of Megistias is μαρτύριον that Leonidas wanted all *kleos* for Spartans); 8.55 (olive tree and spring on akropolis planted as μαρτύρια by Athena and Poseidon); 8.120* (*akinakês* and *tiara* as μαρτύριον that Xerxes took land route back to Persia). In three of these nine instances Herodotus himself provides the μαρτύριον. Instances of μαρτυρέω: 2.18.1*, 4.29*, 5.24.3, 8.94.4.

29 The combination with verb ἀποδείκνυμι draws attention to the fact that these previously existing objects are now invested with a meaning and function differently. See Bakker 2002, esp. 22 on the difference between *epi-deik* and *apo-deik*: "The object of epideixis is always shown as it is; it existed before it was shown or displayed and is not changed or modified by it. . . . What is 'shown' in an act denoted by *apo-deik*, by contrast, is always changed in the act, and may not even have existed before. The person or thing pointed at in an act of *apodeiknunai* acquires a new function according to the requirements of the context."

the region), are invested with a significance and become signs. In the same way, the Crotoniates point to (ἀποδεικνῦσι, 5.42.2) land set aside and given to Kallias, and the absence of such given to Dorieus and his descendants. The parcels of land become signifying objects that become part of the active proof.

Objects used as signifiers and μαρτύρια play a role in another passage, 8.120. The context is again a dispute, and this time Herodotus is directly involved as one of the disputants.[30] Herodotus rejects as false the *logos* (8.118) that Xerxes returned to Asia separately from his army and by sea, but affirms the other *logos*, namely that he went by land with the rest of his army. As a μαρτύριον, he points to the guest-friendship (ξεινίη) which Xerxes showed the people of Abdera, whose city lay on the route of his march homeward, and, in particular, to two distinctive objects:

> μέγα δὲ καὶ τόδε μαρτύριον· φαίνεται γὰρ Ξέρξης ἐν τῇ ὀπίσω κομιδῇ ἀπικόμενος ἐς Ἄβδηρα καὶ ξεινίην τέ σφι συνθέμενος καὶ δωρησάμενος αὐτοὺς ἀκινάκῃ τε χρυσέῳ καὶ τιήρῃ χρυσοπάστῳ.
>
> 8.120
>
> And this too is a great *marturion*: for Xerxes clearly did come to Abdera on his return voyage, both concluding an agreement of guest-friendship with them and giving them as presents a golden *akinakês* and a Persian hat sprinkled with gold.

These objects are able to work as a μαρτύριον for the *logos* that Herodotus endorses and become signs invested with a particular meaning: both are characteristically Persian items, as Herodotus makes clear elsewhere, and the fact that the one is made of gold, the other sprinkled with gold, presumably marks them further as royal, and so likely to have been given by the king.[31] As objects

30 See Nagy 1990b:314–321 on the combination of dispute and investigation by *historia* using *marturia* and *marturiai.*

31 The *akinakês* is specifically described at 7.54.2 as a "Persian sword" (though Scythians have them too, 4.62.2–3 and 4.70, as do the Kaspioi 7.67.1) and appears almost exclusively in connection with Persians (1.132.1; 3.12.4, 7.61.1). At 9.80.2 golden *akinakai* are found on the Persian dead at Plataiai. Masaracchia 1990 *ad* 8.120 compares Xenophon *Anabasis* 1.2.27: δῶρα ἃ νομίζεται παρὰ βασιλεῖ τίμια ... καὶ ἀκινάκην χρυσοῦν καὶ στολὴν Περσικήν, "gifts which are considered honorable by the king ... a golden *akinakês* and a Persian garment." For the object in gift exchange as signifier, see below, ch. 2.8.2. For other golden objects, and the function of gold as a signal of the special status of the object, see the same chapter, esp. on 4.5.3–4 (golden objects fall from the sky in Scythia), 4.162.5 (Euelthon's gift of a golden spindle and distaff), and 3.22.2 and 3.23.4 (golden chains). Cf. also Kurke 1995 and 1999 on the "language of metals" in Herodotus.

associated with the king, their presence is a sign of the presence of the king himself.[32]

A sign of a different kind lies behind the μαρτύριον that appears at 5.92.η.3, a passage we have already looked at above (ch. 1.1.2) in connection with the συμβόλαιον. Melissa gives Periandros a μαρτύριον that it is really her ghost by means of a riddling utterance, which Herodotus then refers to as a πιστὸν συμβόλαιον. The sign is an enigma which only Periandros can solve, but Herodotus intervenes for us and provides the key with which to solve it.

The verbal expression μαρτυρέει μοι functions as an equivalent to Herodotus' usage of the noun μαρτύριον with the dative of the personal pronoun. An oracle, itself a complex of signs, acts as a μαρτύριον for Herodotus' theory about the true extent and borders of Egypt:

> μαρτυρέει δέ μοι τῇ γνώμῃ, ὅτι τοσαύτη ἐστὶ Αἴγυπτος ὅσην τινὰ ἐγὼ ἀποδείκνυμι τῷ λόγῳ, καὶ τὸ Ἄμμωνος χρηστήριον γενόμενον, τὸ ἐγὼ τῆς ἐμεωυτοῦ γνώμης ὕστερον περὶ Αἴγυπτον ἐπυθόμην.
>
> 2.18.1
>
> The oracle of Ammon, which I learned about after I had come to my own opinion, acts as witness for my opinion that Egypt is the size which I show it to be in my *logos*.

A line (*epos*) of Homer can have the same authority,[33] as is shown when Herodotus expounds his theory that heat encourages the growth of horns:[34]

> δοκέει δέ μοι καὶ τὸ γένος τῶν βοῶν τὸ κόλον διὰ ταῦτα οὐ φύειν κέρεα αὐτόθι. μαρτυρέει δέ μοι τῇ γνώμῃ καὶ Ὁμήρου ἔπος ἐν Ὀδυσσείῃ ἔχον ὧδε·
>
> καὶ Λιβύην, ὅθι τ' ἄρνες ἄφαρ κεραοὶ τελέθουσι.
>
> 4.29

32 Cf. the gold coins Dareios issues as a *mnêmosunon* of himself as associated directly with the person of the king himself, 4.162.1–2: discussion in ch. 2.8.8 below.

33 In Thucydides, Homer is also used as evidence, but is adduced as a *tekmêrion* and never as a *marturion*: 1.3.3 (Homer as evidence [τεκμηριοῖ] that the term Hellenes postdates the Trojan War); 1.9.4 (Homer as evidence for great size of Agamemnon's navy, εἴ τῳ ἱκανὸς τεκμηριῶσαι); 3.104.6 (*Homeric Hymn to Apollo* acts as evidence [ἐτεκμηρίωσεν] of antiquity of festival to Apollo on Delos). The implication is that for Thucydides the authority of Homer can be used only as inferential evidence but not as a direct proof. For *epos* in Herodotus as significant or authoritative utterance, cf. Hollmann 2000.

34 At 2.41.4, the horns of dead bulls act as another kind of sign: the Egyptians mark the location of the cattle they bury by leaving one horn (or both) projecting above the earth σημηίου ἕνεκα.

It seems to me that the hornless variety of cattle for this reason [i.e. the cold] do not grow horns in that region [Scythia]. A line (*epos*) of Homer in the *Odyssey* acts as witness for my opinion:

> And Libya, where the lambs are born with horns forthwith.

1.2 Transmission of Signs

1.2.1 σημαίνω

Herodotus uses different terms for different stages of the transmission and reception process: as a marked verb indicating the *transmission* of a sign, of whatever sort, he often uses σημαίνω. As its derivation from the stem *sêm-* suggests, the basic meaning of this verb is to convey a message through the medium of a sign, but a number of developments of this general meaning can be distinguished in the text.

1.2.1.1 σημαίνω of encoding and transmission of sign

In the *Histories* σημαίνω can refer to both the *encoding* and the subsequent *transmission* of a message, where the receiver of the transmission must perform the operation of decoding in order to understand the message. So, for example, the Persian Artayktes claims that by means of the τέρας of the jumping fish, the hero Protesilaos is conveying an encoded message addressed to him alone:[35]

> οὐ γὰρ σοὶ πέφηνε, ἀλλ' ἐμοὶ σημαίνει ὁ ἐν 'Ελαιοῦντι Πρωτεσίλεως...
>
> 9.120.2
>
> [This portent] is not intended for you, rather Protesilaos of Elaious is sending a sign to me.

Or, to use an example involving another sign system, that of dreams, Kroisos reports having a dream which relays (σημαίνει, 1.34.2) to him the message that his son will die after being hit by an iron spear. The verb is also often used of the communication of prophetic or oracular messages. In these instances the

[35] The passage is discussed at greater length in ch. 3.1.3.3 below.

verb carries with it the idea of authoritative communication "from a metaphorically superior vantage point" informed by a connection with the divine.[36] As I will point out below (ch. 1.2.1.3), Herodotus' first-person use of this verb harnesses some of this feeling of divine authority. We have already seen above how Melissa, the dead wife of Periandros, refuses to deliver oracular utterances to him (οὔτε σημανέειν ἔφη ἡ Μέλισσα, 5.92.η.2) via the Thesprotian oracle of the dead. The verb is also used to describe the encoded communication of Apollo and the Delphic oracle, just as in the famous fragment of Herakleitos:

> ὁ ἄναξ οὗ τὸ μαντεῖόν ἐστι τὸ ἐν Δελφοῖς οὔτε λέγει οὔτε κρύπτει, ἀλλὰ σημαίνει.
>
> DK 22 B 93
>
> The lord whose oracle is in Delphi neither speaks nor conceals, but indicates.

At 6.123.2, for example, the Pythia (though here corrupted by the Alkmaionidai) is said to προσημαίνειν, and at 7.142.2, "the god" is said to indicate by the term "wooden wall" that the Athenians are to trust in their fleet: οἱ δ' αὖ ἔλεγον τὰς νέας σημαίνειν τὸν θεόν.[37] Herodotus does not, however, invariably use this verb of oracles: other verbs used of the Delphic oracle and other oracles are, for example, the marked φράζω and χράω, and (*pace* Herakleitos) the unmarked λέγω (see ch. 2.3 below).

One may also encode and transmit a message using a system of signals based on gestures or non-verbal sounds, and Herodotus also uses σημαίνω for this type of sign system, often in military contexts, where the content of the message is an order to carry out a certain action, or information about movements.[38] At 4.113.2 we see an Amazon and young Scythian overcome their lack

36 See Nagy 1990b:165 (who relies here on Hartog 1988 for the metaphor): "In Greek usage someone *sêmainei* 'indicates', that is, 'makes a sign [*sêma*]', when speaking from a superior vantage point, as when a scout goes to the top of a hill and then comes back down to indicate what he saw (Herodotus 7.192.1, 7.219.1). By extension, someone *sêmainei* 'makes a sign [*sêma*]' when he or she speaks from a metaphorically superior vantage point, as when an authoritative person makes a pronouncement that arbitrates between contending points of view (Herodotus 1.5.3). But the ultimate voice of authority belongs to the god of the Oracle at Delphi, whose supreme vantage point confers upon him the knowledge of all things, even the precise number of all grains of sand in the universe (Herodotus 1.47.3; cf. Pindar Pythian 9.44–49)."

37 More on the latter passage in ch. 2.3.3. Complete list of instances of divine or supernatural communication using σημαίνω: 1.45.2 (god προεσήμαινε to Kroisos); 1.78.2 (Telmessians work out what τέρας of snakes and horses σημαίνει); 4.179.3 (prophetic utterance of Triton); 5.92.η.2 (Melissa refuses to σημανέειν); 6.27.1 (gods are wont to προσημαίνειν); 6.123.2 (corrupted Pythia); 7.142.2 (the god Apollo through his oracle at Delphi); 9.120.2 (the hero Protesilaos).

38 Instances: 1.21.2; 1.116.4; 6.77.3; 7.8.δ.1; 8.11.1(*bis*); 9.42.4; 9.56.1; 9.118.2.

of comprehension of each other's language by using sign language.[39] The young Amazon uses her hand to encode and transmit the message (σημαίνουσα, 4.113.2) that each should bring another companion and should meet on the next day.[40]

1.2.1.2 σημαίνω as relaying or retransmission of already transmitted sign

σημαίνω can be used not only to refer to the *encoding* and conveying of a message in the medium of a sign: it can also be used of the relaying or retransmission of an already transmitted message.[41] In such instances, the transmitter is no longer identical with the encoder of the original message, but merely passes on the message in the medium of a sign, with or without decoding it.[42] Thus a shaken Artabanos advises Xerxes to tell the Persians of the threatening dreams the gods have sent: σὺ δὲ σήμηνον μὲν Πέρσῃσι τὰ ἐκ

[39] See discussion in ch. 2.7. below. As will be seen there, the Scythians' incomprehension of the Amazons lies in the field of both behavior and culture, the signs of which they cannot interpret or understand (οὐκ εἶχον συμβαλέσθαι τὸ πρῆγμα, 4.111.1).

[40] For another instance of σημαίνω applied to gestures, cf. 5.20.2, where the Persian guests at the court of Amyntas are encouraged to signal out (ἀποσημανέετε) those women they wish to sleep with. On gesture as a sign system, see ch. 2.7.

[41] List of instances of σημαίνω applied to the relaying of an already transmitted sign, both in coded and decoded form: 1.108.2 (dream-interpreters of Astyages relay meaning of his dream); 1.209.3 (Kyros relates proof from dream); 2.2.4 (herdsman relates to Psammetikhos the first word of children in cave); 2.53.2 (Homer and Hesiod relay the εἴδεα of gods); 2.57.2 (Dodonians indicate by detail of blackness that priestess was Egyptian); 3.14.8 (Psammenitos' strange behavior reported to Kambyses); 3.69.6 (Otanes' daughter relays details of earless nature of Smerdis); 4.76.5, 4.79.5 (Scythian spies report foreign rites and clothing of Anakharsis and Skyles); 5.51.3 (Aristagoras prevented from relaying further details on his map); 7.18.3 (Artabanos tells Xerxes to relay to the Persians details of dream); 8.37.2 (Delphic *prophêtês* relays to Delphians the *teras* he has seen); 8.41.3 (priestess of Athena relays portent of honey-cake untouched by snake in temple); 8.138.1 (courtier relays to Macedonian king Perdikkas' action of circling the sun's image on the floor).

[42] With the following instances of σημαίνω the meaning of relaying or reporting becomes primary, while the connection with sign encoding may become secondary or not apparent: 1.43.3 (messenger tells Kroisos of death of his son); 2.109.2 (*klêros* holder tells king of erosion of land by Nile); 3.72.3 (Dareios suggests one of the Seven request to relay *epos* to the Persian king); 7.173.3 (messengers from Alexander convey size of Persian army and fleet); 7.192.1 (watchers report details of Persian shipwreck off Artemision); 7.219.1 (messengers report movement of Persian army); 8.8.3 (Skyllias the swimmer reports Persian shipwreck); 8.21.1 (Polyas under orders to report any Persian naval disaster to troops at Thermopylai); 8.62.1 (Themistokles conveys his plan in a speech); 8.75.3 (Sikinnos relays Themistokles' message to the Persians); 8.79.4 (Aristeides orders message to be relayed that the Greek fleet is surrounded); 8.80.2 (Themistokles asks Aristeides to relay message to the fleet); 8.110.3 (Sikinnos and others relay Themistokles' message to Xerxes); 9.1 (Alexander relays Athenian response to Mardonios); 9.33.4 (Melampous relays offer to Spartans); 9.49.1 (herald relays Spartan response to Mardonios).

τοῦ θεοῦ πεμπόμενα (7.18.3).[43] The dreams Artabanos speaks of have already been transmitted to Xerxes and himself by the god, a process that could have been described by the verb σημαίνω, which is here, however, applied to the process of retransmitting an original message.

Similar instances occur at 8.37.2 and 8.41.3. In the former passage, as the Persians move toward Delphi, the προφήτης of the Delphic oracle finds weapons, which no one is allowed to remove from the temple, piled up outside it, and then communicates this portent to the Delphians:

> ὁ μὲν δὴ ἤιε Δελφῶν τοῖσι παρέουσι σημανέων τὸ τέρας.
>
> 8.37.2
>
> He went off to convey the *teras* to those of the Delphians who were present.

Here it is not the τέρας itself that signifies (σημαίνει), as is however the case in the passage where sacred ambassadors are sent by Kroisos to the Telmessians to find out what message the τέρας of the snakes and horses in Sardis conveys, τὸ θέλει σημαίνειν τὸ τέρας (1.78.2). The verb is instead applied to the relaying of the coded message by the προφήτης, who is only the conveyer of the message (as he indeed is when it comes to the oracle), not its originator. The same is true for the portent involving the sacred snake on the Athenian akropolis, which for the first time refuses to touch its honey-cake. The priestess communicates this sign to those of the Athenians still remaining in the city:

> σημηνάσης δὲ ταῦτα τῆς ἱερείης μᾶλλόν τι οἱ Ἀθηναῖοι καὶ προθυμότερον ἐξέλιπον τὴν πόλιν ὡς καὶ τῆς θεοῦ ἀπολελοιπυίης τὴν ἀκρόπολιν.
>
> 8.41.3
>
> After the priestess had indicated these things, the Athenians began to leave the city considerably more eagerly, on the basis that even the goddess had deserted the akropolis.

It is not the goddess who is described as transmitting a message via the sign of the snake's refusal to eat (though that is certainly how the citizens interpret it): instead, the subject of the verb is the priestess, who relays the original sign.[44]

43 The dream is discussed below, ch. 2.2.3.

44 These two portents are discussed below, ch. 2.1.

The relayer of the already transmitted message may or may not append a decoded version, an interpretation, to the retransmission of the original sign. When Artabanos tells Xerxes to relay (σὺ δὲ σήμηνον, 7.18.3) to the Persians "the things sent by the god," he presumably means that Xerxes should not just relate the content of the dreams, but also include an interpretation of these dreams, i.e. that the god demands that Xerxes march on Europe. An extremely clear example of the retransmission of a sign without decoding can be found in the account where an Egyptian herdsman relays the first meaningful verbal sign (i.e. not an ἄσημον κνύζημα [2.2.3]) produced by the isolated children of Psammetikhos' linguistic experiment: the word βεκός. He relays it (σημήνας, 2.2.4) in its coded form, which is opaque both to him and to the Egyptian king, until the latter has it decoded by experts and finds out that it is the Phrygian word for 'bread'.[45]

1.2.1.3 Herodotus' use of σημαίνω in first person

An important subset of σημαίνω in the sense of relaying an already transmitted sign, or an interpretation of a sign, is Herodotus' own usage of the verb in the first person, where he becomes an intermediary between the signs he relates and his audience. He is thus in a position to control this flow of information for which he is a conduit. As Nagy has well described, the connotations of this verb are of someone speaking "from a metaphorically superior vantage point, as when an authoritative person makes a pronouncement that arbitrates between contending points of view."[46] The example Nagy goes on to cite is in fact Herodotus' first use of the verb in the work (1.5.3), which is also his first use of the verb in the first person. In this first great narrative act after dismissing the accounts of the stealing of various women by Easterners and Greeks, he relays the name of the man he considers responsible for initiating hostilities against the Greeks:

> ἐγὼ δὲ περὶ μὲν τούτων οὐκ ἔρχομαι ἐρέων ὡς οὕτως ἢ ἄλλως κως ταῦτα ἐγένετο, τὸν δὲ οἶδα αὐτὸς πρῶτον ὑπάρξαντα ἀδίκων ἔργων ἐς τοὺς Ἕλληνας, τοῦτον σημήνας προβήσομαι ἐς τὸ πρόσω τοῦ λόγου, ὁμοίως μικρὰ καὶ μεγάλα ἄστεα ἀνθρώπων ἐπεξιών.
>
> 1.5.3

[45] For the motif of messengers carrying signs without understanding them, cf. e.g. 1.123.3–124.3 (message of Harpagos to Kyros concealed in hare carried by messenger) and discussion in ch. 3.1.2.7 below. On the *bekos* passage, cf. Gera 2003:68–111 and Munson 2005:19–23.

[46] Nagy 1990b:165, who cites Hartog 1988 for this image.

> Concerning these matters I am not going to s[illegible]
> in this way or some other way, but rather, ha[illegible]
> I know to be the first to undertake unjust a[illegible]
> shall advance to the further part of the l[illegible]
> the small and the great cities of men.

The authority Herodotus demonstrates here is seen [illegible]
nouncement of οἶδα (Apollo's claim to know the number of g[illegible]
and the measure of the sea will also be prefaced by an emphatic οἶδα, 1.47.3),
but also in his use of σημαίνω (also used, as we have seen above, of Apollo's communication with mortals).[47] This striking collocation with Kroisos (whose name is, however, postponed for effect until 1.6.1) as the direct object of the verb presents us with the sign of his name but also hints that Kroisos himself forms the nexus of a complex of signs.

A striking example of the control wielded by Herodotus as transmitter comes in the Egyptian *logos*, at 2.20.1.[48] Here he says he will indicate (σημῆναι) two interpretations formulated by Greeks wanting to become ἐπίσημοι ("signaled out, marked") for their σοφίη, which here consists in interpreting and explaining the peculiar behavior of the Nile.[49] He seems to play on the term: these Greeks are attempting to become ἐπίσημοι, "marked by a sign", precisely for their work in decoding and interpreting signs. What he relays is an already decoded message in the form of readings made by certain Greeks of a set of geographical phenomena, namely the yearly flooding of the Nile in summer, a phenomenon not observable in the case of any other river. But Herodotus does not act as an uncritical conduit: at the same time as transmitting the readings, he interferes with the process in two ways. As controller of the channel, he withholds the names of those responsible for the interpretations (as he does, but only temporarily, with the name of Kroisos at 1.5.3, discussed above), passing on only their theories:

47 Cf. Hartog 1999:193–196 on *sêmainein*, esp. 195: "By endowing himself with the capacity to *sêmainein*, the first historian retains something (not the content, but rather the form) of the ancient knowledge of the diviner."

48 This is in keeping with the general increase in first person, polemical, and methodological statements in book 2, as noted by e.g. Marincola 1987, Thomas 2000, and Darbo-Peschanski 1987:108–109 (cf. also 107–112 on first-person statements in the *Histories*).

49 For other instances in the work of the connection between σοφίη and the ability to interpret and manipulate signs, see e.g. discussion of 1.68.3 and συμβάλλομαι, below ch. 1.3.1, and 4.131.1, where the Persians are told that they will be able to find the νόος behind the gifts of the Scythians if they are σοφοί (see discussion below, chs. 1.3.2 and 2.8.2).

ν τὰς μὲν δύο οὐκ ἀξιῶ μνησθῆναι εἰ μὴ ὅσον σημῆναι βουλόμενος μοῦνον.

2.20.1

Two of these theories I do not deem worthy of reproducing here, except only to indicate them.

By not mentioning their names in his narrative, he is withholding from them both recognition and immortality, the bestowal of which we know to be one of Herodotus' aims:[50]

... ὡς μήτε τὰ γενόμενα ἐξ ἀνθρώπων τῷ χρόνῳ ἐξίτηλα γένηται, μήτε ἔργα μεγάλα τε καὶ θωμαστά, τὰ μὲν Ἕλλησι, τὰ δὲ βαρβάροισι ἀποδεχθέντα, ἀκλεᾶ γένηται.

proem

... so that the things which arise from humankind not become evanescent with time, and works and deeds both great and wondrous, some displayed by Greeks, others by barbarians, not become without *kleos*.

The following is another example of Herodotus' narrative use of the verb in the first person: for those who have not seen the figureheads the Phoenicians have on the prows of their ships, Herodotus will relay what these look like: ἐγὼ δέ σημανέω (3.37.2). Herodotus is not simply relaying an image or visual sign, but in a sense also decoding it for his audience, since he only mentions the Phoenician figureheads as an aid to understanding what the ἄγαλμα of Egyptian Hephaistos looks like. And what does the Phoenician figurehead look like? Herodotus answers with another comparison: it is a representation (μίμησις) of a pygmy.[51] He is able to offer the reader not just one but two equivalences, lending him an air of control and superior knowl-

50 The general connection between "remembering" in a literary form (stem μνη-: cf. e.g. οὐκ ἀξιῶ μνησθῆναι, 2.20.1) and fame, *kleos*, is essential to the poetics of the epic tradition, which Herodotus clearly draws on: cf. e.g. Nagy 1979:95–97. See below ch. 2.6 on names and *kleos*, ch. 2.8.8 on the idea of the monument (μνημόσυνον) as perpetual conveyer of *kleos*, and cf. also Bakker 2002 on this, esp. 26–28.

51 On *mimêsis* and *mimeisthai* in Herodotus cf. ch. 2.6 on Kleisthenes of Athens imitating Kleisthenes of Sikyon (5.67.1, 5.69.1) and ch. 2.8.8 on Aryandes' imitation of Dareios' coinage (4.166.1). As Munson (2001a:52n30) comments, the verb "does not necessarily imply awareness or intention to imitate." It is rather that Herodotus directs our attention to similarities that may not have been noted before.

edge. As panhellenic traveler, he is in a position to interpret and draw explanatory parallels between the exotic and the familiar for a parochial audience, as he does, for example, when describing the shape of the Crimean peninsula in terms of either Attika with Sounion at its tip or, for those that have not been there, the heel of Italy (4.99.4–5). As will be argued in ch. 3.2, this is a typical feature of Herodotus' distinctive narrative persona: not only is he interested in the ability of others to encode, transmit, and decode signs, but he himself engages in this activity, at the same time drawing attention to his own competency.[52]

1.2.2 φράζω

Herodotus' use of the verb φράζω in many ways parallels his use of σημαίνω: both are used to describe the transmission of signs, and in fact φράζω seems to act at times as a functional equivalent of σημαίνω, as will be discussed later. That the main meaning is that of showing or pointing out is clear from its use in Homer and the Suda's gloss (φράζουσι· σημαίνουσι, δηλοῦσι). Its connection with signs and communication by signs is demonstrated already in the *Odyssey*, where it is used several times with σήματα as its object. Odysseus, for example, by describing the construction of their marital bed, conveys to Penelope unmistakable signs of his identity:

> ὣς φάτο· τῆς δ' αὐτοῦ λύτο γούνατα καὶ φίλον ἦτορ,
> σήματ' ἀναγνούσῃ τά οἱ ἔμπεδα πέφραδ' Ὀδυσσεύς.[53]
>
> *Odyssey* 23.205–206

52 List of passages where Herodotus uses σημαίνω in first person: 1.5.3* (H. will indicate [σημήνας προβήσομαι] the one he knows to be responsible for beginning unjust actions against the Greeks); 1.75.1* (H. will relay the reason [αἰτίη] Kyros overthrew Astyages); 2.9.2* (H. will relay distance from sea to Thebes); 2.20.1* (H. will relay, but not reproduce in full, theories about Nile); 3.37.2* (H. will relay appearance of statue of Egyptian Hephaistos); 3.106.2* (H. relays account of snatching of gold from Indian ants); 4.99.2* (H. will go ahead and relay [ἔρχομαι σημανέων] measure of Scythian coastline); 5.54.1* (H. will relay exact measurement of distance to Sousa); 6.39.1 (H. will relay how death of Kimon occured); 7.77* (H. will at a later stage relay description of Cilician σκευή); 7.213.3* (H. will later relay another αἰτίη for Athenades' murder of Epialtes); 9.71.2* (H. unable to mark out [ἀποσημήνασθαι] outstanding group at Plataiai). See esp. Nagy 1990b:228–249 for Herodotus' use of the terms αἴτιος and σημαίνω and his authoritative pronouncements. Further discussion and bibliography in ch. 3.2.2.

53 For φράζω + σήματα in the *Odyssey*, see also *Odyssey* 19.250 (details of Odysseus' cloak) and 24.346 (Odysseus' scar and details of Laertes' orchard). Cf. also the expression σῆμα ἀριφραδές, e.g. *Iliad* 23.326 (Nestor's advice on the turning post of the chariot race, which is a σῆμα in the sense of a tomb, but which also has a broader meaning); *Odyssey* 23.73 (scar of Odysseus). Cf. discussion of φράζω in Svenbro 1993:15–17 and Steiner 1994:16–29.

> Thus he spoke: and right away her knees gave way and her heart, too, when she recognized the sure signs [*sêmata*] which Odysseus had shown her.

In Herodotus, the association of the verb with signs and communication is also clear. In an episode already discussed above this is the verb he uses to describe oracular activity of the *eidôlon* of Periandros' dead wife, Melissa, when, satisfied by new offerings, she finally decides to reveal through the Thesprotian *nekuomantêion* the whereabouts of the money Periandros has been looking for:

> ταῦτα δέ οἱ ποιήσαντι καὶ τὸ δεύτερον πέμψαντι ἔφρασε τὸ εἴδωλον τὸ Μελίσσης ἐς τὸν κατέθηκε χῶρον τοῦ ξείνου τὴν παρακαταθήκην.
>
> 5.92.η.4
>
> When he had done this and sent to her a second time, the ghost of Melissa relayed to him the place where he had put his guest-friend's deposit.

Here ἔφρασε functions as an equivalent of σημαίνω, the verb with which, as we have seen, Herodotus describes the oracular activity that Melissa initially refused to perform.

The two verbs also appear in the same context in a passage already discussed above under σημαίνω: the meeting of a Scythian youth and an Amazon. There, φράζω describes the transmission of a message by means of sign language, and σημαίνω appears in a participial clause referring to the girl's transmission of another message in sign form that the youth should bring a companion (σημαίνουσα δύο γενέσθαι, καὶ αὐτὴ ἑτέρην ἄξειν, 4.113.2).

When the citizens of Apollonia consult the oracles both at Delphi and at Dodona about the sudden sterility of their animals and land, the verb with which Herodotus describes the reply of the προφῆται, who base their responses on signs from the god, is φράζω:[54]

> πρόφαντα δέ σφι ἔν τε Δωδώνῃ καὶ ἐν Δελφοῖσι ἐγίνετο, ἐπείτε ἐπειρώτων τοὺς προφήτας τὸ αἴτιον τοῦ παρεόντος κακοῦ, οἱ δὲ αὐτοῖσι ἔφραζον ὅτι ἀδίκως τὸν φύλακον τῶν ἱρῶν προβάτων Εὐήνιον τῆς ὄψιος ἐστέρησαν.
>
> 9.93.4

[54] I deviate here from the text of Hude, who follows Stein in bracketing both τοὺς προφήτας and οἱ δὲ αὐτοῖσι ἔφραζον. Cf. here the collocation of αἴτιον and ἔφραζον with *ait-* and *sêmain-* above.

> They received prophesies both in Dodona and at Delphi, and when they asked the *prophêtai* the cause of the present evil, they indicated to them that they had unjustly deprived Euenios, the guard of the sacred sheep, of his sight.

Likewise, the verb used of the Pythia's revelation to Lykourgos of a new κόσμος for the Spartans is a form of φράζω (φράσαι αὐτῷ τὴν Πυθίην, 1.65.4). We also find the verb in connection with the transmission of a sign in the form of name when Krios the Aeginetan tells Kleomenes his name (ὁ δέ οἱ τὸ ἐὸν ἔφρασε, 6.50.3), and Kleomenes plays on its etymology: Ἤδη νῦν καταχαλκοῦ, ὦ Κριέ, τὰ κέρεα, ὡς συνοισόμενος μεγάλῳ κακῷ ("Better cover your horns in bronze, Mr. Ram, because you're in for big trouble").[55]

1.2.2.1 φράζω used of retransmission of signs

Just as σημαίνω appears in connection with the retransmission of a sign or set of signs which have already appeared, so φράζω is used to describe the retelling (οὗτοι μέν νυν ταῦτα ἔφρασαν, 8.55) by those ordered by Xerxes to sacrifice on the Athenian akropolis of the miraculous appearance of a shoot from the burned stump of the sacred olive tree. Herodotus tells how the seer Megistias sees in the entrails of the sacrificial animals the signs of the Spartans' death and then relays this mantic interpretation (ἔφρασε, 7.219.1) to the Greeks at Thermopylai.[56] As a final example, Likhas' reporting of his discovery of the bones of Orestes and his interpretation of the oracle (συμβαλόμενος … ἔφραζε, 1.68.5, discussed at greater length below, ch. 1.3.1) is described using this verb.

1.2.2.2 φράζω used in first person by Herodotus

As with σημαίνω, φράζω is frequently used by Herodotus himself in the first person in contexts where he presents himself as intermediary between source and audience. He is in a position to pass on the names of rivers that have "shown mighty works" (ἔργα ἀποδεξάμενοι μεγάλα, 2.10.3),[57] or a θῶμα μέγιστον (use by Babylonians of coracles, 1.194.1), or to communicate his

55 Further discussion of this passage in ch. 2.6.1 on names and naming.

56 See ch. 2.4.1 below on this incident.

57 Here the rivers themselves are portrayed as doing precisely what the human beings singled out by Herodotus for inclusion in his work do; cf. ἔργα μεγάλα τε καὶ θωμαστά, τὰ μὲν Ἕλλησι, τὰ δὲ βαρβάροισι ἀποδεχθέντα (proem), "works and deeds both great and wondrous, some displayed by Greeks, others by barbarians." For *erga megala* and the concept of *apodexis*, see Bakker 2002, esp. 24–28.

reading of the Nile's strange behavior (2.24.1), or to relate and explain puzzling phenomena which others have not even noticed: what, for example, happens to all the empty wine jars in Egypt (3.6.1)? All of this lends him a distinctive narrative persona which is connected with his ability to control and interpret signs.

1.3 The Reception, Decoding, and Interpretation of Signs

1.3.1 συμβάλλομαι

A distinctive verb in Herodotus for the decoding and interpretation of signs is συμβάλλομαι, whether the signs are in the form of an oracle, a dream, a portent, or human behavior, or a landscape.[58] In each case, a process of comparison is involved, and the metaphor behind the action of reasoning is that of the putting together of pieces,[59] as happens literally with the *sumbola* in the account discussed above of Glaukos the Spartan and the money deposited with him by a wealthy Milesian (6.85.α.2–δ).[60]

The process of comparison by analogy is frequent in Herodotus' work. In geographical contexts, he mostly uses the active συμβάλλω when comparing rivers and other topographical features with each other; in historical contexts, figures may be compared and contrasted with one another.[61] Sometimes the

58 On the prevalence and distribution of this term in other writers, see discussion in ch. 3.2 below.

59 Cf. the following usages of the similarly prefixed verbs συλλαμβάνω and συνίημι, where a process of combination is likewise involved, and where signs and their decoding are also involved. συλλαμβάνω: oracular decoding (1.63.1: Peisistratos understands Amphilytos' oracle about the tuna; 1.91.4–5: Kroisos fails to understand oracle, understands his mistake; 3.64.5: Kambyses understands oracle about Agbatana; 7.143.2: correct understanding of referent in oracle about Salamis); decoding of language (2.56.3: priestess at Dodona; 4.114.1: Scythians and Amazons); use of ritual (2.49.1: Melampous). συνίημι: oracles (5.80.1: anonymous Theban interprets; 5.92.γ.1: Bakkhiadai interpret); decoding language in general (1.47.3: Delphic oracle understands the deaf; 3.46.1: Spartans cannot understand words of Samian exiles; 4.113.2, 4.114.2: Scythians and Amazons; 5.19.2: Amyntas and words of Alexandros).

60 On συμβάλλομαι and the idea of combination and comparison see Hohti 1977:10; Lloyd 1966: 341–343; Lloyd 1979:134n47; Thomas 2000:200–211; Munson 2001a:83–85.

61 2.10.1 (comparison of reclaimed land around Ilion, Teuthrania, and Ephesos and the plain of the Maiandros River with Nile delta: ὥς γε εἶναι σμικρὰ ταῦτα μεγάλοισι συμβαλεῖν, "to compare these trifles with great things, as it were"). The comparative method is also used with plotting the course of the Nile (2.33), using the known to explain the unknown (see below and under τεκμαίρομαι, ch. 1.3.5). Here, however, the middle of συμβάλλω is used. At 2.10.2 the context is the same, but a negative comparison is used: the other rivers mentioned are not

purpose of comparison is to explain: the familiar may help one to understand the unknown, as for example when Herodotus explains the origins of the Nile on the basis of its supposed resemblance to the Istros:[62]

> καὶ ὡς ἐγὼ συμβάλλομαι τοῖσι ἐμφανέσι τὰ μὴ γινωσκόμενα τεκμαιρόμενος…
>
> 2.33.2
>
> And as I conjecture by inferring what is not known from what is manifest…

Or the small may illuminate the big, as when he compares the delta regions of rivers in Asia Minor with the Nile delta (ὥς γε εἶναι σμικρὰ ταῦτα μεγάλοισι συμβαλεῖν [2.10.1], "to compare small things with great ones") or the Crimea with Sounion:

> λέγω δὲ ὡς εἶναι ταῦτα σμικρὰ μεγάλοισι συμβαλεῖν. τοιοῦτο ἡ Ταυρική ἐστι. ὃς δὲ τῆς Ἀττικῆς ταῦτα μὴ παραπέπλωκε, ἐγὼ δὲ ἄλλως δηλώσω· ὡς εἰ τῆς Ἰηπυγίης ἄλλο ἔθνος καὶ μὴ Ἰήπυγες ἀρξάμενοι ἐκ Βρεντεσίου λιμένος ἀποταμοίατο μέχρι Τάραντος καὶ νεμοίατο τὴν ἄκρην.[63]
>
> 4.99.4
>
> I say this comparing small things with great ones, as it were. The Crimea is of this sort. For anyone who has not sailed past these parts of Attika, I shall explain it another way: it is as if some other people and not the Iapygans were to cut off the area for themselves, starting from Brindisium as far as Tarentum, and to inhabit this promontory.

"worthy of comparison" (ἄξιος συμβληθῆναι). 3.125.2: no other Greek tyrant can be compared to Polykrates in terms of magnificence; 3.160: no Persian dares to compare himself to Kyros; 4.50.1: comparison of volumes of Nile and Istros; 4.53.1: comparison of rivers; 4.99.4: comparison of Crimea with region around Sounion (ὡς εἶναι ταῦτα σμικρὰ μεγάλοισι συμβαλεῖν: cf. 2.10.1, translated above). The purpose of the comparison here is not to find an unknown, but simply to explain an unfamiliar region in terms of a familiar one. On analogy and comparison in Herodotus cf. Corcella 1984; Lloyd 1992; Thomas 2000; and Munson 2001a:45–133.

62 On explaining the unseen by means of the seen, see ch. 3.2.2 below and Thomas 2000:200–212 and Corcella 1984.

63 This interchangeability of the large with the small can be related to Herodotus' famous observation on the fates of cities: τὰ γὰρ τὸ πάλαι μεγάλα ἦν, τὰ πολλὰ αὐτῶν σμικρὰ γέγονε, τὰ δὲ ἐπ' ἐμεῦ ἦν μεγάλα, πρότερον ἦν σμικρά (1.5.4), "For as for those that were of old mighty, most have become small, and those that in my time were mighty were previously small."

An Athenian can thus understand the shape and population distribution of the Crimea if he imagines Cape Sounion (4.99.4): or if someone has not sailed around that part of the world, Herodotus can explain it using the model of Cape Iapygia in southern Italy (4.99.5). Herodotus is in a central position, controlling the comparison, issuing the pieces of information and putting them together, as his use of forms in the first person (λέγω, δηλώσω) and the emphatic use of the personal pronoun ἐγώ underline.

When the process of comparison moves beyond simply placing two items next to each other and involves an additional process, that of deduction based on comparison, Herodotus may use συμβάλλω in the middle voice. The basic function of the middle voice has been described as indicating that action takes place within the subject or is reflected on the subject: "the action envelopes the agent and the agent remains immersed in the action."[64] With the verb συμβάλλομαι the action of comparison involves and envelopes, so to speak, the subject, and this involvement and additional reflection result in deduction and interpretation. An important use by Herodotus of this verb in the middle voice is to describe the decoding and interpretation of signs of all sorts.[65] I list here under separate categories instances of Herodotus' use of the verb relating to signs:

Oracles:
- 1.68.3 (Likhas interprets oracle about the bones of Orestes);
- 5.1.3 (Paionians interpret oracle about Perinthians calling them by name);
- 6.80 (Kleomenes interprets conditions of oracle's fulfillment at Argos);
- 7.143.1 (Themistokles says the *khrêsmologoi* do not interpret the oracle about the wooden walls correctly);
- 7.189.2 (Athenians come to interpretation that the "son-in-law" in the oracle is Boreas).

64 Palmer 1980:292. This also applies to the verbs φράζομαι and τεκμαίρομαι, discussed below.

65 Apart from a fragment of Herakleitos (μὴ εἰκῇ περὶ τῶν μεγίστων συμβαλλώμεθα [DK B 47], "Let us not conjecture rashly about the most important matters"), συμβάλλομαι is not often attested, though not as rarely as Hohti 1977:5, 14 suggests: see ch. 3.2.2 for some interesting examples from the Hippocratic Corpus. Pausanias' use of συμβάλλομαι, especially in combination with τεκμαίρομαι, follows a Herodotean model. Cf. e.g. εἰ δὲ Λυσίππου τοῦ ποιήσαντος τὴν εἰκόνα τεκμαιρόμενον τῇ ἡλικίᾳ συμβάλεσθαι δεῖ με τὸν πόλεμον ἔνθα ὁ Χίλων ἔπεσεν . . . (6.4.7), "If using as evidence the age of Lysippos, who made the statue, I must make an inference about the war in which Khilon was killed . . ."; εἰ δὲ Ὁμήρου χρὴ τεκμαιρόμενον τοῖς ἔπεσι συμβαλέσθαι γνώμην, τὸν ὄφιν τοῦτον δράκοντα εἶναι πείθομαι (8.8.5), "If I must come up with an opinion using as evidence the poetry of Homer, then I am convinced that this snake was a *drakôn*." This is a direct imitation of Herodotus' style and method: cf. e.g. καὶ ὡς ἐγὼ συμβάλλομαι τοῖσι ἐμφανέσι τὰ μὴ γινωσκόμενα τεκμαιρόμενος (*Histories* 2.33.2). On Pausanias as an imitator of Herodotus, see Habicht 1985:97 with references.

Portents:
- 7.57.1 (Herodotus reckons a portent ignored by Xerxes was εὐσύμβλητον);
- 8.94.2 (Corinthians at Salamis interpret mysterious ship as πρῆγμα θεῖον).

Dreams:
- 6.107.2 (Hippias interprets dream about intercourse with mother as sign he will return to his native land);
- 6.108.1 (Hippias interprets that this dream has been fulfilled).

Human behavior:
- 3.68.2 (Otanes concludes the Smerdis on the throne is not the son of Kyros because he never leaves the palace and allows no visitors);
- 4.111.1 (Scythians unable to understand behavior of Amazons);
- 7.209.1 (Xerxes unable to interpret meaning of Spartans' combing out their hair).

Writing (or lack of writing):
- 7.239.4 (Spartans unable to interpret blank wax tablets sent by Demaratos).[66]

Most of these passages will be discussed individually in the chapters corresponding to these sign types. For the present let us focus on one example to illustrate Herodotus' use of the verb. In the yard of a Tegean blacksmith's shop Likhas the Spartan is able to discover the bones of Orestes, which he confirms as being those of Orestes by reading an oracle (1.67.4) against the surroundings in which they were found (1.68.3). This process is described by Herodotus using the verb συμβάλλομαι in a point-by-point breakdown of Likhas' interpretation:

> ὁ δὲ ἐννώσας τὰ λεγόμενα συνεβάλλετο τὸν Ὀρέστεα κατὰ τὸ θεοπρόπιον τοῦτον εἶναι, τῇδε συμβαλλόμενος· τοῦ χαλκέος δύο ὁρέων φύσας τοὺς ἀνέμους εὕρισκε ἐόντας, τὸν δὲ ἄκμονα καὶ τὴν σφῦραν τόν τε τύπον καὶ τὸν ἀντίτυπον, τὸν δὲ ἐξελαυνόμενον σίδηρον τὸ πῆμα ἐπὶ πήματι κείμενον, κατὰ τοιόνδε τι εἰκάζων, ὡς ἐπὶ κακῷ ἀνθρώπου σίδηρος ἀνεύρεται.[67]
>
> 1.68.3–4

> Realizing what was being said, he conjectured that this [skeleton] was Orestes according to the oracle, conjecturing as follows: seeing

[66] See discussion under φράζομαι and ἐπιφράζομαι, below ch. 1.3.4, and also ch. 3.1.3.7.

[67] See discussion under νόος (ch. 1.3.2) for combination of ἐννοέω and συμβάλλομαι, and ch. 1.3.3 for εἰκάζω.

> the two bellows of the blacksmith he found the two winds, in the anvil and hammer he found the "blow and counterblow," and in the iron being hammered out he found the "woe upon woe," reasoning it out along the following lines, that the discovery of iron was to the detriment of mankind.

What is interesting about Likhas' interpretation is that the relationships he perceives between the words of the oracle and the environment surrounding the bones are all of a particular kind, one of cause and effect. The "two winds" are the product of the smith's bellows, "blow and counterblow" result from the hammer being applied to the anvil, and "woe upon woe" results from the use of iron as weapon by man.[68] In other words, Likhas' reading has its chief basis in the figure of metonymy: instead of looking for two winds, or something similar to them, he looks at what might be associated with them, what might cause them. As we will note during the course of this book, the successful interpretation of a sign or set of signs in the *Histories* often depends on seeing the relationship between signified and signifier in a way that is not immediately obvious, involving an ability to move from the figurative to the literal or vice versa, or from one type of figurative relationship to another, metaphor to metonymy or vice versa.[69]

1.3.1.1 Herodotus' use of συμβάλλομαι in first person

Finally, let us consider a group of passages which constitutes Herodotus' own use of the verb συμβάλλομαι in the first person:

2.33.2
: Herodotus compares known facts about the Nile with the Istros to derive information about unknown parts of the Nile (ὡς ἐγὼ συμβάλλομαι τοῖσι ἐμφανέσι τὰ μὴ γινωσκόμενα τεκμαιρόμενος).

4.15.1
: Herodotus works out the relative period of Aristeas' mysterious disappearance by comparison of different accounts (συμβαλλόμενος . . . εὕρισκον).

68 The pair τύπος-ἀντίτυπος occurs elsewhere in a context of sign-reading, in Aeschylus *Seven against Thebes* 488 and 521, where the devices on the shields of the Seven attacking Thebes are subjected to semiotic analysis. Discussion in Zeitlin 1982:85 and Steiner 1994:54–55, though neither compares the Herodotean passage.

69 See, for example, discussion below (ch. 2.8.2) of the interpretation of the Scythian gifts to Dareios (4.132.1–2), where Dareios' reading relies on metonymy, while that of Gobryas depends on metaphor.

4.45.2
Herodotus cannot work out why one land should have three names (οὐδ' ἔχω συμβαλέσθαι ἐπ' ὅτεο μιῇ ἐούσῃ γῇ οὐνόματα τριφάσια κεῖται).[70]

4.87.2
Herodotus works out the site of Dareios' crossing of the Bosphoros (ὡς ἐμοὶ δοκέειν συμβαλλομένῳ).

4.101.3
Herodotus calculates average daily journey traveling in Scythia (ἡ δὲ ὁδός . . . συμβέβληταί μοι).

7.24
Herodotus deduces that Xerxes' excavations at Athos must arise from his μεγαλοφροσύνη (ὡς μὲν ἐμὲ συμβαλλόμενον εὑρίσκειν).

7.187.2
Herodotus works out food supply needed for Xerxes' army (εὑρίσκω . . . συμβαλλόμενος).

8.30.1
Herodotus deduces that the only reason the Phocaeans did not medize was their hatred of the Thessalians (ὡς ἐγὼ συμβαλλόμενος εὑρίσκω).

It is interesting that these passages, the majority of which come from the second and fourth books of the work, the books which feature the largest number of first-person statements by Herodotus, do not in fact involve the interpretation of the kind of signs we see in the examples listed in ch. 1.3.1 above (oracles, portents, and so forth). Nevertheless, all show a process of authoritative deduction based on comparison and represent a display of mastery and control. As with the examples of his use of σημαίνω and φράζω in the first person, these instances show Herodotus involved in the same process that the figures in his work use.

1.3.2 νόος

In the *Histories* νόος has a role to play in both the transmission the and reception of signs.[71] Herodotus can use the noun to refer to the meaning behind something, in other words, to what is the encoded message.[72] Consider the

[70] On this passage, see Burkert 1985a:130 and ch. 2.6 below on names and naming.

[71] As it does in Homer, for which see Nagy 1990a:202–222.

[72] Herodotus uses the verbal form νοέω when describing Artayktes' ruse to obtain leave from Xerxes to appropriate the shrine of the hero Protesilaos as his own property: ἐπὶ γῆν δὲ τὴν βασιλέος στρατεύεσθαι Πρωτεσίλεων ἔλεγε νοέων τοιάδε· τὴν Ἀσίην πᾶσαν νομίζουσι ἑωυτῶν

Scythians' puzzling gift to Dareios of a bird, a mouse, a frog, and five arrows (4.131.1):[73] the Persians ask the Scythian messenger what the νόος of this gift is, assuming (correctly) that each element is a sign and that the whole forms a coded message. But the only answer they receive is that if they are σοφοί they will know what the gift is trying to say (4.131.2). One might say that to get at the message, the νόος, one needs just that: νόος.[74]

In discussing the Massagetan custom of sacrificing horses to the sun (1.216.4), for example, Herodotus tells us what the νόος behind this strange practice is: to the swiftest of the gods they apportion the swiftest of all mortal things.[75] He distills this meaning for us from the strange and unfamiliar ritual practice, and shows that there is a rationale to be decoded, another instance of his narrative persona of the interpreter of signs. He also uses the term νόος in connection with the process of decoding a sign, employing the expression νόῳ λαμβάνειν, or the verb ἐννοέω. So, for example, the older of the two sons of Periandros claims he cannot remember what his maternal grandfather said to him and his brother about their mother because he could not "grasp" it in his νόος: ἅτε οὐ νόῳ λαβών, οὐκ ἐμέμνητο (3.51.1). The parting words of his grandfather, "Do you know, my lads, who killed your mother?" hold no significance for this brother, but the younger brother, Lykophron, is able to distinguish the real message behind them, which is that Periandros killed their mother.[76] If the older brother cannot grasp the νόος behind the old man's question with his own νόος, then Lykophron can.[77] Once the older brother is eventually able

εἶναι Πέρσαι καὶ τοῦ αἰεὶ βασιλεύοντος (9.116.3), "He said that Protesilaos was marching against the king's land using the following rationale: the Persians consider that the whole of Asia belongs to them and whoever is king at the time."

73 Discussed below in ch. 2.8.2.

74 Cf. Nagy 1990a:202–222 on *noos* as the ability not only to encode and decode signs, but to recognize them in the first place, esp. 205: "the verb *noéô* conveys simultaneously the noticing of signs and recognition of what they mean."

75 The reading νόος is the conjecture of Krüger adopted by Hude and Rosén in their texts; the mss. have νόμος. Other instances of νόος in this sense have been contested at 7.162.2 (considered to be an intrusive gloss by Hude following Wesseling) and 9.98.4 (deleted by Krüger, but retained by Hude).

76 The coded question can be considered as an *ainos*, designed to be intelligible only to those who are the correct and intended recipients: on this passage and the *ainos* in general, see ch. 2.5 below.

77 For the pattern of two brothers, one of whom has impaired ability to interpret signs, cf. the two sons of Kroisos, one of whom is mute, the other normal (1.34.2). Paradoxically, it is the unimpaired son, Atys, who because of a faulty and biased reading of a sign (Kroisos' dream that Atys will be destroyed by something made of iron) ends up paying for it with his life, while the nameless and dumb brother saves Kroisos' life precisely by the ability to speak. When a Persian soldier is about to kill Kroisos, his son cries out, "Don't kill Kroisos!" On the two brothers and their relative abilities to communicate, see Sebeok and Brady 1979. On the Kypselidai and their sign-reading skills, see Gray 1996.

to call to mind (but still not decode) his grandfather's question, Periandros also decodes the purport of the words, and acts accordingly:

> Περίανδρος δὲ νόῳ λαβὼν [καὶ τοῦτο] καὶ μαλακὸν ἐνδιδόναι βουλόμενος οὐδέν, τῇ ὁ ἐξελασθεὶς ὑπ' αὐτοῦ παῖς δίαιταν ἐποιέετο, ἐς τούτους πέμπων ἄγγελον ἀπηγόρευε μή μιν δέκεσθαι οἰκίοισι.
>
> 3.51.2
>
> Periandros, comprehending this too, and not wanting to show any weakness, sent a message to the people where the son whom he had exiled was living and forbade them to receive him in their homes.

It is not the last time we see Periandros using νόος to decode signs. Further on in the *Histories*, Herodotus (through the mouth of Sokles the Corinthian) relates how Periandros is able to interpret Thrasyboulos' non-verbal reply to his question about how best to ensure the safety of his tyranny. The bearer of the message, like the older son of Periandros in the previous example, has no idea of the real significance of the signs he relates (Thrasyboulos wades into a field of wheat and cuts off the tallest ears), but Periandros perceives it well enough:

> ... συνεὶς τὸ ποιηθὲν καὶ νόῳ σχὼν ὥς οἱ ὑπετίθετο Θρασύβουλος τοὺς ὑπερόχους τῶν ἀστῶν φονεύειν.[78]
>
> 5.92.η.1
>
> ... having comprehended the action and grasped in his mind that Thrasyboulos was advising him to kill those prominent among the citizens.

The role of νόος in decoding is also seen in Herodotus' use of the verb ἐννοέω, which in two of its three instances in the work relates directly to the interpretation of signs. The first has to do with Likhas' discovery of the bones of Orestes, a feat he achieves by a mixture of chance and skill, συντυχίῃ and σοφίῃ (1.68.1).[79] Likhas' σοφίη lies in his ability to register the points of

[78] That the bearer of a coded message may transmit without understanding it is an irony that seems to interest Herodotus: see discussion of ἐννοέω below and ch. 3.2.1 on messengers and interpreters. The passage is also discussed in ch. 2.7.2.

[79] For the role of chance (which seems linked sometimes to divine providence) in the interpretation (and sometimes the manipulation) of signs, cf. the stories of Dareios, his groom, and his horse (3.85–86, esp. ὥσπερ ἐκ συνθέτου, 3.86.2) and of Zopyros and the chance remark about a mule giving birth (3.151–153, esp. σὺν γὰρ θεῷ, 3.153.2). The first passage is discussed in chs. 2.1.4 and 3.1.2.2, the second in ch. 2.1.6.

contact between the signs of the oracle and the signs in the blacksmith's story, and then to acquire the blacksmith's land without suspicion and lay claim to the bones.[80] He brings the two halves together like σύμβολα:

> ἐννώσας τὰ λεγόμενα συνεβάλλετο τὸν Ὀρέστεα κατὰ τὸ θεοπρόπιον τοῦτον εἶναι.
>
> 1.68.3
>
> Having grasped in his *noos* what was said, he concluded that this [skeleton] was Orestes, according to the oracle.

He recognizes a significance behind the man's words, namely that the bones of supernatural size must belong to a hero, and that that hero may be Orestes.

The second occurrence of the verb is in the famous scene of Kroisos' narrowly averted immolation, when Kyros recognizes and decodes (μεταγνόντα τε καὶ ἐννώσαντα, 1.86.6) and applies to himself the message of Solon, which has just been passed to him via Kroisos (who has only just himself understood what it was Solon was saying to him) and the interpreters. It is ironic that the latter, whose profession it is to decode, while able to understand Kroisos' language, can only translate and transmit the message without themselves comprehending it.[81] Kroisos' words, though perfectly comprehensible to them on a surface level, seem nevertheless to be incomprehensible and without meaning (ὡς δέ σφι ἄσημα ἔφραζε, 1.86.4), so that they have to ask him to repeat what he is saying.[82] We see that to transmit and relay a message is not necessarily the same as to understand it.

80 The connection between σοφίη and νόος is also clear from the passage concerning the gift of the Scythians (4.131–132), just discussed above. On σοφίη and the ability to encode and decode signs see chapters 3.1.4.1 and 3.2.2 below.

81 On the ἑρμηνεύς and other professional interpreters in the *Histories*, see ch. 3.2.1 below and Munson 2005:74–76.

82 ἄσημος is elsewhere applied to the pre-verbal cries of the children of Psammetikhos' linguistic experiment (ἀσήμων κνυζημάτων, 2.2.3) that simply have no meaning and are not signs. Their first verbal cry of *bekos* (described as a φωνή), though now a sign, will also appear meaningless to the messengers and the king until it is discovered to be Phrygian for 'bread'. At 5.92.β.3, the adjective is used of an oracle relating to Aetion, which the Bakkhiadai cannot understand in the sense that the deeper or concealed meaning of the enigmatic speech is impenetrable to them, so that it is as if it has no meaning. A second oracle (5.92.β.2) provides the key to understanding it. The terms used by Herodotus stress the idea of combination and comparison (and note the use of ἀτέκμαρτον as a variation on ἄσημον): τοῦτο μὲν δὴ τοῖσι Βακχιάδῃσι πρότερον γενόμενον ἦν ἀτέκμαρτον, τότε δὲ τὸ Ἠετίωνι γενόμενον ὡς ἐπύθοντο, αὐτίκα καὶ τὸ πρότερον συνῆκαν ἐὸν συνῳδὸν τῷ Ἠετίωνος (5.92.γ), "When the Bakkhiadai first got this oracle it was uninterpretable, but when they learned of the oracle which Aetion had received, they immediately understood the previous one too as being consonant with Aetion's oracle." Cf. Kurke

1.3.3 εἰκάζω

Herodotus uses this verb of the process of decoding and interpreting signs on the basis of comparison and of what is probable, οἰκός.[83] The idea of comparison is confirmed by the collocation of the word with a form of συμβάλλομαι at 1.68.3, discussed above (ch. 1.3.1). There, the verb εἰκάζω is used to describe Likhas' decipherment of the last part of the oracle about the location of the bones of Orestes, which turns on the perception of the metonymic relationship between the "woe upon woe" (πῆμα ἐπὶ πήματι) of the oracle and the iron of the blacksmith as well as the realization of the significance of iron in the 'language' of metals:[84]

> εὕρισκε . . . τὸν δὲ ἐξελαυνόμενον σίδηρον τὸ πῆμα ἐπὶ πήματι κείμενον, κατὰ τοιόνδε τι εἰκάζων, ὡς ἐπὶ κακῷ ἀνθρώπου σίδηρος ἀνεύρηται.
>
> 1.68.3

> He found . . . in the iron being hammered out the "woe upon woe," reasoning it out along the following lines, that iron the discovery of iron was to the detriment to mankind.

At 4.132.1–2, the verb is used of both Dareios' and Gobryas' readings of the Scythians' gift of the bird, mouse, frog, and five arrows, where once again the interpretation of each man depends on the perception of a certain relationship between the sign and that which it signifies. For Dareios, the relationship is chiefly one of metonymy: the mouse stands for earth, because it lives in the earth, the frog for water, because water is its habitat, the bird is "most like a horse," and the five arrows represent the Scythian submission of their military might to the Persians.[85] The message is thus read altogether in terms

2009:434 on this passage as "a speech permeated with συν- compounds that designate the putting together of evidence and the process of human interpretation" with n39: "Within four-and-a-half OCT pages, we find συμβαλέσθαι, συνῆκαν, συνῳδόν, συνέντες, συνείς, συμβόλαιον (Hdt. 5.92α2–η5)." Further discussion of this passage in ch. 2.3.2 below.

[83] On Herodotus' use of *to oikos* cf. e.g. Thomas 2000:168–212.

[84] Iron and conflict are associated with the Fifth Age of man in Hesiod *Works and Days* 174–179. For the idea of a language of metals in Herodotus influenced by the Hesiodic account of the five ages of man and their associated metals, cf. Kurke 1995 and 1999:154–155, who notes that φυσίζοος αἶα in the first part of this oracle (1.67.4) evokes the necessity of agricultural labor associated with the Age of Iron and forms a contrast to βαλανηφάγοι with its evocation of the Golden Age (note also its association with Arkadia, which has its own Golden Age associations) in the first (disastrously misinterpreted) oracle to the Spartans about Tegea (1.66.2). On gold and its role in significant objects, see below ch. 2.8.1–3.

[85] Discussed again in ch. 2.8.2.

of the traditional Persian symbol of submission, the handing over of earth and water:

> Δαρείου μέν νυν ἡ γνώμη ἦν Σκύθας ἑωυτῷ διδόναι σφέας τε αὐτοὺς καὶ γῆν τε καὶ ὕδωρ, εἰκάζων τῇδε, ὡς μῦς μὲν ἐν γῇ γίνεται καρπὸν τὸν αὐτὸν ἀνθρώπῳ σιτεόμενος, βάτραχος δὲ ἐν ὕδατι, ὄρνις δὲ μάλιστα ἔοικε ἵππῳ, τοὺς δὲ ὀϊστοὺς ὡς τὴν ἑωυτῶν ἀλκὴν παραδιδοῦσι.
>
> 4.132.1
>
> Now Dareios' opinion was that the Scythians were handing themselves as well as [the gift of] earth and water over to them, and he reasoned along the following lines, namely that a mouse lives in earth and eats the same food as man, a frog lives in water, a bird is most comparable to a horse, and that by surrendering their arrows to him they were also surrendering their own strength.

Gobryas' reading assumes a metaphoric relationship between sign and signified:

> συνεστήκεε δὲ ταύτῃ τῇ γνώμῃ ἡ Γωβρύεω, τῶν ἀνδρῶν τῶν ἑπτὰ ἑνὸς τῶν τὸν μάγον κατελόντων, εἰκάζοντος τὰ δῶρα λέγειν· "ἢν μὴ ὄρνιθες γενόμενοι ἀναπτῆσθε ἐς τὸν οὐρανόν, ὦ Πέρσαι, ἢ μύες γενόμενοι κατὰ τῆς γῆς καταδύητε, ἢ βάτραχοι γενόμενοι ἐς τὰς λίμνας ἐσπηδήσητε, οὐκ ἀπονοστήσετε ὀπίσω ὑπὸ τῶνδε τῶν τοξευμάτων βαλλόμενοι." Πέρσαι μὲν δὴ οὕτω τὰ δῶρα εἴκαζον.
>
> 4.132.2–3
>
> The opinion of Gobryas, one of the seven men who deposed the Magos, was in direct opposition to this one. He reckoned that the gifts were saying, "If you do not become like birds and fly up into the heavens, o Persians, or become like mice and sink under the earth, or become like frogs and leap into the lakes, you will not return home again, being shot at with these arrows." This is how the Persians went about interpreting the gifts.

An interesting use of εἰκάζω in this sense of interpretation on the basis of comparison occurs in Herodotus' rationalization of the Scythian view that the land to the north of them is full of feathers. Herodotus' reading of their story (τήνδε ἔχω περὶ αὐτῶν γνώμην, 4.31.1) is that the feathers are simply snowflakes:

> τὰ κατύπερθε ταύτης τῆς χώρης αἰεὶ νίφεται, ἐλάσσονι δὲ τοῦ θέρεος ἢ τοῦ χειμῶνος, ὥσπερ καὶ οἰκός· ἤδη ὦν ὅστις ἀγχόθεν χιόνα ἁδρὴν πίπτουσαν εἶδε, οἶδε τὸ λέγω· ἔοικε γὰρ ἡ χιὼν πτεροῖσι· καὶ διὰ τὸν χειμῶνα τοῦτον ἐόντα τοιοῦτον ἀνοίκητα τὰ πρὸς βορέην ἐστὶ τῆς ἠπείρου ταύτης. τὰ ὦν πτερὰ εἰκάζοντας τὴν χιόνα τοὺς Σκύθας τε καὶ τοὺς περιοίκους δοκέω λέγειν.
>
> 4.31.1–2
>
> The uppermost regions of this land have continual snow, a little less in the summer than in the winter, as one might expect. Now anyone who has seen thickly falling snow knows what I mean: for snow looks like feathers. Because this winter is of such a nature, the northern reaches of this continent are uninhabitable. And so I think that the Scythians and their neighbors say [that the region is full of feathers] because they are comparing the snow to feathers.

What the Scythians have done is to make a metaphorical connection between snowflakes and feathers (τὰ ὦν πτερὰ εἰκάζοντας τὴν χιόνα) and then to refer to the reality by the metaphorical equivalent of the snowflakes, 'feathers'. 'Feathers', then, instead of having its normal referent, points to the snowflakes that fall thick and fast.[86] What Herodotus does is to understand the true nature of the sign and match up once again what is signified with its signifier: another instance of Herodotus' expertise in, and control over, signs.[87]

At 2.104, he discusses the Egyptian idea that the Colchians are their descendants, but proudly claims that he himself had come to this interpretation on his own, before hearing it from anyone (νοήσας δὲ πρότερον αὐτὸς ἢ ἀκούσας ἄλλων λέγω, 2.104.1). A little further on, he makes a statement in the same tone, this time using a form of the verb εἰκάζω. He emphasizes the superiority of his interpretation and reasoning, which relied not on inconclusive signs, but on the evidence of a ritual marking of the body practiced only by the Colchians, Egyptians, and Ethiopians:

[86] Cf. Benardete 1969:101, who compares λευκόπτερος νιφάς, "white-winged snow" (Aeschylus *Prometheus Bound* 993). Benardete sees this as a general tendency of the Scythians to confound "the sign with the object of the sign." For criticism of this view, cf. Munson 2005:40.

[87] There is an interesting parallel for the confusion between the literal and the figurative in the two accounts (διξοὺς λόγους, 9.74.1) which Herodotus knows about Sophanes of Dekelea in Attika. According to one, he carried an anchor on a chain attached to his belt, and would bring it with him into battle, anchoring it in the earth so that the enemy could not move him from his position (9.74.1). According to the other, the anchor was a design (ἐπίσημον) on his shield (9.74.2).

αὐτὸς δὲ εἴκασα τῇδε καὶ ὅτι μελάγχροές εἰσι καὶ οὐλότριχες (καὶ τοῦτο μὲν ἐς οὐδὲν ἀνήκει· εἰσὶ γὰρ καὶ ἕτεροι τοιοῦτοι), ἀλλὰ τοισίδε καὶ μᾶλλον ὅτι μοῦνοι πάντων ἀνθρώπων Κόλχοι καὶ Αἰγύπτιοι καὶ Αἰθίοπες περιτάμνονται ἀπ' ἀρχῆς τὰ αἰδοῖα.

2.104.2

I myself conjectured thus, on the basis that they are both black-skinned and woolly-haired (though this amounts to nothing, because there exist other such peoples) but especially for the following reason, namely that the Colchians, Egyptians, and Ethiopians are the only peoples to have practised circumcision right from the start.

Once more, Herodotus marks himself off from others in the reading and use of signs. What seems to matter is not simply the conclusion that is reached, that the Egyptians and the Colchians are related, but Herodotus' novel use of a sign which others have not noticed.[88] Another example of behavior subjected to the process of comparison and interpretation denoted by verbs with the εἰκ- stem is the unfamiliar tactics of the Athenian hoplites at Marathon that the Persians in terms of their own code can only read as insanity:

οἱ δὲ Πέρσαι ὁρῶντες δρόμῳ ἐπιόντας παρεσκευάζοντο ὡς δεξόμενοι, μανίην τε τοῖσι Ἀθηναίοισι ἐπέφερον καὶ πάγχυ ὀλεθρίην, ὁρῶντες αὐτοὺς ἐόντας ὀλίγους, καὶ τούτους δρόμῳ ἐπειγομένους οὔτε ἵππου ὑπαρχούσης σφι οὔτε τοξευμάτων. ταῦτα μέν νυν οἱ βάρβαροι κατείκαζον.

6.112.2–3

When the Persians saw them starting the attack at a run, they prepared themselves to receive them and put the Athenians' actions down to an utterly fatal madness, seeing that their numbers were few and that they were advancing at a run with neither cavalry nor archers with them. This, then, was the interpretation the barbarians gave.

88 Cf. ch. 2.7 below on ritual as a sign system, and cf. ch. 2.8.6 on markings of the body as signs. The passage concludes with another argument based on signs: Herodotus contends that the Colchians must have adopted circumcision through interaction with the Egyptians (and not the Phoenicians), which he proves by means of a μέγα τεκμήριον: when Phoenicians intermarry with the Greeks, they do not circumcise the sons of these unions (2.104.4).

1.3.4 φράζομαι

The middle, and, in the aorist, the passive forms of φράζω are sometimes used to describe the process of reception and interpretation of signs, in contrast to the active forms, which, as we have seen above, are used of the transmission of signs. The middle points toward a process of internal reflection, as does the verb's etymological connection with φρήν, the organ of mental perception and sense.[89] Φράζομαι shows the meaning of decoding most clearly in oracular contexts, where it is often found in the imperative.[90] The instruction has a meaning that works on two levels: the recipient is instructed to perceive and interpret the contents of the oracle, but also to recognize when a particular set of conditions has been fulfilled (often expressed by the formula ἀλλ' ὅταν, "but when").[91] So, for example, the Delphic oracle given to the Siphnians in response to their question as to whether their newfound wealth will last long calls for an ἀνὴρ φράδμων (3.57.4) to recognize the sign of (φράσσασθαι) a wooden ambush and a red herald (3.57.4).[92] A similar usage occurs in one of the oracles given to the Bakkhiadai of Corinth:[93]

> αἰετὸς ἐν πέτρῃσι κύει, τέξει δὲ λέοντα
> καρτερὸν ὠμηστήν· πολλῶν δ' ὑπὸ γούνατα λύσει.
> ταῦτά νυν εὖ φράζεσθε, Κορίνθιοι, οἳ περὶ καλὴν
> Πειρήνην οἰκεῖτε καὶ ὀφρυόεντα Κόρινθον.
>
> 5.92.β.3

> An eagle in the rocks is pregnant and will give birth to a lion, a mighty eater of raw flesh: he will loosen the knees of many. Look out for this carefully, men of Corinth, who live around fair Peirene and Corinth of the high ridges.

89 Discussion in Steiner 1994:18–19.

90 Parke and Wormell 1956:2.xxviii note the frequency of the verb, especially the imperative φράζου (also φράζευ and φράζεο), in imitations of the oracular style (e.g. Aristophanes *Knights* 1030). See also Fontenrose 1978:170–171 and ch. 2.3.2. below. For the same meaning in a non-oracular context, cf. Hesiod *Works and Days* 448, a passage in which the poet advises his brother to look out for the cry of the crane (φράζεσθαι δ' εὖτ' ἂν γεράνου φωνὴν ἐπακούεις), a σῆμα that it is time to plough.

91 For the formula, cf. 1.55.2 and (without ἀλλά) 8.20.2. Further discussion in ch. 2.3 below.

92 Further discussion of this oracle in ch. 2.3. Asheri et al. 2004 *ad loc.* compare the wordplay with *Iliad* 24.354: φράζεο, Δαρδανίδη· φραδέος νόου ἔργα τέτυκται, "Reflect, son of Dardanos: the action at hand requires a wary mind."

93 Cf. also the oracle given to the Euboeans: φράζεο, βαρβαρόφωνος ὅταν ζυγὸν εἰς ἅλα βάλλῃ | βύβλινον, Εὐβοίης ἀπέχειν πολυμηκάδας αἶγας (8.20.2), "Take care, when one of foreign speech casts a yoke of papyrus onto the sea, to keep the much-bleating goats away from Euboia."

The Bakkhiadai are not, however, able to εὖ φράζεσθαι: Herodotus tells us that the oracle remained ἄσημον (5.92.β.3) and ἀτέκμαρτον (5.92.γ.1), both of which adjectives contain roots prominent in Herodotus' vocabulary relating to signs. The oracle is ἄσημον not in the sense that it has no meaning, but that it seems impossible to move from the surface meaning to the code lying underneath, to which the imperative φράζεσθε draws attention, effectively marking the utterance as coded.[94]

Instances of φράζομαι in contexts other than the oracular do not always have an obvious connection with signs, but it is possible to point to passages where the verb is used of perceiving human actions as significant behavior, and where this recognition and interpretation of the signs of human behavior form the basis of subsequent action.[95] The tears of Xerxes on reviewing his mighty army at Abydos present Artabanos with a conundrum: he perceives (φρασθείς, 7.46.1) Xerxes crying, behavior which is normally a sign of sorrow.[96]

The compound ἐπιφράζομαι ('contrive', 'guess') also demonstrates a connection with the perception and interpretation of signs: it describes the formation of a plan on the basis of (ἐπι-) information from signs. This is strikingly demonstrated in Herodotus' narrative of the siege of Barke, where, thanks to the clever plan of a blacksmith, the inhabitants of the city are quite literally able to undermine the attempts of the besieging army to dig tunnels underneath the city walls:[97]

> τὰ μέν νυν ὀρύγματα ἀνὴρ χαλκεὺς ἀνεῦρε ἐπιχάλκῳ ἀσπίδι, ὧδε ἐπιφρασθείς· περιφέρων αὐτὴν ἐντὸς τοῦ τείχεος προσῖσχε πρὸς τὸ δάπεδον τῆς πόλιος· τὰ μὲν δὴ ἄλλα ἔσκε κωφὰ πρὸς τὰ προσῖσχε, κατὰ δὲ τὰ ὀρυσσόμενα ἠχέεσκε ὁ χαλκὸς τῆς ἀσπίδος· ἀντορύσσοντες δ' ἂν ταύτῃ οἱ Βαρκαῖοι ἔκτεινον τῶν Περσέων τοὺς γεωρυχέοντας.
>
> 4.200.2–3
>
> A blacksmith discovered the tunnels by means of bronze-covered shield, working it out as follows: he carried the shield around

94 For a similar instance in which the adjective ἄσημος refers to the fact that the surface meaning is baffling but that the message contains a deeper meaning, cf. 1.86.4 (Kroisos' reply to Kyros' messengers), discussed in ch. 1.3.2 above and ch. 3.2.1 below.

95 Detienne and Vernant 1978:18n32 characterize φράζεσθαι as "one of the verbs associated with *mêtis.*"

96 For tears and other non-verbal behavior as signs, see ch. 2.7.4 below.

97 The enemy replies with a countermove, which equally depends on the use (or, more accurately, the manipulation) of signs: the Persian commander tricks the inhabitants by means of a false oath into opening the gates of the city (4.201). Cf. ch. 3.1.2.3 below.

> the inner circuit of the wall and kept applying it to the ground. In all the other places to which he applied it, the sound given off was dull, but in the places where there were tunnels, the bronze portion of the shield would echo. The people of Barke would then dig a counter-tunnel in this place and kill the Persian sappers.

Another interesting example concerns the precocious daughter of Kleomenes, Gorgo, who is able to detect signs where others are unable to see any.[98] Demaratos sends a tablet containing a warning to the Spartans of the imminent Persian invasion, but instead of writing on the wax surface, writes on the tablet itself and then covers it with wax, so that his message will escape detection by the Persian roadblocks. The Spartans can find no message or sign in the blank tablet, but Gorgo is able to read a sign in the tablet itself:[99]

> ἐπεὶ δὲ καὶ ἀπίκετο [sc. τὸ δελτίον] ἐς τὴν Λακεδαίμονα, οὐκ εἶχον συμβαλέσθαι οἱ Λακεδαιμόνιοι, πρίν γε δή σφι, ὡς ἐγὼ πυνθάνομαι, Κλεομένεος μὲν θυγάτηρ Λεωνίδεω δὲ γυνὴ Γοργὼ ὑπέθετο, ἐπιφρασθεῖσα αὐτή, τὸν κηρὸν ἐκκνᾶν κελεύουσα, καὶ εὑρήσειν σφέας γράμματα ἐν τῷ ξύλῳ. πειθόμενοι δὲ εὗρον καὶ ἐπελέξαντο, ἔπειτα δὲ τοῖσι ἄλλοισι Ἕλλησι ἐπέστειλαν.
>
> 7.239.4
>
> When the tablet arrived in Sparta, the Spartans were unable to interpret it, until, as I find out, Gorgo, the daughter of Kleomenes and wife of Leonides, worked it out herself and made the following suggestion, ordering them to rub off the wax and find the letters on the wooden surface.

1.3.5 τεκμαίρομαι

Of the five instances of this verb, meaning to judge or conclude on the basis of a τεκμήριον, three are used in a first person context by Herodotus himself, demonstrating his close involvement in the transmission and interpretation

98 Gorgo's intelligence is demonstrated earlier in the *Histories* (5.51), where she rescues her father from falling prey to corruption.

99 Cf. treatment of this passage in ch. 3.1.2.7 below.

of signs.[100] In the famous passage on the course of the Nile, the verb is collocated with another key interpretative verb, συμβάλλομαι. The final conclusion that Herodotus arrives at concerning the unknown course of the Nile is based on a reading of empirical geographical phenomena (τοῖσι ἐμφανέσι), namely the course of the Istros:[101]

> καὶ ὡς ἐγὼ συμβάλλομαι τοῖσι ἐμφανέσι τὰ μὴ γινωσκόμενα τεκμαιρόμενος, τῷ Ἴστρῳ ἐκ τῶν ἴσων μέτρων ὁρμᾶται.
>
> 2.33.2
>
> As I conclude by relying on things that are apparent as indications of what is not perceived, [the Nile] has the same dimensions as the Istros.

Signs of quite a different nature, clothing used as a sign of identity, occur in the conversation of Artabanos and Xerxes in which the former categorically denies the status of signs to dreams, claims that if he were to put on Xerxes' clothes, no dream would be so stupid as to think that he were Xerxes, judging purely by the clothes he was wearing (τῇ σῇ ἐσθῆτι τεκμαιρόμενον, 7.16.γ.2).[102]

100 Uses of the verb by Herodotus himself: 1.57.1–2* *bis* (Herodotus infers on the basis of surviving Pelasgian communities and place names that the Pelasgians spoke a barbarian language); 2.33.2* (Herodotus on the course of the Nile, described above). Other instances: 7.16.γ.2 (dream uses clothing as key to identity, described above); 7.234.1 (Xerxes infers that Demaratos is a good man on the basis that everything he has said so far has come to pass).

101 Lloyd 1989 *ad loc.* compares Solon (Stobaeus 1.79.β Meineke): τὰ ἀφανῆ τοῖς φανέροις τεκμαίρου, "Infer what is unseen on the basis of what is seen." Cf. ch. 3.2.2 below on Herodotus' connection to the language of signs in archaic poetry.

102 Other instances of dress and personal ornament as signs in chs. 2.8.5 and 3.1.2.5 below.

Part 2

Sign Systems

2.1 Portents and Their Interpretation in Herodotus

2.1.1 Definition

Portents are aberrations and departures from the norm which by reason of their unusual nature and unexpected appearance are interpreted as signs declarative or prescriptive of some present or future action. We shall elaborate on the elements of this definition a little later, but let us look first at the vocabulary which Herodotus uses to describe the field of signification which in English is subsumed by the term "portent." "Portent" or "omen" may point to a wide variety of phenomena, and Herodotus also uses such general terms as σημήιον, τέρας, and φάσμα, which can refer to various manifestations (earthquakes, sudden illness, abnormal animal births or behavior, eclipses, disasters, thunder and lightning), together with terms that have a narrower and more specific field of reference: φήμη and κληδών refer to auditory signs, for example.[1]

1 Herodotus also uses the term οἰωνός, which *stricto sensu* refers to the behavior of birds as a means of signification, but in its single occurrence in Herodotus is used in the general sense of an omen: δέκομαι τὸν οἰωνόν (9.91.2), "I accept the omen," says the Spartan Leotykhides when he hears that the name of the Samian messenger is Hegesistratos (see ch. 2.6 below on names and naming). The term κληδών is also, however, used in the same passage. The distinction between τέρατα and φάσματα in Herodotus seems to lie in the following: the five instances of φάσμα in the sense of a portent (it may also refer to an apparition) all involve some kind of meteorological phenomenon (rain, 3.10.3; thunderbolt, 4.79.1; eclipse, 7.37.2 and 7.38.1; κεραυνοί, 8.37.2). It should be noted, however, that the phenomena described at 8.37.2 include non-meteorological phenomena (βοή τε καὶ ἀλαλαγμός, "a shout and war-cry"). In all but one (3.10.3), the expression ἐκ τοῦ οὐρανοῦ "from the sky" or the mention of the divine, ὁ θεός, as agent further confirms the connection with the heavens. On the divine in portents, see discussion below. Τέρατα may include meteorological phenomena (thunder and lightning, 4.28.3) but can involve many other types of portents, such as peculiar animal behavior, earthquakes, and the automatic movement of inanimate objects. Τέρας thus seems a broader term than φάσμα, at least in Herodotus. Cf. Bloch (1963:15–16), who surveys Greek literature in general and comes to the same conclusion, pointing out that the term φάσμα is not confined exclusively to metereological phenomena.

I return now to the definition advanced above, namely that portents are events interpreted as signs declarative or prescriptive of some present or future action, and more specifically, the notion that an event may be regarded as having a significance beyond itself and that it is somehow indicative of something that obtains in the world or that will in the future obtain.

2.1.2 Recognition

A particular phenomenon must be recognized as a portentous sign.[2] This recognition is not always automatic, nor is it always universal. In some of his narratives about portents Herodotus stresses the fact that portents are in the eye of the beholder through the use of verbs such as δοκέω while also concentrating on the moment of realization. Thus the strange appearance of snakes in Sardis and the strange behavior of the horses who eat them "*appeared* to Kroisos *to* be a *teras*, as was in fact the case" (ἰδόντι δὲ τοῦτο Κροίσῳ, ὥσπερ καὶ ἦν, ἔδοξε τέρας εἶναι, 1.78.1). Similarly, the appearance at night of Phocian soldiers whitened with chalk seems in the eyes of the panic-struck Thessalian sentries to be some kind of *teras* (δόξασαι ἄλλο τι εἶναι τέρας, 8.27.3). Recognition that the unusually high rising of bread baked for one of his workers, Perdikkas, who eventually usurps his throne, is a *teras* portending "something big" suddenly "comes upon" the Macedonian king (ἐσῆλθε αὐτίκα ὡς εἴη τέρας καὶ φέροι ἐς μέγα τι, 8.137.3).[3] In speaking of the Egyptians and their practice regarding portents, Herodotus comments that more *terata* have been "found" (ἀνεύρηται) by them than by the rest of humanity (2.82.2).[4] The verb implies a process of careful recognition, selection, and recording.[5] As noted above, this method of interpretation according to precedent and comparison is not one that Herodotus shows the Greeks using.

2 Here Peirce's formulation bears repeating: "Nothing is a sign unless it is interpreted as a sign" (Peirce as quoted in Nöth 1990:42). Cf. Harrison's definition of "omen" as "a miracle with a message" (2000:65). Note the Greek idiom "to receive" (δέκομαι: 1.63.1, 4.15.3, 7.178.2, 8.115.1, 9.91.2) an omen or oracle, which again underlines the process of recognition and acceptance.

3 Other instances of the ingressive aorist of this verb in cases of sudden recognition and realization: 1.116.1 (*anagnôsis* that the shepherd boy is Kyros comes upon Astyages), 3.42.4 (it comes upon Polykrates that the appearance of his ring in the belly of a fish is a sign from the gods).

4 Powell s.v. glosses ἀνεύρηται in this passage as "invent, devise." This understanding of the word appears to be a subjective projection on the scholar's part onto Herodotus of a certain skepticism about the Egyptians and their religious practices.

5 On Greek awe at the vast span of time encompassed by Egyptian record keeping, cf. Herodotus' (and Hekataios') encounter with the priests at Thebes, who show 345 generations of priests (1.143.1–4), and cf. Plato *Timaeus* 22b4–5, where the Egyptian priest cries to Solon that the Greeks are always children.

2.1.3 Code

This brings us to a further aspect of this code: the criterion according to which a portent is recognized as such is culturally determined, as Herodotus emphasizes when speaking of the Egyptians and the Scythians, subjects of his two great ethnographic *logoi* in books 2 and 4 respectively. In both these cases, Egyptian and Scythian practice forms a precise inversion of the Greek norm, as it does in other well-known passages from these books.[6] Thus the fall of rain in Egyptian Thebes in the reign of Psammenitos is a φάσμα μέγιστον for the Egyptians (3.10.3), and is used by Herodotus to foreshadow the unhappy reign of Psamennitos, who will end up seeing his sons and daughters killed or enslaved to the Persians. It further acts as a direct contrast to the reign of the happy-go-lucky Amasis, during which no such shocking event occurred (οὐδέν οἱ μέγα ἀνάρσιον πρῆγμα συνηνείχθη, 3.10.2).[7] Rain in Egyptian Thebes is considered a portent, but would hardly be so in Boeotian Thebes, unless it were to rain blood or frogs. The Scythians marvel (θωμάζεται) at thunder in winter as a *teras*, Herodotus tells us, just the opposite of what is held everywhere else, while thunder in summer is considered unremarkable (4.28.3).[8]

There are also portents that appear in the Greek world and whose interpretation depends on a specifically Greek phrase or context.[9] The portent of a flame which shoots from the breast of a cult image of Hera and which appears only to the Spartan king Kleomenes is interpreted by him as meaning that he will not take Argos. If he were meant to, he argues in self-justification, the flame would have appeared from the statue's *head*, showing he would take the city completely. This ingenious interpretation depends on the phrase κατ' ἄκρης (6.82.2), which has a literal ("from the topmost part") as well as figurative meaning ("utterly"), both of which need to be taken into consideration.[10] It is an interpretation and thus a *teras* wholly specific to the Greek language.

6 The *locus classicus* for Egyptian inversion is 2.35.2–36.4. Cf. Lloyd 1992. On Scythian inversion cf. Hartog 1988.

7 Amasis enjoys great success as a reader and manipulator of signs: cf. e.g. his object lesson in signs involving a golden footbath recast as a holy image (2.172.3–5), discussed below in ch. 2.8.1. See also ch. 3.1 on the manipulators of signs and their general success in the world of the *Histories*.

8 Mikalson (2003:43) notes that in the case of solar phenomena Egyptians do not recognize these as *terata* (2.142.3–4), whereas the Persians and Greeks do.

9 Cf. Ferrari 1997:5 on the culturally specific nature of metaphor. As will be clear from this chapter, the imagery of *terata* overlaps with the metaphorical imagery of oracles and ainetic speech, explored in chapters 2.3 and 2.5.

10 Noted by Benardete 1969:165.

The portentous appearance of a dust-cloud and shout coming from the direction of Eleusis, supposedly abandoned and uninhabited, that Dikaios the Athenian and Demaratos the Spartan (8.65.1) observe points to an even more specific code, one that is not just Greek but purely Athenian. The Athenian has to explain to the Spartan, who for the purposes of this story has no knowledge of the Eleusinian mysteries (8.65.2), the peculiar significance of the mystic cry and the meaning of the portent as a whole.[11]

A portent must thus be recognized and interpreted according to a culturally determined code that attributes meaning to the event. Codes are of course involved in any system of signification, but the code used for the interpretation of portents is a particular one. As Scholes puts it:

> Whenever we "make sense" of an event it is because we possess a system of thought, a code, that enables us to do so. Lightning was once understood as the gesture of a powerful being who lived in the mountains or the sky. Now we understand it as an electrical phenomenon. *A mythic code has been displaced by a scientific one.*[12]

With portents we are dealing with just such a "mythic" (i.e. supernatural) code: this at least is the convention to which Herodotus seems to subscribe on those occasions when he comments on the process directly. According to this code, portents are signs functioning in a chain of communication between god and mortal as sender and recipient respectively.

2.1.4 The Question of the Sender

There are a number of passages where Herodotus presents unusual phenomena as portents issuing from a divine source. The most well-known of these is Herodotus' account of two disasters which befall the Chians, which he views as important signs (σημήια μεγάλα, 6.27.1) of even greater evils to come. The two catastrophes, the deaths from a mysterious illness of all but two members of a chorus of one hundred youths sent to Delphi, and the deaths of 119 children

[11] See Harrison 2000:69–70 on this as an example of what he calls an omen mixed with divination: "Dicaeus—and here is the variation—then puts the apparition to use in a form of impromptu divination: from the direction the procession takes, towards Salamis rather than the Peloponnese, he calculates that it is Xerxes' fleet rather than his land force that would soon suffer." Harrison thus takes this as an instance of someone hijacking a *teras*, much as I do in the case of Artayktes and the *teras* of the fish in the passage discussed below. But one might argue that there is always a divinatory sense to omens.

[12] 1982:142; italics mine. Scholes presumably uses the term "mythic" in the sense of "religious" or "supernatural."

killed when the roof of their school collapses, assume according to this model a significance beyond themselves. The divine (ὁ θεός, 6.27.3) uses these events as signifiers to carry some further message, a forewarning of the disastrous naval defeat they will suffer.[13]

Benardete is the first scholar I know of to approach this passage from an explicitly semiotic point of view, and points out the appropriation by the divine of events which are then made to bear a different meaning. He is however inaccurate in his description of what precisely is used as the signifier or sign vehicle in this example. He argues that both activities in which the two sets of children were engaged involved sets of signs:

> The Chians sent the chorus to dance and perhaps to sing at Delphi; it was designed to propitiate Apollo and gain his favor: and the schoolchildren were learning to read and write the language of their city. As the chorus was meant to signify something to a god, so the schoolchildren were learning what the letters of the alphabet signified. What were already signs with a human sense became signs with another meaning: "the god" made the conversion. The god ignored their original significance—the dance addressed to Apollo and the alphabet to men—and made them foretell the future. He converted human things to a divine end.
>
> Benardete 1969:161

But it is not the *signs* with which the children were originally involved that the god converted to his own end, rather the fact of their deaths while engaged in these activities, and it is precisely this that acts as the signifier or sign vehicle in the semiotic communication which Herodotus describes.

According to Benardete, in this passage and again in his description of the earthquake on Delos (6.98), Herodotus views the portents alternately as intentional signs, with a divine sender, and as non-intentional signs, that is to say with no sender.[14] It is true that both at 6.27 and 6.98 Herodotus expresses

13 ὁ θεός is generally taken here to mean gods in general: cf. 1.31.3 ("God showed man how it might be better to die than to live," though the specific deity involved in the story is Hera) and Mikalson 2003:43 on the question of the specificity of the divine agent: "Herodotus does not specify the divine agents of such omens. We may think that for a thunderbolt it was Zeus (4.79.2), for the earthquake on Delos Apollo (6.97–98), and for the omen we shall see on the Thriasian Plain Demeter (8.65), but the assignment of agent is ours, not Herodotus'. The large majority of omens, whether miraculous or not, cannot be assigned to *any* specific god or divine agency."

14 Ibid. The term "non-intentional sign" is mine; Benardete does not make clear what he understands as a contrast to an intentional sign. Possibly he has in mind so-called natural or diagnostic signs.

himself in two different ways when he comes to speak of the portentous nature of the Chian disasters and the earthquake on Delos. He at first uses an impersonal construction:

> φιλέει δέ κως προσημαίνειν, εὖτ' ἂν μέλλῃ μεγάλα κακὰ ἢ πόλι ἢ ἔθνεϊ ἔσεσθαι· καὶ γὰρ Χίοισι πρὸ τούτων σημήια μεγάλα ἐγένετο.
>
> 6.27.1
>
> There is usually a foreshadowing in some way whenever great evils are about to befall a city or nation: for indeed there were great signs for the Chians before these events [the Chians' disastrous naval defeat].

The addressee is clear enough, but the impersonal construction (φιλέει . . . προσημαίνειν) does not specify the sender. When, however, Herodotus rounds off his account of the σημήια μεγάλα (the deaths of the children on the choral tour to Delphi and of those killed by the collapsing school building), he varies the construction:

> ταῦτα μέν σφι σημήια ὁ θεός προέδεξε.
>
> 6.27.3
>
> The god showed them these things in advance as signs [*sêmêia*].

Here sender and addressee are clearly mentioned, and the incidents are presented squarely in the tradition of Homeric portents, where there is no doubt about the fact that the gods are sending a message. But the impersonal construction Herodotus uses to introduce the passage need not exclude the presence of the divine sender, whom as we see Herodotus refers to so clearly at the end of the passage. In general, such impersonal constructions are not as impersonal as they might seem: the absence of a grammatical subject does not necessarily imply the absence of a logical one.[15] The sentence ταῦτα μέν σφι

[15] Kühner-Gerth II.I §352 and Smyth 934 talk of quasi-impersonal constructions where the subject is clear from the context. Meteorological phenomena in Greek may be expressed by a verb without a subject, or by the same verb with ὁ θεός or a particular deity as a subject. To take an example from Herodotus: cf. ὕει "it rains" (2.22.3; 3.125.4; 4.28.2; 4.50.3; 4.185.2) with ὁ θεὸς ὕει lit. "(the) god rains" (3.117.4). Cf. also ὁ θεὸς ἐνέσκηψε βέλος (4.79.1), "(The) god hurled a dart (of lightning)," as opposed to the impersonal ἀστραπή . . . ἐγένετο (3.86.2), "There was a bolt of lightning." The context of 4.79.1, the destruction of part of Skyles' Greek-style townhouse as a forewarning of his fate, probably determines Herodotus' choice of this highly poetic expression (cf. Pindar *Nemean* 10.8; Aeschylus *Prometheus Bound* 360): further discussion of this passage below.

σημήια ὁ θεός προέδεξε seems in any case designed to round off the passage in typical ring-composition style, except that the introductory clause is not repeated verbatim, but with *variatio* (προσημαίνειν-προέδεξε).

At 6.98 we again meet two slightly different expressions of the significance of an event, when Herodotus describes an earthquake on Delos, previously unshaken by any such disturbances.[16] He uses much the same language as he did in summing up the misfortunes which befell the youth of the Chians:

> καὶ τοῦτο μέν κου τέρας ἀνθρώποισι τῶν μελλόντων κακῶν ἔφηνε ὁ θεός.[17]
>
> 6.98.1
>
> This too, I suppose, the god revealed to men as a *teras* of evils to come.

It is ὁ θεός who reveals (ἔφηνε, cf. προσημαίνειν and προέδεξε) the event as a portent (here τέρας, cf. σημήια), but the addressee is not merely a selected group, as was the case with the Chian portents, but a much wider audience: humankind (ἀνθρώποισι).

In summing up the incident, and the proposition that the combined reigns of Dareios, Xerxes, and Artaxerxes saw more ills for Greece occur than did the previous twenty generations of men, Herodotus says:

> οὕτως οὐδὲν ἦν ἀεικὲς κινηθῆναι Δῆλον τὸ πρὶν ἐοῦσαν ἀκίνητον.
>
> 6.98.3
>
> Thus it was in no way unfitting that Delos, previously unmoved by earthquake, was shaken.

This statement looks at the phenomenon from the viewpoint of probability and appropriateness (*oikos*, cf. οὐδὲν ἦν ἀεικές), a manner of presentation

16 The same combination of earthquakes, divine agency, and *ta oikota* occurs again in Herodotus' discussion of the gorge of the Peneios in Thessaly, where he describes the belief of the local inhabitants that Poseidon caused this gorge as "reasonable" (7.129.4). Cf. Harrison's warning (2000:15) against taking this as a rationalizing explanation that excludes "a parallel divine cause."

17 The indefinite κου does not imply doubt or irony here, but simply seems to be a prefatory softening of an ambitious and bold statement. Cf. Denniston 1996:491n1: "Herodotus is fond of divesting himself of the historian's omniscience, and assuming a winning fallibility . . . This often comes out in his use of κου: cf. i113.3, 114.2." Cf. the similar use of κως at 6.27.1, discussed above, where Herodotus also makes a pronouncement about the participation of the divine as sender of portents. Cf. Powell s.v. κως 5. "*it seems*, in hesitant statement".

which implies a looking back after the fact, an interpretation with hindsight, as Benardete notes. But it would be incorrect to say with him that "to interpret this earthquake as 'fitting' does not mean the same as to interpret it as an intentional sign. The gap between them is as great as between an impersonal and a divine foreshowing at Chios."[18]

What Herodotus does is to look at the matter from another angle: given the magnitude of subsequent events, it was entirely consistent and reasonable that Delos suffered an earthquake. This observation made *post factum* need not exclude an interpretation of the sign as intentional. In fact, the observation seems intended rather as a confirmation of the intentional nature of the sign, using an argument based on what is probable, εἰκός (Ionic οἰκός).[19] Once again Herodotus is rounding off a point he begins with the statement, and so 6.98.3 should be seen as a confirmation of that view, not the introduction of a fundamentally different one. He offers in addition another piece of evidence, drawn from another sign system, the oracle spoken by the same god who sent the *teras*:

> κινήσω καὶ Δῆλον ἀκίνητόν περ ἐοῦσαν.
>
> 6.98.3
>
> I shall shake Delos too, unshaken though it be.

In these two passages, then, Herodotus states that the divine is the sender in the chain of communication. Nowhere else is this expressed quite as clearly by Herodotus as narrator.[20] In fact, the general construction he uses when characterizing something as a *teras* or *phasma* is τέρας (φάσμα) ἐγένετο (ἐφάνη) ("a *teras/phasma* happened/appeared"). This construction does not mention the divine explicitly, but cannot be said to exclude the divine as ultimate sender either. Two figures in Herodotus' narrative speak explicitly of divine senders: Dikaios, son of Theokydes, who witnesses and interprets for Demaratos the mysterious dustcloud and φωνή coming from Eleusis (8.65), and Artayktes the Persian, in a passage we shall return to below when discussing the question of addressee (9.120.2).

18 Benardete 1969:161.

19 For the *eikos* argument as characteristic of the fifth-century techniques of argument and debate, cf. Thomas 2000:168n1.

20 Mikalson 2002:195 notes: "Prophecies from omens and dreams might be credited to 'the gods' or 'the divine' (e.g., 6.27.1–3, 7.12–18), but often involve no deity. For omens the location and circumstances might offer a clue (Demeter near Eleusis? 8.65), but even here we, not Herodotus, make the connection."

Dikaios concludes that the phenomena he and Demaratos see are clearly of divine origin:

> τάδε γὰρ ἀρίδηλα, ἐρήμου ἐούσης τῆς Ἀττικῆς, ὅτι θεῖον τὸ φθεγγόμενον, ἀπ' Ἐλευσῖνος ἰὸν ἐς τιμωρίην Ἀθηναίοισί τε καὶ τοῖσι συμμάχοισι.[21]
>
> 8.65.2
>
> The following is abundantly clear, that the voice is of divine origin, since Attika is deserted, and that it is coming from Eleusis to bring vengeance for the Athenians and their allies.

Herodotus makes no comment on this, but his emphasis on Dikaios' obtaining of witnesses (ταῦτα μὲν Δίκαιος ὁ Θεοκύδεος ἔλεγε, Δημαρήτου τε καὶ ἄλλων μαρτύρων καταπτόμενος [8.65.6], "This is what Dikaios the son of Theokydes said, appealing to Demaratos and others as witnesses") and the placement of the account, foreshadowing and preparing as it does the way for the account of the battle at Salamis, seem to indicate his acceptance of the divine origin of the phenomena. On a narrative level, the account of the portent presents the two possibilities between which the allies will have to decide, namely, retreat to, and defense of, the Peloponnese, or offering battle at Salamis. This passage shows in which way the gods decide, and gives us a foretaste of the outcome of events, while the decision taken in the world of men is presented later, at 8.78.

The second figure, Artayktes, who has been captured by the Athenians, insists that the sender of the portent of the jumping fish is none other than the hero Protesilaos, whose precinct he had defiled, and uses one of Herodotus' key words for communication by means of signs:

> οὐ γὰρ σοὶ πέφηνε, ἀλλ' ἐμοὶ σημαίνει ὁ ἐν Ἐλαιοῦντι Πρωτεσίλεως.
>
> 9.120.2
>
> Not for you has it appeared, rather it is to me that Protesilaos who lies in Elaious is sending a sign.

Once again, Herodotus makes no explicit comment on this, and the account is related at one remove (λέγεται ὑπὸ Χερσονησιτέων, 9.120.1), but whether or not Artayktes actually believes his own statement, he does ultimately pay

21 See Stockinger 1959:16n8 for discussion of Homeric use (*Iliad* 2.318) of the adjective ἀρίζηλος in connection with *terata*.

for the outrages he has committed, in one of the most powerful scenes of the *Histories*.[22]

Lastly, let us consider the case of Dareios' clandestine manufacture of a sign which will make him king, where the question of divine involvement again surfaces. There is no question, of course, of the gods' producing the neighing of Dareios' horse, the sign agreed upon by the seven Persian conspirators: that is the work of the manipulations of Dareios' groom, Oibares, as Herodotus makes clear. But immediately upon the production of this sign, a lightning bolt flashes from a clear sky and a thunderclap sounds, "as if by some arrangement," says Herodotus (ὥσπερ ἐκ συνθέτου τευ γενόμενα, 3.86.2). Herodotus views with irony the apparent confirmation of an artificially produced sign by another sign, one wholly impossible to arrange by human ingenuity; it is almost as if heaven winks at Dareios' deception. The pattern of double sign is one familiar from Homer, where Odysseus, for example, in response to a prayer receives a double portent in the form of thunder from Zeus and a κληδών from a servant, who prays aloud for Zeus to get rid of the suitors (*Odyssey* 20.103–104). The situation described by Herodotus seems to mirror such a combination of portents, yet the first incident is no portent, since Dareios has perverted the principle of chance and accident.[23]

2.1.5 Recipient

Let us move now from the question of sender to that of addressee. The term "addressee" implies, however, a model of communication in which a specific person or group is targeted. Portents in the *Histories* may indeed be presented as directed at a particular person or people, but it is also possible to view them as being presented to a wider audience, namely, all mankind (ἀνθρώποισι, 6.98.1), among whom certain individuals may be affected more than others. In this case we might speak of a recipient, one who happens to witness the portent, rather than an addressee. As we have seen above, a typical construction in Herodotus' portent narratives is "a *teras* happened" (τέρας ἐγένετο), with the person affected or witnessing the event appearing in the dative.

[22] I raise the question of Artayktes' belief in the agency of Protesilaos, because, as will be suggested below (ch. 3.1.3.3), Artayktes attempts to manipulate the situation to his own benefit by his particular interpretation of the portent, but ends up bringing about his own death. On this passage see Nagy 2001.

[23] Contrast this with an unambiguous portent of Homeric magnitude and clarity that appears to the seven conspirators on their way to dethrone the false Smerdis (3.76.3): seven pairs of eagles pursue, pluck, and savage two pairs of vultures.

The occurrence of a portent in the immediate vicinity of someone creates a presumption that the portent is directed at that person. Thus when at Olympia, in the presence of Hippokrates, the contents of a cauldron spontaneously begin to bubble, with no fire underneath, Khilon interprets this *teras* as referring to Hippokrates himself (1.59.1–2).

As we have seen, the question of observer versus recipient is played upon in the case of the *teras* of the jumping fish, which occurs in the presence of an Athenian soldier guarding Artayktes, but which the latter insists is meant for him alone. He uses the verb σημαίνω, with the hero Protesilaos being the sender and himself the exclusive addressee: οὐ γὰρ σοὶ πέφηνε, ἀλλ' ἐμοὶ σημαίνει ὁ ἐν 'Ελαιοῦντι Πρωτεσίλεως (9.120.2).[24] Similarly, in talking of two *terata* that occur while Xerxes is leading his army toward the Hellespont, Herodotus says that the first (a mare gives birth to a hare) occurred to the Persian host as they were setting out (ἐς ὁδὸν ὁρμημένοισι τέρας σφι ἐφάνη μέγα, 7.57.1). When he speaks of the second *teras*, which is also blithely ignored by Xerxes, Herodotus speaks of it as happening to Xerxes specifically: ἐγένετο δὲ καὶ ἕτερον αὐτῷ τέρας ἐόντι ἐν Σάρδισι (7.57.2). The shift in presentation reflects perhaps the distinction between general audience and ultimate recipient while also functioning as a narrowing device, bringing the focus of the divine warnings to bear more sharply on Xerxes, whose personal actions have caused and will continue to cause upset and destruction.

2.1.6 Interpretation

Once a portent has been recognized as such, the next stage is to interpret or decode it. We have already refered to the kind of code involved in portents and the fact that Herodotus specifically points out the culturally determined nature of this code in a number of places. Now let us look at the content of this code, and how its decoding is presented by Herodotus. First, the decoders themselves. It is an interesting fact that while professional decoders and interpreters of portents appear in the work, they do so always in a non-Greek context, for reasons which we will presently explore.[25] For example, Herodotus

24 The question of the recipient vs. ultimate audience of this portent is discussed by Nagy (2001:xx), who does not seem to view Artayktes as the ultimate recipient: "The non-Greek speaker can claim that the meaning of Protesilaos is intended for him, not for the Athenian, let alone the native Greeks of the Chersonesus who worship Protesilaos as their local hero. Who, then, is the intended receiver, the *destinataire*, of the meaning of Protesilaos? The historian does not say, and in this regard his meaning, too, is opaque."

25 The *prophêtês* at Delphi is mentioned in connection with the θῶμα and τέρας of the mysterious appearance outside the temple of Apollo of weapons normally kept inside the temple

mentions the Egyptian practice of committing *terata* and their outcomes to writing in order to make use of them to predict the outcome of similar portents in the future:

> γενομένου γὰρ τέρατος φυλάσσουσι γραφόμενοι τὠποβαῖνον, καὶ ἤν κοτε ὕστερον παραπλήσιον τούτῳ γένηται, κατὰ τὠυτὸ νομίζουσι ἀποβήσεσθαι.
>
> 2.82.2
>
> When a *teras* occurs, they watch for the outcome and write it down, and if something like this ever happens again, they consider that the outcome will be the same.

The use of writing in an Egyptian context implies a professional group of scribes and interpreters. This method of interpretation, an approach which seems to involve the strict use of precedent, is mentioned only here in Herodotus. Nowhere else in the *Histories* do we find reference to the decoding of portentuous signs by reference to written or oral records.[26] In those instances where an explanation of a particular reading or decoding of a portent is offered, or even in cases where an explanation is not offered, the portent seems in each case to be addressed on the basis of its own internal logic, without resorting to a body of collected portents. This is not to say that the Egyptian practice of interpretation according to precedent was unfamiliar to the Greek world: Herodotus simply shows more interest in a technique that calls for skill in perceiving systems of oppositions, similarities, and analogies, and not on the application of precedent. This is in fact a general Herodotean characteristic to be found not just in connection with portents, but with other sign systems as well, as subsequent chapters will make plain.

Other professional interpreters mentioned in the context of portents are the Persian *magoi* (7.37.2) and the Telmessian *exêgêtai* (1.78.2), both of whose interpretations we will look at shortly.[27] But apart from these figures, all the remaining interpreters of portents we encounter in the work are lay people. Some of these may be distinguished by a reputation for *sophiê*, as, for example,

(8.37.1–2), but σημανέων (8.37.1) here could simply mean that he relayed the *teras* and not that he interpreted it. See discussion in ch. 1.2.1.2 above on this sense of σημαίνω, and compare 8.41.3, where the priestess of Athena is depicted as relaying, but not necessarily interpreting, the portent of the sacred snake refusing its honey-cake.

26 Interpretation by reference to collected precedents in written form fits in with what we know of Near Eastern treatment of portents: cf. e.g. Oppenheim 1974, Maul 2003.

27 The *magoi* are not, of course, exclusively interpreters of portents, but are consulted in the decoding of other sign systems, such as dreams (cf. ch. 2.2 below).

Thales (1.74.2), or may demonstrate *sophiê* in their interpretations and use of them, such as Kleomenes (6.82.2) or Zopyros (3.153.1), and it is in these figures that Herodotus shows a particular interest, as we will see over the course of this investigation and in particular ch. 3.2. There is one important interpreter who should not be passed over, and that is Herodotus himself. All the interpretations of portents in the work derive in some sense from Herodotus, whether he relates his own or those of others, and the question of Herodotus' identification with the figures who advance them is one we will encounter later. For the moment, however, we shall focus on those places where he delivers an interpretation in his own voice.[28] Lastly, not all portents receive an explanation, or their explanation may be somehow incomplete, with the audience expected to supply a step in the reasoning.[29] As we shall see, the missing step invariably assumes the knowledge of a cultural convention which is unexpressed. This once more reinforces the fact that portents depend always on a conventional code.

We begin our investigation with one of the few professional interpretations of a portent that Herodotus chooses to relate and that also happens to be one of the most completely presented decodings in the work. The Telmessians, known for their skill in this area, explain, quite correctly as it turns out, a *teras* observed by Kroisos at Sardis:

> ταῦτα ἐπιλεγομένῳ Κροίσῳ τὸ προάστιον πᾶν ὀφίων ἐνεπλήσθη. φανέντων δὲ αὐτῶν οἱ ἵπποι, μετιέντες τὰς νομὰς νέμεσθαι, φοιτῶντες κατήσθιον. ἰδόντι δὲ τοῦτο Κροίσῳ, ὥσπερ καὶ ἦν, ἔδοξε τέρας εἶναι.
>
> 1.78.1
>
> While Kroisos was considering these things, the region in front of the city was filled with snakes. After they appeared, the horses left their usual pastures and came and ate them up. Upon seeing this, Kroisos decided it was a *teras*, which in fact it was.[30]

28 For example, 4.79.1; 6.27; 6.98; 7.57.1; 8.37; 8.55.

29 Cf. Mikalson 2002:195 on how in the case of portents at 8.65 and 4.79.2 "we, not Herodotus, make the connection" between deity and portent.

30 Cf. the intriguing thesis of Griffiths (2001:162–164), who claims that this interpretation is a retrofitting to suit the facts and that "no halfway intelligent person confronted with the prodigy could do other than assume that the horses symbolized the Lydians" (162), since horses are the Lydians' strong suit (cf. 1.27.3–4), whereas the Persians with their scale armor are like snakes. Seen this way, "the interpretation ascribed to the Telmessians prophets can only be understood as a deliberately perverse, paradoxical, and sophistic reversal of the surface meaning of the omen" (163). Griffiths views this manipulation as in fact the work of Herodotus, who for narrative purposes did not want to present the account as a case of Kroisos presuming that horses=Lydians and snakes=Persians, only to find out that he had made the wrong assumption after his disas-

The narrative fully describes the transmission by messengers of the details of the *teras* from Kroisos to the Telmessians, and the transmission of their reply back to the king. The interpretation of the experts is quite correct, but arrives too late to be of use to Kroisos, who has already been captured by the Persians and who seems fated to derive no benefit from expert advice, whether through his own lack of comprehension (cf. the famous encounter with Solon, 1.29–33) or a failure to receive messages in time. This narrative motif may be contrasted with another scenario (7.37.2), to be discussed below, where advice from experts is provided immediately, without any interference in the chain of communication, but the interpretation advanced by the *magoi* is flawed.

How do the Telmessians interpret the portent? Herodotus, no doubt for greater narrative effect, presents us with their interpretation first, postponing slightly the presentation of their reasoning:

> Τελμησσέες μέντοι τάδε ἔγνωσαν, στρατὸν ἀλλόθροον προσδόκιμον εἶναι Κροίσῳ ἐπὶ τὴν χώρην, ἀπικόμενον δὲ τοῦτον καταστρέψεσθαι τοὺς ἐπιχωρίους, λέγοντες ὄφιν εἶναι γῆς παῖδα, ἵππον δὲ πολέμιόν τε και ἐπήλυδα.
>
> 1.78.3
>
> This was the reading of the Telmessians, that Kroisos could expect a foreign army to come against his country and that once it arrived it would defeat the native inhabitants. They said that a snake was the child of the earth and that a horse was hostile and an invader.

In the report of the reasoning behind their interpretation what is presented is the significance of the agents in the portent, the snakes and the horses. We are left to ourselves to combine the elements: no great task, to be sure, but nevertheless a narrative technique that we encounter elsewhere in Herodotus' narratives concerning the interpretation of signs.[31] What could be regarded as a separate *teras* in its own right, the sudden appearance of snakes in Sardis, is passed over in favor of the even more striking *teras* of the horses devouring the snakes, and it is this that forms the object of the interpreters' attention. Three separate *terata* combine to form a complex here: the appearance of snakes in

---

trous defeat. Griffiths suggests that this was because Herodotus had already used this motif with Kroisos' famous misinterpretation of the "You will destroy a great empire" oracle. I am not convinced by this part of Griffiths' argument, but the idea that the Telmessians' interpretation is paradoxical and that this ultimately reflects on Herodotus' ingenuity is attractive.

31 Cf. e.g. below on the portent of the mule giving birth (7.57.2).

Sardis, the horses' desertion of their normal pastures and their arrival in the *proastion*, and, thirdly, their devouring of the snakes,

The key to the decoding of this complex, as presented by Herodotus' narrative, lies in making a connection between the snakes and the Lydians on the one hand, and the horses and the enemy on the other. The stress in Herodotus' account may thus be said to fall on the axis of selection (or substitution) and the relation between individual elements in the *terata* and what they correspond to.[32] The first connection is made via the identification of snakes with "children of the earth" (ὄφιν εἶναι γῆς παῖδα, 1.78.3). This does not receive any further elaboration, but the point in common must be the autochthonous origin of both snakes and the Lydians. Once pointed out, the transference is a natural and instinctive one for a Greek audience at least, since the claim of national autochthony and the serpentine appearance and chthonic origins of autochthonous ancestors are familiar themes in Greek mythology and art.[33] One could say that snakes are literally children of the earth, but that as applied to the Lydians the expression is metaphorical.[34] The semantic marker of autochthony thus links the two. This marker becomes clear if one considers the *teras* from the point of view of space and a system of oppositions of types of space. The snakes do not come from anywhere, but simply are suddenly there, filling the *proastion* (τὸ προάστιον πᾶν ὀφίων ἐνεπλήσθη, 1.78.1). If one views the physical layout of the situation described by Herodotus in terms of the opposition foreign vs. native, or rural vs. urban,

32 "Axis of selection" and "axis of combination" are terms developed by Jakobson (1960) on the basis of the two structural relations in language, which Saussure characterized as paradigmatic and syntagmatic relations. Paradigmatic relations (envisaged along a vertical axis) exist between elements which can be substituted for each other in a particular sign complex (e.g. between the snakes of the portent and the Lydians, or the horses and invaders), the "possible alternatives of and oppositions to a sign" (Nöth 1990:444). Syntagmatic relations, envisaged along a horizontal axis, govern the combination of the elements of a sign complex (e.g. horses eat snakes = enemy overrun Lydians). Cf. Munson 2001a:46 in the context of Herodotus' use of analogy: "Comparison and analogy may be activated 'horizontally' to bind overlapping, concentric, or parallel classes of similar objects. But they also work 'vertically,' through indices and symbols across different levels of reality, as in inductive prophecy."

33 For discussion of this motif in an Athenian context, cf. Loraux 1993 (introduction, and ch. 1). The contrast between αὐτόχθονες "autochthonous people" and ἐπήλυδες "immigrants" is made by Herodotus in discussing the population of Libya (4.197.2), also at 8.73.1–2 in connection with the peoples of the Peloponnese. He speaks of Erekhtheus as "earthborn" (γηγενής, 8.55).

34 There is in fact a tradition of autochthonous origin linked to the city of Sardis in which it is described as πρωτόχθων (e.g. *SEG* 36, 1096 where Sardis is ἡ πρωτόχθων καὶ μητρόπολις τῆς Ἀσίας καὶ Λυδίας ἁπάσης, "the first land and mother-city of Asia and all of Lydia") and αὐτόχθων: epigraphic and literary references in Chuvin 1991:104 and Herrmann 1993:238–239. I am grateful to Prof. C. P. Jones for these references.

the *proastion* here falls into the latter category.[35] In this way, it becomes easy to understand the identification of the horse as an enemy and invader (ἵππον δὲ πολέμιόν τε καὶ ἐπήλυδα, 1.78.3). The horses abandon their normal areas and normal activities and frequent an unaccustomed area, and indulge in abnormal behavior, the eating of snakes (οἱ ἵπποι μετιέντες τὰς νομὰς νέμεσθαι, φοιτῶντες κατήσθιον, 1.78.1).[36] The horse in this interpretation thus has the semantic marker |foreign|. Once the necessary substitutions have been made, the elements can be combined and read horizontally along the axis of combination to produce the total message (Figure 2).

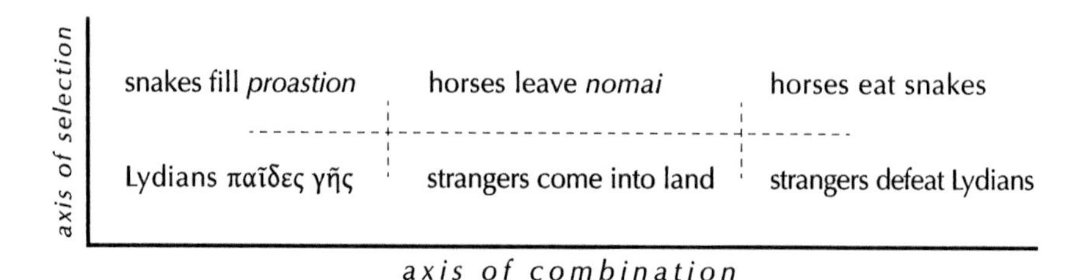

Figure 2. Diagram of the *teras* of 1.78

The other instance of a professional interpretation illustrates an approach which is based a flawed premise. While setting out with his army for Abydos, Xerxes witnesses a total eclipse of the sun by the moon:

> ὁρμημένῳ δέ οἱ ὁ ἥλιος ἐκλιπὼν τὴν ἐκ τοῦ οὐρανοῦ ἕδρην ἀφανὴς ἦν οὔτ' ἐπινεφέλων ἐόντων αἰθρίης τε τὰ μάλιστα, ἀντὶ ἡμέρης τε νὺξ ἐγένετο.
>
> 7.37.2

[35] The *proastion* is of course capable of being contrasted with the *astu* or *polis* proper, as it is indeed at 4.78, where Skyles pursues his Greek lifestyle in the *polis*, while his Scythian comrades are left behind in the *proastion*. Cf. Audring 1981:223–224: "Man darf sich daher eine unsichtbare Grenzlinie denken, die das *proastion* von der eigentlichen Stadt, im speziellen Falle des Skyles das Skythische vom Griechischen, schied." This opposition does not seem to be at work here, and the *proastion* should be regarded rather as space associated with the city. Audring, surveying evidence referring to the Archaic period, defines the *proastion* as "Landzone in unmittelbarer Nähe der Stadt" (228), so that it is an area capable of being viewed alternatively as outside the city or as closely linked with it.

[36] Apart from the etymological connection between νομή and νέμεσθαι which Herodotus plays upon here, there is of course a play on νόμος ("custom") and νομή ("pasture, customary area").

> As Xerxes was starting off, the sun left its place in the sky and was invisible, even though there were no clouds and the sky was exceptionally clear, and it became night instead of day.

When he approaches the *magoi* for an interpretation, they reply that it is a divine foreshadowing for the Greeks of the destruction of their cities:

> οἱ δὲ ἔφασαν ὡς Ἕλλησι προδεικνύει ὁ θεὸς ἔκλειψιν τῶν πολίων, λέγοντες ἥλιον εἶναι Ἑλλήνων προδέκτορα, σελήνην δὲ σφέων.
>
> 7.37.3

> They said that the god was pointing out in advance the eclipse of their cities to the Greeks and that the sun was an indicator of the Greeks while the moon referred to themselves.

As with his presentation of the Telmessians's decoding, Herodotus relates first the total reading of the φάσμα, the combination of the sign components, and then analyzes the individual components (the sun and moon) in terms of the axis of selection. The idea that a literal eclipse in the heavens should indicate a metaphorical eclipse on the earth, and that the divine should be the transmitter of such a sign complex (cf. προδεικνύει ὁ θεός), follows naturally once one has recognized the phenomenon as a portent, but it is the connection that the *magoi* draw between sun and moon as signifiers (or, as Herodotus in a once-off usage calls them, προδέκτορες) and the Greeks and Persians respectively as the signified that is problematic. Unlike the decoding of the Telmessians, which relies on a system of internal oppositions present and detectable in the sign complex, the interpretation of the *magoi* seems to be predicated on an arbitrary assumption: why should the sun be a symbol of the Greeks and not of the Persians? Their reading is perhaps motivated by a desire to remove the sense of unease which the portent engenders in their leader, who is described as becoming "worried" (τῷ Ξέρξῃ ἐπιμελὲς ἐγένετο, 7.37.3). Their pronouncement is in fact an apotropaic gesture and a reflection of what they *hope* will be. As members of the king's entourage, they do not enjoy the same independence as the Telmessians, and their partiality leads them to an ill-considered reading, a phenomenon observable also in their interpretations of dreams (cf. ch. 2.2 below).[37]

Herodotus' account of the φάσμα ignored by the philhellenic Scythian king Skyles illustrates well his occasional practice of omitting a full explanation of elements of the portent, leaving it to the audience to make the final

37 The question of influence and self-interest in interpretation is considered in ch. 3.2.1 below.

connection. As we have already seen with the portent of the snakes at Sardis, these connections are perhaps easier for an ancient Greek audience to make than a contemporary one, and are interesting for what they reveal of the cultural conventions and code according to which the portent is understood. Herodotus sets the portent squarely in a framework of divine warning: ἐπείτε δὲ ἔδεέ οἱ κακῶς γενέσθαι, ἐγένετο ἀπὸ προφάσιος τοιῆσδε (4.79.1), "A misfortune was bound to befall him, and it came about for the following reason." A lightning bolt (Herodotus chooses to frame the sentence with ὁ θεός, "the god," as subject of an active verb) strikes and destroys Skyles' town house, built in Greek style, just as he is preparing to be initiated into the rites of Dionysos:

> μέλλοντι δέ οἱ ἐς χεῖρας ἄγεσθαι τὴν τελετὴν ἐγένετο φάσμα μέγιστον. ἦν οἱ ἐν Βορυσθενεϊτέων τῇ πόλι οἰκίης μεγάλης καὶ πολυτελέος περιβολή . . . τὴν πέριξ λευκοῦ λίθου σφίγγες τε καὶ γρῦπες ἕστασαν· ἐς ταύτην ὁ θεὸς ἐνέσκηψε βέλος· καὶ ἡ μὲν κατεκάη πᾶσα, Σκύλης δὲ οὐδὲν τούτου εἵνεκα ἧσσον ἐπετέλεσε τὴν τελετήν.
>
> 4.79.1–2

> As he was about to undertake his initiation a most striking manifestation [*phasma*] took place. He owned in the city of the Borysthenites a large and costly walled house . . . about which were placed sphinxes and griffins made of marble. Onto this [house] the god let fall a bolt of lightning, and it burned down entirely, but despite this Skyles still went ahead with his initiation.

Skyles is eventually put to death by the Scythians for his desertion to foreign ways (ξεινικοὶ νόμοι, 4.80.5).

There is a detail of Skyles' house that Herodotus provides in his description that seems to be relevant but is not explained: the sphinxes and griffins of white stone. How do these sphinxes and griffins function in the sign complex? The connection between signifier and signified seems to be one between an item associated with the cult of a god and the cult itself: since the *phasma* occurs just before Skyles' initiation into the rites of Dionysos, it might be natural to assume the sphinxes and griffins are symbols of Dionysiac cult.[38] Yet griffins and sphinxes are not the first creatures which spring to mind as part of Dionysiac iconography of

[38] Interestingly enough, a marble statue of what is either a sphinx or a griffin (head and upper thorax missing), dating from the fifth century, was found in excavations at Olbia at the beginning of the century. Description in Koshelenko et al. 1984:213 and photograph ibid., tab. 98.1. Koshelenko et al. see the object as an example of the influence of local environment on art.

the fifth century at any rate.[39] We must either revise our opinions about Dionysiac iconography of the fifth century in the light of this passage, or seek an alternative explanation. More likely is that the combination of sphinxes and griffins constitutes a typically Greek decorative motif, and that they are in this way linked to Greek culture and cult, and thus to Dionysiac cult, which in this narrative is viewed by Scythian eyes as somehow representative and typical of Greek culture (4.79.3). The connection to Dionysos according to this model would then be a more indirect one. It is interesting that what for the Scythians is most typically Greek, the rites and madness of Dionysos and his followers, or, in the account of Anakharsis (4.76.1–5), those of the Great Mother, is precisely that which the Greeks themselves could at times choose to depict as foreign and "other."[40] There are in fact several examples of sphinxes and griffins depicted together (a naturally attractive combination for an artist, since both are *Mischwesen*), both in vase painting and in the plastic arts, dating from the Archaic to the Classical periods.[41] The griffin admittedly is not Greek in origin, nor the sphinx, but they are common decorative motifs on Greek artifacts of the archaic and classical periods, and it is in this way that they can act as symbols of Greekness.[42] As symbols, the link between them

39 In Herodotus, griffins are associated with Apollo as guardians (χρυσοφύλακες} of the hyperborean gold from the one-eyed Arimaspoi: 4.13.1 and 4.27. Griffins are found in Dionysiac iconography of the fourth century, as animals who draw his chariot (e.g. fourth-c. pelike in Paris [Louvre MNB 1036] and situla in New York [MMA 56.171.64], reproduced in *LIMC* s.v. *Dionysus*, 461 and 462), as well as in other Dionysiac contexts of the same period which seem to suggest their role as guardians of the dead (discussion in Delplace 1980, esp. 365–385). But Delplace 1980 (who does not, however, consider this passage) maintains that this development is to be found only in the Hellenistic period. Sphinxes seem even less likely as Dionysiac symbols. It is true that Chian coinage from the fifth century depicts a sphinx in front of an amphora covered by grapes, which seems to argue a connection with the cult of Dionysos, but this seems an isolated practice, and there does not seem to be any extant representation of sphinxes and griffins together in a Dionysiac context. For examples of this motif on the coins of Chios see Kraay 1976, nos. 888–892.

40 See Corcella 1993:293–294; Hartog 1988:61–84; Henrichs 1994:47–51.

41 "Kolonnettenkrater" (Attic) British Museum B 101, Naukratis (Abb. 41 in Dierichs 1981); pyxis (Corinthian) St. Louis, Collection of Washington University 600.WU 3263 (Abb. 13 in Dierichs 1981); "Kesselkrater mit Ringhenkeln" (northern Ionia), Paris, Louvre E659 (Abb. 76 in Dierichs 1981); gold sheet from Delphi (Abb. 110 in Dierichs 1981); terra cotta plaque from Lokroi, Sackler Museum 1980.2, ca. 570 BCE (*LIMC* s.v *Sphinx*, ill. 232).

42 The "white stone" (i.e. marble) from which the sphinxes and griffins are sculpted also acts as an indication of Greekness. Herodotus himself mentions griffins as decorative devices on a Greek artifact: a bronze vessel like a krater which is decorated with the heads of griffins in a row (4.152.4), a description which matches well with finds of *protomoi* in the shape of griffins (examples in Delplace 1980 and Dierichs 1981). My use of the term *symbol* follows the definition established by Peirce and followed by Sebeok of an arbitrary and conventional sign, where the link between the sign and what it denotes is based on convention and not on similarity or contiguity (discussion in Nöth 1990:108 and 115–120).

and what they signify is based on convention, on a fashion in the Greek decorative arts which here becomes a sign of Greek culture.[43]

A more direct link between cultic item and divinity exists in two other portents in the *Histories*, both relating to the goddess Athena and the Athenian akropolis. As with the mysterious dust-cloud seen coming from Eleusis (8.65), they are all portents in which the code against which they are to be read is a local and narrow one, one which must be explained to a panhellenic audience. In the first, the sacred snake in the temple of Athena leaves its honey-cake untouched:

> λέγουσι Ἀθηναῖοι ὄφιν μέγαν φύλακα τῆς ἀκροπόλιος ἐνδιατᾶσθαι ἐν τῷ ἱρῷ. λέγουσί τε ταῦτα καὶ δὴ καὶ ὡς ἐόντι ἐπιμήνια ἐπιτελέουσι προτιθέντες· τὰ δ᾽ ἐπιμήνια μελιτόεσσά ἐστι. αὕτη δ᾽ ἡ μελιτόεσσα ἐν τῷ πρόσθε αἰεὶ χρόνῳ ἀναισιμουμένη τότε ἦν ἄψαυστος.
>
> 8.41.2–3
>
> The Athenians say that a great snake lives in the sanctuary as guardian of the akropolis. They also say they perform a rite of setting out monthly offerings for it, believing it to exist: the offerings consist of honey-cake. This honey-cake, which up till then had always been consumed, at that time remained untouched.

When this is announced by the priestess (as has already been noted in ch. 1.2.1.2, σημηνάσης as applied to the priestess refers rather to the secondary conveying of sign information than to interpretation, which the Athenians seem to provide for themselves), the Athenians are all the more willing to abandon the city "since the goddess too had left the akropolis" (ὡς καὶ τῆς θεοῦ ἀπολελοιπυίης τὴν ἀκρόπολιν, 8.41.3). Thus the snake functions as an index of the goddess, being a guardian (φύλαξ, 8.41.2) of her sanctuary.[44]

Another example of a portent involving the relationship between an item associated with the goddess and the goddess herself follows soon after his account of the snake. Again, in order to explain the portent, Herodotus must explain the cultural code against which it is to be read. Thus he explains

[43] Sphinxes and griffins are found on Scythian artifacts (a gold mirror, for example, from the *kurgan* of Kelermes in southern Russia shows that the motif of the griffin and the sphinx was popular in Scythian art as early as the seventh/sixth c. BCE [reproduction in Corcella 1993, ill. 4–5]).

[44] I use the term *index* of a sign which points to the presence of something else by virtue of association with the signified either through contiguity or a relationship of part and whole. This is the sense established by Peirce and followed by Sebeok (discussion in Nöth 1990:107–114).

the significance of the sacred olive tree in the Erekhtheion, before relating the portent of the tree:

> ἔστι ἐν τῇ ἀκροπόλι ταύτῃ Ἐρεχθέος τοῦ γηγενέος λεγομένου εἶναι νηός, ἐν τῷ ἐλαίη τε καὶ θάλασσα ἔνι, τὰ λόγος παρὰ Ἀθηναίων Ποσειδέωνά τε καὶ Ἀθηναίην ἐρίσαντας περὶ τῆς χώρης μαρτύρια θέσθαι. ταύτην ὦν τὴν ἐλαίην ἅμα τῷ ἄλλῳ ἱρῷ κατέλαβε ἐμπρησθῆναι ὑπὸ τῶν βαρβάρων· δευτέρῃ δὲ ἡμέρῃ ἀπὸ τῆς ἐμπρήσιος Ἀθηναίων οἱ θύειν ὑπὸ βασιλέος κελευόμενοι ὡς ἀνέβησαν ἐς τὸ ἱρόν, ὥρων βλαστὸν ἐκ τοῦ στελέχεος ὅσον τε πηχυαῖον ἀναδεδραμηκότα.[45]
>
> 8.55
>
> There is on this akropolis a temple which is said to be that of Erekhtheus the Earthborn, and in it there is an olive-tree and a source of salt water, which the story told by the Athenians says Poseidon and Athena set up as *marturia* when they fought over the area. Now it happened that this olive tree was set on fire along with the rest of the sanctuary by the barbarians. On the second day after the fire, when those Athenians who were commanded by the king to offer sacrifice went up to the sanctuary, they saw that a shoot, as long as a cubit, had shot up from the stump.

Here the olive tree functions as a sign in several ways: firstly, the tree itself is metonymically a symbol of Athena and a *marturion* testifying to her gift of the tree to the Athenians, her victory over Poseidon, and her claim to be their goddess.[46] It also acts as an index, since its rapid growth from seeming destruction presumably points to the renewed presence of the goddess. We may think for example of the *Homeric Hymn to Dionysos* and the sudden appearance and growth of the vegetation associated with that divinity when the ship on which he has been kidnapped by pirates is suddenly overrun with vines and ivy (38–41). Herodotus does not need to label this explicitly as a *thôma* or *teras*, but the narrative steers us in this direction, with the introductory sentence "I shall now relate why I mentioned these things" (τοῦ δὲ εἵνεκεν τούτων ἐπεμνήσθην, φράσω, 8.55) promising us a good story, and the details of the account are suggestive and portentous enough in themselves.[47]

45 This sign is linked by Herodotus' narrative to a sign of a different nature: Herodotus tells us Xerxes had ordered Athenian exiles in his retinue to make sacrifices on the akropolis, giving as a reason two alternatives, one of which suggests as a motivation a dream, 8.54 (cf. discussion of this motif in ch. 2.2 below).

46 See ch. 1.1.4 above on *marturia*.

47 On Herodotus' use of the verb φράζω in contexts of sign transmission, see above, ch. 1.2.2.

Finally, let us consider an interpretation advanced by Herodotus himself. After describing the Persian crossing of the Hellespont, he relates the *teras* of a mare giving birth to a hare, which he characterizes as εὐσύμβλητον (7.57.1), "easy to interpret," an adjective formed from the verb συμβάλλομαι, one of the verbs he uses in particular to describe the process of decoding a sign by a process of analogy.[48] The incident contains a variation of a narrative motif common in Herodotus' descriptions of the interpretation of signs: a breakdown in communication between interpreter and recipient of signs. The reason for breakdown varies: so, for example, one could compare the narrative of 7.57.1 with that of 1.78, the portent of the snakes at Sardis. In both accounts, powerful leaders cannot avail themselves of valuable information afforded by an interpretation of a portent. In the case of Kroisos, the distance between Sardis and the abode of the Telmessians and the time this journey takes conspire against him, though he has of course the desire to interpret the portent; Xerxes, on the other hand, is simply not interested in the portent, considering it of no account (τὸ Ξέρξης ἐν οὐδενὶ λόγῳ ἐποιήσατο, 7.57.1). Herodotus claims the portent is easy to interpret, but one suspects this is more a rhetorical tactic on his part *ad maiorem Herodoti gloriam*: his ingenious interpretation shines all the more brightly for the disclaimer. His reading revolves around the transference of both the horse's and the hare's traditional characteristics to the army, and the realization that the horse and the hare are tangible and actual manifestations of a metaphorical and figurative description of Xerxes and his army:

> ἵππος γὰρ ἔτεκε λαγόν. εὐσύμβλητον ὦν τῇδε [τοῦτο] ἐγένετο, ὅτι ἔμελλε μὲν ἐλᾶν στρατιὴν ἐπὶ τὴν Ἑλλάδα Ξέρξης ἀγαυρότατα καὶ μεγαλοπρεπέστατα, ὀπίσω δὲ περὶ ἑωυτοῦ τρέχων ἥξειν ἐς τὸν αὐτὸν χῶρον.[49]
>
> 7.57.1

48 See ch. 1.3.1 above.

49 The characteristics of the proud horse and timorous hare need not necessarily be regarded as specific to the Greek cultural tradition, but there is much in the image of both horse and hare that is reminiscent of Homeric descriptions. Cf. *Iliad* 6.506–514, Paris' return to battle, where he is compared to a magnificent horse (ὡς δ' ὅτε τις στατὸς ἵππος . . .), supremely confident in himself (ἀγλαΐφι πεποιθώς; cf. *Histories* 7.57.1: ἀγαυρότατα καὶ μεγαλοπρεπέστατα) and with shining armor (τεύχεσι παμφαίνων), but who is elsewhere also quick to display the characteristics of a hare (though he is not specifically compared to one). The hare appears in a famous simile from *Iliad* 22, where in another example of how one entity can bear two different images, Hektor is imagined as an eagle about to pounce on a cowering hare (ἁρπάξων . . . πτῶκα λαγωόν, 22.310), but elsewhere is portrayed as just such another timorous creature, a dove (τρήρων πέλεια, 24.140) or a fawn (νέβρος, 24.189), "cowering down under a thicket," καταπτήξας ὑπὸ θαμνῷ (24.191), a man running for his life (περὶ ψυχῆς, 24.161; cf. περὶ ἑωυτοῦ τρέχων, *Histories* 7.57.1).

> A horse gave birth to a hare. This was easy to interpret: Xerxes was going to lead an expedition against Greece in a most proud and magnificent fashion, but would return to his own land running for his own dear life.

The relationship between signifier and signified is thus seen by Herodotus as an iconic relationship, where characteristics of the horse and the hare are shared by the army of Xerxes.[50] But this is only part of the reading, a consideration only of the elements of the total message and the relationship between signifier and signified in terms of the axis of selection or substitution. What is vital to Herodotus' reading is his combination of the elements of the *teras* (along the axis of combination) and his revelation that the horse and the hare are in fact one and the same, or, to put it another way, that they are two different signs in the complex that ultimately have the same referent. The action of birth then does not just function to create a separate entity, a hare out of a horse, a cowering, timorous, and fugitive army out of a proud and majestic one, but is also an equation of two disparate and seemingly contradictory elements. For Herodotus, the difference in level or hierarchy between parent and offspring in the *teras* functions on a temporal level to show the present and the future.

Herodotus caps his *tour-de-force* exposition by listing another portent to which Xerxes could have paid attention had he chosen to: a mule gives birth to a mule, which in itself is enough to constitute a portent, as the story of Zopyros and the siege of Babylon (3.153.1) makes clear.[51] Not only does the offspring of this *teras* bear a double set of genitalia, male and female, but the male genitalia appear *above* the female (7.57.2). Herodotus never explains the portent, presumably considering it to be as εὐσύμβλητον as the preceding one, another manifestation of his technique of leaving the audience to make connections for themselves. We are probably intended to transfer patterns of thought and oppositions that Herodotus uses in his discussion of the portent of the horse and the hare. The motif of birth does not seem to be used in the same way, however, to mediate temporally between a "before" and an "after" picture of Xerxes and his army and to draw an equivalence between two different creatures: instead, the *adunaton* of a mule giving birth simply seems to draw atten-

50 On iconic relationships and similarity (real, or recognized by convention) between signifier and signified cf. Nöth 1990:121–127.

51 During Kyros' siege of Babylon the Persian Zopyros is inspired when, after hearing a taunt that the Persians will only take the city when a mule gives birth, he learns of a *teras*: the actual birth of a mule from a mule. Cf. discussion below, ch. 2.8, of another semiotic aspect to this story, Zopyros' use of self-mutilation, to produce the impression that he has been punished by the Persians, in order to penetrate the ranks of the Babylonians.

tion to the theme of inversion and abnormality. The motif of the possession of two opposite qualities by one individual, rather than being expressed, as in the first *teras*, by the device of two separate entities (the horse and the hare) with a common referent (Xerxes and his army), is here expressed in the dual nature of the offspring with its double identity as male and female (διξὰ ἔχουσαν αἰδοῖα, τὰ μὲν ἔρσενος, τὰ δὲ θελέης, 7.57.2). The qualities associated with the horse in the first *teras* may here be viewed in the male nature of the creature, while the negative connotations of the hare are expressed in the female sexual identity of the mule. Finally, the relative physical positioning of two sets of genitalia, male above female (instead of female above male, one presumes?) suggest the function of inversion, and through inversion, the disastrous outcome of the expedition, the conversion of the army from the proud horse to the cowardly hare.[52]

[52] For the dominance of female over male as ominous, cf. the opening of the oracle given to the Milesians and Argives: ἀλλ' ὅταν ἡ θήλεια τὸν ἄρσενα νικήσασα | ἐξελάσῃ καὶ κῦδος ἐν Ἀργείοισιν ἄρηται, | πολλὰς Ἀργείων ἀμφιδρυφέας τότε θήσει (6.77.2), "But when the female conquers and drives off the male and wins glory among the Argives, then this will cause many of the Argives to tear both their cheeks in mourning."

2.2 Dreams and Their Interpretation in Herodotus

2.2.1 Herodotean Dreamers

There are surprisingly few dreams reported in Herodotus' work as compared, for example, to portents and oracles. They are not only limited in number: they are distributed among a small number of dreamers who are further defined by two important categories, those of ethnicity and power. Of the eighteen dreams mentioned by Herodotus, no less than fourteen are dreamed by non-Greeks. Furthermore, the dreamers themselves belong to an exclusive club of rulers, tyrants, and high officials, the main players on the stage of the *Histories*: Kroisos; Astyages; the Persian kings Kyros, Kambyses, and Xerxes; the Persian high officials Datis, Artabanos, and Otanes; the Egyptian kings Sabakos and Sethon; the Greek tyrants Hipparkhos, Hippias, and Polykrates (though the dream itself is experienced by his daughter).[53]

Why should Herodotean dreamers be so specifically defined in terms of ethnicity and power? The reason for the first limitation has a direct connection with the second: the most powerful individuals in the *Histories*, and the ones whose actions have the most far-reaching effects, are precisely those figures from outside the Greek world who come into contact with it and change it and who are all absolute rulers. Beginning with Agamemnon's dream in the second book of the *Iliad*, it is a convention in Greek literature, as well as in oneirocritical manuals, that the dreams of rulers have a special significance for the whole of society.[54] Since the leading Greek states in Herodotus' work

53 Cf. the characterization of these dreams in Bichler 1985 as "Reichsträume" and the more specific classification in Köhnken 1988:24 of "Königsträume." The only dream of a "democratic" ruler is the dream of Agariste (Perikles' mother) in which she gives birth to a lion (6.131.2). Dareios is the only Persian king not to appear in the work as a dreamer (see below for further comment on this). He does, however, appear as the subject of Kyros' dream (1.209.1).

54 *Iliad* 2.80–82 and Artemidorus 1.2, who cites among others Panyasis of Halikarnassos (not, it seems, the Panyasis who was Herodotus' uncle) for this proposition. Panyasis does however recognize the significance of a dream dreamed by many members of the *dêmos*.

are not ruled by absolute rulers, it follows from this that there are few, if any, dreams recorded in connection with those states. Such states, as will be seen in a later chapter, are more often associated with a different system of signs, that of the oracle.[55]

The prominence accorded to the dreams of absolute rulers is thus in direct proportion to the prominence of the latter in the narrative structure of the work. The position of the dreams themselves in the narrative shows that for Herodotus they are a vital narrative tool for marking transitions in power and exploring choices. The dreams generally occur at highly significant and critical junctures in the narrative, a prime example being the complex of three dreams (though, as it appears, it is actually one and the same dream) that dramatizes in striking fashion the making of Xerxes' decision to invade Europe.[56] The insistent dream that demands that Xerxes mount an expedition against the Greeks forms one pole of the debate, while Artabanos, ever the counselor of restraint, moderation, and good sense, forms the other. "Debate" is perhaps not the correct word, since the interpretative issue is not resolved by the triumph of one γνώμη over another, as is the case, for example, with the discussion between Dareios and Gobryes about the meaning of the Scythian gifts (4.132.3, discussed in ch. 2.8 below), but by the sheer force of terror and power of the dream, which with its threats of hot irons and torture bullies even the sceptical Artabanos into supporting the expedition (7.18.1). The divine origin of the dream is not explicitly stated by Herodotus: instead we see in his speech to Xerxes after seeing this dream how Artabanos has come haltingly to this conclusion:[57]

55 Mikalson 2003:41–42 considers the question, "Why does Herodotus give most and the most elaborate dreams to the Persians?" His answer is that this "may have been for literary reasons" (he does not elaborate on this here) but also considers the possibility that this reflects actual Persian practice: "as Georges … notes, Persian gods apparently had no voice or form (and hence no oracles), and 'therefore the dream is the characteristic medium of divine communication among Medes and Persians.'"

56 Cf. Baragwanath 2008:249–253 on the role of this dream in the account of Xerxes' motivations for invasion.

57 Note the use of the indefinite τις and ὡς οἶκε and cf. Herodotus' use of particle κως in his conclusions about the presence of the divine and the portents involving Delos (φιλέει δέ κως προσημαίνειν, εὖτ' ἂν μέλλῃ μεγάλα κακὰ ἢ πόλι ἢ ἔθνεϊ ἔσεσθαι, 6.27.1), discussed above in ch. 2.1.3. Cf. Mikalson 2003:42 on the two strands of divine and human motivation for the campaign, with references in n115 to Harrison 2000:132–137 and 231; Evans 1991:15, 28, and 37; Pelling 1991:139–140; Fornara 1990:36–37, 43–45; Lloyd-Jones 1983:61–63; Pritchett 1979:96–98; Pohlenz 1973:117–118, Immerwahr 1954:33–36. Munson 2001b examines the vocabulary of necessity and compulsion in this account, in particular the expression τὸ χρέον γενέσθαι (7.17.2). On the basis of her investigation of ἀναγκ- words and constructions using δεῖ and χρή (35) she concludes (43) that this expression, which is used by the dream to Artabanos ("You will

ἐπεὶ δὲ δαιμονίη τις γίνεται ὁρμή, καὶ Ἕλληνας, ὡς οἶκε, φθορή τις καταλαμβάνει θεήλατος, ἐγὼ μὲν καὶ αὐτὸς τράπομαι καὶ τὴν γνώμην μετατίθεμαι.

7.18.3

Since some kind of divine impulse has come about and some kind of god-driven destruction seizes hold of the Greeks, so it seems, I am turned and am changing my mind.

In the account of Kroisos' downfall, the first manifestation of divine nemesis begins with a dream:

ἔλαβε ἐκ θεοῦ νέμεσις μεγάλη Κροῖσον ... αὐτίκα δέ οἱ εὕδοντι ἐπέστη ὄνειρος, ὅς οἱ τὴν ἀληθείην ἔφαινε τῶν μελλόντων γενέσθαι κακῶν κατὰ τὸν παῖδα.

1.34.1

A great divine vengeance overtook Kroisos. . . . A dream stood over him as he slept and revealed to him the truth of the evils which were going to happen with regard to his son.

The downfall of the Medes and the rise of Persians are marked by Astyages' dreams about his daughter (1.107.1; 1.108.1). Kyros' dream about the rise of Dareios (1.209.1) occurs shortly before his fatal encounter with Tomyris' army and has the narrative function of signaling firstly Kyros' insecurity and unrestrained desire for power: he does not realize that the dream signifies not an attempt on the part of Dareios to seize power, but a vision of what will be after his death, which is close at hand. Secondly, the dream acts as a pointer forward toward Herodotus' subsequent account in book 3 about Dareios' rise to power.[58]

Even those dreams about whose contents Herodotus tells us nothing function to provide motivation for certain types of actions. These are actions

---

not escape with impunity, averting that which is supposed to happen"), "is likely to include a non-supernatural component and indicate 'what is supposed to happen' according to the predispositions of the parties involved." For Munson it is the force of *nomos* (in particular, the Persian royal *nomos* of expansion and increase of power) that is the compulsion here, focalized through Artabanos.

58 Another dream which has a major narrative function is the dream of Kambyses about his brother Smerdis (3.30.2), which leads Kambyses to have him killed, an act which is described as the first of his evils (πρῶτα τῶν κακῶν, 3.30.1). A similar phrase marking a decisive moment in a narrative is seen again in the account of the Ionian Revolt, where Herodotus says the ships the Athenians sent were the ἀρχὴ κακῶν (5.97.3) for both Greeks and barbarians.

in which the behavior of the agent seems in some way surprising, unusual, or irrational, so that the influence of a dream is invoked by Herodotus to explain it. The Persian commander Datis, for example, while at Mykonos on his way back to Asia, is suddenly moved by a dream to seek out a gilded statue of Apollo amongst his spoils and have it returned to the temple from which it was plundered (6.118.1). The influence of the divine is not specifically mentioned, but is not far away: after all, the dream occurs to Datis just a few miles from Apollo's sacred island of Delos, and the name of the sanctuary in Boiotia from which the statue was stolen is Delion. Xerxes' request, on the day after he has set fire to Athens, that the Athenian exiles in his army go up onto the akropolis and sacrifice (presumably to the goddess Athena) "according to their own fashion" (τρόπῳ τῷ σφετέρῳ θῦσαι τὰ ἱρά, 8.54) can be explained by Herodotus only in terms of a dream (ὄψιν τινὰ ἰδὼν ἐνυπνίου) or a sudden scruple (ἐνθύμιον) after burning the temples. Similarly, the Persian general Otanes, who ignores Dareios' command to spare the lives of the Samians and kills the male population even in temples and sanctuaries, is motivated to resettle the island of Samos by a strange combination of factors, a dream and an illness which affects his private parts (ἔκ τε ὄψιος ὀνείρου καὶ νούσου ἥ μιν κατέλαβε νοσῆσαι τὰ αἰδοῖα, 3.149).[59]

2.2.2 Vocabulary of Dreams

Herodotus refers to the dream itself variously as ὄνειρος, ὄνειρον (stem ὀνειρατ- in oblique cases), ἐνύπνιον, ὄψις ὀνείρου, ὄψις ἐνυπνίου, ὄψις ἐν τῷ ὕπνῳ, or simply ὄψις on its own. The different words for "dream" do not seem to indicate any fundamental difference in type. As far as the masculine and neuter forms ὄνειρος and ὄνειρον are concerned, both may be used to describe the same dream (e.g. ὄνειρον at 7.14, but ὄνειρος at 7.16.β.1), but the two forms may have different connotations. Kessels suggests the masculine form may be perceived as more Homeric and "poetic" (1978:178), on the basis of the fact that three of the five instances of the masculine form appear in the narrative describing the dream of Kroisos, which is particularly Homeric in its vocabulary and presentation.[60] He concludes (183) more generally that,

[59] The dream and the disease are presented as two distinct factors, but they are probably joined by an aetiological connection: the dream explains to Otanes the cause of his illness. Mikalson 2003:42 with n111 comments that these dreams involving religious expiation are an exception to the general tendency in Herodotus for dreams to be signs or causes of future misfortunes.

[60] Cf. Herodotus' description of Kroisos' dream about Atys, whose figure stands over him as he sleeps (αὐτίκα δέ οἱ εὕδοντι ἐπέστη ὄνειρος, 1.34.1) with similarly hovering Homeric dream-figures, e.g. κακὸν γὰρ ὄναρ κεφαλῆφιν ἐπέστη (*Iliad* 10.496).

apart from Homer and the lyric poets, "the masculine form was sometimes used as an epic reminiscence, but was generally replaced by the neuter." This may explain why in the narrative at 7.14 the dream of Xerxes is referred to as an ὄνειρον (neuter), but Artabanos refers to it as an ὄνειρος (masculine) θεοῦ τινος πομπῇ ("a dream [sent] through the guidance of some god") at 7.16.β.1. Artabanos is arguing against the divine nature of this particular dream, and emphasizes the vague nature of most dreams by referring to them as "wandering" (ἐνύπνια . . . πεπλανημένα, 7.16.β.2) and as "visions of dreams" (ὄψιες ὀνειράτων), contrasting this with Xerxes' belief in its divine origin. In this context it would make perfect sense for Artabanos to characterize Xerxes' belief with the marked form ὄνειρος, further emphasizing this with the expression θεοῦ τινος πομπῇ, while himself using more neutral expressions.

As far as the connotations of of ὄνειρος/ν vs. ἐνύπνιον are concerned, Kessels' survey (190–192) reveals that the former is almost exclusively confined to tragedy and lyric, while the latter seems to be confined to prose literature, with ἐνύπνιον being the only term for "dream" in medical literature.[61] In Herodotus, ὄνειρος/ν is used 23 times, while ἐνύπνιον is found 16 times (Kessels 1978:191), suggesting he has a preference for the more elevated and epic connotations of the former.[62]

2.2.3 Structure of Dreams

Herodotus' dreams fall into two main structural types: the first relies predominantly on signs of an auditory nature, the other on visual signs.[63] I say "predominantly" because every dream in Herodotus has a visual component: after all, in the Greek idiom one "sees" a dream, εἶδον ὄνειρον, or "a vision of a dream," ὄψιν ὀνείρου.[64] The dream is something seen, but what is seen? In the

61 In Artemidorus (1.1) there is a distinct difference in meaning between the two, the ἐνύπνιον being a dream about present conditions (what one is at present occupied with, cf. Artabanos' theory at *Histories* 7.16.β.2), the ὄνειρος being revelatory of future events.

62 Cf. the similar conclusion of Vinagre 1996:274–275.

63 The two types are equally represented in Herodotus' work, occurring seven times each (unlike Frisch 1968:60, I see the dream of Sabakos as belonging to the first type: further discussion below), with neither type being privileged and with no sense that the one is more reliable than the other. As Frisch (1968:60) points out, Herodotus uses both types within a short space of each other in the complex of dreams seen by Xerxes at 7.12–19, "als wollte die Gottheit alle ihre Möglichkeiten ausschöpfen, ihn beim Kriegsentschluss zu halten." The typology is found in Artemidorus and has been used by scholars of ancient Near Eastern dreams: see Noegel 2007:6–7, who cautions against excessive reliance on this typology and shows that there is overlap between the types.

64 ὁρᾶν ὄψιν ἐν τῷ ὕπνῳ (2.139; 3.30; 6.107; 6.118; 6.131); ὁρᾶν ὄψιν ἐνυπνίου (3.124; 5.55; 8.54); ὁρᾶν ὄψιν (1.108; 1.209; 7.12); ἐνύπνιον ὁρᾶν (4.172.3; 4.184.4). The other construction used by

first type, a male figure, sometimes described as being of preternatural size and beauty (ἀνὴρ μέγας τε καὶ εὐειδής[65]), stands over the dreamer (ἐπιστῆναι: 1.34.1, 1.38.1, 2.139.1, 2.141.3, 5.56.1, 7.12.1, 7.14; ὑπερστῆναι: 7.17.1)[66] and addresses him, sometimes with a challenging reproach.[67] As a type, these dreams correspond extremely closely to dreams in the Homeric corpus, where a dream-figure typically stands at the dreamer's head and addresses him, and where the message of the dream is conveyed through signs in an auditory medium, not a visual one.[68] The dream-figure is personified to such an extent that at 7.13.1 and

Herodotus is δοκεῖν with nominative or accusative plus infinitive: 1.107; 1.108; 1.209; 2.139.1; 2.141.3; 3.30; 3.64; 5.56; 6.107; 7.12.1. The use of δοκεῖν implies nothing about the validity of the dream or the dreamer's report, as Kessels 1978:200–203 and van Lieshout 1980:26–27 demonstrate. Particularly interesting is Kessels' comparison (202) of Herodotus' usage with that found in the inscriptions from the Asklepieion at Epidauros, where much the same terminology appears.

65 ἀνὴρ μέγας τε καὶ εὐειδής: 5.56.1; 7.12.1. See discussion below of the presence of the divine in Herodotean dreams.

66 The choice of ὑπερστῆναι (stand *over*) as opposed to the more commonly found (in Herodotus) ἐπιστῆναι (stand *near*) expresses the exceptionally threatening and insistent nature of the dream-figure which appears to Artabanos. But cf. Homeric ὑπὲρ κεφαλῆς (*Iliad* 2.20, 2.59, 23.68; *Odyssey* 4.803, 6.21, 20.32, 23.4).

67 The series of dreams which visit Xerxes and Artabanos all begin with an address and challenging question: μετὰ δὴ βουλεύεαι, ὦ Πέρσα, στράτευμα μὴ ἄγειν ἐπὶ τὴν Ἑλλάδα, προείπας ἁλίζειν Πέρσῃσι στρατόν; (7.12.1), "Are you changing your decision, Persian, so as not to lead an army against Greece?"; ὦ παῖ Δαρείου, καὶ δὴ φαίνεαι ἐν Πέρσῃσί τε ἀπειπάμενος τὴν στρατηλασίην καὶ τὰ ἐμὰ ἔπεα ἐν οὐδενὶ ποιεύμενος λόγῳ ὡς παρ' οὐδενὸς ἀκούσας; (7.14), "Son of Dareios, are you manifestly renouncing the campaign in front of the Persians and paying no attention at all to my utterances, as if you have heard from a nobody?"; σὺ δὴ κεῖνος εἷς ὁ ἀποσπεύδων Ξέρξην στρατεύεσθαι ἐπὶ τὴν Ἑλλάδα ὡς δὴ κηδόμενος αὐτοῦ; (7.17.2), "Are *you* the one who is advising Xerxes against invading Greece, as if you are concerned for him?"

68 E.g. *Iliad* 2.20: στῆ δ' ἄρ' ὑπὲρ κεφαλῆς Νηληΐῳ υἷι ἐοικώς, "It stood above his head, looking like the son of Neleus"; *Iliad* 10.496: κακὸν γὰρ ὄναρ κεφαλῆφιν ἐπέστη, "An evil dream stood over his head"; *Iliad* 23.68: στῆ δ' ἄρ' ὑπὲρ κεφαλῆς καί μιν πρὸς μῦθον ἔειπεν, "He stood above his head and spoke to him" (=*Iliad* 24.682; *Odyssey* 4.803; *Odyssey* 6.21). Challenging reproach: *Iliad* 2.23–25: εὕδεις . . . οὐ χρὴ παννύχιον εὕδειν βουληφόρον ἄνδρα . . ., "You are sleeping . . . a man who gives counsel ought not to sleep all night . . ." and *Iliad* 23.69: εὕδεις, αὐτὰρ ἐμεῖο λελασμένος ἔπλευ, Ἀχιλλεῦ, "You are sleeping, but you have become forgetful of me, Achilles." Penelope's dream about the geese and the eagle (*Odyssey* 19.535–553) is the one Homeric dream which uses visual signs as opposed to purely acoustic ones. It is also exceptional in that it offers its own decoding when the eagle speaks and identifies itself with Odysseus and the geese with the suitors: nothing like it is found in Herodotus. On the interpretation of this dream, see now Levaniouk 2011. Herodotean dream-figures differ from Homeric ones in one important respect: while they have a strong connection with the divine, as is the case with Homeric dream-figures, their appearance is different. In the Homeric corpus, as Kessels 1978:219–221 and van Lieshout 1980:15–16 point out, emphasis is placed on the dream-figure's resemblance to the person whose appearance it assumes: *Iliad* 2.20 (the dream-figure assumes the likeness of Nestor); *Odyssey* 4.796 (Athena looks like Iphthime); *Odyssey* 6.22 (Athena looks like the daughter of Dumas), whereas in Herodotus the dream-figures are generally of a supernatural size and beauty, and unidentified (the one exception being the dream-figure in Sethon's dream

7.15.3, for example, the dream can be described as flying up to (ἐπιπτήσεται) or away from (ἀποπτάσθαι) the dreamer.[69] Artabanos, while expressing skepticism about the divine nature of the dream visiting Xerxes, in fact credits the apparition, "whatever it be," with the ability to distinguish between him and Xerxes and not be misled by judging simply on the basis of attire:

> οὐ γὰρ δὴ ἐς τοσοῦτό γε εὐηθίης ἀνήκει τοῦτο, ὅ τι δή κοτέ ἐστι τὸ ἐπιφαινόμενόν τοι ἐν τῷ ὕπνῳ, ὥστε δόξει ἐμὲ ὁρέων σὲ εἶναι, τῇ σῇ ἐσθῆτι τεκμαιρόμενον.
>
> 7.16.γ.2
>
> Whatever this thing is that keeps appearing to you in your sleep, it has not reached such a level of stupidity that it will see me and think it is you, making an inference on the basis of your attire.

The subject of the verb τεκμαίρεσθαι, to which attention has been drawn in ch. 1.3.5 as a term connected to drawing of conclusions on the basis of signs, is here none other than the dream itself, which is imagined as able to use the signs conveyed by royal clothing, or rather, not to rely exclusively on these signs as indices of the royal presence.[70]

The appearance of the dream-figure acts as an authentication and sign of dream-status (though not necessarily, as we shall see, of the dream's veracity), but the actual message of the dream is conveyed through the dream-figure's speech, not through any action or visual signs. Artabanos' dream, however, forms a striking exception, since it combines speech with action:[71]

> ταῦτά τε δὴ ἐδόκεε Ἀρτάβανος τὸ ὄνειρον ἀπειλέειν καὶ θερμοῖσι σιδηρίοισι ἐκκαίειν αὐτοῦ μέλλειν τοὺς ὀφθαλμούς.
>
> 7.18.1

[2.141.3], who is said to be the god Hephaistos). Such supernaturally large and beautiful dream-figures, which do appear in authors other than Herodotus (e.g. Aeschylus *Persae* 181–199, Plato *Crito* 44a–44b), are closer to the dream-figures found in dream records from the Near East, who sometimes have gigantic proportions and are also depicted as standing at the bedside of the dreamer. There are examples of both features in Oppenheim 1956:129, e.g. an Akkadian dream (§8 no.14 in his collection), in which the dream-figure is "a man, surpassing in size, of glorious form, beautifully [?] clad."

69 Again, this owes much to the Homeric presentation of dreams: cf. Agamemnon's dream, . . . ὣς ὁ μὲν εἰπὼν | ᾤχετ' ἀποπτάμενος (*Iliad* 2.70–71).

70 For clothing functioning as signifier elsewhere in the *Histories*, see ch. 2.8.

71 The dream sequence has been identified by some (e.g. Reinhardt 1966:171; Solmsen 1982:89–90) as having "Oriental motifs" or, as Baragwanath 2008:251 sees it, distinctly Persian motifs: these include the exchange of clothing, the donning of the king's robe, and the terrible punishments the dream threatens.

> The dream seemed to Artabanos to make these threats and to be on the point of burning out his eyes with hot irons.

In the second type of Herodotean dream, the message is conveyed purely through a complex of visual signs, with no dream-figure framing the dream or delivering a pronouncement. Examples of this type are Astyages' dreams involving his daughter Mandane (1.107.1; 1.108.1), or Kyros' dream of Dareios as a winged figure, overshadowing with his wings both Europe and Asia (1.209.1). The difference between the two types of dreams explains, for example, the different use of the word ὄνειρος: in the first type, the dream is the figure that appears to the sleeper (e.g. αὐτίκα δέ οἱ εὕδοντι ἐπέστη ὄνειρος, ὅς οἱ τὴν ἀληθείην ἔφαινε τῶν μελλόντων γενέσθαι κακῶν κατὰ τὸν παῖδα, 1.34.1), while in the second, ὄνειρος refers to the dream experience as a whole (e.g. Hippias' dream about intercourse with his mother, 6.107.1–2). Thus, even though the dreams that Xerxes and Artabanos experience have different contents, Herodotus refers to them as the same dream (τὠυτὸ ὄνειρον, 7.14), since the dream-figure is the same.

The dreams of the great Median and Persian leaders Astyages, Kyros, Kambyses, and Xerxes (with the exception of the dream at 7.12 and 7.14) all fall into the second type of dreams, depending as they do on visual, not acoustic, signs.[72] But they are linked by more than the simple fact of their dependence on visual signs: the Median and Persian kings all dream in a remarkably similar way. The distinctive feature their dreams share is their sheer scale and extent as well as the image of power spreading from a central point. They take place on a stage that has as its limits the continents of Asia and Europe, or even the sky, and at the center stands a figure that seems to dominate this landscape. Let us consider the first of Astyages' two dreams about his daughter:

> καί οἱ ἐγένετο θυγάτηρ τῇ οὔνομα ἔθετο Μανδάνην, τὴν ἐδόκεε Ἀστυάγης ἐν τῷ ὕπνῳ οὐρῆσαι τοσοῦτον ὥστε πλῆσαι μὲν τὴν ἑωυτοῦ πόλιν, ἐπικατακλύσαι δὲ καὶ τὴν Ἀσίην πᾶσαν.
>
> 1.107.1

72 As has been mentioned above, no dreams experienced by Dareios are recorded by Herodotus. The major crisis of interpretation which he confronts in the *Histories* is a different one, and in terms of a different sign system: how to understand the gifts of the Scythians (4.131–132): cf. ch. 2.8 below. As with Xerxes' dreams, the crisis of interpretation is linked to a major decision, whether to continue with the expedition or not.

> He had a daughter named Mandane, whom Astyages seemed to see in a dream urinating so much that his city was filled with it and the whole of Asia inundated.

In the second dream the imagery is once again on a cosmic scale:

> ἐδόκεε οἱ ἐκ τῶν αἰδοίων τῆς θυγατρὸς ταύτης φῦναι ἄμπελον, τὴν δὲ ἄμπελον ἐπισχεῖν τὴν Ἀσίην πᾶσαν.
>
> 1.108.1
>
> It seemed to him that a vine was growing from the private parts of this daughter and that the vine was overshadowing the whole of Asia.

Read along the axis of combination, the syntax of the dreams is the same, even if different elements have been substituted along the axis of selection (the all-encompassing urine becomes the spreading vine in the second dream).[73] The same combination of elements is at work in Kyros' dream of Dareios, where Dareios stands in the center like a winged genie:

> ἐδόκεε ὁ Κῦρος ἐν τῷ ὕπνῳ ὁρᾶν τῶν Ὑστάσπεος παίδων τὸν πρεσβύτατον ἔχοντα ἐπὶ τῶν ὤμων πτέρυγας καὶ τουτέων τῇ μὲν τὴν Ἀσίην, τῇ δὲ τὴν Εὐρώπην ἐπισκιάζειν.
>
> 1.209.1
>
> Kyros seemed to see in his sleep the eldest son of Hystaspes, who had wings on his shoulders and was overshadowing Asia with one of them and Europe with the other.[74]

73 I agree with Asheri 2004 on 1.107.1 that the two dreams are similar, but not that they transmit the same message. As Pelling (1996) points out, the two dreams should be viewed as a series, with the second building on the first, clarifying and specifying (the same phenomenon occurs with the dreams of Xerxes and Artabanos in book 7). The motif of urination is one which has an ambiguous significance, to judge from a fragment from an Assyrian dream-book which analyzes dreams about (male) urination, ranging from the negative to the positive: e.g. "If his urine [expands(?)] in front of (his) penis and [ ] the wall: [he will not have] sons; If his urine ex[pands] in front of (his) penis and [ ] the wall, the street: he will h[ave] sons." Of special interest are the following: "If his urine expands in front of (his) penis and f[ills(?) all] the streets: his property will be robb[ed] and given to the city [ ]; If his urine expands in front of (his) penis [and] he does obeisance in front of his urine: he will beget a son and he (the son) will be king" (Oppenheim 1956:265) and "If he drinks his wife's urine: he will live in great prosperity" (Bottéro 1982:12, citing Oppenheim).

74 The imagery of the dream can be seen as authentically Persian, as Asheri 2004 *ad loc.* shows, citing iconographic evidence for the motif of winged male figures in Achaemenid art and for its significance as symbol of the king chosen by Ahura-Mazda.

Here the physical scope of the dream is even wider, including Europe, as is fitting for Kyros' role as the founder of the Persian empire.

In the fourth of the dreams which Xerxes experiences, the motif of the all-encompassing figure returns: this time, however, the figure is none other than the dreamer himself and the ambit of the dream is wider still:

> ἐδόκεε ὁ Ξέρξης ἐστεφανῶσθαι ἐλαίης θαλλῷ, ἀπὸ δὲ τῆς ἐλαίης τοὺς κλάδους γῆν πᾶσαν ἐπισχεῖν, μετὰ δὲ ἀφανισθῆναι περὶ τῇ κεφαλῇ κείμενον τὸν στέφανον.
>
> 7.19.1
>
> Xerxes seemed to be crowned with the bough of an olive-tree, whose branches seemed to overshadow the whole world, but later the wreath about his head disappeared.

The selection of the olive as the overshadowing and dominating element is significant, given its role elsewhere in the *Histories* as symbol of Greekness.[75] There is an additional variation in the syntax of the dream, ignored by the *magoi* in their interpretation, and left to speak for itself by Herodotus: the wreath *disappears* from Xerxes' head, pointing to the ultimate failure of his domination. The *magoi*, too easily satisfied with a reading that on the face of it seems favorable, do not bother (or dare) to read further along the axis of combination and consider the syntax of the entire dream.[76] They treat it as if it is like the dreams of Astyages and Kyros, which present only one picture, a kind of tableau endlessly repeating the same action, without taking into account the change in the dream's movement and the fact that there is a sequence of elements that need to be combined.

Kambyses' dream of his brother Smerdis may also be viewed as belonging to the same type, but with some variations:

75 "Suspiciously Greek" is the comment of How and Wells. The olive wreath as prize for ἀρετή at the *agônes* of the Greeks comes in for particular Persian scorn and ridicule (8.26.2). Köhnken (1988:35) also points to the Spartans' award of olive wreathes to Eurybiades and to Themistokles after Salamis (8.124.2). He rejects the connection many commentators make between the olive crown in Xerxes' dream and the olive shoot that miraculously appears on Athena's olive tree in the Erekhtheion after it has been burned down (8.55): cf. his arguments at 30–32.

76 Cf. discussion above, ch. 2.1, of their interpretation for Xerxes of the portent of the eclipse of the sun (7.37.3) as possibly motivated by a desire to please the king. Köhnken (1988:29) compares the simple passing over of these dream elements by the *magoi* with Onomakritos' manipulative reading of the oracles of Mousaios to Xerxes, where he surpresses any negative passages and only reads those that forecast success for the Persians (7.6.4).

> ἐδόκεέ οἱ ἄγγελον ἐλθόντα ἐκ Περσέων ἀγγέλλειν ὡς ἐν τῷ θρόνῳ τῷ βασιληίῳ ἱζόμενος Σμέρδις τῇ κεφαλῇ τοῦ οὐρανοῦ ψαύσειε.
>
> 3.30.2
>
> It seemed to him that a messenger came from the Persians and announced that Smerdis was sitting on the royal throne and had touched the sky with his head.

The vision of Smerdis is not seen directly by the dreamer, but through the medium of a messenger, and it is precisely the acoustic nature of this medium that contributes to Kambyses' mistaken interpretation. What Kambyses passes over in his interpretation is that there is no exclusive link between the name Smerdis and his brother, that as a linguistic sign |Smerdis| has more than one referent, a confusion which would not have arisen had a dream-figure of his brother Smerdis appeared directly to him.[77] He ignores the possibility that the Smerdis of his dream could be anyone other than his brother, and has him killed on the strength of it, which, as I have pointed out above, forms an important point in Herodotus' narrative, marking the beginning of Kambyses' voyage into madness (3.30.1).[78]

2.2.4 Interpreters and Interpretation of Dreams

As with portents and oracles, so too in the case of dreams there exists a class of professional interpreters. Herodotus mentions ὀνειροπόλοι and μάγοι (that is, in their capacity as interpreters of dreams) on only three occasions, two of these three being in a non-Greek setting, in connection with Astyages (1.107.1;

77 See ch. 2.6 below on the special nature of names as signs, which as markers of personal identity have an indexical quality, pointing to a particular individual, but which at the same time may point to other bearers of that name, and also may have referents beyond the individual or individuals names: cf. the incident of the Aiginetan Krios and the play Kleomenes makes on its meaning "ram" (6.50.3). The general possibility of more than one referent for a linguistic sign comes into play in the dream of Sethon, the Egyptian king (2.141.3–6). The dream turns on the god's use of the word "avengers, helpers" (τιμωροί), the significance of which remains clear, but whose referent turns out unexpectedly not to be armed men, but mice, who destroy the invaders' weapons. A similar play on the possibility of more than one referent for a linguistic sign is present in Herodotus' account of Aristodikos and his challenging encounter with Apollo (1.158.1–159.4), which revolves around the word "suppliant" (ἱκέτης).

78 The problem of name and identity will arise again later in the same book with the coup of the false Smerdis, who just as he seizes power by the manipulation of signs, will be detected and dethroned thanks to the interpretation of signs. Otanes, judging on the basis of other signs besides (τῇδε συμβαλλόμενος, 3.68.2), has his daughter ascertain whether or not the Smerdis she lives with has ears, and thus establishes that this Smerdis is not the real Smerdis (3.69).

1.108.1; ὀνειροπόλοι and μάγοι, 1.128.2) and Xerxes (μάγοι, 7.19.1).[79] The third occasion is in connection with Hipparkhos (ὀνειροπόλοι, 5.56.2), in an Athenian setting, but it is relevant to note that this is under a tyrannical and not a democratic regime: the former provides an environment hostile to independent interpretation. As in the case of professional interpreters of portents, professional interpreters of dreams in Herodotus' work are either wrong in their readings (the *magoi* in the case of Astyages' dreams, and, as has just been discussed, in the case of Xerxes' fourth dream) or, if correct, it is their fate to be ignored.[80]

In the case of the interpretation of Astyages' two dreams, the *magoi* at first advance the correct interpretation, since with hindsight we know that Mandane's offspring, Kyros, will eventually control all of Asia in his stead. When they are asked to reexamine their interpretation (1.120.1), after the young Kyros has been discovered to be still alive and elected king by his playmates, their new interpretation that all the dream referred to was that Kyros would one day be called "king" in a children's game (1.120.2–3) proves to be incorrect. They read the sign complex of the dream against a much smaller background—a children's playground, rather than the continent of Asia—ignoring the vastness of its range. As with the interpretation of the portent of the eclipse at 7.37.2–3, here too the *magoi* seem to be led to their interpretation by an eagerness to please and an instinct for self-preservation. Herodotus devotes

79 At 1.107.1, 1.108.1–2, 1.128.2, the terms ὀνειροπόλοι and μάγοι are used interchangeably, the latter being a more general term (as the expression τῶν μάγων οἱ ὀνειροπόλοι [1.107.1; 1.108.2; 1.128.2] makes clear) used also of the priestly caste in their capacity as interpreters of portents and interpreters of religious and secular law. Like ὄνειρος, ὀνειροπόλος has distinctly Homeric connotations (*Iliad* 1.63; 5.149). According to Vinagre's study (1996:261–262), the word is not attested (except in Herodotus) after Homer until the first century CE, in Philon of Alexandria (*On Dreams* 2.42). He cites Philostratos *Life of Apollonius* 2.37 as evidence for the specifically poetic connotations of the word: οἱ γοῦν ἐξηγηταὶ τῶν ὄψεων, οὓς ὀνειροπόλους οἱ ποιηταὶ καλοῦσι, "Expounders of dreams, whom the poets call *oneiropoloi*." Vinagre's argument is that Herodotus used ὀνειροπόλος *faute de mieux* because the term ὀνειροκρίτης, which subsequently became one of the most popular terms used to describe interpreters of dreams, did not yet exist in his Ionic dialect (262). As evidence, he cites the fact that Herodotus uses the verb κρίνω in the context of dream interpretation exclusively with ἐνύπνιον (1.120.1) or ὄψις (1.120.1; 7.19.1) or intransitively (7.19.2). But the decision to use ὀνειροπόλος (if ever consciously articulated) could have been made purely on stylistic grounds, just as with ὄνειρος.

80 Herodotus does not actually tell us what the ὀνειροπόλοι said to Hipparkhos, merely that he "rejected" (ἀπειπάμενος, 5.56.2) the dream, and went ahead with the procession. As Mikalson 2003:16 comments, this is an unusual dream for Herodotus: "contrary to his usual practice, he neither has another interpret them nor attempts to do so himself. . . . This prophetic dream is uncharacteristically enigmatic." Some (van Groningen 1949; LSJ s.v. ἀπεῖπον; van Lieshout 1980:172 and 243n97) have seen in the expression ἀπειπάμενος a reference to apotropaic ritual by means of prayer to deflect the ill omen, comparing the Latin *averruncare*.

a fair amount of space to an interesting dialogue (1.120.4–6) between Astyages and the *magoi* after the latter deliver their revised reading. The dialogue reveals the stake the *magoi* have in Astyages' continued rule, suggesting the problem of conflict between political interests and interpretation of signs. Astyages asks them to consider their advice to him carefully, adding perhaps not without a touch of menace, that they should consider what is "safest" (ἀσφαλέστατα, 1.120.4) both for him and them.[81] The *magoi* hastily assure the king that they have a personal stake in the preservation of his rule:

> καὶ νῦν εἰ φοβερόν τι ἐνωρῶμεν, πᾶν ἂν σοὶ προεφράζομεν.
>
> 1.120.6
>
> Now if we foresaw anything awful, we would tell you the whole matter in advance.[82]

Few, then, of the dreams we find in Herodotus are interpreted by professionals, and we have seen that their results either are ignored by those who consult them, or are flawed because of relations of power and dependency in which the interpreters are caught up.

What of interpretations by the dreamers themselves? They fare hardly better than the professionals: Kroisos is persuaded not to observe the dream's warning by the sophistic arguments of his son Atys, who is then killed in a hunting accident (1.34.1–43.3); Kyros misunderstands the appearance of Dareios in his dream as a usurper, not a successor after his death (1.209.1–5); Kambyses, as we have seen, assumes that the Smerdis reported to have "touched the sky" is his brother, and has him murdered (3.30.2–3); the misgivings of the daughter of Polykrates about a dream in which she sees him suspended in midair being washed by Zeus and anointed by the sun (3.124.1) are dismissed by him at the cost of his life; Hipparkhos ignores a dream on the eve of the Panathenaia and refuses to accept it and is assassinated the next day (5.56.1–2); Hippias' optimistic interpretation of his dream about intercourse with his mother as

81 They pay dearly for their interpretation: after Kyros stages a successful uprising against Astyages, Astyages' first act is to have them all impaled, only then to arm those Medes still faithful to him (1.128.2).

82 The *magoi* use the verb προφράζω (found in the work only here), whose simplex, φράζω, is often associated with sign communication, whether referring to the sending of an encoded message or the relaying of an already transmitted message (ch. 1.2): it is thus a highly appropriate verb for the *magoi* to use of themselves, being concerned as they are with the interpretation of signs. The use of the prefix προ- is reminiscent of its use with προδείκνυμι (e.g. 6.27.3, 7.37.3), προσημαίνω (e.g. 1.45.2, 6.27.1), and προλέγω (e.g. 1.53.3), verbs used of divine foreshadowing by means of signs.

meaning his successful return to exile is shattered by a sneeze and the sinking of his loose tooth into the earth, the only piece of Attica he will obtain (6.107.1–4); Xerxes and Artabanos are forced by the insistence of their common dream to go ahead with the invasion of Europe, with disastrous consequences. Only the Ethiopian king of Egypt, Sabakos, as will be seen below, both correctly interprets his dream and takes appropriate action (2.139.1–3). Can the unfortunate consequences following upon the other dreams be ascribed wholly to errors in interpretation? In the case of Xerxes, the dream is so powerful, and threatens such dire consequences if not obeyed, that he might appear to have little choice in the matter. Yet, as Munson has pointed out, "Divine prescriptions as such . . . do not eliminate the agent's freedom to decide as he wishes."[83]

The one instance where Herodotus presents more fully the process of self-interpretation of a dream, namely in his account of the dream of Hippias, is of interest for a number of reasons, the first being the use of the term συμβάλλομαι to describe Hippias' decoding of the dream. In this dream, Hippias sleeps with his own mother. In his interpretation, he perceives an iconic relationship between the sign-element "mother" (τῇ μητρὶ τῇ έωυτου) and the idea of one's native land (ἐν τῇ ἑωυτοῦ), while safely defusing the potentially troubling image of intercourse by reading this too as a metaphoric expression of reunion:

> ἐδόκεε ὁ Ἱππίης τῇ μητρὶ τῇ ἑωυτοῦ συνευνηθῆναι. συνεβάλετο ὦν ἐκ τοῦ ὀνείρου κατελθὼν ἐς τὰς Ἀθήνας καὶ ἀνασωσάμενος τὴν ἀρχὴν τελευτήσειν ἐν τῇ ἑωυτοῦ γηραιός.
>
> 6.107.1–2
>
> Hippias seemed [in a dream] to have slept with his own mother. He therefore conjectured from the dream that he would return to Athens from exile and after getting his rule back would die at an advanced age in his native land.[84]

Hippias, then, is far from ignoring the signs of his own dream, unlike his brother Hipparkhos (5.56.1–2), and applies to them a process of decoding by analogy (συνεβάλετο . . . ἐκ τοῦ ὀνείρου).[85] This is the only dream related by

83 Munson 2001b:35.

84 In Caesar's dream of intercourse with his mother, which receives a positive interpretation from the *coniectores*, the figure of his mother also represents the earth, which will subject itself to him (Suetonius *Life of Julius Caesar* 7.2).

85 The Peisistratidai are presented by Herodotus as particularly interested and involved in the interpretation and manipulation of signs: cf. 5.93, where Hippias is described as τοὺς χρησμοὺς ἀτρεκέστατα ἀνδρῶν ἐξεπιστάμενος, "of all men the one who knew the oracles the most accu-

Herodotus in which the dreamer's interpretive activity is characterized using the verb συμβάλλομαι: here, as generally in instances of sign interpretation, it describes the perception of connections between signifier and signified and the drawing of conclusions from this recognition.[86] All this Hippias does, but he adduces additional meaning which the sign complex of the dream does not itself necessarily support: as presented by Herodotus, there is nothing in the details of the dream to suggest that Hippias will die peacefully and at a ripe old age (γηραιός), only his own wishful thinking.[87]

The second point of interest in the narrative is Hippias' judgment on landing at Marathon that the dream has been fulfilled, and not in the way in which he envisaged. On disembarking with the Persians at Marathon, he sneezes so violently that from his aged mouth a tooth flies out, which hides itself somewhere in the sand. Hippias' reaction is one of distress: he searches for the tooth, is unable to find it, and then declares that the land will never be his, and that the sum total of his share in it consists of the portion his tooth now holds (6.107.3–4).[88] His recognition of completion or fulfillment of the dream is described with the same verb Herodotus uses of Hippias' decoding of his dream:

> Ἱππίης μὲν δὴ ταύτῃ τὴν ὄψιν συνεβάλετο ἐξεληλυθέναι.
>
> 6.108.1
>
> Hippias in this way conjectured that his dream had reached its fulfillment.

---

rately," and cf. their association with the notorious Onomakritos the χρησμολόγος (7.6.3–5). Further discussion in ch. 2.3 and esp. ch. 3.1.

86 Instances and usage discussed in ch. 1.3.1 above.

87 That an ancient audience might not have dismissed Hippias' favorable reading of his dream as completely misguided is demonstrated by Artemidorus' discussion of such dreams (1.79). He stresses that the actual act of intercourse with one's mother does not in itself imply anything bad or good: one has to consider the positions (αἱ συμπλοκαὶ καὶ τὰ σχήματα τῶν σωμάτων) involved. Circumstances surrounding the act in the dream are also important, e.g. whether the mother in the dream is alive or a corpse. If the mother is dead, then such a dream means death for the dreamer. Artemidorus, like Hippias, makes a connection between the figure of the mother and one's native land, saying that such a dream can be favorable for a politician. As Vernant (1990:110–111) points out, it is possible that in Sophocles *Oedipus Rex* Iocasta refers to this sort of positive interpretation when she attempts to reassure Oedipus by saying that many men have slept with their mothers in dreams: "according to Iocasta, either this sign has no meaning that men can possibly interpret in advance (cf. 709) and so should not be given too much importance or, if it does indeed predict something, it is more likely to be a favorable event."

88 Artemidorus 1.31 discusses dreams about teeth falling out, and says that they represent the loss of possessions.

What is being decoded here are not the signs of the dream's sign complex, but signs of a different kind. There is firstly the sneeze, whose unusual magnitude (μεζόνως ἢ ὡς ἐώθεε, 6.107.3) and suddenness point firmly in the direction of the portentous, then the disappearance of his tooth into the sand. The putting together of these signs draws from Hippias a groan (ἀναστενάξας, 6.107.4), a non-verbal marker that elsewhere in the *Histories* introduces moments of dramatic revelation and sudden recognition of the meaning of signs.[89] But there is no authorial confirmation of Hippias' reading: Herodotus lets it stand without comment, and just as Hippias constructs his hopes on the basis of his interpretation of signs, so too does he relinquish them on the basis of signs of a different kind.[90] In this instance, and in the case of Kleomenes, the self-interpreters seem to stand alone on the narrative stage, and Herodotus leaves us to decide whether the signs that these characters react to, and accept as signs, really are such.

Herodotus does not, as a rule, provide interpretations of dreams in his own right, preferring to let the figures of his work provide their own, which subsequent events confirm or deny. The dream of Polykrates' daughter forms an exception, where it is Herodotus himself who explains the significance of the dream.[91] In the dream she sees her father suspended in midair, washed by Zeus and anointed by the sun (3.124.1). Herodotus structures his narrative of Polykrates' end at the hands of the unscrupulous Oroites so that the dream and its final interpretation frame Polykrates' death, acting as almost the final word on the life of Polykrates after his unusually long epitaph (3.125.2–4). Polykrates' daughter reacts instinctively to the dream and attempts to prevent her father from leaving, but at this stage no interpretation is advanced (3.124.1–2).[92] It is only after reporting the impalement of Polykrates by Oroites that Herodotus

89 Kroisos on the pyre finally understanding Solon's use of the term ὄλβιος (1.86.3); Kleomenes realizes that the Argos mentioned in the oracle refers not to the city but to the grove he has just destroyed (6.80). The parallel to Hippias' groan is particularly close in the case of Kleomenes, since here too συμβάλλομαι is used in connection with judging the fulfillment (συμβάλλομαι δ' ἐξήκειν μοι τὸ χρηστήριονἐξήκειν, 6.80; cf. ἐξεληλυθέναι, 6.82.1, 6.108.1) of one sign on the basis of another sign (in the case of Kleomenes, the response that the name of the place he has destroyed is Argos).

90 Similarly, in the case of Kleomenes (6.80), cited in the previous footnote, Herodotus does not confirm or deny Kleomenes' reading, and states this explicitly: "I cannot definitively say whether he was lying or telling the truth" (οὔτε εἰ ψευδόμενος οὔτε εἰ ἀληθέα λέγων, ἔχω σαφηνέως εἶπαι, 6.82.1). Kleomenes claims to receive an additional sign in the form of a flame projecting forth from a cult image of Hera (6.82.2): see discussion above, ch. 2.1.3.

91 Mikalson (2003:16n2) notes the rule and its exceptions.

92 She attempts to restrain her father by means of signs of a different kind, with words of ill omen (ἐπεφημίζετο, 3.124.2) spoken in a context where they should carry even greater power, the beginning of a journey by sea.

reveals the connections between the dream's complex of signs and what they signify. The actions of washing and anointing are removed from the context in which they most naturally belong, that is, the reception and honoring of a guest, and placed in a plainer and more literal one: the "washing" refers only to the action of the rain, and "anointing" only to the appearance of exudations on Polykrates' corpse as it is exposed to the sun (3.125.4).[93] Herodotus reveals that the connection between the signifier and its signified is one of metonymy, an association of cause and effect: "Zeus" turns out not be the god himself, but that which he causes, namely rain, while "Helios" likewise is not the god himself, but that which is caused by his activity, sweat and moisture drawn out of the body.

2.2.5 Dreams and the Divine

As with Herodotean portents, the hand of the divine is often revealed in the dreams that appear in the work, sometimes implicitly, on occasion explicitly.[94] If dreams are viewed against the background of a convention that presents them as a means of communication between the divine and the human, then the divine itself may be presented as the sender in this chain of communication.[95] This is exceptionally explicit in the dream of the Egyptian king Sethon (2.141.3), where it is not simply any dream-figure who appears to him in his dream, but the god Hephaistos himself, who acts both as sender and sign-carrier.[96] Elsewhere, the dream is presented as a sign-carrier sent by the divine, almost like a messenger: this is the case, for example, with the dream that visits both Xerxes and Artabanos. The dream is described by them as "divine" (θεῖος, 7.16.γ.2), and it claims to carry with it a knowledge of "what must happen" (τὸ χρεὸν γενέσθαι, 7.17.2). Kroisos' dream about Atys is also placed in a divine context, appearing as it does after Herodotus' ominous comment that divine nemesis overtook him after Solon's visit (ἔλαβε ἐκ θεοῦ νέμεσις

93 The combination of λούειν and χρίειν occurs frequently in the *Odyssey* in the context of the reception of guests and the treatment of honored persons: e.g. 3.466, 4.252, 8.364, 19.320, 23.154. But it is also relevant that these verbs can also be used of the care of a corpse: cf. e.g. Zeus' orders that the body of Sarpedon be removed from the battlefield and washed and anointed (λοῦσον ποταμοῖο ῥοῇσι χρῖσον τ' ἀμβροσίῃ, *Iliad* 16.669–670). The imagery of the dream thus plays on the two contexts in which the verbs may be used.

94 Cf. above, ch. 2.1.4.

95 Mikalson 2003:42n110 refers to Fornara 1990 and Frisch 1968:47–52 for the claim that a divine origin would have been assumed for all dreams in the *Histories*.

96 The account of the dream is, however, related by Herodotus at one remove, since he is repeating in extensive indirect discourse what the Egyptian priests say (2.136.1 and 2.99.1).

μεγάλη Κροῖσον, 1.34.1). When described, the appearance of the dream-figures points in the direction of the divine: they are remarkable for their size and beauty (μέγας τε καὶ εὐειδής), a combination which elsewhere in Herodotus also signifies the divine (or at least the appearance of the divine, as 1.60.4, the Peisistratid parading of the woman Phye as the goddess Athena, demonstrates) and the supernatural.[97]

Dreams, then, may be presented as an instrument for communication between the divine and human realms. Only in one place is the possibility explicitly mentioned that dreams may not be bearers of signs: Artabanos' discussion with Xerxes concerning the dream that persistently urges him to invade Europe. It has been noted that here there is also some uncertainy as to whether the gods are the senders of the dream. But while it is true that Artabanos here articulates a theory that dreams are the remnants of one's daytime activities that wander at random through one's mind at night, and thus do not consitute signs with meaning, it should be emphasized that he by no means intends this as a universal theory.[98] He does admit the possibility that certain dreams are θεῖα, divinely sent and significant, but demands that they be submitted to a test, advocating in effect the use of one type of sign to determine the genuineness of another set of signs.

Connected with the convention of the divine origin of dreams is the convention that dreams contain signs not simply of what is, but of what will be. Herodotus introduces the dream of Kroisos as one "that revealed to him the truth of the evils to come with respect to his son" (ὅς οἱ τὴν ἀληθείην ἔφαινε τῶν μελλόντων γενέσθαι κακῶν κατὰ τὸν παῖδα, 1.34.1). But the divine nature of the sender does not necessarily guarantee the ἀληθείη of the message: the divine is equally capable of sending signs which are deliberately false and

97 Supernatural figures: the φάσμα of the gigantic hoplite at Marathon (6.117.3); Phye, who plays the part of Athena in Peisistratos' procession (1.60); two hoplites "having a greater than human appearance" terrify the Persians at Delphi and are regarded as sent by the divine (cf. θεῖα, 8.38). In the case of the dream-figure which appears to Hipparkhos, Nenci 1994 *ad* 5.56 argues that this is in fact the ghost (εἴδωλον) of Harmodios, just as he would have appeared in the famous sculptural group of the Tyrannicides. But given the ambiguous quality of the dream-figure's words, it seems unlikely that the dream-figure should be so clearly defined and have so specific an identity. The height and beauty of the figure should simply be seen as generic attributes of the divine. Height and beauty are common features in descriptions of divine epiphanies in Greek literature in general: cf. passages collected by Richardson 1974 in his commentary on lines 188–190 and 275–280 of the *Homeric Hymn to Demeter*.

98 Nor should this be necessarily seen as Herodotus' own view, as is assumed by van Lieshout (1980:41): "The very mention of this theory in its generality—admittedly to give a dramatic turn to his story—can well betray that for Herodotus dreams were taken to be significant only in exceptional cases." Cf. Harrison 2000:135 on the fruitlessness of attempting to determine whether Herodotus subscribes to Artabanos' view.

designed to mislead, like Agamemnon's ὄνειρος in *Iliad* 2.6, described variously in the manuscripts as θεῖος ("divine") or οὖλος ("destructive").[99] A most striking example of this in Herodotus is the dream of Sabakos, the Ethiopian king of Egypt, who is advised by a dream-figure to assemble the priests of Egypt and chop them in half (2.139.1).[100] There is a plan behind this potentially destructive advice, as Sabakos realizes, namely to contrive the downfall of his kingship, in order that he may not exceed the time allotted by fate to his reign. It is interesting that Sabakos resists falling into the gods' trap because he has knowledge derived from another sign system, an Ethiopian oracle which sets the limit of his rule at fifty years. By reading the two messages against each other, he is able to withdraw voluntarily (ἑκών, 2.139.3) and unscathed by the gods, a remarkable figure in Herodotus, and a testament to the benefits of an ability to interpret signs.

99 Likewise, the vividness (ἐνάργεια) of a dream has nothing necessarily to do with its veracity (ἀληθείη) or its comprehensibility: the latter is clear from Hipparkhos' dream, which is described as extremely vivid (ἐναργεστάτην, 5.55), but which is couched in the riddling language of the *ainos* and oracle (cf. αἰνίσσεσθαι, 5.56.1). Cf. discussion in van Lieshout 1980:18–19. On the *ainos* see ch. 2.5, and on ambiguity in oracles, ch. 2.3.2.

100 Compare also the account of the oracle of the Brankhidai to Aristodikos (1.159.4), which deliberately seeks to mislead him, as Apollo admits: ναὶ κελεύω, ἵνα γε ἀσεβήσαντες θᾶσσον ἀπόλησθε, ὡς μὴ τὸ λοιπὸν περὶ ἱκετέων ἐκδόσιος ἔλθητε ἐπὶ τὸ χρηστήριον, "Yes, I order [thus], so that you may act impiously and be destroyed all the sooner, so that in future you will not consult the oracle about giving up suppliants."

2.3 Oracles and Their Interpretation in Herodotus

In comparison with the other mantic systems mentioned by Herodotus, oracles are by far the most frequently mentioned type of prophetic sign in the work, with more than sixty instances mentioned, and constitute one of the most familiar features of Herodotus' writing. As with dreams, oracles often mark critical junctures in the narrative, perhaps the most familiar example being the key role played by oracles in the account of the rise and fall of Kroisos, who begins a campaign against the Persians on the strength of his mistaken interpretation of an oracle (1.53), ignores the Pythia's warning of a mule on the Persian throne (1.55), and complains bitterly to Apollo through her when his empire is shattered (1.90–91).[101] But, unlike dreams, which by their nature allow only for revelation to the individual (though this revelation may have relevance not just for the dreamer, but for the community as well), oracular signs are revealed to the collective as well as the individual, with both *polis* and private citizen consulting the god.

Thus Herodotus is able to use oracles to frame his introductory account of the Spartan state, for example, marking critical events in its growth: the establishment of good government (εὐνομίη, 1.65.2) by Lykourgos is introduced by the famous oracle which hesitates whether to address him as god or mortal (1.65.3), and oracles concerning Arkadia and Tegea are presented as vital factors in the failures and successes of the Spartan campaigns against those states (1.66.2; 1.67.4). Dreams, as we have seen, are almost exclusively the preserve of absolute rulers, and, consequently, largely of non-Greek figures, while oracles are consulted largely by citizens of Greek *poleis*, though also by absolute rulers of both Greek and non-Greek origin.[102] But oracles may not only be consulted by collective bodies: they are capable also of being inter-

[101] Other oracles associated with Kroisos: 1.47; 1.85.2. For the idea that oracles in the *Histories* not only confer meaning on the narrative action, but also have a cognitive function, compensating for the shortcomings of prose in a work that aspires to be epic, cf. Calame 2003:153.

[102] Roughly a third of those who consult oracles in the work are non-Greeks.

preted collectively, as the Pythia on one occasion instructs the Thebans to do, ordering them to bring the question before their assembly (ἐς πολύφημον, 5.79.1).[103]

Apart from the major role which oracles play in Herodotus' narrative, they also provide the motivation for actions of a particular kind by an individual or community, often the performance of a ritual act, sometimes one which the community would be otherwise disinclined to perform: thus the citizens of Amathous in Cyprus are instructed by an oracle to initiate a hero cult in honor of their enemy Onesilos, in whose severed head a swarm of bees has taken up residence (5.114.2). The Delphians are enjoined on the basis of an oracle (ἐκ θεοπροπίου, 2.134.4) to submit themselves to anyone concerned for retribution for the killing of Aesop.[104] Actions of this kind may be compared with ritual actions motivated by dreams, as in the example of Xerxes' decision to send a party of Athenians to sacrifice on the akropolis (8.54), discussed in ch. 2.2.1 above. An important subsection of activity motivated by oracular precept is the foundation of colonies: Herodotus' narrative of the foundation and history of Cyrene, for example, is punctuated by a chain of oracular pronouncements.[105]

2.3.1 Oracle as Mediator between Divine and Recipient

Oracles have in common with other mantic sign systems the assumption of a chain of communication between the sphere of the divine and that of the human, with the sender being the divinity itself and the receiver the consultant.[106] The communication takes place by means of signs, as with the other

103 Discussed further below, ch. 2.3.2. The Athenians are also shown on two occasions deciding the meaning of an oracle by debate: 7.142.1–143.3 and 7.189.1.

104 Other instances of the expression in connection with the performance of ritual activity: colonization of Sardinia by citizens of Phokaia (1.165.1); foundation of sanctuary of Erinyes by the Aigeidai of Sparta (4.149.2); return of cult image of Apollo to Boiotia (6.118.3); institution of hero cult of Artakhaies by Akanthioi (7.117.2); sacrifice to Boreas by Athenians (7.189.1); ritual exclusion of descendants of Athamas from prytaneum by Akhaioi (7.197.1); attempted sacrifice of Athamas as scapegoat (καθαρμός) by Akhaioi (7.197.3); guarding of sheep sacred to Apollo by leading citizens of Apollonia (9.93.1). Cf. also the expression ἐκ τῶν λογίων, "on the basis of oracles" at 1.64.2 (purification of Delos by Peisistratos).

105 4.150.3; 4.151; 4.155.3; 4.157.2; 4.159.3; 4.161.2; 4.163.2–3. Other examples in the *Histories* of oracles relating to colonization: 1.165.1 (Kyrnos); 4.178 (Phla); 5.43 (Herakleia in Sicily). On colonization oracles, see Malkin 1987; Malkin 1989 (on Cyrene: 139–140); Malkin 2003; Parker 1985:306–307; and Dougherty 1992.

106 Mikalson (2002:195) makes the point that "[o]nly oracles have a named divine agent." On the unspecified divine in portents and dreams, see chapters 2.1.4 and 2.2.5 above.

mantic systems, but the flow of communication between god and man is mediated by an important intermediary, the oracular institution (χρηστήριον, μαντήιον) and its personnel, the πρόμαντις and προφήτης. While portents and dreams present themselves directly to their recipients, the oracular system requires the mediation of a figure who communicates directly with the divinity on the one hand, and with the human realm by means of the sign system of language on the other. The oracle encodes the god's response into a system of signs intelligible to men, translating, but not, however, interpreting. The foundation myth (2.55) which Herodotus claims to have heard from the Dodonian προμάντιες about the oracles of Zeus at Dodona and at Siwah in Libya perfectly demonstrates in mythic fashion the ability of the πρόμαντις to communicate in both non-human and human form. According to this version, two black doves fly from Egyptian Thebes, the one to Dodona, the other to Libya. The doves speak in human speech (αὐδάξασθαι φωνῇ ἀνθρωπηίῃ, 2.55.2) to the inhabitants of both places and instruct them to found an oracle of Zeus. In Herodotus' rationalizing interpretation of the myth, we may view the avian identity of the mythic figures as a metaphor of their "otherness." For Herodotus, their "otherness" lies in the fact that they are swarthy Egyptian priestesses, who at first cannot speak the local language (ἐβαρβάριζε, 2.57.2) and whose foreign speech is characterized as bird-like (ὄρνιθος τρόπον), hence their appearance in the reports of the locals as black doves:

> μέλαιναν δὲ λέγοντες εἶναι τὴν πελειάδα σημαίνουσι ὅτι Αἰγυπτίη ἡ γυνὴ ἦν.
>
> 2.57.2
>
> In saying that the dove was black they indicate that the woman was Egyptian.

Blackness is interpreted by Herodotus as a sign of the priestess' Egyptian origin, just as it is for his theory that the Colchians are Egyptians (2.104.2), and it is a sign which the Dodonians transmit (σημαίνουσι) even if they do not recognize it as such.[107] One might say that at the root of the myth lies an expression of the dual nature of the oracle, its ability to communicate with the divine (the language of birds is characteristic not only of barbarians, but also of the divinely inspired poet) and simultaneously speak a language intelligible to humans.[108]

[107] Discussed in ch. 3.2.1 below. For σημαίνω in the sense of the transmission of a sign without decoding it, see ch. 1.2.1.2 above.

[108] Cf. Munson 2005:67–69 on this passage, and esp. 68n3, presenting evidence for the voice of

How the oracle communicates with the divinity is not explored by Herodotus. The oracle at times displays the omniscience of a god, as when at Delphi the Pythia anticipates a consultant's question before it has escaped his lips (5.92.β.2), or when she knows precisely what Kroisos is doing with a tortoise and a cauldron:

> οἶδα δ' ἐγὼ ψάμμου τ' ἀριθμὸν καὶ μέτρα θαλάσσης,
> καὶ κωφοῦ συνίημι καὶ οὐ φωνεῦντος ἀκούω.
> ὀδμή μ' ἐς φρένας ἦλθε κραταιρίνοιο χελώνης
> ἑψομένης ἐν χαλκῷ ἅμ' ἀρνείοισι κρέεσσιν,
> ᾗ χαλκὸς μὲν ὑπέστρωται, χαλκὸν δ' ἐπίεσται.
>
> 1.47.3

> I know the number of grains of sand and the measure of the sea,
> and I understand the dumb and hear the one who does not speak.
> A smell comes to my senses of a hard-shelled tortoise being boiled
> with lamb in bronze which has bronze underneath it and bronze
> on top.

Even more striking is the πρόμαντις of Apollo Ptoos, who is suddenly able to dispense with translators and delivers a response in perfect Carian to the consultant, Mys (8.135.2). This might be taken as some form of possession by the god, but there is no specific description of the prophetic μανία for which the Pythia, for example, is elsewhere so renowned.[109] Herodotus' description of the oracle of Apollo at Patara in Lykia (1.182) mentions the physical association of the god and the πρόμαντις, who is locked in the temple overnight whenever the god visits, the only time at which the oracle is active.[110] Only

---

birds as metaphor for the voice of the poet, "who produces speech that is abnormal but close to that of the gods." She cites Alcman *PMG* 39, 40 as an example, referring to Nagy 1990b:88. The combination of birdsong, foreign women, and prophecy is especially vivid in Aeschylus *Agamemnon* 1050–1052 and the picture of Cassandra. Cf. Harrison 2000:128n26 for further passages that make this association.

109 For an etymological link between μαντική and μαίνομαι cf. Plato *Phaedrus* 244b6–c5. The question of the Pythia's μανία and what it amounts to is still a vexed one. Maurizio 1995 has recently surveyed the problem and evidence, and convincingly argues that it was the Pythia herself, and not her male attendants, who issued the oracular response directly, without intervention, and in the form in which it eventually reached the consultant. She also accepts that the Pythia had the ability to prophesy in verse form, and suggests that the Pythia's altered state was not one of uncontrollable raging and maenadic frenzy.

110 According to Parker 1983:93n77, "The conception of the prophetess as the god's bride . . . is hinted at mythologically, esp. in the figure of Cassandra . . . , but was certainly not enacted ritually in Greece; the sacred marriage in Patara is for Hdt. a foreign custom, tinged with charlatanism."

in Herodotus' description of Amphilytos, the χρησμολόγος ἀνήρ who relates to Peisistratos the oracle of the swarming tuna, is there what seems to be an explicit reference to divine presence:[111]

> ὁ μὲν δή οἱ ἐνθεάζων χρᾷ ταῦτα.
>
> 1.63.1
>
> He delivered the following oracle while in a state of possession.

The conduit-like nature of the oracle means that its identity may at times be depicted as bound up with that of the god. Thus in the *Histories* the deliverer of an oracle may be presented as the oracular medium (e.g. ἡ Πυθίη ἔχρησε, 4.156.2), but also as the god himself (e.g. δοκέω . . . τὸν θεόν χρῆσαι, 5.80.1).[112] This is also reflected in the use of the verb σημαίνω in connection with oracles, which may have as its subject the god or the oracle.[113] The "I" of oracular utterances is sometimes indistinguishable from that of the god, as in the Pythia's reply to the Spartans:[114]

[111] χρησμολόγοι are normally purveyors and interpreters of oracles whose authority derives from an oracular source such as Bakis, Mousaios, or Laios, but not themselves creators of mantic utterances (with the exception of fraudulent practitioners, such as the notorious Onomakritos, 7.6.3, discussed in ch. 3.1 below). The passage could be interpreted to mean that the *selection* and subsequent performance of an apposite oracle was made under divine influence. Cf. 1.62.4 ἐνθαῦτα θείῃ πομπῇ χρεώμενος παρίσταται Πεισιστράτῳ Ἀμφίλυτος ὁ Ἀκαρνὰν χρησμολόγος ἀνήρ, "Then, under divine guidance, Amphilytos, the seer from Akarnania, stood by Peisistratos." What strikes Peisistratos is the timing and circumstance of the oracle's utterance by Amphilytos, and this is reflected in Herodotus' description of his actions: he "receives" (δέκεσθαι, 1.63.1) the oracle, the expression used of the recognition of an utterance as a κληδών or omen (discussion and references in ch. 2.1.2 above). The craft of the *mantis* Euenios is described as "inborn" (ἔμφυτος, 9.94.3): for more on this figure cf. ch. 2.4.2 below.

[112] Other instances of the god as subject of the verb: 1.69.2; 1.91.5; 1.159.2; 5.1.2; 6.80. The majority of these instances occur in the direct or reported speech of figures in the work, with 5.1.2 and 1.159.2 being spoken by Herodotus himself. Cf. Mikalson 2003:55 on the question of oracular voice: "In the first of the two oracles to the Athenians the Pythia orders the Athenians to 'leave my sanctuary,' and in the second she says, 'I will tell you this.' The question here and elsewhere is who is the 'I' of the oracular voice from Delphi. In some cases it is umistakably Apollo; in others, as for the 'wooden wall' oracle, recipients react as though it is Apollo; and in no case need we assume it is the Pythia herself. Clearly the oracular 'I' is Apollo. . . . [The Pythia] spoke the words, but the words were Apollo's."

[113] The Pythia (albeit corrupted by the Alkmaionidai, on which see ch. 3.1) is said to προσημαίνειν (6.123.2), while the god is said to σημαίνειν (7.142.2) by the term "wooden wall" that the Athenians are to trust in their fleet.

[114] The oracular first person is also found in the reply of the Delphic oracle to Kroisos: οἶδα δ' ἐγὼ ψάμμου τ' ἀριθμὸν καὶ μέτρα θαλάσσης (1.47.3), "I know the number of grains of sand and the measure of the sea." Parke and Wormell 1956:2.xxii–xxiii take this as a sign of authenticity in oracles: "Again, at any rate until period VII [i.e. down to 300 BCE] the Pythia when prophesying was regarded as possessed by the god. Her own personality was lost and replaced by that of

> Ἀρκαδίην μ' αἰτεῖς; μέγα μ' αἰτεῖς· οὔ τοι δώσω.
>
> 1.66.2
>
> Do you ask me for Arkadia? You ask much of me. I shall not give it to you.

In other instances, however, Herodotus chooses to distinguish the identity of the god from that of his oracle. This is what he does in his presentation of the confrontation between Kroisos and Apollo, where the Pythia justifies the ways of the god to the defeated and disgruntled Lydian. She makes no reference to her own identity, but speaks of Apollo in the third person:

> προθυμεομένου δὲ Λοξίεω ὅκως ἂν κατὰ τοὺς παῖδας τοῦ Κροίσου γένοιτο τὸ Σαρδίων πάθος καὶ μὴ κατ' αὐτὸν Κροῖσον, οὐκ οἷός τε ἐγένετο παραγαγεῖν Μοίρας.
>
> 1.91.2
>
> Though Loxias was eager that the disaster at Sardis happen in the time of Kroisos' descendants and not during Kroisos' time, he was not able to dissuade the Fates.

Reference to the god in the third person by an oracle is also found in the oracle given to Arkesilaos:

> ἐπὶ μὲν τέσσερας Βάττους καὶ Ἀρκεσίλεως τέσσερας, ὀκτὼ ἀνδρῶν γενεάς, διδοῖ ὑμῖν Λοξίης βασιλεύειν Κυρήνης.
>
> 4.163.2–3
>
> For four Battoi and four Arkesilaoi, eight generations of men, does Loxias grant you rule of Cyrene.

It may be significant that only in these two passages is Apollo referred to as Loxias, a name which the ancients understood to refer to the enigmatic and "crooked" nature of his oracular speech (cf. Plutarch *Moralia* 511b6). By referring to Apollo by this title, the Pythia alludes to the enigmatic nature of the god's communication with mortals precisely at the moment when he is defending himself against Kroisos' charges of deception.[115]

Apollo. It was not she but the god in her who spoke. Thus authentic oracles down to period VII always allude to Apollo in the first person, and any which refer to him in the third person may confidently be rejected." The vexed question of "authenticity" and dating of oracles is probably incapable of resolution in this manner.

115 Further discussion of the enigmatic nature of oracular communication below. As Pucci (1996:

The oracular chain of communication is not exclusively unidirectional, flowing only from god to mortal. It does, in a limited fashion, at times allow for interchange between human and divinity, since the oracle comes in response to a question from the consultant, unlike portents and dreams, which appear, in Herodotus at any rate, unsolicited.[116] There are a number of occasions in the work where the format of question and response even approaches something like a dialogue, as when Kroisos complains through the Delphic oracle about Apollo's ingratitude and deception and receives a lengthy discourse on fate, the gods, and human responsibility for interpretation (1.91.2), or when Mykerinos in a similar fashion protests against the fact that his impious predecessors were granted years of rule, while he, a pious man, has been granted only six more years of life, and receives the reply that the end of his life has been quickened because he has not played his part in fulfilling Egypt's destiny to suffer one hundred and fifty years of ills (2.133). In the case of Aristodikos of Kymai, who questions Apollo's oracular instruction to deliver the refugee Paktyes into the hands of the Persians, the dialogue is an even more confrontational one. Interchange between god and mortal leaves the oracular format and enters the realm of direct communication in unmediated human speech when Aristodikos, by driving away all the sparrows and injured birds sheltering in the god's temple at Didyma, provokes a vocal response in the form of a voice (φωνή, 1.159.3) which issues from the *aduton*. Aristodikos then challenges the god to explain why he comes to the aid of his suppliants (ἱκέται) in this case, but not in the case of the ἱκέτης Paktyes, and receives the reply, "So that the Kymaioi may perish the more quickly for their impiety."[117] In all these instances, the oracular

159) points out, there is another similarity between the two passages in that Apollo is presented in connection with the fates in both passages: at 1.91.2–3, he holds back, and wins concessions from, the Moirai, arranging for the fall of Sardis to be put off for three years, while at 4.163.2 he grants (διδοῖ) the Battiadai rule for eight generations of men.

[116] An exception is formed by collections of oracles of figures such as Bakis (8.20; 8.77; 8.96.2; 9.43), Mousaios (7.6.3; 8.96.2; 9.43), and Laios (5.43), which relate to a wide variety of matters and are not promulgated in response to any particular question. Another exception is the phenomenon of the ἐπίκοινον χρηστήριον, an oracle given at the same time to the Argives and Milesians (6.19; 6.77.2). Herodotus presents the two oracles as distinct and unrelated to each other, but they are delivered simultaneously, the one relating to the Milesians being unrequested and delivered in their absence, and described as an addition (παρενθήκη) to the main body, which relates to the Argives (6.19.1). Cf. Piérart 2003 on this, who sees it as "a single oracle bearing upon a single theme," originally aimed at the Milesians, here termed "Argives" in the Homeric sense of Greeks in "general."

[117] Are we to imagine this response too to have been delivered by the mysterious voice coming from the temple, or is this once more an oracular communication? In any case, Herodotus creates the impression of a direct and unmediated dialogue between Aristodikos and Apollo.

system seems to step outside itself, revealing information about the methods of the gods and the link between their actions and fate.[118]

Herodotean oracles, for the most part, are directed toward a specific recipient, and the question of the correct addressee is an important one. In several oracles in verse form the name of the recipient is woven into the oracular utterance, acting as a kind of stamp which has the double function of marking off something, showing possession or destination, and protecting the contents against access by an inappropriate person.[119] The question of correct recipient arises when Herodotus, in speaking of an oracle which Mardonios takes as relating to the Persians, is concerned to point out that it actually had to do with another group entirely, the Illyrians and Enkheleans:

> τοῦτον δ' ἔγωγε τὸν χρησμόν, τὸν Μαρδόνιος εἶπε ἐς Πέρσας ἔχειν, ἐς Ἰλλυριούς τε καὶ τὸν Ἐγχελέων στρατὸν οἶδα πεποιημένον, ἀλλ' οὐκ ἐς Πέρσας.
>
> 9.43.1
>
> But I know that this oracle, which Mardonios said related to the Persians, was composed with reference to the Illyrians and Enkheleis, not the Persians.

By pointing out this mistake, Herodotus demonstrates that Mardonios' confidence in the oracle is unfounded, and in this way he is able to strike yet another note of imminent doom in his narrative leading up to the Battle of Plataiai.[120] The proud and emphatic first-person usage (ἔγωγε . . . οἶδα)[121] echoes the Delphic oracle's proud reply to Kroisos:

118 Another instance is the Athenian request (backed by a threat not to leave the temple) for a more favorable oracle after they have received an unremittingly gloomy response from the Pythia (7.140.2–3). The second oracle explains Athena's attempts to persuade Zeus to arrange a better outcome for the Athenians: οὐ δύναται Παλλὰς Δί' Ὀλύμπιον ἐξιλάσασθαι, | λισσομένη πολλοῖσι λόγοις καὶ μήτιδι πυκνῇ (7.141.3), "Pallas is not able to placate Olympian Zeus, though she begs him with many speeches and shrewd cunning." Cf. Apollo's attempts to intercede with the Moirai on Kroisos' behalf (1.91.2).

119 Cf. e.g. the Pythia's address to Kroisos as a "big fool" (μέγα νήπιε Κροῖσε, 1.85.2), the form and tone of which recall the Hesiodic μέγα νήπιε Πέρση (*WD* 633, noted by Parke and Wormell 1956:2.xxv) and the Hesiodic tradition of advice and blame by means of *ainos*. On the figure of Kroisos and the *ainos* tradition, see Nagy 1990b:274–313. For literal stamps and seals (σφρηγίς, σήμαντρον) in Herodotus and their function as sign-bearers, see ch. 2.8.4 below.

120 Another foreshadowing: the banquet of Thebans and Persians in which a Persian guest weeps in impotent foreknowledge of the disaster about to befall them (9.16.3).

121 Cf. Herodotus' avowal that he knows "these and many other similar oracles of Mousaios relating to the Persians" (ταῦτα μὲν καὶ παραπλήσια τούτοισι ἄλλα Μουσαίου ἔχοντα οἶδα ἐς Πέρσας, 9.43.2) and cf. ch. 3.2 on Herodotus' self-presentation as a master of signs. In a way,

οἶδα δ' ἐγὼ ψάμμου τ' ἀριθμὸν καὶ μέτρα θαλάσσης.

1.47.3

I know the number of grains of sand and the measure of the sea.

2.3.2 The Oracular Code

The sign system of the oracle is one based on linguistic signs, involving not simply encoding into the sign system of language, but also an additional level of encoding into a special language, marked by its format, lexis, and a figurative and, at times, ambiguous and riddling mode, which in turn calls for recognition and an additional process of decoding on the part of the recipient. Roughly half of the oracles in the *Histories* are of this type, though not all are of equal difficulty. It is clear from the attention that he devotes to such oracles that Herodotus has a great interest in the potential for difficulties and misunderstanding that such a double-encoding carries with it. Let us look in more detail at how this language is marked. One immediately perceptible feature is the poetic format of certain of the oracles, which are framed in dactylic hexameter or iambic trimeter.[122] Connected with this format is a particular dialect and lexis, the language of epic and didactic poetry. It is a language which is panhellenic, incorporating the features of distinct and local dialects, but aiming at the widest possible Greek audience.[123] Thus, by adopting this language, the oracle is able to address all Hellas using a common dialect. In some instances, the oracle may go further than this and adapt its language to the dialect or language of the recipient. The Pythia addresses Battos and his colonists partly in the Doric dialect:

αἰ τὺ ἐμεῦ Λιβύην μηλοτρόφον οἶδας ἄμεινον,
μὴ ἐλθὼν ἐλθόντος, ἄγαν ἄγαμαι σοφίην σευ.

4.157.2

Herodotus does know the "measurements of the sea" (μέτρα θαλάσσης): at 4.86.4, he gives the dimensions of the Black Sea (ὁ μέν νυν Πόντος οὗτος καὶ Βόσπορός τε καὶ Ἑλλήσποντος οὕτω τέ μοι μεμετρέαται), as noted by Nagy (1990b:235).

[122] 25 total, the majority from Delphi. The sole oracle in iambic trimeter is at 1.174.5. Of the remaining oracles reported in indirect speech by Herodotus it is difficult to say whether we are invited to assume an "original" in prose or in verse form. At 4.163.2–3, for example, Herodotus presents the oracle to Arkesilaos III as direct speech and in prose form, but Parke and Wormell (1956) see evidence of metrical patterns here, and reproduce the passage (no. 70 in their collection) in reconstructed verse form (the handiwork of Diels 1897:19–20). The interlocutor Theon in Plutarch's dialogue about why the Delphic oracle no longer prophesies in verse reminds us that prose oracles were issued as well as ones in verse (*Moralia* 403A).

[123] Cf. Colvin 1999:60 on epic-Ionic in quotations of poetry and oracles.

> If you, who have never been there, know sheep-raising Libya better than I, who have been there, then I greatly admire your *sophiê*.

The Pythia's general appeal for colonists in Libya is also partially in Doric:

> ὃς δέ κεν ἐς Λιβύην πολυήρατον ὕστερον ἔλθῃ
> γᾶς ἀναδαιομένας, μετά οἵ ποκά φαμι μελήσειν.
>
> 4.159.3

> Whosoever comes to lovely Libya after the land has been portioned out, I warrant that he will regret it one day.

If one subscribes to Herodotus' opinion, the oracle at 4.155.3 contains one word in Libyan, βάττος, having the meaning 'king' in that language. The oracle of Apollo Ptoos in Boiotia is even able to speak to a non-Greek in his own tongue: the πρόμαντις speaks directly to Mardonios' ambassador, Mys, in his native Carian, dispensing with the intermediary figures of the local citizens (8.135.2).

All of these examples demonstrate the adaptability of oracles and their ability to speak with the tongues of men. They seem to offer the possibility of understanding by all men, yet, on the other hand, the message of the god may be encrypted in a fashion which seems more designed to hide than to reveal. This brings us to the ambiguous, riddling style for which oracles (in literary contexts, at any rate) are notorious. A glance at the epithets used by figures in the *Histories* as well as by Herodotus himself to describe oracular pronouncements is revealing: κίβδηλος ('false', 'counterfeit'), ἀμφιδέξιος ('cutting two ways'), ἄσημος ('meaningless'), ἀτέκμαρτος ('insoluble'), ψευδής ('false'). Yet in many instances the oracles described with these epithets are not in themselves 'counterfeit'. Of the three oracles described as κίβδηλος (1.66.3; 1.75.2; 5.91.2), only in the last instance is the oracle absolutely false to the core or counterfeit in the sense of a forged coin with a center of base metal covered over by a slip of precious metal: the Alkmaionidai have corrupted the Pythia in order to produce oracles which will persuade the Spartans to depose the Peisistratidai (5.63.1). In the other two oracles referred to (the Spartans will measure the Tegean plain with chains [1.66.2–3]; Kroisos will destroy a great empire [1.53.3, 1.75.2]), the oracle is true, and the description reflects the gap between what the oracle actually means and the recipient's interpretation.[124] What links them, as Kurke points out, is the "failure of delibera-

124 See now Kurke 2009, an incisive exploration of the connections between coinage and oracles and the term κίβδηλος.

tion."[125] As applied to oracles (and other matters) she finds in the term κίβδηλος the traditional Greek idea that the good and the bad, the false and the true are so mixed and so resemble each other, or are so concealed, the one under or over the other, that it is extremely difficult to distinguish one from the other and find a touchstone to make a test of authenticity.[126]

The terms ἀμφιδέξιος (5.92.ε.1), ἄσημος (5.92.β.3), and ἀτέκμαρτος (5.92.γ.1) cluster around the oracles concerning the birth and fate of Kypselos and the fortunes of the Bakkhiadai. ἀμφιδέξιος means here I think not so much "ambiguous" (the definition advanced by How and Wells), nor "favorable" (Nenci 1994). The literal meaning—"cutting both ways" (Powell), "sharp on both sides" (cf. Euripides *Hippolytus* 780, where it is used of a sword)—and its context in Herodotus—the oracle which promises success to Kypselos, but limits power to the second generation—show that it refers to the positive and negative aspects of the message, as Kirchberg (1965:77) points out. We are here again close to the idea of the package delivered by the gods to mortals in which both good and ill are mixed in such a way that mortals cannot separate them out clearly. Ἄσημος and ἀτέκμαρτος are terms used by the Bakkhiadai to describe an oracle that seems to them to have no sense, but which they are in fact later able to decode by placing alongside a subsequent oracle (5.92.γ.1).[127] As Kurke points out, it is no accident that these terms attach themselves to this part of the work, the speech of Sokles the Corinthian to the Spartans (the longest given to any individual), in which he asks them not to install tyranny in Athens and in which oracular and sign interpretation figures four times (the above-mentioned passages involve oracles from Delphi, as well as Periandros' encounter with Melissa at the Thesprotian *nekuomantêion* [5.92.η.2–4]). She characterizes this as "a veritable disquisition on the reliability of oracles—even those that seem most opaque—given the proper interpretation" and underlines its paradigmatic nature:

125 Kurke 2009:436: "If we return to the passages in Book 1 to see what these counterfeit oracles have in common with the sequence in Book 5, we find that, paradoxically, it is the failure of deliberation that makes them counterfeit. In both cases in Book 1, the text exposes what a counterfeit oracle lacks by retroactively supplying a twofold process of deliberation or consultation: first, the recipient of a riddling or ambiguous oracle should consult the god again; second, the recipient should engage in communal discussion and interpretation (or, at the very least, accept advice from human advisors). Thus both narratives reveal the need for the same dual intervention—both divine and human, inextricably implicated in each other (like *phusis* and *nomos* wedded in civic coin)."

126 Cf. Kurke 2009:426, citing Theognis 117–124 on the κίβδηλος ἀνήρ, esp. 123–124 on the gods themselves as counterfeiters: τοῦτο θεὸς κιβδηλότατον ποίησε βροτοῖσιν | καὶ γνῶναι πάντων τοῦτ' ἀνιηρότατον, "This is the most counterfeit thing the divine has contrived for mortals, and the hardest of all to find out."

127 For discussion of the term ἄσημος, see ch. 1.3.2 above.

> Thus, I would suggest that Socles' speech is engaged in a process of duelling oracular interpretation before the assembly of allies—a process that it flags through a meta-discourse on the reliability of oracles when subjected to the proper forms of human interpretative activity. And notably, all of this is repeatedly troped through the imagery of signs and/or coinage.[128]

The term ψευδής is used by Amasis at 2.174.2 in opposition to "true oracles" (ἀληθέα μαντήια). Once again, the term reflects the point of view of the user: here, ψευδής in Amasis' eyes refers to the fact that a particular oracle has not succeeded in detecting the thefts he has made, not to any deception on its part, and ἀληθής is here literally the sum of its components (α-privative and λαθ-), since the thefts do not escape the notice of the oracle.

But what is the purpose of the ambiguity and enigma if the function of the oracle is after all communication between god and mortal? More than one figure in the *Histories* accuses the deity of deception (ἀπάτη): in a remarkable passage, discussed above in connection with dialogue between divinity and mortal, Kroisos asks Apollo whether he is in the habit of deceiving those who have honored him with gifts (εἰ ἐξαπατᾶν τοὺς εὖ ποιεῦντας νόμος ἐστί οἱ 1.90.2).[129] The god, via the Pythia, denies the charge of deception, claiming that Kroisos should have looked more closely and asked the additional question, "Whose great empire will I destroy?"

Apollo thus squarely places the responsibility for adequate interpretation of his response on Kroisos' shoulders. His oracular statements are not designed to mislead, but are signs which demand interpretation.[130] Herakleitos' dictum bears repeating:

> ὁ ἄναξ, οὗ τὸ μαντεῖόν ἐστι τὸ ἐν Δελφοῖς, οὔτε λέγει οὔτε κρύπτει, ἀλλὰ σημαίνει.
>
> DK B 93

> The lord whose oracle is at Delphi neither speaks nor conceals, but indicates with signs.

128 Kurke 2009:433.

129 Kleomenes also protests against Apollo's deception: ὦ Ἄπολλον χρηστήριε, ἦ μεγάλως με ἠπάτηκας φάμενος Ἄργος αἱρήσειν (6.80), "O Apollo of the oracles, you have deceived me greatly indeed, claiming that I would take Argos."

130 Cf. Mikalson 2002:195: "Oracles in particular might appear misleading and be so initially, but in the most flagrant such cases Herodotus takes pains to have the recipients themselves ultimately acknowledge the oracle's correctness (e.g. 1.91.4–6, 6.76.1 and 80)."

Confronted with the uncertainty of human knowledge, men approach the oracle with a desire for the exact knowledge which is the property of the divine, but "the ambiguity of the responses given by the Delphic Oracle does not replace their lack of knowledge of the future with specific predictions, but with a different kind of uncertainty."[131] This is not to say that the uncertainty is irresolvable: of the total number of what I have referred to as doubly-encoded oracles in the *Histories* (37), only one quarter do not receive a decoding or are misinterpreted by the recipient.[132]

The god's encoding forces the recipient in effect to construct his own response.[133] The additional level of encoding ensures that the response is capable of being understood only by those whom it is to benefit and becomes on occasion a test of the worthiness of the consultant.[134] There is much in common between the format of the oracle and that of the riddle (αἴνιγμα) and, related to it, the *ainos*, a genre which, as Nagy has demonstrated, also relies on a second encoding, a deeper level of meaning which underlies a surface meaning and is decipherable only by those who are σοφοί.[135] In Plutarch's dialogue "Why the Pythia no longer gives oracles in verse," the interlocutor Theon refers to the connection between the riddle (αἴνιγμα) and oracle and Apollo's discrimination between the σοφοί and the stupid (σκαιοί):

131 Dougherty 1992:43, summarizing the view of Vernant 1974.

132 The misinterpretation of oracles in the *Histories* is sometimes overstated in secondary literature, e.g. Harrison 2000:61 ("frequent misinterpretation"). Cf. ch. 3.2.1 below.

133 Parker 1985:301. See also Maurizio 1997:316–317 on 7.140–144; interpretation by the community as a "collection of experts" who validate the oracle, cf. Kurke 2009, esp. 434–436.

134 This idea is articulated clearly in Plutarch's dialogue "Why the Pythia no longer gives oracles in verse." One of the participants, Theon, develops the idea that in previous times the god cloaked his message in ambiguity: τούτοις οὖν περιέβαλον ὑπονοίας καὶ ἀμφιλογίας, αἳ πρὸς ἑτέρους ἀποκρύπτουσαι τὸ φραζόμενον οὐ διέφευγον αὐτοὺς οὐδὲ παρεκρούοντο τοὺς δεομένους καὶ προσέχοντας (*Moralia* 407E), "He surrounded these things [information in his oracles] with hidden meanings and ambiguities, which hid the message from others but did not escape them or deceive those who needed to know and who concentrated." Note Plutarch's use of φράζομαι to describe the encoded message of the god: see ch. 1.3.4 above on this verb as marker and discussion of the oracle of the Siphnians (3.7.3) below.

135 Thus at 5.56.1 the verb αἰνίσσεσθαι is used of the words of a dream-figure which delivers a message in oracular dactylic hexameters to Hipparkhos on the eve of the Panathenaia. Though riddling, the dream itself can be referred to as "extremely clear" (ἐναργεστάτην, 5.55). See ch. 2.2 above and cf. Munson 2001a:196: "These words exemplify both the value of verbal signs from the gods and the problems they create for the inquirer." On the *ainos*, double-encoding, and the σοφός, see Nagy 1990b, esp. 146–150, and on the connection between αἴνιγμα and the oracle, Pucci 1996:9–16; Manetti 1993; Struck 2005:160–165.

εὖ γὰρ εἰδέναι χρὴ τὸν θεόν, ὥς φησι Σοφοκλῆς [=Sophocles fr. 771 Radt], σοφοῖς μὲν αἰνικτῆρα θεσφάτων ἀεί, σκαιοῖς δὲ φαῦλον κἀν βραχεῖ διδάσκαλον.

Moralia 406E

One should be well aware that the god, as Sophocles says, is always a riddler of prophecies for the wise, but for the stupid an inferior though concise teacher.

In Herodotus, the connection between σοφίη and the interpretation of oracles is drawn at 1.68.1, where Likhas is credited with decoding the oracle about the bones of Orestes by a mixture of συντυχίη and σοφίη.[136] The Delphic oracle's disdain for the Libyan colonists' σοφίη may also reflect disdain for their ability to interpret the signs of the oracle (4.157.2, quoted above). The oracle itself at times draws attention to this double-encoding and by means of internal clues reminds the recipient of the need for careful consideration: a Delphic oracle to the Siphnians calls for a φράδμων ἀνήρ to φράσσασθαι (3.57.3), to recognize the signs of the fulfillment of oracle.[137] Similarly, an oracle of Bakis to the Euboians begins with the imperative of the same verb, φράζεο (8.20.2; see ch. 1.3.4, n93 above). The Bakkhiadai are instructed in an oracle to "watch out for these things carefully" (ταῦτά νυν εὖ φράζεσθε, 5.92.β.3). The command seems to work on two levels, constituting both advice to do something (for the Siphnians, to look out for a "wooden ambush" and a "red herald," for the Euboians, to keep their goats away from the island) as well as a coded instruction to look closely and to interpret both the signs of the oracle and the signs of its fulfillment.

2.3.3 Decoding and Interpreting Oracles

Responsibility for the interpretation and decoding of the oracle thus rests with the recipient, who must judge whether the oracle has only one level of encoding and so may be understood at face value, with no further decoding, or whether it is doubly encoded and thus demands further interpretation. There are few professional interpreters of oracles in the *Histories*: the προφήτης

136 For σοφίη and the interpretation of signs, see ch. 1.3.2 above. Cf. Struck 2004:90–96 on the idea of coincidence and meaningfulness involved in the term σύμβολον. He notes (90) that the verb συμβάλλειν "also carries with it a notion of meeting, as in bumping into someone or something."

137 See ch. 1.3.4 for discussion of φράζομαι and its use by Herodotus in contexts relating to the interpretation of signs. The oracle is discussed shortly below.

seems only to relay the message of the god, not to interpret it.[138] Χρησμολόγοι, however, are also interpreters: we will shortly see their role in the Athenian debate about the oracle of the wooden wall, a debate in which their γνώμη is defeated and, as events prove, rightly so.[139] Onomakritos, the χρησμολόγος and arranger (διαθέτης, 7.6.3) of the oracles of Mousaios, is able to influence the interpretations of others, not so much through his own interpretations, as by his interference with oracular messages. This he achieves in two ways, either by inserting spurious material into the body of oracles regarded as authoritative, as he does when he introduces an oracle that the islands off Lemnos will vanish beneath the sea (7.6.3), for which he is expelled by the Peisistratidai, or by presenting only the favorable parts of an oracle, as he does at the court of Xerxes:

> εἰ μέν τι ἐνέοι σφάλμα φέρον τῷ βαρβάρῳ, τῶν μὲν ἔλεγε οὐδέν, ὁ δὲ τὰ εὐτυχέστατα ἐκλεγόμενος ἔλεγε . . .
>
> 7.6.4

138 Instances: 7.111.2 (προφητεύοντες, whose activity is clearly contrasted with that of the πρόμαντις); 8.36.2; 8.37.1; 8.135.3; 9.93.4. At 8.135.3 it may seem as if the πρόμαντις of the oracle of Apollo Ptoos is identical with the προφήτης: καὶ πρόκατε τὸν πρόμαντιν βαρβάρῳ γλώσσῃ χρᾶν. καὶ τοὺς μὲν ἑπομένους τῶν Θηβαίων ἐν θώματι ἔχεσθαι ἀκούοντας βαρβάρου γλώσσης ἀντὶ Ἑλλάδος, οὐδὲ ἔχειν ὅ τι χρήσωνται τῷ παρεόντι πρήγματι· τὸν δὲ Εὐρωπέα Μῦν, ἐξαρπάσαντα παρ' αὐτῶν τὴν ἐφέροντο δέλτον, τὰ λεγόμενα ὑπὸ τοῦ προφήτεω γράφειν ἐς αὐτὴν, φάναι δὲ Καρίῃ μιν γλώσσῃ χρᾶν, "And straightaway the *promantis* began to deliver an oracle in a foreign language, and those of the Thebans that had accompanied [Mys] were greatly astonished to hear a foreign language instead of Greek, and did not know what to make of the present situation. But Mys snatched the writing tablet which they were carrying and began to write down the words of the *prophêtês* and said that he was speaking in Carian." The expression τὰ λεγόμενα ὑπὸ τοῦ προφήτεω could refer to repetition by the *prophêtês* of the authoritative oracular utterance of the *promantis*. The verbs of speaking used to describe the utterance of each (χρᾶν and λέγω respectively) reflect this, λέγω, as opposed to χρᾶν, showing unmarked speech. λέγω can of course be used of oracular speech (1.47.2; 1.65.2; 1.67.3) (cf. εἰπεῖν: 1.85.2; ἔφη: 5.79.1, 6.86.γ.2) but in such cases the context rather than the verb of speaking always makes the oracular nature of the utterance clear. Maurizio 1995:70 (who does not mention this passage) argues against "the division of labor" between Pythia and προφήτης, pointing to the fact that the Pythia may be called προφῆτις (e.g. Euripides *Ion* 42, 321, 1322; Plato *Phaedrus* 244b) as well as πρόμαντις and that the distinction is perhaps "one of emphasis, rather than function. The word *prophetes* emphasizes the announcement of the divine message, while *mantis* emphasizes contact with the divine" (70n14). See also Nagy 1990b:162–167, who explores how the distinction between προφήτης and μάντις can sometimes be collapsed, and cf. Mikalson 2003:56n164 on *promantis*.

139 I return to the χρησμολόγοι in ch. 3.1. On their role and status, see Dillery 2005; Bowden 2003; Pritchett 1971–1979:3.318–321; Shapiro 1990, and Garland 1990:82–85. Bowden (2003:261n30) considers the possibility that the reference to οἱ χρησμολόγοι in 7.142.3–143.3 can be "analysed as a construction of definite article with plural adjective, referring to an indefinite group of people, 'those who engaged in oracle interpretation.'"

> Whenever there was something in [an oracle] spelling disaster for the Persians, of this he would make no mention, but would select the most optimistic parts and recite those.

We find, in short, what we have already found to be the case with other professional interpreters in the *Histories*, namely that professional interpreters of oracles are either wrong or corrupt.[140] The majority of Herodotean oracles, when their interpretation is described, are interpreted by nonprofessionals, who enjoy both success and failure in their interpretative endeavors. As has been mentioned above, successes in the interpretation of oracles in the *Histories* far outweigh failures.

How do the figures of Herodotus' work go about interpretation? In a number of the interpretations found in the *Histories*, the process of decoding is described using the verb συμβάλλομαι, a verb often used by Herodotus in other contexts involving the decoding of signs.[141] Likhas' interpretation of the Delphic oracle relating to the location of the bones of Orestes is described with this verb (1.68.3) and the activity is one of "putting together" signifier and signified, and perceiving the relationship between them, which is there one of cause and effect. The verb is used of the Paiones' recognition of the fulfillment of the oracle given to them, which instructs them to attack the Perinthioi when they hear them call out their name. In this case, the Paiones are able to recognize the sign of their name in the victorious shouts of the Perinthioi as they sing the paean:

> νικώντων δὲ τὰ δύο τῶν Περινθίων, ὡς ἐπαιώνιζον κεχαρηκότες, συνεβάλοντο οἱ Παίονες τὸ χρηστήριον αὐτὸ τοῦτο εἶναι.
>
> 5.1.3

> When two [of the three sets of] Perinthian [fighters] were gaining the upper hand and the Perinthians in their joy began to sing the paean, the Paiones reckoned that this was exactly what the oracle meant.

They are able to separate the signifier from the signified, dissociating the sound |paion| from its context in the Perinthians' cry of triumph to the god

140 Cf. Mikalson 2002:195n18: "Interpreters of oracles and dreams, whether Greek *chresmologoi* or Persian priests, however, are often in error."

141 See ch. 1.3.1 above.

Apollo, and associating it with the signification it carries in another sign system involving the god, namely his oracle.[142]

Συμβάλλομαι is also the verb used by Kleomenes to describe his recognition of the fulfillment of the oracle that he would take Argos: he realizes that the Argos of the oracle refers to not the city of the Argives but the hero Argos, whose sacred grove he has just destroyed, in other words that as a signifier, |Argos| has more than one referent (6.75.3).

The oracle of the "wooden wall" shows the process described by συμβάλλομαι being practiced in two different ways: the χρησμολόγοι (the only reference in Herodotus to interpreters of oracles as a group) identify the referent of the term ξύλινον τεῖχος as the ancient fence which once encircled and protected the Athenian akropolis, while an opposing group, for which Themistokles becomes the spokesman, sees its referent as the ships of the Athenian fleet:

> οὗτος ὡνὴρ οὐκ ἔφη πᾶν ὀρθῶς τοὺς χρησμολόγους συμβάλλεσθαι.
>
> 7.143.1
>
> This man said that the χρησμολόγοι were not putting this together correctly at all.

In other words, the readings (γνῶμαι, 7.142.1) of the two groups rest respectively on a literal connection between signifier and signified (a wall is a wall), and on a figurative one, in which the ships substitute metaphorically for the wooden wall, both wall and ship having the function of defense and being composed of wood.[143] Themistokles' contribution is not the drawing of this metaphoric connection between signifier and signified (from the passage cited immediately below it is clear that this type of connection had already been suggested), but his appeal to the internal consistency of the oracular text to resolve a question of reference on which previous attempts to argue this interpretation had foundered:[144]

[142] Munson 2005:83, who comments that the Perinthians sing the paean "oblivious to the language of the Paeonians. They only hear pure Greek as conveying meaning." She compares the position of the Thereans and Cyrenaeans, who can only see in the name Battos the Greek meaning of 'stutterer' (4.155.1–3), while Herodotus insists that the word is actually the Libyan for 'king'. For names and naming see ch. 2.6 below.

[143] One could also argue that an additional relationship of metonymy is at work, since wood, the material from which the ship is made, comes to represent the idea of ship, as in the oracle given to the Siphnians, discussed below.

[144] Cf. Johnston and Struck 2005:22 and Dillery 2005 on Plutarch's presentation of Themistokles' actions and use of sign interpretation.

τοὺς ὦν δὴ τὰς νέας λέγοντας εἶναι τὸ ξύλινον τεῖχος ἔσφαλλε τὰ δύο τὰ τελευταῖα ῥηθέντα ὑπὸ τῆς Πυθίης.

7.142.2

What kept on tripping up those who said that "wooden wall" meant "ships" were the two things said by the Pythia at the end of the oracle.

The reference is to the second oracle given to the Athenians, in which the Pythia addresses the island of Salamis:

ὦ θείη Σαλαμίς, ἀπολεῖς δὲ σὺ τέκνα γυναικῶν
ἤ που σκιδναμένης Δημήτερος ἢ συνιούσης.

7.142.2

O divine Salamis, you will destroy the children of women either when the corn is being sown or when it is being brought in.

Themistokles resolves the disturbing expression "You will destroy the children of women" by a semiotic sleight of hand: he simply transfers the referent of "children" from the Athenian people to the enemy. His argument is hardly based on divine inspiration or on a special vision, but on a rhetorical appeal to the internal logic and consistency of the text: if the referent of τέκνα γυναικῶν is the Athenians, then Salamis could hardly be addressed as θείη ("divine") but would be called σχετλίη ("cruel"). As Manetti comments,

> Themistocles . . . puts forward as his final argument an interpretation which tends more to the positive proof of his own reasoning than the demonstration of the falsity of the basic premiss of his opponents. . . . It could well be that the discussion so far has caused us to lose sight for a moment of the fact that the object of debate is a prophecy of Apollo. This is significant, for the logic applied to the interpretation of the divinatory response is precisely the same as that which governs political assemblies.[145]

145 Manetti 1993:34. For the use of reasoning in forecasting the future, cf. Euripides F973 N (μάντις δ' ἄριστος ὅστις εἰκάζει καλῶς) and Thucydides on Themistokles (τῶν μελλόντων ἐπὶ πλεῖστον τοῦ γενομένου ἄριστος εἰκαστής, *Histories* 1.138.3). Cf. ch. 1.3.3 above on εἰκάζω and interpretation in Herodotus. Cf. Harrison 2000:245: "As for the alleged erosion of divination by democracy, the interpretation of oracles in no way precludes such rational deliberation but rather depends upon it. As is illustrated most graphically by the story of Themistocles and the wooden wall, the democratic assembly of Athens—the sanctum sanctorum of Greek secular rationality—was also a fitting venue for the textual analysis of the advice of Apollo. . . . There is no necessary reason then why democratic decision-making and divination should have been incompatible." See also ibid., 194–195.

Interpretation by debate occurs also amongst the Thebans, who are in fact instructed by the oracle to put their question about the possibility of revenge on the Athenians to their own assembly:

> ἡ δὲ Πυθίη ἀπὸ σφέων μὲν αὐτῶν οὐκ ἔφη αὐτοῖσι εἶναι τίσιν, ἐς πολύφημον δὲ ἐξενείκαντας ἐκέλευε τῶν ἄγχιστα δέεσθαι.
>
> 5.79.1
>
> The Pythia said that they would not get vengeance on their own and ordered them to bring the matter to the assembly and ask their nearest for help.

Here, too, Herodotus presents the debate as one in which the connection between signifier, the expression τῶν ἄγχιστα δέεσθαι ("ask your nearest"), and signified is explored first as a literal one ("nearest" referring to the Thebans' neighbors) and then as a figurative one ("nearest" in terms of kinship, referring to the island of Aigina, named after one of the daughters of Theban Asopos). He does not merely report the debate, but dramatizes it as two successive speeches in *oratio recta*, with an anonymous Theban citizen (εἶπε δή κοτε μαθών τις, 5.80.1) presenting the winning reading (γνώμη, 5.80.2). Just as in the case of the oracle about the wooden wall, the assembly must vote on which is the *better* of the two interpretations, as if an ultimate interpretation cannot be reached:[146]

> καὶ οὐ γάρ τις ταύτης ἀμείνων γνώμη ἐδόκεε φαίνεσθαι, αὐτίκα πέμψαντες ἐδέοντο Αἰγινητέων . . .
>
> 5.80.2
>
> As nobody seemed to have a better interpretation than this, they sent to the Aiginetans immediately and asked them for help.

[146] Cf. Manetti 1993:23, who notes that "the formula normally used by the oracle when giving ritual advice reflects that which was used to record decisions of democratic assemblies." See also Kurke 2009 and Maurizio 1997:316–317 on interpretation by the community as a sign of authenticity: "[T]he community is a collection of experts who, in some crucial sense, author this oracle and in so doing deem it authentic—that is, they accept it as a divine utterance with predictive value, and their acceptance facilitates the remembrance and introduction of this oracle into the Delphic tradition. Authenticity as defined by the ancient audience/authors of oracles, then, was implicitly conferred (or denied) during the complex and contested exchanges of an oracular performance. In this context, authenticity means that an oracle was judged relevant or true and hence a bona fide member of the Delphic tradition."

ταύτῃ Θεμιστοκλέος ἀποφαινομένου Ἀθηναῖοι ταῦτα σφίσι ἔγνωσαν αἱρετώτερα εἶναι μᾶλλον ἢ τὰ τῶν χρησμολόγων.

7.143.3

After Themistokles set forth his opinion in this way, the Athenians decided that this seemed preferable to that of the χρησμολόγοι.[147]

Herodotus shows himself directly as interpreter in his account of an oracle given to the inhabitants of wealthy Siphnos. The oracle is given in response to the question whether the Siphnians' prosperity will be long-lasting:

> ἀλλ' ὅταν ἐν Σίφνῳ πρυτανήια λευκὰ γένηται
> λεύκοφρύς τ' ἀγορή, τότε δὴ δεῖ φράδμονος ἀνδρὸς
> φράσσασθαι ξύλινόν τε λόχον κήρυκά τ' ἐρυθρόν.
>
> 3.57.4
>
> But when on Siphnos the buildings of state turn white, and the marketplace white-browed, then there is need of a shrewd man to look out for a wooden ambush and a red herald.

The account contrasts the Siphnians' lack of understanding of the oracle, both upon receiving it and upon its fulfillment (τοῦτον τὸν χρησμὸν οὐκ οἷοί τε ἦσαν γνῶναι οὔτε τότε ἰθὺς οὔτε τῶν Σαμίων ἀπιγμένων, 3.58.1), with the interpretative skills of Herodotus, who is able to provide the solution. The form of the oracle is a familiar one (ἀλλ' ὅταν . . . τότε δή, "but when . . . then"), demanding the appearance of a sign as condition for its fulfillment. The task of the interpreter thus becomes not just the interpretation of the oracle, but also the recognition of the set of circumstances which signify the coming into being of the predicted action.[148] The oracle itself draws attention to this and to the double-encoding of the utterance by calling for a "shrewd man" (φράδμων

147 At 7.189, the Athenians' interpretation of an oracle that instructs them to call upon their brother-in-law as an ally is also presented as a collective endeavor, and their association of the γαμβρός of the oracle with Boreas, husband of Erekhtheus' daughter, Oreithyia, is once more described by the verb συμβάλλομαι.

148 Other examples in Herodotus: 1.55.2; 6.77.2; 8.77.1; and, without ἀλλά, 8.20.2. See Fontenrose 1978 ("Definite Signs") 166–170 and 185 for examples of this construction, which is one of the most highly imitable stylistic features of the oracular style, as its parodic use by characters in Aristophanic comedy demonstrates (e.g. *Birds* 983–988; *Knights* 198). *Pace* Crahay 1956:200 and Parke and Wormell 1956:2.xxii ("Without prejudice to their authenticity all such responses [i.e. beginning with ἀλλά] must be held to be incomplete in their present form"), ἀλλά need not indicate that the oracle is part of a larger text. On the question of fulfillment of oracles cf. Harrison 2000:138–139 and index s.v. *fulfilment*.

ἀνήρ) to "be on the lookout" (φράσσασθαι). As at 5.92.β.3 and 8.20.2, the verb φράζομαι can itself be taken as a coded utterance, alerting the recipient to the necessity of reading the oracle on two levels.[149]

On the one hand, the recipients are told to be beware of (φράσσασθαι, cf. φυλάξασθαι, 3.58.2 as gloss and *variatio*) a "wooden ambush" and a "red herald," on the other, they are also instructed to decipher the meaning of these two phrases. No φράδμων ἀνήρ appears among the Siphnians, and so they do not recognize the conditions of the oracle in the arrival of the Samian ships and their dispatch of one ship with ambassadors to extort payment from the Siphnians (3.58.2). In effect it is now Herodotus who assumes the role of φράδμων ἀνήρ as he unravels the enigma.[150] There is much to unravel: as Manetti points out, by means of a double *enallagê* the adjective "wooden" has been detached from its logical referent, the ship in which the Samian ambassadors first approach the Siphnians (3.58.2), and applied to the "ambush" which the Samians have prepared for them, while the redness of their ships becomes a property of those that sail in them, the Samian ambassadors (the "red herald" referred to by the oracle).[151] Furthermore, a relationship of metonymy joins the signifiers "wooden" and "herald" with the idea of "ship" and "ambassadors," wood being the material from which the ship is made, and heralds and ambassadors both being associated with the process of negotiation in hostilities. But Herodotus does not in fact provide a complete reading in these terms. He does what we have seen him do elsewhere, namely, provide a key piece of information from which the rest of the puzzle may be solved:[152]

> τὸ δὲ παλαιὸν ἅπασαι αἱ νέες ἦσαν μιλτηλιφέες· καὶ ἦν τοῦτο τὸ ἡ Πυθίη προηγόρευε τοῖσι Σιφνίοισι φυλάξασθαι τὸν ξύλινον λόχον κελεύουσα καὶ κήρυκα ἐρυθρόν.
>
> 3.58.2

149 Again, cf. ch. 1.3.4 on φράζομαι.

150 The comment of Crahay (1956:260) on the φράδμων ἀνήρ could thus be applied to Herodotus: "Il y a dans cette prophétie un élément qui n'apparaît pas dans la solution de la devinette: δεῖ φράδμονος ἀνδρός. Le sens en paraît clair: seul un sage peut comprendre les menaces et les pièges de la prosperité. Tel est biên l'enseignement qui se dégage de toutes les fictions analogues. Et n'expriment-elles pas toutes les leçons de morale pratique qui constituent la doctrine des Sept Sages?"

151 Manetti 1993:26. The "ambush" (λόχος) works on two levels. On one level it is the place of concealment, reminding one of the famous κοῖλος λόχος, the wooden horse at Troy (*Odyssey* 4.277), and on another it includes the group of men who perpetrate the "ambush".

152 Cf. discussion of 7.57.2 in ch. 2.1.6.

> Long ago all ships were painted with ochre: it was this that the Pythia was warning the Siphnians about in advance when she ordered them to look out for a wooden ambush and a red herald.

The oracle given to Arkesilaos III of Cyrene also contains elements which remain uninterpreted, though clear enough when read against Greek cultural conventions:

> ἢν δὲ τὴν κάμινον εὕρῃς πλέην ἀμφορέων, μὴ ἐξοπτήσῃς τοὺς ἀμφορέας ἀλλ' ἀπόπεμπε κατ' οὖρον· εἰ δὲ ἐξοπτήσεις τὴν κάμινον, μὴ ἐσέλθῃς ἐς τὴν ἀμφίρρυτον· εἰ δὲ μή, ἀποθανέαι καὶ αὐτὸς καὶ ταῦρος ὁ καλλιστεύων.
>
> 4.163.3

> If you find the oven full of amphorae, do not fire them, but send them on their way with a fair wind. If you fire the oven, do not go to the place surrounded by water. If you do, you will die, both you and the finest-looking bull.

It becomes clear what the oven and amphorae refer to when Arkesilaos has several of his opponents, who have barricaded themselves in a tower, burned alive: the connection between signifier and signified is a metaphorical one, with the tower substituting for the oven, and the unfortunate men for the pots within it.[153] Arkesilaos realizes the connection too late, but attempts to comply with the rest of the oracle's conditions by avoiding "the place surrounded by water" (ἡ ἀμφίρρυτος). Here perceiving the signified is not the difficulty, since, as it turns out, Arkesilaos is quite right in his assumption that the feminine adjective ἀμφίρρυτος qualifies a city, but rather determining the referent (*which* city?).[154] He understands the referent to be Cyrene, and so avoids this city and goes to Barke, the city of his father-in-law, where both men are, however, recognized and killed in the marketplace by exiles from Cyrene. The "finest-looking bull" (ταῦρος καλλιστεύων) is never explained by Herodotus, but clearly refers to Alazeir, Arkesilaos' father-in-law.[155] As with Skyles' griffins

153 For another instance of an oven to be taken in a metaphorical sense, cf. the *marturion* and *sumbolaion* which the ghost of Melissa sends to Periandros, 5.92.η.2 (referred to in ch. 1.1.2 and 1.1.4 above).

154 The feminine gender of the expression in Greek and its general use in the poetic tradition (e.g. *Odyssey* 1.50; Pindar *Isthmian* 1.8) would most naturally lead one understand it as an adjective qualifying an island.

155 For Manetti (1993:27), however, the referent remains a mystery: "This is never explained and thus remains incomprehensible to us, too."

(4.79.1, discussed in ch. 2.1.6 above), here too Herodotus takes for granted the cultural code against which the animal imagery of the oracle must be read,[156] a code in which the mention of the physically perfect bull, the largest and costliest victim offered in cult, would be likely to activate associations of sacrifice and the well-known image of the death of Agamemnon, slain like a bull at the manger (βοῦς ἐπὶ φάτνῃ, *Odyssey* 4.534–535=11.411).[157]

Arkesilaos' dilemma is different from that of the Siphnians, who are simply unable to make sense of the Pythia's utterance. The former is able to achieve partial comprehension, at least, moving through a state of ignorance, then knowledge, and ignorance once more. At first, he ignores the oracle because of his desire to gain power again (ἐπικρατήσας τῶν πρηγμάτων τοῦ μαντηίου οὐκ ἐμέμνητο, 4.164.1). He then realizes too late the meaning of the oracle's warning and attempts to comply with the oracle's warning by voluntarily removing himself from Cyrene, but because of his misinterpretation of the referent of ἡ ἀμφίρρυτος, ends up fulfilling the oracle:

> Ἀρκεσίλεως μέν νυν εἴτε ἑκὼν εἴτε ἀέκων ἁμαρτὼν τοῦ χρησμοῦ ἐξέπλησε μοῖραν τὴν ἑωυτου.
>
> 4.164.4
>
> And so Arkesilaos, whether deliberately or unwillingly, fell short of the oracle and fulfilled his own fate.

Herodotus underscores the connection between Arkesilaos' involuntary mistake in interpretation (ἁμαρτὼν τοῦ χρησμοῦ) and his own death, and referring to his willful disregard of the oracle on the one hand (cf. οὐκ ἐμέμνητο, 4.164.1), and his attempt to comply with it on the other by willingly keeping away from Cyrene (ἔργετο ἑκὼν τῆς τῶν Κυρηναίων πόλιος, 4.164.3).

These are elements and patterns also recognizable in Herodotus' accounts of Kroisos and Kambyses, both of whose errors in interpretation also involve confusion concerning the referent of the oracular signifier. In the case of the oracle given to Kroisos about destroying a mighty empire (1.91.4), what is signified is clear enough; it is the particular referent of the expression "great empire" (μεγάλη ἀρχή) that is at stake. In the case of Kambyses, the referent

[156] Cf. Munson 2001a:244–251 on cultural code and animals.

[157] Corcella (Asheri et al. 2007 *ad loc.*) compares *Iliad* 2.480–481, comparison of Agamemnon to the finest-looking bull of the herd, where the sacrificial overtones are not however as obvious. For καλλιστεύω in a sacrificial context, again involving a human victim, compare *Histories* 7.180, where the Persians sacrifice the most handsome. See further ch. 2.6 below. For an actual example of βόες καλλιστεύοντες in a sacrificial context in a fourth-century BCE inscription from Athens, see Sokolowski 1969 (33B 21).

of the signifier "Agbatana" provides the difficulty: he receives an oracle that he will die in Agbatana (3.64.4), and he assumes that refers to the imperial capital in Persia. By a strange turn of events he finds himself lying mortally wounded outside a city in Syria and asks what it is called, only to find out that it is Agbatana. In all three instances (Kroisos, Kambyses, Arkesilaos), the involuntary error in interpretation is described using a form of the root ἁμαρτ-:

> Κροῖσος δὲ ἁμαρτὼν τοῦ χρησμοῦ . . . (1.71.1);
> Kroisos, failing to understand the oracle . . .
>
> παντὸς δὲ τοῦ μέλλοντος ἔσεσθαι ἁμαρτών . . . (3.65.4);
> [Kambyses,] failing to understand what was going to happen . . .
>
> ἁμαρτὼν τοῦ χρησμοῦ ἐξέπλησε μοῖραν τὴν ἑωυτοῦ. (4.164.4)
> [Arkesilaos] in failing to understand the oracle fulfilled his own fate.[158]

This combination of *hamartia* and involuntariness is at the heart of Aristotle's formulation of the hero of tragedy in the *Poetics* (1453a8–10), and is one of the several ways in which Herodotus' work and tragedy in general overlap.[159] The statement of Kroisos after he has listened to Apollo's self-defense of his actions is revealing for its assessment of the role of personal responsibility borne by humans for the interpretation of signs:

> ὁ δὲ ἀκούσας συνέγνω ἑωυτοῦ εἶναι τὴν ἁμαρτάδα καὶ οὐ τοῦ θεοῦ.
>
> 1.91.6
>
> After he heard this he recognized that the mistake was his own and not caused by the god.

The limitations of human knowledge and the obscure and sometimes unknowable plans of the gods are familiar themes both in the *Histories* and in Greek literature of the Archaic and Classical periods. Yet figures in the *Histories* are nevertheless able to avail themselves of information sent by the gods via oracular signs.

158 Cf. also Teisamenos' error (ἁμαρτὼν τοῦ χρηστηρίου, 9.33.2) in interpreting the oracle which tells him that he will win five "contests" (ἀγῶνες). Teisamenos takes the referent of ἀγῶνες to be athletic contests, not military ones. On Teisamenos as *mantis*, see ch. 2.4 below.

159 Cf. Schütrumpf 1989 on this passage and the combination of *hamartia* and involuntariness in Aristotle and this tradition in earlier authors. For a summary of scholarship on Herodotus, tragedy, and the tragic, see Saïd 2002.

2.4 Other Types of *Mantikê*

IN THIS CHAPTER WE SHALL CONSIDER OTHER TYPES OF *MANTIKÊ* besides oracular utterances. As with oracles, these systems of divination involve the active solicitation of signs revelatory of the future, as opposed to portents and dreams, which, though revelatory of the future, generally appear unsolicited.[160] Oracles, however, rely on the sign system of language, whereas the forms of *mantikê* to be discussed here rely on a system of signs which are visual in nature. The forms of *mantikê* practiced in the ancient world were numerous, but only a few varieties appear in Herodotus' work.[161]

2.4.1 *Mantikê* by Animal Sacrifice

The type which Herodotus mentions most frequently is divination by means of animal sacrifice, that is, the inspection of the internal organs of a sacrificial victim for signs regarded either as favorable or unfavorable for a military action about to be undertaken. The terms used for this kind of consultation (θύεσθαι, σφαγιάζεσθαι, καλλιερέεσθαι) show that sacrifice is at its kernel.[162] The parts of the sacrificed animal which form the object of consultation are termed ἱρά or σφάγια, which may be qualified by the following adjectives: χρηστά (9.62.1; with negative, 5.44.2, 9.61.3), καλά (6.112.1), ἐπιτήδεα (with negative, 9.37.1), καταθύμια (9.45.2).[163] Positive results may also be described

[160] For this distinction in antiquity, cf. e.g. Servius on *Aeneid* 6.190, where a distinction is made between *auguria impetrativa* (solicited signs) and *auguria oblativa* (unsolicited signs).

[161] Other types of *mantikê* are surveyed in Halliday 1913 and Bouché-Leclerq 1879-1882, still the fullest account of divination in the ancient world. Recent overview of Greek divination by Bremmer 1996; cf. Johnston and Struck 2005 and now Flower 2008b.

[162] θύεσθαι (5.44.2; 7.134.2; 7.167.1; 9.10.3, 9.33.1; 9.38.1; 9.62.1), σφαγιάζεσθαι (6.76.1; 7.180; 9.61.2; 9.72.1), καλλιερέεσθαι (6.82.2; 7.113.2; 7.167.1; 9.92.2). For descriptions of and distinctions between these terms, see Jameson 1991:200–201.

[163] The distinction between ἱρά and σφάγια is discussed by Pritchett 1971–1979:1.109–115 and 3.73–90. According to him, the former are "for divination purposes, which might be taken in camp before setting out, in the course of which the omens had to be interpreted as favorable

by the impersonal third-person singular active of καλλιερέειν (6.76.2; 7.134.2; 9.19.2; 9.38.2; 9.96). The type of sacrificial victim is described only once, at 7.113.2, and there, the victims (white horses sacrificed by the *magoi*) appear to be mentioned precisely to demonstrate the "otherness" of the Persian practice. It is also interesting that Herodotus mentions no details of extispicy or of the organs themselves: contrast, for example, Xenophon *Hellenica* 3.4.15 and 4.7.7, where the historian describes in detail why the signs are unfavorable: the victim's liver is missing the part known as the lobe (λοβός).[164]

The workings of the system are never shown or explained. This is presumably because it is a cultural "given" for a Greek audience, and, as a general rule, Herodotus passes over details of ritual unless they are particularly striking and differ from standard Greek practice.[165] Questions of the interpretation of

---

before the action could be begun," while the latter are "of a propitiatory nature, performed immediately before the action began and sometimes even after the troops had been committed" (3.73–74); "σφάγια were not necessarily, if at all, for divination purposes" (1.110). He is forced to admit, however, that this distinction will not hold for Herodotus, where the same consultation of sacrificial signs can be described at 9.37.1. as ἱρά, but is referred to as σφάγια at 9.41.4. Jameson (1991:201) suggests the following relationship between the two terms, in which ἱρά may have both a broader sense, covering a variety of practices, including σφάγια:

hiera "rites"

hiera "special parts of the victim"	*sphagia* "rites focused on bloodletting"
hiera "signs derived from the parts of the victim"	*sphagia* "signs derived from bloodletting"

Jameson also rejects the idea that σφάγια were propitiatory rather than divinatory in nature (204) and stresses the concentration on the action of the killing of the victim and bloodletting (205): "In effect, the *sphagia* narrow down to a single action and an observation—the killing of the victim with a stab into the neck and the observing of the flow of blood that results." See now Flower 2008b:159–165, who thinks one distinction between the two may be that in the case of σφάγια "the nature of the ritual may have necessitated that the seer slit the animal's throat with his own hands" (163) and thinks that the seer wore different clothing and acted differently for each type (165). On the spirit surrounding the σφάγια, cf. Henrichs 1981:215–216.

164 Further examples in Pritchett 1971–1979:3.73–78. Pritchett (1971–1979:3.83) believes that the σφάγια of Pausanias at Plataiai (9.61.3, discussed below) did not involve extispicy, and from this attempts to derive a general theory: "Clearly, the method of taking omens from the *sphagia* was entirely different from the complicated procedure involved in extispicy." Granted, to sacrifice and inspect the σπλάγχνα ("vital organs") must have been extremely difficult under a hail of arrows, but is this not precisely the point of Herodotus' mentioning this detail, to show Pausanias' piety under extreme conditions, and contrast it with Mardonios' decision to dispense with the σφάγια (τὰ σφάγια ἐᾶν χαίρειν, 9.41.2)? This is not to say that other signs connected with sacrifice may not have been noted, such as the movement of the victim or the flow of blood, perhaps; discussion and evidence in Pritchett 1971–1979:3.83–87.

165 See ch. 2.7 on ritual accompanying oaths. Cf. Burkert 1990 in general on the implicit Greek model that Herodotus notes variances from but does not articulate, and Mikalson 2002:197: "Standard features of his many ethnological surveys of non-Greek peoples are descriptions of the gods they worshipped, their major sanctuaries, and unusual cultic or burial practices, all usually noted because of their variance from the Greek."

a set of signs obtained by this form of *mantikê* are never entered into as they are in the case of oracles. We are shown the *mantis* Megistias on the eve of battle at Thermopylai "looking into" the sacrificial victims (ἐσιδὼν ἐς τὰ ἱρά, 7.219.1) and then relaying (ἔφρασε) the message of his coming death, but are not told what the signs are from which he derives his reading.[166] Herodotus gives us only the results of readings, never the process of decoding. Perhaps this is because as an art or discipline (τέχνη), this kind of *mantikê* has its own set of rules and uses a more straightforward application of principles (a certain shape in a certain quadrant of the liver is either favorable or not) that appears as unremarkable when compared to the decoding of an oracle.[167] Making the connection between the signs glimpsed in the sacrifice and what they signify appears to be unproblematic; no polysemy, ambiguities, or confusions between literal and figurative referents are presented, and no aporia in decoding is ever shown—quite the opposite of what we have seen in the case of portents, dreams, and oracles. The readings resulting from this form of divination yield "yes/no" responses: we learn only that a particular sacrifical consultation has been favorable or unfavorable, or at most, as happens at Plataiai, that the signs for one side are favorable for defending, but not for attacking.[168] The sole and striking exception to this may be the case of Megistias, mentioned above, who is able to foresee in the victim something quite specific: the death of the Spartan contingent in the battle to come at Thermopylai (τὸν μέλλοντα ἔσεσθαι ἅμα ἠοῖ σφι θάνατον, 7.219.1). The pathos of the story of the seer who knows his own imminent death but nevertheless chooses to fight (of which the mythical paradigm is the seer Amphiaraus) may well explain this exception.

[166] For another instance of "looking into" the mantic signs, cf. 4.68.3, where Scythian *manties* are shown ἐσορῶντες ἐς τὴν μαντικὴν, "looking into the divination": here the signs do not reside in animal organs but sticks of willow. Possibly Herodotus transfers the familiar image of looking into the insides of a victim to the unfamiliar Scythian practice of rhabdomancy.

[167] A distinction between natural or intuitive divination (μαντικὴ ἄτεχνος, i.e. "inspired" divination through dream, vision, and divine possession, *mania*) and artificial divination (μαντικὴ τεχνική, interpretation of portents, extispicy) is drawn by Plato in the *Timaeus* (71e–72b) and in the *Phaedrus* (244c–d). (The Greek terms I have used do not occur in exactly this form in these texts.) In these passages, Plato dismisses artificial divination and champions inspired divination in accordance with his theory of knowledge. For discussion of this distinction and caution against taking it as a hard and fast one, see Flower 2008b:84–91. In Herodotus, absence of detail about artificial divination is motivated perhaps not by disdain, but, as I have suggested above, by the fact that the interpretation of other types of signs is more challenging and of greater interest.

[168] Μαρδονίῳ δὲ προθυμεομένῳ μάχης ἄρχειν οὐκ ἐπιτήδεα ἐγίνετο τὰ ἱρά, ἀμυνομένῳ δὲ καὶ τούτῳ καλά (9.37.1), "Though Mardonios was keen to begin battle the sacrificial signs were not favorable for this, but they were favorable for resisting an attack."

2.4.2 *Manties*

Herodotus seems to reserve his interest for the professional interpreters of these signs, the *manties*, but not for their interpretations. This is not to say that the results of their interpretations are of no importance: the services of Herodotean *manties* are in high demand, as the remarkable biographies of the figures discussed below show, and the concern on both sides at Plataiai about the unfavorable signs for attack (9.38.2) and their repeated sacrifices under ever-increasing hardship show that such consultations are not an empty formality either for the participants or for the narrator.[169] Mardonios' eventual decision to say "to hell with the sacrifices" (τὰ σφάγια ἐᾶν χαίρειν, 9.41.4) and to proceed with the attack is directly characterized by Herodotus as an overly forceful, ill-considered, and inflexible plan of action (γνώμη . . . ἰσχυροτέρη τε καὶ ἀγνωμονεστέρη καὶ οὐδαμῶς συγγινωσκομένη, 9.41.4). Mardonios' dismissal of the σφάγια finds a parallel in his boast that an unfavorable oracle, which predicts the total destruction of the Persians after their occupation of the Delphic sanctuary, will not come to pass, since the Persians will not attempt to seize the holy site (9.42.3). This is immediately undermined by Herodotus with his revelation that this oracle was meant for the Illyrians and Enkheleans, not the Persians (9.43.1–2).[170] In discussing the Greek contingent at Plataiai, Herodotus by way of contrast stresses Pausanias and the Spartans' scrupulous attention to the σφάγια and shows them sacrificing again and again to obtain favorable signs, but making no offensive action, despite the heavy loss of men under the steady hail of Persian arrows (9.61.3). Only the

169 Nor, as Pritchett well points out, should it be assumed that if generals abandoned or delayed an enterprise because of unfavorable signs this was merely a tactic. Thus Pritchett 1971–1979:3.68 mentions Macan's interpretation of Kleomenes' aborted crossing of the Erasinos into Argive territory (6.76), who says that Herodotus here has given "in this passage an imperfect and distorted tradition of a brilliant and strategic combination, projected and carried out by Kleomenes, the demonstration of the Erasinos being a feint to draw the Argives from the city." Again, Pausanias' refusal to give battle until the σφάγια are favorable has also been seen as a manipulatory tactic to draw the enemy infantry closer or keep his men in hand (see collection of quotations in Pritchett 1971–1979:3.78–80, which includes Nilsson, Hignett, and Burn). But neither in the case of Kleomenes at the Erasinos nor in that of Pausanias at Plataiai is there the slightest hint of this in Herodotus' presentation. Herodotus is perfectly aware that signs can be manipulated (see ch. 3.1 below), but he points to this quite plainly when he wants us to see it (for example, by his use of the verb μηχανάομαι and its compounds, e.g. 1.59.3: other instances discussed in ch. 3.1). See also Flower 2008b in general for the necessity of taking ancient divination "seriously."

170 Cf. ch. 2.3.1 on the question of correct recipient.

use of a different kind of sign communication, in the form of prayer to Hera (9.61.3–62.1), is able to produce a change in the visual signs of the σφάγια.

Herodotus thus presents this form of *mantikê* as a familiar part of Greek experience, as his omission of details seems to indicate. Only in a few instances do we see non-Greeks using sacrifice as a means of divination, and in each of these cases Herodotus draws attention to how these sacrifices differ from Greek practice or how, in the case of Mardonios, Greek practice is consciously and explicitly adopted. Thus the Carthaginian general Amilkas is shown performing divinatory sacrifice, and while his actions are described using verbs familiar to Greek ears (ἐθύετο καὶ ἐκαλλιερέετο, 7.167.1), the manner of sacrifice shown is the holocaust, the consumption of the entire victim by fire (ἐπὶ πυρῆς μεγάλης σώματα ὅλα καταγίζων), a practice that is not used by the Greeks in divinatory sacrifice, and that seems designed to give the scene a wholly exotic and non-Greek atmosphere.[171] Before the Persian army under Xerxes crosses the Strymon, the *magoi* pause for sacrificial consultation. Once again a familiar and unmarked verb is used of their sacrifice (ἐκαλλιερέοντο σφάζοντες, 7.113.2), but here the sacrificial victims are white horses, which do not form part of the repertory of animals used by Greeks for this kind of sacrifice. Furthermore, the blood from their throats flows directly into the waters of the river, as opposed to over the stone of an altar or over a hearth or into a pit: ἐς τὸν [sc. Strymon] οἱ μάγοι ἐκαλλιερέοντο σφάζοντες ἵππους λευκούς (7.113.2). Finally, when the Persian commander Mardonios consults the omens on the eve of the battle of Plataiai, he uses Greek sacrificial practices (Ἑλληνικὰ ἱρά, 9.37.1), and has specifically engaged a Greek *mantis*, Hegesistratos, for this purpose.

The only other forms of *mantikê* which Herodotus mentions are confined to his descriptions of non-Greeks. He describes two Scythian methods of divination, one using willow sticks, the other using strips of bark from the linden tree. Here he does provide some details of the technique, something which he does not do in the case of Greek sacrificial *mantikê*: willow sticks (ῥάβδοι) are gathered together in large bundles, which are then placed on the ground and unrolled while the *manties* pronounce oracular utterances (θεσπίζουσι). The

[171] It may be used in descriptions of Greek sacrifice in hero cult: cf. καταγίζω used of thigh pieces burned to ashes and deposited in the tomb of Opis and Arge (4.35.4), ἐναγίζω used of sacrifice to heroized Phocaean dead on Kyrnos (1.167.2) and to Herakles ὡς ἥρωι (2.44.5). These are not divinatory sacrifices. All other instances of καταγίζω in Herodotus are found in the context of non-Greek ritual practices. This may be compared with Herodotus' general descriptions of Egyptian, Persian, and Scythian sacrifice, which are presented explicitly and implicitly as departures from Greek sacrificial ritual, and which also increase the impression of exoticism: cf. e.g. Burkert 1990 on Herodotus' accounts of non-Greek religion and ritual.

sticks are then gathered together again, with the *manties* continuing to make pronouncements (4.67.1). In the case of divination by strips of bark, a practice of the androgynous Enarees, a length of bark is twisted about the fingers (4.67.2). In both cases, there is much that remains obscure in the description: how the readings are arrived at, and what in each case constitute the signifiers, are not explained.[172] But the consequences of the readings both for those who are singled out by them and for the professional interpreters are of the highest importance, and, as will be discussed shortly below, demonstrate Herodotus' interest in the figure of the *mantis* in general, and in the effects of the interpretation of signs.

The other description of non-Greek *mantikê* comes from the other major ethnographic excursus of book 4, Herodotus' account of Libya and its peoples and *nomoi*.[173] The Nasamones practice divination using a kind of incubation:

> μαντεύονται δὲ ἐπὶ τῶν προγόνων φοιτῶντες τὰ σήματα καὶ κατευξάμενοι ἐπικατακοιμῶνται· τὸ δ' ἂν ἴδῃ ἐν τῇ ὄψι ἐνύπνιον, τούτῳ χρᾶται.
>
> 4.172.4
>
> They practice divination by frequenting their ancestors' tombs and sleeping upon them after uttering prayers: they make use of whatever they see in their dreams.

Here the ancestors are directly involved in the process of signification, acting presumably as mediators between divine and human planes and as transmitters of signs. Their tombs, themselves signs in the sense of markers (σήματα), act as a channel for the mantic signs of the dreams.[174]

Apart from these descriptions of non-Greek *mantikê*, Herodotus nowhere else devotes attention to the mechanism of *mantikê* or the interpretative

172 Cf. Corcella in Asheri et al. 2007 *ad loc.*

173 Herodotus' description of the Immortalizing Getai, who every four years dispatch an unfortunate messenger with a list of requests to the god Salmoxis, might be included as another instance of non-Greek *mantikê*, though he does not explicitly describe it as such. They throw the messenger up into the air above a set of three spears pointed upwards. If the man is killed, it is a sign that the god is pleased and has accepted the messenger; if he is not killed, they take this as a sign that he is a bad man and expell him (4.94.2–4).

174 Noted by Benardete 1969:126. For Homeric interplay between σῆμα as grave marker and as sign in a broader sense, see Nagy 1990a:202–222. As mentioned in ch. 1.1.1 above, in Herodotus σῆμα does not generally appear in the general sense of "sign" as it does in Homer, but this usage should not be excluded as a possibility. The tombs and ancestors function in another process of signification mentioned in the very same passage by Herodotus, that of oath-making. Cf. ch. 2.7 for ritual accompanying oath and ch. 3.1 for manipulation by oath.

process. It is rather the professional interpreters of such signs, the *manties*, on whom the spotlight falls. Herodotus mentions ten Greek *manties* by name, a substantial number of whom are members of famous mantic families.[175] There is firstly the prototypical figure of Melampous of Pylos, whom Herodotus credits as the founder of *mantikê* for the Greeks:

> ἐγὼ μέν νύν φημι Μελάμποδα γενόμενον ἄνδρα σοφὸν μαντικήν τε ἑωυτῷ συστῆσαι καὶ πυθόμενον ἀπ' Αἰγύπτου ἄλλα τε πολλὰ ἐσηγήσασθαι Ἕλλησι καὶ τὰ περὶ τὸν Διόνυσον, ὀλίγα αὐτῶν παραλλάξαντα.
>
> 2.49.2
>
> It is my opinion that Melampous was a wise man who acquired a knowledge of *mantikê* and after learning a good many things, including the rites of Dionysos, brought them from Egypt to the Greeks, making a few changes.

Amphiaraus is also mentioned briefly in connection with his oracle in Boiotia and his presenting the Thebans with the choice of having his services either as an ally (σύμμαχος) or as a *mantis* (8.134.2). Descended from Melampous (7.221) is Megistias of Akarnania, who, as we have seen, foresees his own death and that of others at Thermopylai, but will not leave the field. Elis is the place of origin of several of the *manties* who are all members of one of the two great mantic families, the Telliadai and the Iamidai: Tellias (presumably a Telliades, 8.27.3); Kallias (Iamides, 5.44.2); Hegesistratos (Telliades, 9.37.1); Teisamenos (Iamides, 9.33.1).[176] Other *manties* are Hippomakhos of Leukas (9.38.1); Kleandros of Phigaleia in Arkadia (6.83.2); Euenios and his son, Deiphobos, of Apollonia in Illyria (9.92.2). All the *manties* mentioned by Herodotus thus have

[175] Burkert (1992:41–46) discusses the organization of seers into family-like groups, where the relationship between members is by either natural or artificial affinity, and provides Near Eastern parallels for this type of structure. See also Flower (2008b:37–50), who is insistent that membership in mantic families was more a matter of blood descent and not adoption (38): "In the case of seers, however, adoption could not have been as acceptable a substitute for biological descent. This was because mantic knowledge was inherently different from medical knowledge; like medical knowledge is was technical and teachable, but unlike medical knowledge it was also an innate gift." But see 46: "The qualification of descent, however, does not exclude the possibility of adoption, which was common in ancient Mesopotamia." On the prosopography of *manties*, see Kett 1966. Cf. Dillery 2005 on the independent diviner in myth and in the Archaic and Classical periods.

[176] The other famous mantic family of Elis, the Klutiadai (Cicero *De Divinatione* 1.41.91), is not mentioned by Herodotus. Κλυτιάδην at 9.33.1 is generally agreed to be spurious. Cf. Dillery 2005:174, 192 on the three families of seers and Flower 2008a on the Iamidai.

their origin in the western part of maainland Greece and the central Peloponnese, ranging from Apollonia to Phigaleia.[177] These *manties* have however much more in common than their place of origin and lineage: many are distinguished by a mixture of ingenuity verging on the unscrupulous and an extreme courage, and find themselves driven into exile because of unfavorable readings they have given the ruler or city by whom they are employed.[178]

To begin with the first feature, the characteristic of cunning ingenuity, Herodotus shows this as present already in the mythical founder of *mantikê*, the ἀνὴρ σοφός, Melampous of Pylos (2.49.2).[179] He makes a direct connection between his behavior and that of Teisamenos of Elis, whom he describes as "imitating" the latter (οὗτος ἐμιμέετο Μελάμποδα, 9.34.1).[180] Melampous is approached by the citizens of Argos to find a cure for the madness which has descended upon their women (τῶν ἐν Ἄργεϊ γυναικῶν μανεισέων, 9.34.1). He demands as payment half of the kingship, which the Argives refuse to consider, but when still more of their womenfolk are afflicted by madness, they agree to his terms, only to find that Melampous, knowing he has the upper hand, now demands that his brother Bias be given a one-third share of the kingship.

177 On this interesting phenomenon cf. Dillery 2005:184, who notes that this region lacks large urban settlement and connects this with the independence of the *mantis* (or chresmologue): "His activities might be in the service of powerful chiefs, or, in the case of fifth-century Athens and Sparta, of an entire *polis*, but he seems always positioned outside the political structure of the state, essential to but also separate from the governance of the *polis*."

178 Cf. Johnston's general remarks (Johnston and Struck 2005:19) on the friction between diviner and ruling elite, both in mythic accounts and in accounts from the Archaic and Classical periods, where the problem of the authority of the independent diviner in the context of the *polis* arises (for which cf. Dillery 2005:183–219, esp. 208–209). On the mobility of the Greek seers, see Burkert 1992:41–46. On the *mantis* as "problem-solver," see Bremmer 1996:98, and on his bravery see ibid., 99. Cf. also Munson 2001a:59–73 on Herodotus' three seer narratives and Dillery 2005, esp. 183–219. The resourcefulness of seers forms part of what Burkert ("migrant charismatic specialists," 1992:42) and Flower (2008b:29–30) have termed the seer's "charisma".

179 The connection between σοφίη and the ability to interpret and manipulate signs has already been raised in ch. 1.3 in connection with Likhas the Spartan, and is discussed again in ch. 3.1 and 3.2. For the application of the phrase ἀνὴρ σοφός to a *mantis*, cf. a fourth-century BCE funerary inscription from the deme of Myrrhinous in Attika in honor of Kalliteles, son of Meidoteles, himself a *mantis*: μάντεος ἐντίμο μάντιν, σοφὸν ἄνδρα, δίκαιον (*SEG* 23.161), "a *mantis*, son of a respected *mantis*, a wise man, just."

180 Cf. Munson 2001a:52n30 on *mimêsis* statements in Herodotus, and 60–61 on this *mimêsis* and 52–59 on the *mimêsis* of the two Kleisthenes (5.67.1, 5.69.1). She argues that in both cases, the analogy between imitated and imitator works vertically and that they both involve an analogy between the citizen of a Greek *polis* and a monarchical ruler: "By using Melampus to interpret Tisamenus, the text emphasizes the invasive character of Tisamenus' request and paradoxically transforms his achievement of citizenship into a metaphor for the acquisition of kingly power" (61).

It is Melampous' services as a healer that are sought after: the *mantis*' ability to interpret signs means that he is in a position to find the cause of disease and thus to cure it, which mirrors the dual abilities of his patron god Apollo.[181] This ability is not shown in any of the other Greek *manties* mentioned by Herodotus, but it does emerge in his description of the Scythian *manties*, discussed further below, whose divinatory abilities enable them both to determine the cause of the king's illness (perjury by one of his subjects) and to find the offending perjurer.[182] The madness of the Argive women, described by the Argives as a disease (νοῦσος, 9.34.1), is caused by an offense to Dionysos, as we know from other sources (e.g. Diodorus 4.68.4, Apollodorus 1.9.12, Pausanias 2.18.4): it is more than fitting, then, that Melampous, whom Herodotus presents as the introducer of Dionysiac rite and cult to Greece (2.49–50), should be the one to cure destructive Dionysiac madness. The knowledge of ritual and the name of the god, and the ability to interpret them for a different audience, are further aspects of Melampous' mastery and control of signs.[183]

Melampous' bargaining technique with the Argives is precisely what Teisamenos uses when the Spartans approach him at the time of Xerxes' invasion to act as their *mantis* (9.35.1). They offer him the position of commander (ἡγεμών) alongside the Heraklid kings, but he demands full Spartiate status. As in the case of the Argives, there is initial reluctance on the part of the Spartans, but eventual agreement to these terms, and, in a fashion similar to Melampous, Teisamenos is fully conscious of his position of strength and extracts from them Spartiate status for his brother Hagias as well. We do not see Teisamenos at work as a *mantis*, but he is shown interpreting signs of a different sort in the form of an oracular response. It is ironic that Teisamenos, expert in *mantikê*, misinterprets this oracle, which tells him that he will win five great "contests" (ἀγῶνες). These "contests," as the Spartans are the first to realize, must not be read against the background of athletic competition, but have as their referent military combat:

> Λακεδαιμόνιοι δὲ μαθόντες οὐκ ἐς γυμνικοὺς ἀλλ' ἐς ἀρηίους ἀγῶνας φέρον τὸ Τεισαμενοῦ μαντήιον, μισθῷ ἐπειρῶντο πείσαντες Τεισαμενὸν ποιέεσθαι ἅμα Ἡρακλειδέων τοῖσι βασιλεῦσι ἡγεμόνα τῶν πολέμων.
>
> 9.33.3

[181] Cf. Burkert 1985b:147: "The god of purifications must also be an oracle god."

[182] On healing as part of a seer's competency, for which there is more evidence in the Archaic period than in the Classical, see Flower 2008b:27–29.

[183] Cf. ch. 2.6 below on the introduction of the names of the gods from Egypt.

> Once the Spartans realized that the oracle given to Teisamenos referred not to athletic contests but to military ones, they attempted by means of money to persuade him to become a military commander alongside the Heraklid kings.

Herodotus' account of Euenios of Apollonia (9.92.2–9.94.3) provides an interesting variation of this narrative pattern of the cunning *mantis* who tricks the king or community, where this time it is the *mantis* who is outsmarted in the deal.[184] The citizens of Apollonia put out Euenios' eyes for failing to watch over the flock of sheep sacred to Apollo, but, after a period of infertility and crop failure, they are now instructed by the god to give Euenios whatever compensation he chooses. The Apolloniates approach Euenios, and, without telling him anything of the god's instructions, ask him hypothetically what compensation he would accept. Euenios chooses, and the Apolloniates then reveal the reason they have asked him, and hold him to his word, though he is furious and considers himself cheated (ἐξαπατηθείς, 9.94.3). Compensation from the gods follows, however, in the form of an inborn mantic ability (ἔμφυτον μαντικήν, 9.94.3).

The motifs of resourcefulness and profit are shown in the accounts of Tellias and Hegesistratos, both of Elis. Tellias, acting as *mantis* for the Phocians, develops a scheme (σοφίζεται αὐτοῖσι τοιόνδε, 8.27.3) for them against the Thessalians, who are besieging them on Mount Parnassos.[185] He whitens the bodies and weapons of a select band of men with chalk, so that in a night attack they will be able to recognize one another and kill anyone who is not so marked. The trick has the additional effect of terrifying the outlying Thessalian guardposts, who believe that they are witnessing something supernatural (ἐφοβήθησαν, δόξασαι ἄλλο τι εἶναι τέρας, 8.27.4). Tellias' cunning scheme (σοφίζεται . . . τοιόνδε, 8.27.3) is based on the manipulation of signs, but a different kind of sign from those used in *mantikê*. The whiteness of the soldiers' bodies becomes a sign invested with two meanings: for the Phocians, it is a sign which serves to indicate that these soldiers are from the same side;

184 Cf. Munson 2001a:70–73 on the episode and in particular her observation (70) that the narrative concerning Euenios separates this issue of compensation from the profession of seer, but "maintains the theme of the individual's blackmail of the city by translating it into an ethical and juridical question of *dike*." She points out that the episode differs from the others in its closer connection to mythical motifs, such as the Cattle of the Sun (*Odyssey* 12.127–133) and the punishment of the community by the gods (cf. Hesiod *Works and Days* 242–244).

185 See ch. 3.1 for other instances of σοφίη in connection with the manipulation of signs, and cf. 9.37.2 for the similar concept of μηχανή, discussed shortly below.

for the Thessalians, however, the whiteness signifies the supernatural, and is interpreted accordingly as a fearful *teras*.[186]

Hegesistratos, a member of the same *genos*, the Telliadai, acts as *mantis* for Mardonios at Plataiai out of a mixture of hatred (ἔχθος) for the Spartans, from whom he has barely escaped with his life, and a desire for profit (κέρδος):

> μεμισθωμένος οὐκ ὀλίγου ἐθύετό τε καὶ προεθυμέετο κατά τε τὸ ἔχθος τὸ Λακεδαιμονίων καὶ κατὰ τὸ κέρδος.
>
> 9.38.1
>
> Receiving a considerable wage, he read the sacrificial omens [for the Persians] and supported them keenly both because of his hatred for the Spartans and because it was profitable.

Herodotus' narrative stresses the man's ingenuity as well as his courage: Hegesistratos runs afoul of the Spartans, possibly because of his unfavorable readings or possibly because of manipulations of readings, and is condemned to death by them.[187] He devises a plan which Herodotus describes in language he reserves for exceptional acts of cunning and bravery:[188]

> αὐτίκα δὲ ἐμηχανᾶτο ἀνδρηιότατον ἔργον πάντων τῶν ἡμεῖς ἴδμεν.
>
> 9.37.2
>
> He contrived the bravest deed of any that we know of.

Using a knife that has somehow come into his possession, he calculatedly cuts off part of his foot which has been clamped in the stocks, digs his way out of the room, and manages to reach Tegea, traveling by night and successfully

186 Also discussed in ch. 2.1.2 above. The figure of the strategically resourceful *mantis* emerges again in Thucydides, who describes (3.20.1–4) how the ἀνὴρ μάντις Theainetos, son of Tolmides, and Eupompides come up with a plan of escape from the besieged city of Plataiai. The attempt involves the making of ladders, but the length of these has to be calculated by counting the layers of bricks in the enemy's siege-wall and estimating (εἰκάσαντες τὸ μέτρον, 3.20.4) the height of an average course of bricks. The themes of resourcefulness, measuring, and conjecture are highly reminiscent of Herodotean *manties*.

187 The reasons for the Spartans' anger are not spelled out by Herodotus: the idea that Hegesistratos may have given unfavorable readings, whether deliberately or not, is my interpretation, based on the case of Kallias (5.44.2). All Herodotus says is that the Spartans sentenced him to death because, according to them, they had suffered many terrible things (πολλά τε καὶ ἀνάρσια, 9.37.1) at his hands.

188 For the formula τῶν ἡμεῖς ἴδμεν used to flag the remarkable cf. e.g. 3.60.4 (temple of Hera on Samos the largest ever); 8.105.1 (Hermotimos' revenge the greatest ever); 9.64.1 (victory at Plataiai the finest ever). On μηχανάω and μηχανή in contexts involving cunning and sometimes the manipulation of signs, see ch. 3.1 below.

avoiding Spartan search parties. It is quite remarkable how Hegesistratos carefully calculates (σταθμησάμενος, 9.37.2) how much of his foot to cut off.[189] The verb σταθμάομαι is used several times by Herodotus of his method of interpretation and conclusion on the basis of comparison, as when he introduces Dareios' famous experiment in comparative anthropology:

> ὡς δὲ οὕτω νενομίκασι τὰ περὶ τοὺς νόμους οἱ πάντες ἄνθρωποι, πολλοῖσί τε καὶ ἄλλοισι τεκμηρίοισι πάρεστι σταθμώσασθαι, ἐν δὲ δὴ καὶ τῷδε . . .
>
> 3.38.2

> That all men have this custom concerning their practices may be measured by many *tekmêria*, and in particular by the following . . .

Especially comparable for the element of cunning intelligence and calculation is Herodotus' account of the Assyrian thieves in the city of Ninos, who dig a tunnel leading from their homes to Sardanapallos' underground treasure-chambers, computing the distance exactly (σταθμούμενοι, 2.150.3). Teisamenos' decision to cut off part of his own body finds a parallel in the story of the Egyptian master thieves, one of whom gets caught in a trap in an underground treasure-chamber and instructs his brother to cut off his head, so that they will not at least be identified (2.121.β.2).[190] Equally courageous is the action of Megistias, who sees (ἐσιδὼν ἐς τὰ ἱρά, 7.219.1) the unfavorable outcome of the coming action at Thermopylai, clearly recognizing "the goddesses of Doom approaching," as the epitaph attributed to Simonides by Herodotus puts it (Κῆρας ἐπερχομένας σάφα εἰδώς, 7.228.3), but does not leave the field, even though he is not a Spartan, and has been excused from the battle by Leonidas (7.221).[191] This is one of several places in the *Histories* where the gap between knowledge of the future gained through the interpretation of signs and the inability (or, as here, willing refusal) of those who possess this knowledge to avoid the foreseen evil evokes a pathos which functions much like tragic irony.[192]

189 Cf. the calculation of the *mantis* Theainetos in Thucydides 3.20.1–4, mentioned above.

190 The verb μηχανᾶσθαι, often an indication of σοφίη in the *Histories* (see ch. 3.1), figures prominently in this account (2.121.α.1; 2.21.γ.2; 2.121.ε.1).

191 For the theme of the *mantis* who foresees his own death, but does not leave his post, cf. Dillery 2005:204–206 on the anonymous *mantis* in Xenophon *Hellenica* 2.4.18–19 at the Battle of Munychia in 403 and the mythical figures of Amphiaraus and of Idmon (Apollonius Rhodius *Argonautica* 1.140, 143).

192 Cf. the tearful remarks of Thersandros' Persian neighbor at a dinner given at Thebes some time before the Battle of Plataiai (9.16.4–5). Other places where a similar sentiment occurs are: 1.91.1; 3.43.1; 3.65.3; 7.17.2. Cf. ch. 2.3.1.3 above on oracles and the tragic.

The account of Kallias of Elis demonstrates simultaneously the motifs of persecution and gain we have already come across in Herodotus' treatment of *manties*.[193] Kallias has to flee (ἀποδράντα, 5.44.2) Telus, the tyrant of Sybaris, because of unfavorable readings for the city's campaign against Kroton (ἐπείτε οἱ τὰ ἱρὰ οὐ προεχώρεε χρηστὰ θυομένῳ ἐπὶ Κρότωνα, 5.44.2), and assists the Crotoniates in their successful campaign against Sybaris. For this he receives a grant of land for himself and his descendants:

> οἱ δ' αὖ Κροτωνιῆται ἀποδεικνύουσι Καλλίῃ μὲν τῷ Ἠλείῳ ἐξαίρετα ἐν γῇ τῇ Κροτωνιήτιδι πολλὰ δοθέντα, τὰ καὶ ἐς ἐμὲ ἔτι ἐνέμοντο οἱ Καλλίεω ἀπόγονοι.
>
> 5.45.2
>
> The Crotoniates for their part point to many plots of land in Crotoniate territory set aside and given to Kallias of Elis, areas which the descendants of Kallias were still working up to my time.

Finally, as an example of the influence and negative power of persuasion of *manties*, there is Kleandros of Phigaleia (6.83.2). After the destruction of most of the adult male population of Argos by the Spartans under Kleomenes, the Argive slaves assume and keep control of the state, until the sons of the Argives who lost their lives in battle grow to adulthood and take back their power, expelling the slaves. The slaves retreat to Tiryns and manage to capture it, and from then on a state of peaceful relations exist between the two groups, which is broken, however, by Kleandros, a *mantis* who persuades the slaves to attack their masters once more (6.83.2). Kleandros is thus responsible for the lengthy war which follows after this and in which the freeborn Argives eventually gain the upper hand with difficulty.

What emerges strongly from a consideration of these Herodotean *manties* is that, for Herodotus, their skill does not seem to lie so much in the interpretation of mantic signs (of which we see almost nothing) as in the manipulation of signs of various kinds. This does not involve the falsification of signs on the part of the *manties* (there is no direct mention of this by Herodotus), but rather exploitation of the demand for their services and semiotic competency to obtain power and gain. Their ability is much sought after, as we have seen in the case of Melampous, Teisamenos, and others, and carries with it the possibility of power and profit (κέρδος), but this ability and power also

[193] The motif is also found in accusations hurled against seers in tragedy: e.g. Sophocles *Oedipus Rex* 380–389, Euripides *Bacchae* 255–257; and cf. Dillery 2005:199, 208–209 on the themes of greed, *misthos*, and self-interest in descriptions of what he terms "independent religious experts."

contain a potentially lethal charge that may at any time blow up in the face of the user. An unfavorable reading, or the perception of an unfavorable reading, can result in the expulsion (Kallias) or even execution (Hegesistratos) of the *mantis*.

Nowhere are these high stakes made clearer than in Herodotus' ethnographic excursus on Scythian *mantikê*, where the themes associated with Greek *manties* manifest themselves in extreme form, perhaps another instance of Herodotus' principle that the extremes of the earth are accompanied by extremes in terms of climate, natural resources (gold, spices), and human behavior.[194] Scythian *manties* wield vast power, but at the same time they are subject to the ultimate penalty of death if they are shown to be false diviners (ψευδομάντιες, 4.69.2). Whenever the king falls ill, the three most prominent *manties* are sent for, who by divination normally establish that someone has sworn falsely by the king's hearth (4.68.1).[195] Their function here is to determine the cause of illness and to recommend a cure, just as Melampous is asked to do in the case of the frenzied women of Argos (9.34). But as Hartog has commented, their function then changes from healer to judge as divination is now used to ascertain the identity of the culprit, who is then arrested and brought in (4.68.2).[196] If he denies the charge, a second set of *manties*, six in number, are summoned, and if their consultation confirms the guilt of the suspect, he is immediately executed by decapitation, and his goods become the property of the first *manties* (4.68.3). If, however, their reading establishes his innocence, then still more *manties* are summoned (4.68.4), and if a majority reading still maintains his innocence, then the first set of *manties* are condemned to death as ψευδομάντιες (4.69.2).

This use of *mantikê* to determine the king's illness and sniff out the offending oath-breaker is described by Herodotus as a foreign practice, yet despite its exotic dress and the gruesome descriptions of execution (the ψευδομάντιες are shackled, bound, gagged, and strapped to a oxcart piled high with fuel, which is then lit and sent on its way [4.69.1]), it contains the very elements we have already seen as associated with Greek *manties*: the potential for power, profit, and ruin.

194 Cf. 3.106.1 for the theme of the extremities (ἐσχατιαί), which contain both the most precious and finest things and the largest and most monstrous animals and the strangest human beings and customs. Cf. in general Romm 1994 on this theme.

195 Here oath-making and divination are once again connected: cf. discussion of Nasamones (4.172) above.

196 Hartog 1988:129.

2.5 The *Ainos*

In ch. 2.3 we spoke of the phenomenon of double-encoding, whereby certain oracular utterances have, along with a surface meaning, an additional and deeper level of meaning underlying that surface meaning. As was seen there, it is in this second encoding that the message of the oracle lies. Double-encoding is not, however, confined to oracular contexts: it may also take place in non-oracular contexts where a verbal utterance carries a secondary meaning underneath a primary one and where the recipient must perform an additional decoding in order to get at the message of the utterance. Herodotus has no particular word for such utterances (λόγος and ἔπος are, however, used at 1.141.1 and 3.50.3, 6.37.2 respectively),[197] nor are they invariably introduced by characteristic narrative markers, but they amount to what we may call αἶνοι, a term used by the Greeks to describe a variety of speech ranging from poetic praise to criticism to the fable, all having in common the notion of "an allusive tale containing an ulterior purpose," "a code that carries the right message for those who are qualified and the wrong message or messages for those who are unqualified."[198]

[197] For the use of the term ἔπος in Herodotus, see Hollmann 2000. Whenever Herodotus uses the term (81 instances) it always refers to some kind of "marked" speech, that is, utterances set aside from normal speech either by form (verse, whether Homeric, oracular, or that of Aristeas' *Arimaspeia*) or, by far the larger category, by content (e.g. gnomic utterance, *ainos*, insult, promise, threat, *bon mot*). What all of these instances have in common is that they are utterances which have consequences of some sort or another: thus, for example, the words purporting to be those of Dareios and ordering the killing of Oroites are described as ἔπεα (3.128), and the analogy Kambyses' sister draws between the fight of a lion cub and a puppy and Kambyses' murder of Smerdis is described as an ἔπος and leads directly to her death (3.32; and see n212 below). Looked at this way, ἔπος when used of an utterance in verse implies more than the simple fact that words have been arranged in a metrical pattern but refers to the authority that resides in it, as in the case of the pronouncement of an oracle or a line of Homer used as a μαρτύριον (e.g. 4.29).

[198] The first definition is that of Verdenius (1962:389), and the second that of Nagy (1990b:148). Pindar's praise poetry refers to itself as *ainos* or *epainos*, but "*ainos* can also refer to the narrower concept of a speech of admonition, or *parainesis* . . . or it can designate animal fables,

Perhaps the most well-known Herodotean *ainos* is Kyros' *logos* (so described by Herodotus, 1.141.1) about the *aulos*-player and the fish.[199] When the Ionians and Aeolians approach Kyros and ask to be on the same terms with him as they were with Kroisos, Kyros by way of answer tells them a story:

> ὁ δὲ ἀκούσας αὐτῶν τὰ προΐσχοντο ἔλεξέ σφι λόγον, ἄνδρα φὰς αὐλητὴν ἰδόντα ἰχθῦς ἐν τῇ θαλάσσῃ αὐλέειν, δοκέοντά σφεας ἐξελεύσεσθαι ἐς γῆν. ὡς δὲ ψευσθῆναι τῆς ἐλπίδος, λαβεῖν ἀμφίβληστρον καὶ περιβαλεῖν τε πλῆθος πολλὸν τῶν ἰχθύων καὶ ἐξειρύσαι, ἰδόντα δὲ παλλομένους εἰπεῖν ἄρα αὐτὸν πρὸς τοὺς ἰχθῦς· "Παύεσθέ μοι ὀρχεόμενοι, ἐπεὶ οὐδ' ἐμέο αὐλέοντος ἠθέλετε ἐκβαίνειν ὀρχεόμενοις."
>
> 1.141.1–2

> After he heard what they were proposing, he told them a *logos*, saying that an *aulos*-player once caught sight of some fish in the sea and began to play his pipe, thinking that they would come out onto the land. When he was cheated of his expectation, he took a net and cast it around a great number of the fish and hauled it out, and upon seeing them leaping about, he said to the fish, "Stop dancing for me: you didn't want to come out and dance before, when I played my *aulos*."

Herodotus immediately steps in to explain the point of Kyros' story: when Kyros had previously asked the Ionians and Aeolians to revolt from Kroisos' control, they did not do so, but now that everything has changed and Kroisos been deposed, they are prepared to obey him. The Ionians and Aeolians are thus the fish, and Kyros the *aulos*-player.[200] But this is not the whole of the

---

such as those by Archilochus to admonish his friends or blame his enemies" (Nagy 1990b:149). Other modern definitions of *ainos* are listed by van Dijk (1997:78–82).

199 For *logos* as a designation for fable, see e.g. Aristophanes *Wasps* 1399: further references in van Dijk 1997:82–83. Ancient rhetoricians specifically cite this Herodotean passage as an example of *muthos* (in the sense of fable: cf. other examples in van Dijk 1997:84–88) used by historians: Theon *Progymnasmata* 2 (=van Dijk G20b), Doxapater *Commentarium in Aphthonium* (II 147 Walz = van Dijk 31T2), scholiast *in Aphthonium* (II 10 Walz = van Dijk 31T3). Doxapater claims that Herodotus used *muthos* in many places (ἐν πολλοῖς), Thucydides rarely (σπανίως). *Ainos*, *logos*, and *muthos* may all be used of fables.

200 As Hirsch 1985:226 notes, the structural opposition between sea and land in the *ainos* corresponds to dominance of the Greeks as a sea power and of the Persians as a land power, so the link between the signifier (fish, *aulos*-player) and signified (Ionians and Aeolians, Kyros) is not a difficult one to make. Hirsch (223) also points out the Near Eastern evidence for referring to conquered people as being captured like fish, especially a document of Sargon II in which he

message: what are its implications for the Ionians and Aeolians? How do they understand Kyros' *logos*? Kyros does not say what he will do to them, but we hear that their reaction is to build walls around their cities and gather at the Panionion (1.141.4), and we are later told of Harpagos' subjugation of the Ionian cities, the second enslavement of Ionia (1.169.2). The verb used by Herodotus to decribe the Ionians' construction of city walls, περιεβάλοντο, literally to 'cast around', cleverly mirrors the verb used by Kyros to describe the *aulos*-player's casting of a net about the fish, περιβαλεῖν, translating the figurative into the literal. Instead of waiting for the net of Kyros to surround them, they surround themselves with a wall, showing that they received and understood the message in Kyros' *ainos*.[201]

Why does Kyros choose this method of reply? It is not that he wishes his message to be completely hidden: he wants the Ionians and Aeolians to "get the message" and Herodotus tells us that he is very angry indeed with them (ὀργῇ ἐχόμενος, 1.141.4). The *ainos* with its image of the expiring and gasping fish and the triumphant and sarcastic *aulos*-player conveys a sinister threat much more effectively than an angry and strongly worded refusal in unadorned and unmarked speech would. Metaphor is stronger at times than plain speech. The comparisons of the Ionians and Aeolians to helpless fish and Kyros to the fisherman act as potent reminders of the relative positions of power between the two. The stronger warns the weaker with an *ainos* that serves to reveal the iron fist under the velvet glove.[202]

Much the same technique of threatening via the medium of the *ainos* is used by Kroisos in his message to the people of Lampsakos when he learns that they are holding Miltiades (grandfather of the famous Miltiades, commander at Marathon) captive:

> πυθόμενος ὦν ὁ Κροῖσος ταῦτα πέμπων προηγόρευε τοῖσι Λαμψακηνοῖσι μετιέναι Μιλτιάδην· εἰ δὲ μή, σφέας πίτυος τρόπον ἀπείλεε ἐκτρίψειν.
>
> 6.37.2

boasts that he "drew the Iamanean (i.e. Ionian) from out of the sea of the setting sun, like a fish." Cf. also Ceccarelli 1993.

201 Meuli 1975:2.729 sees the mention of the net as an allusion to the Persian military practice of using the net to round up prisoners (σαγηνεύειν, described at 6.31.1–2, the Persian capture of Khios, Lesbos, and Tenedos).

202 The *ainos* is also used as a weapon of the weaker against the stronger, as will be seen in instances below, but here it is a tool used by the stronger against the weaker. Cf. Meuli 1975: 2.744: "Besonders als Waffe des Kleinen, Schwachen gegenüber dem Mächtigen haben wir die Fabel kennengelernt; nun bedient sich aber auch der Mächtige gelegentlich dieser Redeform, die er so oft hat hören müssen, gegenüber dem Kleinen, und dann nimmt sie gern ironisch drohenden Ton an."

> When Kroisos heard this, he sent the following message to the people of Lampsakos and warned them to let Miltiades go: if they did not, he threatened to wipe them out like a pine tree.

It is clear that Kroisos wants Miltiades released, but the expression "like a pine tree" throws the Lampsacenes into confusion. What does it mean? An old man eventually provides the key:[203]

> πλανωμένων δὲ τῶν Λαμψακηνῶν ἐν τοῖσι λόγοισι τί θέλει τὸ ἔπος εἶπαι τό σφι ἀπείλησε ὁ Κροῖσος, πίτυος τρόπον ἐκτρίψειν, μόγις κοτὲ μαθὼν τῶν τις πρεσβυτέρων εἶπε τὸ ἐόν, ὅτι πίτυς μούνη πάντων δενδρέων ἐκκοπεῖσα βλαστὸν οὐδένα μετιεῖ ἀλλὰ πανώλεθρος ἐξαπόλλυται.[204]
>
> 6.37.2

> While the citizens of Lampsakos were adrift in their discussions about what the message [*epos*] behind Kroisos' utterance was in which he threatened to wipe them out like a pine tree, one of the elders at last understood it and said what it really meant: the pine is the only tree which if chopped down does not send forth any new shoot but is completely destroyed.

In fear they release Miltiades.[205] As in the case of Kyros' *logos*, Kroisos' *epos* is told in a diplomatic context, an exchange between two foreign powers, and is related by the stronger to the weaker. Once again, the threat lies in the imagery used, drawn this time not from the animal but the plant world, which communicates more effectively than direct and unmarked speech.[206] In this

203 For the pattern of general confusion and subsequent resolution by an anonymous τις, cf. the debate concerning the oracle received by the Thebans (discussed in ch. 2.3 above): τοιαῦτα ἐπιλεγομένων εἶπε δή κοτε μαθών τις . . . (5.80.1), "While they were discussing such matters, someone came up with an idea and said . . ." and cf. 6.52.5–7. Cf. Harrison 2000:194: "The old man, the outsider, coming forward with the correct interpretation is almost a cliché of the interpretation of oracles."

204 The βλαστός, or shoot, appears as a sign in a different sign system, in the portent of the olive tree on the Athenian akropolis (8.55), where it signifies the regrowth of the city and the return of the goddess: see ch. 2.1 above. Cf. also the verbs βλαστάνω and ἀναβλαστάνω, used exclusively in the *Histories* in a metaphorical sense of the flourishing of a city (7.156.2) but also of the blooming of evil (3.62.4, 5.92.δ.1). Vegetal imagery is also at play in the *ainos* about Glaukos, whose line is destroyed "root and branch" (πρόρριζος, 6.86.δ; and in Solon's *ainos* to Kroisos, 1.32.9).

205 Fear as a reaction to an *ainos* is also found at 6.2.1: Histiaios flees in fear (δείσας) after Artaphrenes delivers his metaphor about Histiaios stitching the shoe of the Ionian Revolt (see below).

206 Ancient discussions of the *ainos* mention the plant realm as well as the animal world as settings: cf. the definition in e.g. Eustathius on *Iliad* 11.430 (= van Dijk 4T35): ὁ μὲν αἶνος λόγος ἐστὶ

instance the *ainos* is not framed, as with other *ainoi*, as an extended metaphor, but resides concisely in a simile (πίτυος τρόπον).[207]

The interaction between Artaphrenes and Histiaios reveals another aspect of the *ainos*, the relationship between speaker and audience founded on a basis of tacit understanding: the speaker expects that his audience will grasp his meaning and will understand the coded utterance. Artaphrenes knows full well that Histiaios is lying (τεχνάζοντα, 6.1.2) when he affects innocent surprise at the news of the Ionian Revolt, and replies to him:

> οὕτω τοι, Ἱστιαῖε, ἔχει κατὰ ταῦτα τὰ πρήγματα· τοῦτο τὸ ὑπόδημα ἔρραψας μὲν σύ, ὑπεδήσατο δὲ Ἀρισταγόρης.
>
> 6.1.2
>
> This is how you stand in relation to these matters, Histiaios: you stitched this shoe, and Aristagoras put it on.

The reply is designed to show Histiaios that Artaphrenes knows precisely what is going on, and Artaphrenes chooses to use code to convey this point more effectively ("I know that you know that I know") and to match Histiaios' cunning with a cunning of his own. The signifiers in Artaphrenes' coded reply are carefully chosen and highly appropriate to the figure of Histiaios: the image of the craftsman stitching is suggestive of the traditional image of the trickster as stitcher, weaver, and contriver of plans.[208] As with Kroisos' *ainos*,

---

μυθικὸς ἐκφερόμενος ἀπὸ ἀλόγων ζῴων ἢ φυτῶν πρὸς ἀνθρώπων παραίνεσιν . . . ("An *ainos* is a made-up [*muthikos*] story transferred from speechless animals or plants for the instruction of men"); cf. Munson 2001a:240–241 on discussion of Kallimakhos' dispute of the laurel and the olive, which is in a specifically Lydian setting (Mt. Tmolos). Cf. Munson 2001a:244 (cf. 251) on the role of animals in metaphors and symbolic code between divine and human: "As a field on which god operates more directly, the animal world represents an intermediary between the divine and human realms. Translated into historical terms, this view encompasses the idea that, on the one hand, animal events reflect human events and, on the other hand, the ways in which they do so mysteriously register divine reaction."

207 Benardete (1969:168) notes that "the simile of the pine-tree becomes a real threat when the deed which it suggests is grasped." Both Macan 1895 and How and Wells 1928 seem to miss the point of the image of the pine tree: "No adult Lampsakene could have been at a loss for an explanation of the bitter jest of Kroisos: nor could Hdt. had he read—or remembered—the passage in Charon." The relevant passage in Kharon of Lampsakos (FGH i.33 fr.6; Strabo 589) tells us that the old name of Lampsakos was Pituousa, "the place of pines," but, while appropriate for Kroisos' image, it does not explain the threat behind the simile: if anything, it helps to mask it. "

208 The connection between the verb ῥάπτω ('stitch together') and δόλος ('guile, trick') is made for example at *Odyssey* 3.118–119: εἰνάετες γάρ σφιν κακὰ ῥάπτομεν ἀμφιέποντες παντοίοισι δόλοισι, "For nine years we carefully contrived evil for them with all sorts of tricks." At *Histories* 9.17.4 ῥάπτω is combined with φόνος: ἀλλὰ μαθέτω τις αὐτῶν ὅτι ἐόντες βάρβαροι ἐπ' Ἕλλησι

the reaction to Artaphrenes' coded message upon decoding is fear and action: in a panic (δείσας, 6.2.1) Histiaios flees to the coast that same night.

Tacit understanding between speaker and recipient and expectation of understanding according to a common code are also at the basis of a remark made by Prokles, the father of Periandros' murdered wife, Melissa, to his grandchildren. He knows that Periandros murdered Melissa and wishes to convey this fact to his grandchildren. At the end of a visit to their grandfather, he asks them a parting question: "Do you know who killed your mother?" (3.50.3). The reactions of the two grandsons demonstrate precisely the coded nature of the utterance (described here as an *epos*, as in the case of Kroisos' utterance at 6.37.2),[209] which is more than a simple question. The elder of the two pays no attention to it, but the younger, Lykophron, immediately perceives that his grandfather is in fact telling him that Periandros murdered his mother, as is clear from his reaction of distress and his refusal to speak to his father on his return home:

> ἤλγησε ἀκούσας οὕτω ὥστε ἀπικόμενος ἐς τὴν Κόρινθον ἅτε φονέα τῆς μητρὸς τὸν πατέρα οὔτε προσεῖπε.
>
> 3.50.3
>
> Upon hearing this he became so aggrieved that on his return to Corinth he did not address his father because he was his mother's murderer.

The grandfather uses the question as an *ainos* to convey his message for two reasons: he must obviously use caution in so sensitive a matter, and he must be sure that the message falls on suitable ears. The allusive nature of Prokles' speech acts as an automatic device of testing and selection, since only the

ἀνδράσι φόνον ἔρραψαν, "But let one of them know that they, barbarians, have contrived murder against Greeks." One may also compare the role that stitching plays in Harpagos' secret message to Kyros (1.123.4, discussed further in ch. 3.1). Weaving and cunning are combined in the figure of Amestris, the wife of Xerxes, who weaves an intricately embroidered cloak for her husband by means of which she tricks her husband into revealing his infidelity, 9.109.1: ἐξυφήνασα Ἄμηστρις ἡ Ξέρξεω γυνὴ φᾶρος μέγα τε καὶ ποικίλον καὶ θέης ἄξιον διδοῖ Ξέρξῃ, "Amestris, the wife of Xerxes, wove a great cloak, embroidered and worth seeing, and gave it to Xerxes." Cf. discussion in ch. 2.8 and 3.1 below. For the shoe in a context of deception one may compare Hermes' sandals in the *Homeric Hymn to Hermes*. Hermes, the arch-trickster, plaits (διέπλεκε, 80) a pair of sandals for himself in order to conceal his own baby footprints when stealing Apollo's cattle (cf. καταπλέκω, 4.205 and discussion in ch. 2.8 below). As Detienne and Vernant (1978:302) show, the weaving of the sandals is intimately connected with the weaving of wiles: "the *metis* of Hermes at no time makes any distinction between the most sophisticated methods of twisting plant fibres together and the construction of the traps he intends to set."

209 Cf. Hollmann 2000.

one who feels concern at the mother's death and the identity of the killer will decode the surface question not as a question but as a statement of Periandros' guilt. The distinction between the two brothers lies in this ability to decode, and it is clearly shown when Periandros asks the elder brother what his grandfather said to them:

> ἐκείνου δὲ τοῦ ἔπεος τό σφι ὁ Προκλέης ἀποστέλλων εἶπε, ἅτε οὐ νόῳ λαβών, οὐκ ἐμέμνητο.[210]
>
> 3.51.1
>
> He did not remember the utterance [*epos*] which Procles had made when seeing them off because he did not comprehend it [literally, 'grasp it with his *noos*'].

Eventually he remembers, and repeats his grandfather's words, still presumably with no understanding, but Periandros has *noos* enough to realize the encoded nature of the utterance and the message lying under the surface:[211]

> Περίανδρος δὲ νόῳ λαβὼν [καὶ τοῦτο] καὶ μαλακὸν ἐνδιδόναι βουλόμενος οὐδέν, τῇ ὁ ἐξελασθεὶς ὑπ' αὐτοῦ παῖς δίαιταν ἐποιέετο, ἐς τούτους πέμπων ἄγγελον ἀπηγόρευε μή μιν δέκεσθαι οἰκίοισι.
>
> 3.51.2

210 The elder brother is later referred to as νωθέστερος (3.53.1), "stupid." The motif of two brothers, one in some way "handicapped" in terms of the ability to communicate by signs, the other unimpaired and even talented in this regard, can be seen in the two sons of Kroisos, Atys and his brother, who is mute. But which of these is impaired and which is not is put into question by subsequent events: Atys produces a reading of Kroisos' dream by which he convinces his father that the death by an iron spear which the dream warns of cannot possibly arise in a hunting context. As it turns out, this is precisely where Atys meets his death, and his reading of the dream is in a way responsible for his death. The son who is "damaged" and "dumb" (διέφθαρτο, ἦν γὰρ δὴ κωφός, 1.34.2; Sebeok and Brady [1979:289n5] suggest that the problem would today be diagnosed as autism) and who seemingly has no ability to use signs (and is given no name in the narrative) ends up saving his father's life when he shouts to a Persian soldier not to kill Kroisos (1.85.4).

211 As has been shown in ch. 1.3.2 above, the ability to decode is often associated with *noos*. Periandros proves himself a competent reader of signs in several contexts: he decodes (συνεὶς τὸ ποιηθὲν καὶ νόῳ σχών [5.92.η.1], "understanding what had been done and grasping it in his *noos*") the visual message which his friend and fellow tyrant, Thrasyboulos, sends him (walking through a field of wheat and cutting off the highest stalks). He is also able to decode the message which his dead wife sends him as an authentic guarantee that she is really the sender (πιστὸν συμβολαῖον, 5.92.η.3): she accuses Periandros of putting his loaves in a cold oven. Only Periandros is in a position to decode this message and only Melissa could have sent it, since it refers to his sexual violation of her corpse. In this sense it comes close to the "I know that you know that I know" kind of *ainos* which Artaphrenes relates to Histiaios. Cf. ch. 3.2 below on tyrants and signs.

> Periandros, comprehending this too and not wanting to show any weakness, sent a message to the people where the son whom he had exiled was living and forbade them receive him in their homes.

When in the hands of the stronger the *ainos* may threaten, as in the case of Kyros and Kroisos, but it may also warn and persuade in a more diplomatic fashion when the encoder of the *ainos* is in a weaker or equal position.[212] The Spartan king Leotykhides, for example, who wishes to persuade the Athenians to release a group of Aeginetan hostages which they are refusing to return, resorts to the rhetorical strategy of an extended *ainos* and tells the story of Glaukos the Spartan.[213] Glaukos accepts a deposit of money from a wealthy Milesian and retains a set of σύμβολα, tokens. He undertakes to turn over the deposit to anyone who produces a matching set of σύμβολα (6.86.α). After a number of years, the sons of the Milesian come to Sparta to reclaim the money (6.86.β.1). When they produce the σύμβολα, Glaukos claims that he remembers nothing of the agreement and the deposit, and sends them away, telling them to come back after four months, during which time he will investigate whether or not he ever accepted such a deposit (6.86.β.2). He asks the Delphic oracle whether he should keep his oath to the Milesian and return the money to the bearer of the σύμβολα. The oracle tells him that he can certainly pretend to know nothing of the agreement and profit by it, but reminds him that his descendants may be visited with the awful consequences of oath-breaking. He then asks the god for forgiveness, but the Pythia tells him that to have considered breaking his oath is the same as having actually done so (6.86.γ.1–2).

212 For another example of this, cf. 3.32.1, a passage Munson (2001a:251n67) describes as an "enacted *ainos*": in a fight staged by Kambyses, a puppy is set against a lion cub. The puppy's brother breaks its chain to take part in the fight and they are able to subdue the lion. Kambyses' wife and sister cries because her brother Smerdis has no one to come to his aid. This reply (significantly described as an *epos*) is in the Greek view directly responsible for her death at the hands of Kambyses (3.32.3).

213 The technique is that used by Phoinix in his attempt to persuade Akhilles to yield to the entreaties of Agamemnon (*Iliad* 9.434–605). He relates the story of Meleagros as an *ainos*, as Nagy (1979:105, 240) points out: just as Meleagros eventually yielded to the pleas of the one closest to him (his wife) when the enemy was already in the city, so too Akhilles should yield to the requests of those near to him. Phoinix's inclusion toward the end of his speech of a description of the Litai (502–512) is paralleled by Leotykhides' quotation of the oracle to Glaukos which speaks of the "child of Oath" (6.86.γ.2). Like Ate, who is associated with the Litai and who quickly pursues and finds those who spurn them (ἡ δ' Ἄτη σθεναρή τε καὶ ἀρτίπος [505], "Ate is strong and sound of foot"), the child of Oath also moves swiftly and catches up with those who break their oaths: κραιπνὸς δὲ μετέρχεται, εἰς ὅ κε πᾶσαν ᾧ συμμάρψας ὀλέσῃ γενεὴν καὶ οἶκον ἅπαντα, "Swiftly he comes after them, until he seizes and destroys their entire line and house."

Leotykhides does not let his *ainos* speak for itself, as Kyros, Kroisos, and Artaphrenes do, but immediately provides an interpretation of it: the house of Glaukos no longer exists in Sparta but has been utterly wiped out, roots and all (ἐκτέτριπταί τε πρόρριζος ἐκ Σπάρτης, 6.86.δ), an expression that recalls Kroisos' threat to the Lampsacenes and the image of the pine tree (πίτυος τρόπον ἐκτρίψειν, 6.37.2). If the Athenians do not return the men, they may suffer the same fate as Glaukos: the utter extinction of their line.[214] Leotykhides' speech is the one example of an unsuccessful *ainos* in the *Histories*: it may be that the Athenians, elsewhere so gullible (cf. Herodotus' comments on the Phye episode at 1.60.3 and on Aristagoras' persuasion of the Athenians, 5.97.2), do not allow themselves to be persuaded by a man who himself has been guilty of making false oaths and has played a part in corrupting the Pythia (6.65–66). Of the dire consequences with which he threatens the Athenians we read nothing further.[215]

Even when an *ainos* is decoded for the recipient by the person who relates it, this does not guarantee that the recipient will accept or understand its message. The Athenians simply ignore and discount Leotykhides' *ainos*, and so too does Kroisos in the case of the *ainos* which Solon relates to him in answer to his question whether he has seen any one in his travels whom he would call most fortunate of all (πάντων ὀλβιώτατος, 1.30.2). Solon's reply, which awards first place to Tellos the Athenian (1.30.3) and second to Kleobis and Biton of Argos (1.31.1), is in the form of an *ainos*, revolving, as Nagy has shown, around the meaning of the word ὄλβιος.[216] To Kroisos, to be ὄλβιος simply means being wealthy and fortunate, whereas Solon understands something very different by the term, and his accounts of Tellos and of Kleobis and Biton are designed, when read correctly, to illustrate the real meaning of the term.

In both of Solon's *exempla*, the figures deemed ὄλβιοι enjoy a sufficient means of life up to the moment of their death and complete their lives in a noble fashion, enjoying honor (τιμή) after their death: Tellos is killed while fighting for his city and receives a public burial at the very spot where he fell (1.30.4–5); Kleobis and Biton bring honor to their mother and themselves by pulling her in an oxcart to the temple of Hera, then die a mysterious death which comes upon them in their sleep after they have been fêted by their

214 For οὕτω as a characteristic bridge between the *ainos* and its application to the context in which it is told, cf. Nagy 1990b:310 and references there.

215 Cf., however, Munson 2001a:90: "But given the context, that omission does not necessarily imply that they have avoided divine punishment, nor does having the message on divine justice conveyed by an individual who will himself be a historical exemplum for it impugn its validity."

216 Nagy 1990b:244.

community, and become the recipients of statues at Delphi and of a hero cult (1.31.1–5).[217]

Kroisos cannot interpret Solon's *ainos*, as is shown by his indignant reproach at having his own great good fortune and prosperity so lightly dismissed (1.32.1). In a lengthy speech, Solon attempts to make clear what ὄλβος really entails and how it differs from material wealth and from good fortune (εὐτυχίη). His warning lies in the fact that material prosperity may at any time disappear and that even if it is present and endures up to the moment of death, one may still not be called ὄλβιος unless one has ended one's life well, εὖ (1.32.7). This message Kroisos chooses to ignore, being convinced only of Solon's stupidity (1.33).

But there is something further in Solon's words: what he leaves unsaid is how this may affect Kroisos and what the consequences of thinking oneself ὄλβιος are. *Atê*, destruction as a result of hubristic thinking, is mentioned indirectly in Solon's statement that the very rich man is better able to endure its attack than the fortunate man (εὐτυχής) who is moderately well off (1.32.6), but Solon gives no direct warning to Kroisos, "Beware of *hubris* and its attendant *atê*!"[218] Rather, as Nagy has pointed out, the *hubris* and *atê* are shown in direct action as narrated by Herodotus, beginning with the story of Atys and Adrastos:[219]

> μετὰ δὲ Σόλωνα οἰχόμενον ἔλαβε ἐκ θεοῦ νέμεσις μεγάλη Κροῖσον, ὡς εἰκάσαι, ὅτι ἐνόμισε ἑωυτὸν εἶναι ἀνθρώπων ἁπάντων ὀλβιώτατον.
>
> 1.34.1

217 It is interesting that Solon assigns Kleobis and Biton second place in terms of ὄλβος, yet he devotes much more attention to their achievements than to Tellos' simple death; they seem to exemplify Solon's message about ὄλβος and the end more clearly and in a more extreme form.

218 By contrast Hesiod, for example, in *Works and Days* 213–216 describes how not even the good man (ἐσθλός), let alone the inferior (δειλός), is capable of withstanding *hubris* combined with *atê*: this follows a direct warning to Perses not to incur *hubris*. The Herodotean Solon describes the visitation of *atê* (ἄτην μεγάλην προσπεσοῦσαν, 1.32.6) but never includes an explicit warning against the behavior that attracts it. Nagy 1990b:248 compares the Solon of his own poetry (F 13.11–18 W) with the Solon of Herodotus: "In the actual poetry of Solon, then, the teaching of the Sage about this topic is direct: *hubris* is a cause of *atê*... the *atê* and *hubris* of Croesus are not confronted directly by Solon in the encounter dramatized by Herodotus. In his own poetry, Solon can speak in his juridical role as lawmaker. In his encounter with a tyrant, however, he is more diplomatic." On the Herodotean Solon and the poetry of Solon, cf. Chiasson 1986.

219 Nagy 1990b:248. Following Immerwahr 1966:157–158, he suggests that the names of Atys and Adrastos can be interpreted as pointing precisely to *atê* and *nemesis*, the former name because of its resemblance to the noun, the latter via a more indirect path: Adrastos suggests the adjective ἄδραστος, "from which one cannot run away," which in turn suggests the idea of *nemesis*, who is in fact is called Ἀδράστεια in Aeschylus *Prometheus Bound* 936. On significant names in Herodotus, see ch. 2.6 below.

> After Solon's departure, a great divine *nemesis* took hold of Kroisos, because, to make a conjecture, he considered himself to be the most *olbios* of all mankind.

Kroisos fails to understand both Solon's explicit statements about the nature of ὄλβος and the implicit warning about his conduct, both the surface meaning and the underlying meaning. Understanding, revelation, and the final solution to Solon's *ainos* come only later, as Herodotus shows in the dramatic scene of Kroisos on the pyre, when he calls out Solon's name and recalls his teaching (1.86.3–5). The interaction between Kroisos, the interpreters, and Kyros now reminds one of that first interchange between Solon and Kroisos. Kroisos' utterances on the pyre are just as puzzling as Solon's once were, and to the interpreters (ἑρμηνέες), who can translate his language but not the meaning of his words, what he says is ἄσημα, without meaning or sense (1.86.4).[220] Yet Kyros is able to make sense of Kroisos' words, to grasp the message in his *noos* (1.86.6).[221]

Solon's *ainos* and its final interpretation by Kroisos seem to show the hand of Herodotus even more than the other *ainoi* discussed in this chapter. Solon's message lies stretched over a considerable narrative terrain instead of being concentrated in one place, and it is Herodotus who is responsible for this. We have seen that the *atê* and *hubris* that accompany the consideration of oneself as ὄλβιος are not directly mentioned by Solon, something that he does, however, do in his own poetry, but are allowed by Herodotus to emerge later, in the story of Atys and Adrastos:

> Without the narration of Herodotus, neither the guilt of Croesus nor the meaning of Solon the sage could be manifest. The words of the Sage have been ambiguously spoken in the mode of an *ainos*, the true meaning of which can only be brought out by the turn of events as narrated by Herodotus.[222]

In other words, we see Herodotus here in his role of transmitter, marshaler, and interpreter of signs.

220 On these and other interpreters and their failure to interpret, see ch. 3.2.1 below.
221 See ch. 1.3.2 above on *noos* and the interpretation of signs.
222 Nagy 1990b:248.

2.6 Names and Naming

2.6.1 Meaning of Names, Action of Naming

It has long been recognized that personal names form a distinctive and special type of linguistic sign. They mark out and point to a particular individual, just as personal pronouns are indexical signs whose function it is to point to a referent. But names, unlike personal pronouns, which have no semantic content, have the capacity to convey additional information in that they do not simply point beyond themselves but have sense in their own right.[223] This is especially observable in the case of Greek names, which are made of elements readily recognizable and understandable to speakers.[224] A connection may therefore be perceived to exist between the meaning of a name and its bearer or referent, and a transference of qualities made from the meaning of a name to its bearer which may reflect positively, negatively, or ironically on the person so named.[225] Krios is the name of an individual from Aigina, yet his name has a meaning quite apart from its function of indicating and marking out its bearer: it means 'ram', and it is on this connection that Kleomenes the Spartan king seizes when, stung by Krios' rejection of his authority, he makes the following threat:

> ἤδη νῦν καταχαλκοῦ, ὦ κριέ, τὰ κέρεα, ὡς συνοισόμενος μεγάλῳ κακῷ.
>
> 6.50.3

223 See Peradotto 1990:95–99, summarizing the modern debate on names, meaning, and reference.

224 Cf. Svenbro 1993:18n46: "The nature of their onomastic system facilitated interpretation and reinterpretation, as most Greek proper names are composed of semantically identifiable elements."

225 It is significant that ὄνομα may refer to both a common and a proper noun. Cf. Munson 2005:31–32, who notes (32n11) that Herodotus does distinguish the category of proper names of individual persons from that of ethnic names in his description of the Atarantes of Libya, described as ἀνώνυμοι (4.184.1).

> "Cover your horns in bronze, Mr. Ram, because you're in for big trouble."[226]

Herodotus thus shows himself fully aware of the double capacity of names both to point and identify and to have meaning in themselves, drawing our attention to the possibility of connections between the bearer and the meaning of the name.[227] That comparison between the two may reveal an ironic or humorous dissonance has already been seen in the case of Krios, but the experience of Leon shows that the connection may have more serious consequences. Leon ("Lion") is the name of an Aeginetan sailor on the first Greek ship to be captured by the Persian fleet near Skiathos. As the finest looking on board, he is executed over the ship's prow by the Phoenician crew as a kind of sacrificial victim:

> καὶ ἔπειτα τῶν ἐπιβατέων αὐτῆς τὸν καλλιστεύοντα ἀγαγόντες ἐπὶ τὴν πρῴρην τῆς νεὸς ἔσφαξαν, διαδέξιον ποιεύμενοι τὸν εἷλον τῶν Ἑλλήνων πρῶτον εἶναι κάλλιστον.
>
> 7.180

> Then they led the finest looking of the crew to the prow of the ship and slit his throat, considering it a favorable omen that their first Greek captive should be the finest.

Herodotus grimly suggests, "Perhaps he benefited to some extent from his name as well" (τάχα δ' ἄν τι καὶ τοῦ οὐνόματος ἐπαύροιτο, 7.180), presumably meaning that just as the man's beauty marked him out for slaughter in the

226 Presumably the layer of bronze is meant as protection (instances of the adjective κατάχαλκος listed in LSJ all have to do with bronze used as an overlay for protective armor, e.g. Euripides *Heraclidae* 376, of a wicker shield, ἰτέα). Cf. Stein 1889–1896 *ad loc.*: "Krios soll seine Hörner zur Abwehr der ihm bevorstehenden Unglückes verstählen lassen." The name is also played on by Simonides *PMG* 507 (referred to by Aristophanes *Clouds* 1355–1356): ἐπέξαθ' ὁ Κριὸς οὐκ ἀεικέως | ἐλθὼν ἐς εὔδενδρον ἀγλαὸν Διὸς | τέμενος, "Krios got a proper shearing when he came to the well-wooded and splendid sanctuary of Zeus." One of the scholiasts to Aristophanes explains that Krios was a wrestler (παλαιστής) from Aigina. Ἐπέξατο "was shorn" seems to be meant ironically, and Krios may be presumed to be an unsuccessful competitor against Simonides' patron. Page (1951:140–142) argues that Simonides' Aiginetan wrestler and Herodotus' Aiginetan statesman are in fact one and the same man. The name also appears in an Attic verse inscription of about 400 BCE, which also seems to play on the double reference of κριός: οὗτος, ὃς ἐνθάδε κεῖται | ἔχει μὲν τὄνομα κριο, | φωτὸς δὲ ψυχὴν ἔσχε | δικαιοτάτο (*GVI* i.1785), "The one who lies here has the name Krios, but had the soul of a most righteous man."

227 The significance of names is played upon already in the Homeric poems, where such genealogies as Phemios Terpiades (*Odyssey* 22.330) or Noemon, son of Phronios (*Odyssey* 2.386), appear. The etymology of Odysseus' name, one version of which is explained at 19.407–409, plays an important role in the *Odyssey* as a whole: cf. e.g. Austin 1972; Peradotto 1990; and Breed 1999.

way in which the finest animal in a herd is chosen as a sacrificial victim, so too did the nobility of his name, "Lion," contribute to the Phoenicians' decision, being a kind of omen.[228] The ominous connection between the meaning of a name and its bearer may also be experienced in a more positive and less baneful fashion, as with the name of Hegesistratos ('Leader of the army'). When Hegesistratos of Samos asks Leotykhides for assistance, Leotykhides asks for his name and upon hearing it accepts it as a (good) omen (δέκομαι τὸν οἰωνόν, 9.91.2) and so agrees to give his help.[229] As Munson (2005:49) puts it, "Herodotus' etymologies have the mantic character of Leotychides' discovery of Hegesistratus' name and of the creation and interpretation of names as represented in Plato's *Cratylus*."

The connection may be revealed accidentally and assume a sudden significance in a given situation, as in the instances above, or the connection may be forged in a conscious fashion, right at the occasion of naming. The parents of Demaratos ('Prayed for by the people'), for example, give him this name to reflect the fact that this is the male child whom the Spartan people have prayed and hoped for (πανδημεὶ Σπαρτιῆται . . . ἀρὴν ἐποιήσαντο, 6.63.3).[230]

228 A comparison between a human being and a sacrificial victim, also revolving around the verb καλλιστεύω, lies behind the oracle given to Arkesilaos of Cyrene (4.163.3, discussed in ch 2.3 above), where the ταῦρος ὁ καλλιστεύων ("most handsome bull") of the oracle turns out to be Arkesilaos' father-in-law, who is killed by the people of Barke. Here Leon literally becomes a sacrificial victim. Lions are not of course sacrificial victims either in Greek or Persian tradition, but sacrificial victims are the finest (κάλλιστος) of their kind, and the lion enjoys the highest status amongst the animals, being the prey of kings in depictions of Persian hunting scenes and the animal which reigns supreme in Homeric similes (e.g. *Iliad* 3.23–26). In the *Histories* the lion appears as symbol for absolute ruler in the oracular dream of Hipparkhos (5.56.1) and in an oracle about Kypselos (5.92.β.3). Macan's comment on 7.180 surveys the different possibilities in a way that does justice to Herodotus' sense of humor and irony: "There is no doubt a touch of irony here, but how exactly does Hdt. mean it? Did the Phoenicians ascertain that the name of this Adonis was 'Lion' and did this discovery seal his fate? Or does not Hdt. mean that such grand names are dangerous, and provocative of φθόνος, νέμεσις? Or, short of that, does he simply mean, 'much good his grand name did him!' " Immerwahr (1966:260n69) sees a play on Leonidas' name at 7.225.2: "The significance of the name Leonidas, 'son of Lion,' is emphasized by the alliteration that occurs at the mention of his tomb: ὅκου νῦν ὁ λίθινος λέων ἕστηκε ἐπὶ Λεωνίδῃ." Cf. also Munson 2005:47.

229 Cf. ch. 2.1.2 above on the recognition of omens and portents.

230 Compare the name of Alkinoos' wife, Ἀρήτη, 'Prayed for' (discussion in Peradotto 1990:108, where he also considers the possibility of the meaning 'Accursed'), and the epithet πολυάρητος, applied to the infant Odysseus by Eurykleia as she presents him to Autolykos for naming (*Odyssey* 19.403–404). Cf. discussion in Peradotto 1990:138–139, who points out the ambiguity: 'Much-prayed-for' but also 'Much-cursed,' a "close synonym . . . for the very word, *odyssamenos*, which motivates the name Autolycus chooses." Considering Demaratos' subsequent expulsion and rejection by the Spartan people (at the instigation of Kleomenes and Leotykhides), perhaps we may find the same ambiguity in his name as Peradotto sees in Ἀρήτη and πολυάρητος.

A subsequent naming may supplant an original naming, as in the case of Oiolykos and Battos, where a by-name reflects a connection between the bearer of the name and the circumstances surrounding him. Oiolykos' original name (not preserved by Herodotus) is changed when he refuses to follow his father, Theras, to found a colony on the island, subsequently named after him. Theras warns that he will be left as a sheep among wolves (ὄϊς ἐν λύκοισι, 4.149.1), and from this utterance a name arises which somehow becomes dominant, taking over from his original name. In the case of Battos, according to Herodotus at least (ὡς μέντοι ἐγὼ δοκέω, 4.155.1), he is renamed by the Delphic oracle:

> Βάττος δὲ μετωνομάσθη, ἐπείτε ἐς Λιβύην ἀπίκετο, ἀπό τε τοῦ χρηστηρίου τοῦ γενομένου ἐν Δελφοῖσι αὐτῷ καὶ ἀπὸ τῆς τιμῆς τὴν ἔσχε τὴν ἐπωνυμίην ποιεύμενος. Λίβυες γὰρ βασιλέα βάττον καλέουσι, καὶ τούτου εἵνεκα δοκέω θεσπίζουσαν τὴν Πυθίην καλέσαι μιν Λιβυκῇ γλώσσῃ, εἰδυῖαν ὡς βασιλεὺς ἔσται ἐν Λιβύῃ.
>
> 4.155.2
>
> His name was changed to Battos after he came to Libya. He gave himself this name after the oracle given to him at Delphi and the title he had obtained: for the Libyans call their king *battos*, and it is for this reason, I think, that the Pythia when delivering her oracle addressed him in the Libyan tongue, knowing that he would be king in Libya.[231]

The action of naming goes beyond simply attaching a new sign to the bearer, but may constitute a speech act, since it produces an actual result, making him king (or at least predicting that he will be). Herodotus shows us naming as an act which produces or confirms the status of kingship also in his account of the rise of Kyros. The giving of the name "king" (βασιλέος ὀνομασθέντος, 1.120.4) to Kyros in a children's game has far-reaching consequences, since by various twists and turns it ends up fulfilling Astyages' dream that the offspring of his daughter will rule in his stead. To Astyages and the *magoi*, the context of Kyros' being named king—a children's game—limits the sense in which he is "king" and safely defuses the dream's prophecy (ἐς ἀσθενὲς ἔρχεται, 1.120.3), but Herodotus seems to show that the naming is an absolute act which, once performed (under whatever circumstances), has an enduring effect.

[231] The other version, told by the people of Thera and Cyrene (4.155.1), which Herodotus preserves, is that Battos got his name from his stuttering.

The same *logos* shows another facet of names and the uses to which they may be put. When Kyros has been restored to his true parents, Kambyses and Mandane, they discover that the name of the herdsman's wife who brought up Kyros in his infancy is Kuno ('Bitch'). Kuno, as Herodotus points out, is a translation of the Median "Spako" (1.110.1), and from this they weave a story that Kyros was raised by a bitch:

> οἱ δὲ τοκέες παραλαβόντες τὸ οὔνομα τοῦτο, ἵνα θειοτέρως δοκέῃ τοῖσι Πέρσῃσι περιεῖναί σφι ὁ παῖς, κατέβαλον φάτιν ὡς ἐκκείμενον Κῦρον κύων ἐξέθρεψε.
>
> 1.122.3
>
> His parents adopted this name so that their son might seem to the Persians to have survived through providence, and they broadcast a report that a bitch had raised Kyros when he was exposed.

Their manipulation consists in the appropriation (παραλαβόντες) and conversion of a proper name into an ordinary noun, from Κυνώ to κύων, just as Kleomenes converts Κριός to κριός. In the former instance, the distinction is reflected in a formal change, the change from a form with a suffix indicative of a female personal name (cf. Γοργώ) to one with a suffix indicative of a common noun. With the Κριός to κριός change there is no formal change observable, but the context (the mention of horns) makes the change clear. In both cases, the referent is no longer regarded as a person but the very thing which is signified by the signifier. In other words, there is no longer a distinction between the signified ("dog," "ram") and the referent (the woman Kuno, the man Krios), and the manipulators reduce the referents to the position of animals, each for their own purposes.

Herodotus directly addresses the issue of the connection between the meaning of a name and its referent or bearer precisely in the case of Persian names, which all, without exception, end in sigma, and which resemble their bearers in terms of physical appearance (σώματα) and magnificence (μεγαλοπρεπείῃ):

> καὶ τόδε ἄλλο σφι ὧδε συμπέπτωκε γίνεσθαι, τὸ Πέρσας μὲν αὐτοὺς λέληθε, ἡμέας μέντοι οὔ· τὰ οὐνόματά σφι ἐόντα ὅμοια τοῖσι σώμασι καὶ τῇ μεγαλοπρεπείῃ τελευτῶσι πάντα ἐς τὠυτὸ γράμμα, τὸ Δωριέες μὲν σὰν καλέουσι, Ἴωνες δὲ σίγμα. ἐς τοῦτο διζήμενος εὑρήσεις τελευτῶντα τῶν Περσέων τὰ οὐνόματα, οὐ τὰ μέν, τὰ δὲ οὔ, ἀλλὰ πάντα ὁμοίως.
>
> 1.139

> The following thing also happens to be the case among them, which has escaped the notice of the Persians themselves, but not us: their names resemble their bodies and their grandeur and all end in the same letter, which the Dorians call *san* and the Ionians *sigma*. If you look into it, you will find all Persian names ending in this letter, not just some of them, but all of them alike.[232]

Persian names, then, do not simply identify or mark their bearers, but describe them, presumably not necessarily as they are but as they would like to be regarded. In other words, there is a natural relationship between sense and referent. Herodotus in fact illustrates this principle of Persian onomastics later in the *Histories* when he gives Greek equivalents for the names Dareios, Xerxes, and Artaxerxes, all of which are fitting names for kings and leaders:

> δύναται δὲ κατὰ Ἑλλάδα γλῶσσαν ταῦτα τὰ οὐνόματα, Δαρεῖος ἐρξίης, Ξέρξης ἀρήιος, Ἀρτοξέρξης μέγας ἀρήιος.[233]
>
> 6.98.3
>
> These names have the following meanings in Greek: Dareios means "doer," Xerxes means "warrior," and Artaxerxes means "great warrior."

These are the only Persian names whose significance he reveals (apart from the Median Spako), but there are indications that he treats certain other Persian names as if they contained Greek roots, and plays on connections between these familiar roots glimpsed in foreign names and the refer-

[232] That all Persian names end in -s is only true of course of the Hellenized forms of masculine names: Persian (masculine) names ending in -*a* or -*â* are regularly interpreted by Greeks as names of the second declension ending in -ης or -ος (see following footnote). The tone of Herodotus' declaration (Πέρσας μὲν αὐτοὺς λέληθε, ἡμέας μέντοι οὔ, "It has escaped the Persians' own notice, but not ours") is typical of his "master of signs" persona: cf. ch. 3.2 below.

[233] Herodotus' translations, however, bear little resemblance to the actual meanings of these names (all translations from Schmitt 1967:120–121): *Dârayavauß* = "das Gute festhaltend"; *Xßayârßâ* = "über Helden herrschend"; *Artaxßaça* = "das Arta zur Herrschaft habend." Cf. the ingenious treatment of this question in Chamberlain 1999:267–272; cf. also Munson 2005:48–51. Herodotus' point about the magnificence (μεγαλοπρεπείη) of Persian names still holds though, as a glance through the names explained by Schmitt 1967 shows. The passage should also be considered in its context, coming as it does after Herodotus' statement about the significance of the earthquake on Delos (6.98.1) and his report of the oracle that predicted this earthquake (6.98.3). As Munson (2005:49) puts it: "As a third order of signs, he inserts the passage cited above, with his translation of the mighty names that 'name' the epoch. The context is prophetic as is the substance of the narrator's 'beginning of evil' pronouncement."

ents of these names.[234] μεγαλοπρεπείη ('magnificence, grandeur') is visible in the numerous Persian names in Herodotus beginning in *Mega*-, to the Greek ear suggestive of μέγας ('great'), e.g. Megabates as if from μέγα- and βαίνω ('walk'), Megadostes as if from μέγα- and δίδωμι ('give'), or in those ending in *-phrenes*, suggestive of Greek φρήν and its plural, φρένες ('mind, senses'), e.g. Artaphrenes as if ἀρτίφρων ('sound of mind').[235] The name Harpagos resembles the Greek ἅρπαγος ('hook') and other words built on the root ἁρπ- ('grasp, seize'), a not inappropriate description of his character.[236] The first element of the name of Prexaspes suggests Ionic πρηξ- (πρήσσω, 'do, act'), as found in the Greek names Πρηξίλεως (9.107.2) and Πρηξῖνος (7.180), and Herodotus seems in one place to play on this perceived connection:

> Πρήξασπες, οὕτω μοι διέπρηξας τό τοι προσέθηκα πρῆγμα.
>
> 3.62.2
>
> "So, Prexaspes, this is how you have performed the task I assigned you!"[237]

The pronouncing of a name, whether as an initial act of bestowal (ὀνομάζειν, οὔνομα τιθέναι) or as an act of recollection (μνῶμαι, ἐπιμνῶμαι, μνήμην ποιέεσθαι), is a highly significant, not to say semiotic, activity. To bestow a name is to bring about a certain change in reality, or at least to attempt to bring about a change, as when parents harness the glory of a former bearer of a name to the present bearer: so the Athenian tyrant is named Peisistratos after the famous son of Nestor (5.65.4).[238] The renaming of tribes by Kleisthenes

234 Discussion in Schmitt 1967, esp. 142–143. Some suggestions as to how Persian names may have been subjected to Greek folk etymology are made by Armayor 1978:156 and *passim*, but a good many of these are simply too far-fetched (e.g. "GOBRYAS really was a wail-teemer as the father of Mardonius," presumably from γόος and βρύω; and "HYMAIES thy-man?"). It may be argued that this is in the nature of folk etymologies (cf. those made by Socrates in Plato's *Cratylus*), but even so, Armayor's are often not based on any natural or probable basis.

235 The *Mega*- prefix is a hellenization of Persian *baga*- ('god'): thus Megabates = **Bagapâta* "von Gott geschützt" (Schmitt 1967:130). The *-phrenes* suffix is a hellenization of Persian *-farnâ* ('fame': thus Artophrenes = **Artafarnâ* "das Arta als Ruhm habend" (Schmidt 1967:129). Both names have "magnificence" (μεγαλοπρεπείη), in both their Greek and Persian versions. For a name reflecting on the σῶμα of its possessor, at least to Greek ears, cf. the name Abrokomes, suggestive of ἁβροκόμης ('delicate-haired') and Greek notions of oriental softness (ἁβρότης) and luxury (τρυφή).

236 Armayor 1978:151 and 156.

237 Bencsik 1994:40; Powell 1937:104. Iranian form as yet (Schmitt 1967:135n124) unreconstructed.

238 The naming of the earlier Peisistratos can in turn be seen as a reflection of his father Nestor's powers of leadership and persuasion and a transference of these powers to the child. Greek names are often comments on qualities of the parent rather than the child, as Peradotto 1990 and Svenbro 1993:64–79 show.

of Sikyon and, in imitation of his maternal grandfather, by Kleisthenes the Athenian demonstrates the connection between naming and the exercise of power and imposition of will. Kleisthenes of Sikyon changes the traditional names of the four Doric tribes (φυλαί), used also in Argos, because of his hatred of Argos and all things Argive:

> ἵνα δὴ μὴ αἱ αὐταὶ ἔωσι τοῖσι Σικυωνίοισι καὶ τοῖσι Ἀργείοισι, μετέβαλε ἐς ἄλλα οὐνόματα.
>
> 5.68.1
>
> So that the Sicyonians might not have the same tribes as the Argives, he changed their names to different ones.

Three of the four names which he substitutes, however, are, according to Herodotus at least, an expression of tyrannical caprice, designed to humiliate his own citizens (πλεῖστον κατεγέλασε τῶν Σικυωνίων, 5.68.1). He names them after the swine, the ass, and the sucking pig:[239]

> ἔνθα καὶ πλεῖστον κατεγέλασε τῶν Σικυωνίων· ἐπὶ γὰρ ὑός τε καὶ ὄνου <καὶ χοίρου> τὰς ἐπωνυμίας μετατιθεὶς αὐτὰ τὰ τελευταῖα ἐπέθηκε, πλὴν τῆς ἑωυτοῦ φυλῆς· ταύτῃ δὲ τὸ οὔνομα ἀπὸ τῆς ἑωυτοῦ ἀρχῆς ἔθετο. οὗτοι μὲν δὴ Ἀρχέλαοι ἐκαλέοντο, ἕτεροι δὲ Ὑᾶται, ἄλλοι δὲ Ὀνεᾶται, ἕτεροι δὲ Χοιρεᾶται.
>
> 5.68.1
>
> And then he enjoyed a big laugh at the Sicyonians' expense, for he gave [the tribes] names based on the words "pig," "ass," <and "sucking pig"> with just a change in the endings, all except his own tribe: to this he gave a name based on his own rule [*arkhê*]. And so these were called the Arkhelaoi, while the others were called the Hyatai ["Swinites"], Oneatai ["Assites"], and the Khoireatai ["Piglingites"].

The grandson named for him also brings about changes in the names of the four traditional φυλαί in Athens, and also does so in order not to use the same names as a despised people, in this case the Ionians in general (5.69.1).

[239] Herodotus' interpretation of Kleisthenes' motives is not the only one possible, and in fact seems unlikely. Nenci 1994 *ad loc.* notes that the names of the tribes properly interpreted refer not to the animals themselves but those who raise them and that these are not *nomina foedantia* "ma di denominazioni chi riflettono diversificazioni di carattere economico e probabilmente territoriale." He compares the names of the old Athenian *phulai* (5.66.2): Ὅπλητες ('warriors'), Ἀργαδῆς ('laborers'), Γελέοντες ('cultivators'), Αἰγικορεῖς ('herdsmen and shepherds'). On the meaning of the name Ἀρχέλαοι, see Nagy 1990b:179–180.

The name changes involved are, however, different in that they are accompanied by structural changes: not only are the names changed (to those of nine Attic heroes and the Aeginetan hero, Aias) but the number of the φυλαί are increased to ten and their composition changed, with the demes being distributed among the ten φυλαί in such a way as to break up local allegiances (5.69.2). The results of their renaming are thus quite distinct. As Benardete puts it,

> While the tyrant gives meaningful names, the democrat gives names that have a local rather than an etymological significance; and while the tyrant attempts to alienate the people from themselves, the democrat imposes on them a stronger sense of belonging to Athens.
>
> 1969:146

Both use names and renaming as a form of social engineering.[240] The fact that Kleisthenes the Athenian is named after Kleisthenes of Sikyon (ὁμώνυμος, τὸ οὔνομα ἐπὶ τούτου ἔχων, 5.69.1) goes hand in hand with, and seems to explain, his "imitation" (ἐμιμέετο, 5.67.1) of his name changing.[241] Identity of name is intimately connected with identity of behavior: this may be seen in Herodotus' treatment of the two queens named Nitokris, one of whom is Babylonian, the other Egyptian.[242] Apart from sharing the same name, they also have in common a cunning scheme (μηχανή): both lure unsuspecting but deserving victims into a trap involving a closed space.[243] In the case of the

240 In the case of Kleisthenes of Sikyon, the engineering extends to signs of a different sort: the attempted removal of the *hêrôon* and grave of the hero Adrastos the Argive. Herodotus frames this in the same terms as the expulsion of a living person: ἐκβαλεῖν ἐκ τῆς χώρης (5.67.1), "expel from the country." Note also the control of signs of yet another sort: rhapsodic contests are stopped, because the Argos and the Argives are praised too much in the Homeric poems (5.67.1).

241 As another case of *mimêsis* cf. what Herodotus describes as Teisamenos' imitation (ἐμιμέετο, 9.34.1) of Melampous' trick in obtaining citizenship for his brother. The two do not share the same name of course, but they do share the same profession of *mantis* (see ch. 2.4). On homonymy as revelatory of a significant commonality between name-bearers cf. Munson 2005:47n83.

242 While the Egyptian Nitokris' name is attested (*Nt-ikr.ti*, 'Neith is excellent'; Lloyd 1989), there is (so far) no attestation of the name Nitokris in a Babylonian context. Asheri 2007 *ad* 1.185–187 discusses various possibilities: that this refers to Adad-guppi, mother of Nabonido, the last king of Babylon, who appears in inscriptions to have been an influential person at court; that this refers to Nebuchadnezzar (change of sex?) or to Naquî-a-Zakutun, wife of Sannacherib. It may be that comparison with the Egyptian queen reshaped the name into an identical form. In any case, it is clear that identities of name and of deed are connected in the Herodotean version.

243 Nitokris of Babylon: ἡ δ' αὐτὴ αὕτη βασίλεια καὶ ἀπάτην τοιήνδε τινὰ ἐμηχανήσατο (1.187.1), "This same queen also contrived the following plan of deception." Nitokris of Egypt: τὴν

Babylonian Nitokris, it is a trap which operates after her death: she has her tomb built into one of the city gates of Babylon with an inscription inviting any future king of Babylon to open her tomb if he be in need of money, but not to open it otherwise (1.187.1–2). When Dareios conquers the city, he is inflamed by the inscription and opens the tomb, only to find a body and a further inscription telling him that if he were not insatiate and sordidly avaricious he would not open the tombs of the dead (1.187.3–5). The Egyptian Nitokris' trap is more deadly: in order to revenge her husband, she invites his murderers to a feast in an underground chamber, which she suddenly floods with water through a hidden pipe.[244]

That the bestowal of names brings with it a corresponding change and division in reality may be seen in the relationship between the names of the gods and the gods themselves, something especially prominent in the second book of the *Histories*. The Pelasgians of old, Herodotus tells us, used to sacrifice to the gods without using any names, knowing and using only the general term θεοί, so called because of their function in establishing the kosmos (κόσμῳ θέντες, 2.52.1), until they adopted the names of the Egyptian gods with the approval of the oracle at Dodona (2.52.2–3). It seems clear that Herodotus does not mean that they simply began to use the sounds and forms of Egyptian divine names, applying them to their gods: after all, he does not think the names Artemis, Apollo, etc., are Egyptian, since he provides the actual Egyptian names of many of these deities.[245] The passage should be understood in a different sense, suggested already by Stein and Linforth and more recently persuasively defended by Burkert, whose arguments and insights will be found paraphrased here: the acquisition of the οὐνόματα of the gods involves the transference of the peculiar types, characters, and cults of the Egyptian gods (following Stein) and the mapping of this system of distinctions and divisions onto the undifferentiated θεοί of the Pelasgians.[246] That the οὔνομα of a god carries with it a

ἔλεγον τιμωρέουσαν ἀδελφεῷ ... πολλοὺς Αἰγυπτίων δόλῳ διαφθεῖραι. ποιησαμένην γάρ μιν οἴκημα περίμηκες ὑπόγαιον καινοῦν τῷ λόγῳ, νόῳ δὲ ἄλλα μηχανᾶσθαι (2.100.2–3), "They said that out of revenge for her brother ... she destroyed many of the Egyptians by a trick. For she had an enormous underground chamber built and held what was ostensibly an opening feast, but she plotted other things in her mind [*noos*]." Cf. discussion of ἀπάτη, δόλος, and μηχανή in ch. 3.1 below.

244 The Babylonian Nitokris is also renowned for her hydraulic engineering, and though this does not form part of her trap, it does form part of her defense of the city (1.185–186).

245 Zeus=Amun (2.42.5); Apollo=Horos (2.144.2; 2.156); Dionysos=Osiris (2.42.2; 2.144.2); Demeter=Isis (2.59.2; 2.156.1); Artemis=Boubastis (2.137.5; 2.156); Pan=Mendes (3.46.3); Epaphos=Apis (2.153.2). See the table in Harrison 2000:210–211 for a full list of Herodotus' equations of Greek and foreign gods.

246 Stein 1889–1896 *ad loc.*; Linforth 1924:283–286; Burkert 1985a. Cf. Harrison 2000:251–264 for

recognition of the existence and distinctive character of that god is clear from another passage in book 2, where Herodotus says that the Egyptians do not know the *names* of Poseidon or the Dioskouroi:

> Αἰγύπτιοι οὔτε Ποσειδέωνος οὔτε Διοσκούρων τὰ οὐνόματά φασι εἰδέναι, οὐδέ σφι θεοὶ οὗτοι ἐν τοῖσι ἄλλοισι θεοῖσι ἀποδεδέχαται.
>
> 2.43.2
>
> The Egyptians deny any knowledge of the names of either Poseidon or the Dioskouroi, and say that these gods have not been received among the other gods.

Ignorance of their names goes together with the fact that there is no place for them in the Egyptian pantheon. In addition, according to Herodotus, the names of Hera, Hestia, Themis, the Kharites, and the Nereidai are unknown to the Egyptians (2.50.2): the implication is that the deities themselves are not worshiped either and that the Egyptians do not have divisions in their system of gods corresponding to the bearers of these names. Furthermore, Herodotus says that all these gods were named by the Pelasgians, except Poseidon, and this god they learned of from the Libyans:

> τῶν δὲ οὔ φασι θεῶν γινώσκειν τὰ οὐνόματα, οὗτοι δέ μοι δοκέουσι ὑπὸ Πελασγῶν ὀνομασθῆναι, πλὴν Ποσειδέωνος. τοῦτον δὲ τὸν θεὸν παρὰ Λιβύων ἐπύθοντο· οὐδαμοὶ γὰρ ἀπ' ἀρχῆς Ποσειδέωνος οὔνομα ἔκτηνται εἰ μὴ Λίβυες, καὶ τιμῶσι τὸν θεὸν τοῦτον αἰεί.
>
> 2.50.2

a reexamination of the question with further bibliography. I am unconvinced by Harrison's objections to the broader significance of the term οὔνομα in the sense of a place or category to which a name corresponds. He argues (253), for example, that at 2.43.1–4 "it is surely very unlikely that he could mean that the Greeks picked up from the Egyptians 'the practice of giving a name' to a mortal already recognized as an individual." But it does not seem unlikely at all if one understands by οὔνομα 'place or category to which a name corresponds': it is Harrison's particular phrasing "the practice of giving a name" that makes the proposition unlikely. His conclusion is that the passage must mean that Herodotus really thought that the Greeks did borrow the Egyptian names, but that these names underwent significant change after they were borrowed (264): "The names of the gods that came from Egypt might, in Herodotus' view, have arrived in a rather different form from that in which he knew them in his own day." This is, I suppose, a possible theory, but an unnecessary and unlikely one, and requires one to believe that Herodotus could consider that from e.g. Boubastis the name Artemis came about a result of a series of phonological changes. Harrison cites (264n52) in support of this idea Hekataios FGH 1 F 21 (the Phoenicians pronounce Danaë as Dana), but this phonological change is nowhere near as extreme as the changes required to produce Artemis from Boubastis.

> Those gods whose names they claim not to know seem to me to have been named by the Pelasgians, with the exception of Poseidon. This god they learnt of from the Libyans: for no one else except for the Libyans has used the name of Poseidon right from the start, and they have always worshiped this god.

So Poseidon was *named* by the Libyans: but then Herodotus says they learned of *the god* (he does not say *name*) from the Libyans. To learn the name of a god is to also to recognize his existence as a distinct entity and recipient of cult: in one sentence Herodotus can say that the Libyans named Poseidon, and in another that they gave the knowledge of the god himself to the Pelasgians. It is in this sense that the Pelasgians, and thus the Hellenes, took the names of the gods from the Egyptians: as Burkert puts it, we are not dealing with the individual and precise correspondence of phonemes, but the fact that one system of signification and meaning clearly reflects another.[247] Burkert links Herodotus' statement about the origin of the names of the gods (οὐνόματα τῶν θεῶν) with another passage in the *Histories* where Herodotus uses οὐνόματα in a context of dividing and defining. Herodotus cannot understand (συμβαλέσθαι, 4.45.1) amongst other things why there should be three names (Europa, Libya, and Asia) for what is one undifferentiated object, the earth (ἐπ' ὅτεο μιῇ ἐούσῃ γῇ οὐνόματα τριφάσια κεῖται, 4.45.1).[248] He does not believe that the divisions made by the names correspond to any divisions in reality. From this it appears that for each name there ought to exist an appropriate category, an approach which Burkert rightly says must be viewed against the background of contemporary fifth-century speculation about the philosophy of language and the belief in the natural and correct relationship between signifier and signified. Burkert compares two passages from Anaxagoras and the Derveni Papyrus in which the actions of differentiation and naming are clearly linked.[249] Herodotus on one occasion draws attention to a certain correctness

247 Burkert 1985a:130: "Es geht nicht um einzelne, punktuelle Entsprechung von Lautgebilden, sondern darum, dass ein System von Bedeutungen ein anderes eindeutig abbildet."

248 As with the other instances of συμβάλλεσθαι discussed in ch. 1.3.1 above, the verb is used in the context of matching the signifier to referent.

249 Anaxagoras, DK 59 A 52 (Aristotle *Physics* 187b2): διό φασι πᾶν ἐν παντὶ μεμῖχθαι, διότι πᾶν ἐκ παντὸς ἑώρων γιγνόμενον· φαίνεσθαι δὲ διαφέροντα καὶ προσαγορεύεσθαι ἕτερα ἀλλήλων ἐκ τοῦ μάλισθ' ὑπερέχοντος διὰ πλῆθος ἐν τῇ μίξει τῶν ἀπείρων, "For this reason [all writers on nature say] that everything was mixed up in everything else, because they saw that everything came from everything. But things appear different one from another and are called different things on the basis of the thing that predominates in terms of quantity in the mixture of limitless things." Derveni Papyrus col. XVII 13–14 (*ZPE* 47 [1982]): ἦμ μὲγ γ[ὰρ καὶ πρ]όσθεν, ὠνομάσθη δὲ γενέσ[θαι] ἐπεὶ διεκρίθ[η. Burkert's (1985a:129) translation: "Die Dinge

or rightness (ὀρθότης) in the relationship between name and bearer which is reminiscent of the doctrine of the "correctness" of names mentioned above: in relaying the Scythian names of various divinities, he comments that Zeus is most correctly called Papaios in Scythian (ὀνομάζεται δὲ σκυθιστὶ ... Ζεὺς ... ὀρθότατα κατὰ γνώμην γε τὴν ἐμὴν καλεόμενος, Παπαῖος, 4.59.2). The name probably suggests to Herodotus πάππας ('papa', e.g. *Odyssey* 6.57) and so Zeus' role as father of gods and men. In this sense, the application of the name Papaios to the deity reflects the nature of the god accurately, and so is "correct."[250]

2.6.2 Transmission of Names

So much for the assignation and bestowal of names, the primary act of signification when signifier is attached to referent. Let us now consider the secondary act of signification, the transmission of names by figures in the *Histories* and by Herodotus himself as narrator, in whose hands the ultimate control of the channel of communication lies. Herodotus' narrative power over the transmission of names will be discussed shortly, but for the moment we consider the control exercised by figures within the work. The instances under consideration all have to do with the suppression of the transmission of names. The desire for suppression results from the close connection between the name as signifier and the bearer of the name. Just as the meaning of a name may act on the bearer, whether positively (Peisistratos, 5.65.4) or negatively (the names of the tribes given by Kleisthenes of Sikyon, 5.68.1–2), so too the actions of the bearer may be seen to act upon the name, investing it with associations both good and ill. Names may inspire such fear and hatred through recollection of the actions of the bearer that they become subject to suppression. Because of such a hatred (ὑπὸ μίσεος, 2.128), the Egyptians refuse to mention the names of Kheops and Khephren, during whose combined reign of 106 years every type of ill befell the Egyptians and the temple precincts remained closed. They

---

waren schon vorher da, die Benennung aber, dass sie geworden seien, erhielten sie, als sie sich abgesondert hatten." Creation and naming occur together, for example, in Herodotus' description of Arion, inventor of the dithyramb, who is described as διθύραμβον πρῶτον ἀνθρώπων τῶν ἡμεῖς ἴδμεν ποιήσαντά τε καὶ ὀνομάσαντα καὶ διδάξαντα ἐν Κορίνθῳ (1.23), "the first man we know of to have created, named, and produced a dithyramb in Corinth." The actions of invention (ποιήσαντα) and naming (ὀνομάσαντα) form a unit joined by the conjunctions τε and καί, with the second καί joining the activity of performance (διδάξαντα) to that of composition.

250 Cf. Munson 2005:43–46 on the idea of the correctness of names in Herodotus and in fifth-century thought about language.

accordingly say that the pyramids of these kings belong to a local herdsman, Philitis, who used to pasture his animals in the area (2.128). By so doing, the Egyptians frustrate the intentions of those who built these pyramids, since they are no longer monuments to them and no longer perpetuate their name and memory.[251] This is not all that the Egyptians do, since besides simply suppressing the names of Kheops and Khephren and denying them recognition after death, they actively insult them by attaching to their magnificent monuments the name of one on the opposite end of the social scale, a mere herdsman.

Hatred for past deeds is according to Herodotus the reason why Carian women married to Ionians did not address their husbands by name (or eat with them):

> διὰ τοῦτον δὲ τὸν φόνον αἱ γυναῖκες αὗται νόμον θέμεναι σφίσι αὐτῇσι ὅρκους ἐπήλασαν καὶ παρέδοσαν τῇσι θυγατράσι μή κοτε ὁμοσιτῆσαι τοῖσι ἀνδράσι μηδὲ οὐνόματι βῶσαι τὸν ἑωυτῆς ἄνδρα, τοῦδε εἵνεκα ὅτι ἐφόνευσαν σφέων τοὺς πατέρας καὶ ἄνδρας καὶ παῖδας καὶ ἔπειτε ταῦτα ποιήσαντες αὐτῇσι συνοίκεον.
>
> 1.146
>
> On account of this killing [by the first Ionian settlers in Karia], these women, instituting a custom amongst themselves, swore and handed down to their daughters oaths that they would never take food together with their husbands and would never address their husband by name out loud, because they had slain their fathers, husbands, and children, and having done so, had taken them as wives.

Name taboo may lie behind Herodotus' curious report of a Libyan tribe, the Atarantes, who are said to be the only people who are without names (ἀνώνυμοι, 4.184.1). It is not that the tribe as a whole has no name, merely that they do not have personal names (ἑνὶ δὲ ἑκάστῳ αὐτῶν οὔνομα οὐδὲν κεῖται, 4.184.1). Herodotus suggests no reason for this (just as he has no further comment on the Libyan tribe that has no dreams, 4.184.4) but behind it may lie the practice of name-avoidance, attested in several cultures, and in particular among the Tibbus, a people living in the Tibesti range, the very area which Herodotus is describing here.[252]

[251] For the pyramid as a means to perpetuate the glory and name of its builder (μνημόσυνον), cf. e.g. 2.136.3–4 (pyramid of Asykhis) and discussion below, ch. 2.8.

[252] Carpenter 1956:237, following a report of the German explorer Nachtigal (from 1869): "A Tibbu married woman (who, like the Carian women in Herodotus, may not eat with her husband)

Prohibition of a different sort may be encountered in regard to names of divinities, where the divine name is so closely identified with its divine bearer that it becomes the subject of religious taboo. Herodotus subjects himself to such a prohibition concerning the name of Osiris, but in a limited fashion. Since he preserves the name of Osiris a number of times in both its Egyptian form (2.42.2, 2.144.2, 2.156.4) and its Greek "translation," Dionysos (e.g. 2.144.2), it is not a question of an outright *Namenverbot*. What is at issue is the context in which the god is mentioned. Herodotus suppresses the name in four instances: when mentioning the festival of Isis in Bousiris, during which tens of thousands beat their breasts for one whom "it is not holy for me to mention" (οὔ μοι ὅσιόν ἐστι λέγειν, 2.61.1); when describing the costliest form of mummy decoration, which represents "the one whom I do not consider it holy to name in such a matter" (τοῦ οὐκ ὅσιον ποιεῦμαι τὸ οὔνομα ἐπὶ τοιούτῳ πρήγματι ὀνομάζειν, 2.86.2); when talking of the statue of the kneeling cow at Sais which is brought out every year "when the Egyptians beat their breasts for the god who is not named by me in such a matter" (τὸν οὐκ ὀνομαζόμενον θεὸν ὑπ' ἐμέο ἐπὶ τοιούτῳ πρήγματι, 2.132.2); and when he describes tombs in the precinct of the temple of Athena of "the one whose name I consider it not holy to pronounce in connection with such a matter" (τοῦ οὐκ ὅσιον ποιεῦμαι ἐπὶ τοιούτῳ πρήγματι ἐξαγορεύειν τοὔνομα, 2.170.1). In all of these passages it is clear that the prohibition (οὐκ ὅσιον) is on mentioning Osiris' name, which is replaced by a tabu periphrasis, either in the form of an extended articular phrase (τὸν οὐκ ὀνομαζόμενον θεὸν ὑπ' ἐμέο ἐπὶ τοιούτῳ πρήγματι, 2.132.2) or a relative clause (τοῦ οὐκ ὅσιον ποιεῦμαι τὸ οὔνομα ἐπὶ τοιούτῳ πρήγματι ὀνομάζειν, 2.86.2). This occurs precisely in connection with the death of Osiris and the mourning for him at religious festivals in his or Isis' honor, a connection Herodotus paraphrases with an expression which itself is a circumlocution, ἐπὶ τοιούτῳ πρήγματι ("in connection with such a matter," 2.170.1).[253]

---

turns her face away when she speaks to her man and will not utter his name in the presence of others. Save in direst emergencies, the woman's sisters and parents will not allow the man's name to pass their lips. In consequence, when a young man marries, his name is thenceforth so seldom uttered that it virtually disappears, to be replaced by some circumlocution." Parallels in other cultures: the practice of *isihlonipho* among the Xhosa of South Africa, where a new wife may not use words containing any syllable of her husband's name or those of his family (Finlayson 1995); North and South American Indian practices described in Austin 1972:3.

253 There is no need to speculate on Herodotus' reasons for silence beyond his own statement that it is not holy to mention the name of the god in these circumstances, "an unmistakable religious scruple" as Linforth puts it (1924:281). Lateiner (1989:65), however, treats these passages together with places where Herodotus will not relay ἱροὶ λόγοι ('sacred accounts': 2.46–48; 2.51; 2.62; 2.65; 2.81) and calls his reticence "an elegant excuse for avoiding an excursus into the irrelevant." Leaving aside the question of the ἱροὶ λόγοι, it does not appear irrelevant to

That Herodotus exercises a conscious choice in this activity will be shown shortly, but first a brief look at the implications of the retransmission of names. To mention a name in a public context is to reactivate and perpetuate the actions of the bearer of that name. This is the concern of epic and praise poetry, the due recognition and transmission of the glorious actions of men (κλέα ἀνδρῶν), in the case of epic those of the remote past, and in the case of praise poetry, those of the present as well. Both perpetuate the fame and glory of men (*kleos*) through the medium of poetry, which acts as intangible monument, recollecting and transmitting the *kleos* of the hero or *laudandus* every time it is performed. Herodotus follows in this tradition. Already in the prooemium to his work he shows his concern that the great deeds (ἔργα μεγάλα) of men not become without *kleos* (μήτε . . . ἀκλέα γένηται, proem). This is also seen in places where Herodotus makes it a point to preserve the names of those who have "shown great deeds" (ἀποδέξασθαι) and "become brave men" (ἄνδρες ἀγαθοὶ γενόμενοι).[254] After each of the great battles described in the *Histories*, Herodotus devotes attention to relaying the names of those who were the most distinguished in the action (ἄριστοι): for example, after his description of the battles of Marathon (6.114), Artemision (8.17), Thermopylai (7.224–228), Salamis (8.93), and Plataiai (9.71–75). The proper assignment and perpetuation of *kleos* necessarily involves the recollection of names, which act as focal points for *kleos*, ensuring that it reaches the appropriate recipient.[255] Name and *kleos* may become so intimately connected that a certain name, because of its association with the *kleos* of a previous bearer, is bestowed on a subsequent bearer in an attempt to harness the predecessor's *kleos*.[256]

mention directly the name of Dionysos-Osiris in the four instances discussed, something that would take up less space that the circumlocutions Herodotus resorts to. For examples of tabu periphrasis as a phenomenon in descriptions of ritual, cf. Nagy's study of the fire ritual of the Atiedian Brethren, 1990a:164–170.

254 ἔργον + ἀποδείκνυσθαι: 1.16.2; 1.59.4; 1.174.1; 2.10.3; 3.134.3; 3.155.6; 6.15.1; 7.139.3; 8.17; 8.89.2; 8.90.4; 8.91; 9.71.3; 9.72.2; 9.72.3. ἀπόδειξις of ἔργα: 2.101.1. ἀνὴρ ἀγαθὸς γενέσθαι: 1.95.2; 1.169.1; 5.2.1; 5.109.3; 6.14.1; 6.14.3; 6.114; 6.117.2; 7.53.1; 9.17.4; 9.71.3; 9.75. On the meaning of *apodexis* in Herodotus, cf. Bakker 2002.

255 Thus Odysseus cannot help but shout his real name as he makes his escape from Polyphemos (*Odyssey* 9.502–5) so that *kleos* for his ingenious and daring exploits in the cave may be recognized as his alone. The episode simultaneously reveals the other use that names may be put to, namely as focal points for curses, since it is through his knowledge of Odysseus' true name that Polyphemos is able to tell his father Poseidon who is responsible for putting out his eye and so ensure that Poseidon's wrath will fall upon Odysseus. Cf. Austin 1972:4 on name magic in the *Odyssey*.

256 Hippokrates names his son Peisistratos the Athenian in memory of (ἀπεμνημόνευσε, 5.65.4) the son of Nestor. Note the use of the μνημ- stem and the idea of the name as monument activating *kleos*. As we have seen, Kleisthenes the Athenian is named after his Sicyonian grandfather and in fact "imitates" his actions. Cf. Svenbro 1993:77: "The name of Cleisthenes the Athenian was

The verbs used by Herodotus for the recollection and mentioning of names (μνῶμαι, ἐπιμνῶμαι, παραμνῶμαι, μνήμην ποιεῦμαι) all bear the same root that is found in words describing physical monuments and funerary markers (μνῆμα, μνημήιον, μνημόσυνον), and so Herodotus' text in those places where he mentions names using these verbs may be said to constitute a verbal monument in itself.[257] In several places he consciously draws attention to the mentioning of names in his work, especially when passing over the mention of certain people in favor of others.[258] Thus, in moving his narrative from Gyges to Ardys, Herodotus says:

> ἀλλ' οὐδὲν γὰρ μέγα ἀπ' αὐτοῦ ἄλλο ἔργον ἐγένετο βασιλεύσαντος δυῶν δέοντα τεσσεράκοντα ἔτεα, τοῦτον μὲν παρήσομεν τοσαῦτα ἐπιμνησθέντες, Ἄρδυος δὲ τοῦ Γύγεω μετὰ Γύγην βασιλεύσαντος μνήμην ποιήσομαι.
>
> 1.15
>
> But because no other great deed was done by him in his reign of thirty-eight years, we will bypass him after mentioning this much about him, and I will make mention of Ardys, son of Gyges, who came to power after Gyges.

---

at once a *mnêma* and a hope; when spoken aloud, the name evoked the memory of Cleisthenes the Sicyonian, the grandfather whom it was necessary to resemble. And, Herodotus tells us, Cleisthenes 'did imitate [*emiméeto*] his maternal grandfather, Cleisthenes' in the realm of political organization. The hope to which the name testified was thus realized." Cf. also Samios, the name of the son of Arkhias the Spartan who died fighting (ἀριστεύσας ἐτελεύτησε) on Samos (3.55.1–2) and Svenbro 1993:78 on this: "Far from being an indication of the ethnic origin of its bearer . . . the name Samios here sums up the most glorious of the exploits of the Spartan Archias, Samios' father. Each time that Samios is addressed by name, the *kléos* of his father resounds."

257 On this idea, cf. Immerwahr 1960 and Bakker 2002:26. For an instance of a verbal utterance directly characterized by Herodotus as a μνημόσυνον, cf. the *bon mot* of Dienekes the Spartan: if the hail of Persian arrows will block out the sun, then at least the fighting will be in the shade. Herodotus goes on to say: ταῦτα μὲν καὶ ἄλλα τοιουτότροπα ἔπεά φασι Διηνέκεα τὸν Λακεδαιμόνιον λιπέσθαι μνημόσυνα (7.226.2), "They say that these and other like utterances Dienekes the Spartan left as a monument for himself." Cf. Bakker 2002:26 and Hollmann 2000 on the use of the term *epos* in Herodotus. The concept of the μνημόσυνον is further discussed in ch. 2.8. On μνῆμα as funerary marker and tomb, cf. Henrichs 1993:171–172 and references there.

258 This may also be illustrated by the expression ὀνομαστός, 'renowned', applied to someone whose actions are worthy enough for his name to be mentioned. Thus at 7.224.1 Herodotus mentions other Spartans besides Leonidas who are ὀνομαστοί and says he has found out their names (and those of all three hundred of the Spartans who fell at Thermopylai), even if he does not mention them. At 7.98 he does however list the names of those fighting on Persian vessels who were most worthy of mention (ὀνομαστότατοι).

In talking of the predecessors of Sesostris he says:

> παραμειψάμενος ὦν τούτους τοῦ ἐπὶ τούτοισι γενομένου βασιλέος, τῷ οὔνομα ἦν Σέσωστρις, τούτου μνήμην ποιήσομαι.
>
> 2.102.1
>
> Passing these by, I will make mention of the king who came to power after them, whose name was Sesostris.

He may also express his discretion and freedom in mentioning the names of some but not others by saying that he is under no compulsion (ἀνάγκη) to mention the names of all. So, for example, in his discussion of the commanders of ships and infantry on the Persian side, he says the following:

> τούτοισι πᾶσι καὶ τοῖσι ἐς τὸν πεζὸν τεταγμένοισι αὐτῶν ἐπῆσαν ἑκάστοισι ἐπιχώριοι ἡγεμόνες, τῶν ἐγώ, οὐ γὰρ ἀναγκαίῃ ἐξέργομαι ἐς ἱστορίης λόγον, οὐ παραμέμνημαι· οὔτε γὰρ ἔθνεος ἑκάστου ἐπάξιοι ἦσαν οἱ ἡγεμόνες, ἔν τε ἔθνεϊ ἑκάστῳ ὅσαι περ πόλιες τοσοῦτοι καὶ ἡγεμόνες ἦσαν.
>
> 7.96.1
>
> Each of these [units], including those assigned to the infantry, had native commanders, whom I will not mention, since I am not under compulsion to include them in the account of my research: for not every nation had commanders worthy of mention, and amongst every nation there were as many commanders as there were cities.

For the same reason, he will not mention (οὐ παραμέμνημαι, 7.99.1) the names of all the commanders of ships, but will single out Artemisia.[259]

Just as Herodotus, by being the ultimate conduit for the transmission of names, is in a position to select and then pass on the names of the worthy, he also has the power to exclude the unworthy from his narrative by refusing to transmit their names. Those excluded by Herodotus may be unworthy of mention for reasons other than the absence of remarkable and outstanding deeds. We have already seen in ch. 1.2.1.2 Herodotus' deliberate omission of the names of the three Greeks who proposed theories about the flooding of the

259 Other instances: Herodotus can catalog (καταλέξαι, 8.85.2) the names of many of the commanders of the Greek ships, but will mention only Theomestor, son of Androdamas, and Phylakos, son of Histiaios; he will omit the names of other Egyptian kings, except for that of Moiris, because they displayed no great works (οὐδεμίαν ἔργων ἀπόδεξιν, 2.101.1), and pass on to Sesostris (τούτου μνήμην ποιήσομαι, 2.101.2).

Nile in summer, and how Herodotus by not transmitting their names refuses to contribute to their desire to become famous for their σοφίη:

> ἀλλὰ Ἑλλήνων μέν τινες ἐπίσημοι βουλόμενοι γενέσθαι σοφίην ἔλεξαν περὶ τοῦ ὕδατος τούτου τριφασίας ὁδούς, τῶν τὰς μὲν δύο οὐκ ἀξιῶ μνησθῆναι εἰ μὴ ὅσον σημῆναι βουλόμενος μοῦνον.
>
> 2.20.1
>
> But some Greeks, wanting to be marked out for their ingenuity, relate three paths of explanation concerning this water, of which two I do not deem worthy of mention, except for those parts I am willing to indicate.

Rendering one's opponents anonymous while at the same time criticizing their ideas is one of the chief weapons in the arsenal of any polemicist. Herodotus also refuses to transmit the names of certain Greeks who pass off as their own doctrines about the immortality of the soul and reincarnation, which the Egyptians thought of a long time before them:

> τούτῳ τῷ λόγῳ εἰσὶ οἳ Ἑλλήνων ἐχρήσαντο, οἱ μὲν πρότερον, οἱ δὲ ὕστερον, ὡς ἰδίῳ ἑωυτῶν ἐόντι· τῶν ἐγὼ εἰδὼς τὰ οὐνόματα οὐ γράφω.
>
> 2.123.3
>
> There are certain Greeks who have made use of this doctrine, some further back in time, others more recently, as if it were their own: though I know their names, I [will] not write them down [here].

The suppression of names is an attempt to distribute credit (and *kleos*) where it is due, but also throws Herodotus' own contribution, the recognition that these are in fact Egyptian beliefs, into relief, a tactic we have seen in the previous example. In the case of the Delphian who attaches an inscription claiming the Spartans as dedicants of a golden lustral basin that is actually a gift of Kroisos (1.51.4), and the Samian who seizes the property that the eunuch of Sataspes has absconded with upon learning of his master's execution (4.43.7), Herodotus stresses that he perfectly well knows the name of the person responsible (τοῦ ἐπιστάμενος τὸ οὔνομα, 1.51.4, 4.43.7), but will not mention it (οὐκ ἐπιμνήσομαι, 1.51.4; ἑκὼν ἐπιλήθομαι, 4.43.7). Here I think suppression cannot simply be termed "a purposive desire to consign a small, foul act to oblivion."[260] For how can Herodotus assign an act to oblivion precisely by

[260] Lateiner 1989:69. Cf. Dewald 1987:165.

relating it in his *Histories*? It is rather the agents who are consigned to oblivion, perhaps not because of any distaste on Herodotus' part.[261] The effect of the omissions is to draw attention to the narrator's position of superior knowledge by the very act of his withholding the names.

All those whose names Herodotus does not formally mention suffer the fate that he fights against in the introduction to his work: their achievements become without *kleos* (ἀκλεᾶ), and, by extension, they themselves become ἀκλέες. That names are powerful signs is shown by the place they occupy in the *Histories* and the way they are used by the figures within the work, but especially by Herodotus himself, their ultimate interpreter, transmitter, and controller.

[261] *Pace* Lateiner 1989:69, I do not think ἑκὼν ἐπιλήθομαι can mean 'gladly forget'. It is simply the functional equivalent of οὐκ ἐπιμνήσομαι ('I will not make mention of'). The qualification ἑκών stresses that it is a conscious, voluntary omission (not a lapse of memory, in other words), and ἐπιλήθομαι here means only 'I do not mention', not 'I forget', just as ἐπιμνήσομαι, in this context, means 'I shall mention', not 'I shall remember'. For λαθ- as an equivalent of οὐ μνη-, or οὐ λαθ- as an equivalent of μνη-, cf. Nagy 1990a:210n22.

2.7 Action, Ritual, and Gesture as Signs

THE ACTIONS, RITUAL, AND GESTURES OF HUMAN BEINGS can act as bearers of meaning which call for interpretation as much as any portent or oracle.[262] In Herodotus' work we are constantly reminded of this in a number of ways.[263] To begin with, there is the sheer number of and variety in the customs of the *ethnea* that populate the *Histories*. Each group has its own set of *nomoi*, codes of behavior according to which certain actions assume certain significances among that group. The link between the action as signifier and what the action signifies among that people rests on convention (*nomos*): νόμος πάντων βασιλεύς ("king of all is custom"), as Herodotus says, roughly quoting Pindar (fr. 169 S.-M.). The context of Herodotus' remark shows both the universal power which *nomos* exerts over each society and, more importantly, that the content of *nomos* is not identical from group to group. He demonstrates this by recalling Dareios' famous experiment, in which he assembled Greeks and Indians and asked the former for what price they would eat their dead parents and the latter at what price they would burn theirs. The answer: a resounding refusal from both sides, the Indians crying out and

262 By "action" I have in mind any kind of human activity considered apart from speech. "Ritual" and "gesture" are considered as subcategories of the blanket term "action," both involving action of a formalized nature used and recognized by a particular group. "Gesture" may of course at times form part of "ritual" but may also be used spontaneously. Under "ritual" I will here consider δρώμενα ('things done') rather than λεγόμενα ('things said'). For ritual considered as a sign system, cf. Burkert 1979:35–58, esp. 48–49. Bibliographical references to studies on non-verbal behavior in Lateiner 1987 and Nöth 1990.

263 Lateiner (1987) is the first to have recognized and collected these Herodotean instances under the rubric of what he has termed non-verbal communication. He does not distinguish, however, between types and levels of communication (for example, non-verbal communication between figures in the *Histories* as opposed to communication between author and audience by means of the description of non-verbal signs). Each instance he lists is a *potential* act of communication, but he does not show whether it actually functions as such in the text. There is nothing to suggest, for example, that suicide (Lateiner's category II.Z, 114) is presented as an act of communication in the *Histories* (*pace* Lateiner 1987:93).

bidding him be silent (3.38.4). As Munson (2005:76–77) notes, there are in fact three different cultural codes used in this dialogue:

> a linguistic code, a code of communication (how things are said, including expressions and gestures), and a code of customs, the last representing the substance of the discourse. . . . In this narrative, the cultural codes of communication stand out. The Persian Darius expresses himself in monetary terms, similar to those of his Lydian predecessor Croesus [1.86.4]. . . . The Greeks respond, as we would say, in a "normal" way, and answer the question courtroom-style in the same terms in which it is asked. The Indians (and this is an orientalistic detail) display emotion. As for the code of customs, what the three parties are talking about is funeral rites, in which again each differs from the other two. Finally, the reference to interpreters draws attention to the languages—Persian, Greek and Callatian—specifying that the Greeks had the means to understand *these* codes, and that this item of difference is the least problematic of all. At the level of the *nomoi*, sacred to the ones and repulsive to the others, the exchange reaches a dead end. *Cultural* translation is difficult when people find difference from themselves disturbing.

2.7.1 Reading Encounters

Many more examples could be cited for the relativity of *nomos* in Herodotus, but let us concentrate first on a number of passages in which he describes the moment of encounter between different peoples and the aporia which the encounter produces (generally experienced by only one of the two parties). These examples demonstrate how Herodotus applies to the reading of human action verbs that he uses elsewhere to describe the interpretation of signs.

Xerxes experiences a problem in finding the correct connection (συμβαλέσθαι, 7.208.3) between Spartan behavior and the significance of that behavior when he hears from a spy who is observing the Greek encampment at Thermopylai that the Spartans are sitting outside their defensive wall, exercising and combing their hair. Here Herodotus uses the verb συμβάλλομαι of Xerxes' failure to decode their behavior correctly. To the latter, it only seems to indicate absurdity (γελοῖα), but, as Herodotus and then Demaratos (7.209.3) tell us, it is actually a sign that they are preparing for battle to the death:

> ἀκούων δὲ Ξέρξης οὐκ εἶχε συμβαλέσθαι τὸ ἐόν, ὅτι παρεσκευάζοντο ὡς ἀπολεόμενοί τε καὶ ἀπολέοντες κατὰ δύναμιν· ἀλλ' αὐτῷ γελοῖα γὰρ ἐφαίνοντο ποιέειν, μετεπέμψατο Δημάρητον τὸν Ἀρίστωνος.
>
> 7.209.1
>
> When Xerxes heard this he could not comprehend [their behavior] for what it was, namely that they were preparing themselves to be killed and to kill with all their might: because to him they appeared to be doing ridiculous things, he sent for Demaratos son of Ariston.

When the Persians first encounter the Greek style of hoplite warfare at Marathon, they are at a loss to interpret their tactics: the Athenians are few in number, and they advance at a run, without the covering support of cavalry or archers. This the Persians can only construe as destructive madness (μανίην . . . πάγχυ ὀλεθρίην, 6.112.2).[264] Here the only thing such actions can signify in the Persians' eyes is behavior devoid of sense.

The actions of unfamiliar peoples may challenge interpretation and result in aporia in contacts between different groups, but action itself in the form of gesture may also form a deliberate means of communication between parties who cannot communicate with linguistic or written signs. Mutual unintelligibility of language or distance may make communication by linguistic means impossible or impractical. In Herodotus' account of the origins of the Sauromatai, for example, the Scythian youth and Amazon maiden who meet and have sex have no other means of communication between them save sign language:[265]

> καὶ φωνῆσαι μὲν οὐκ εἶχε (οὐ γὰρ συνίεσαν ἀλλήλων), τῇ δὲ χειρὶ ἔφραζε ἐς τὴν ὑστεραίην ἐλθεῖν ἐς τὠυτὸ χωρίον καὶ ἕτερον ἄγειν, σημαίνουσα δύο γενέσθαι, καὶ αὐτὴ ἑτέρην ἄξειν.
>
> 4.113.2
>
> She was not able to speak (for they did not understand one another), but with her hand she indicated that he should come to the same

264 The verb used of the Persians' reading is κατεικάζω: for the simplex εἰκάζω as one of the verbs characteristically used of sign interpretation by the conjectural matching of signifier to signified, cf. ch. 1.3.3 above.

265 Cf. Aeschylus *Agamemnon* 1060–1061 (Klytemnestra to Kassandra): εἰ δ' ἀξυνήμων οὖσα μὴ δέχῃ λόγον | σὺ δ' ἀντὶ φωνῆς φράζε καρβάνῳ χερί, "If you do not understand and cannot comprehend this speech, signify as much with foreign hand instead of voice."

> spot the following day and bring another with him, signifying there should be two, and that she would bring another with her.

The verbs φράζω and σημαίνω are already familiar as verbs describing the transmission of a message by signs (cf. ch. 1.2.1, 1.2.2 above). As Munson (2005:73) points out, "Just as sex replaces war, here the universal language of gestures overcomes the language barrier." Non-linguistic signs also solve the problem of distance: while the range of linguistic signs is limited, because with increasing distance words can no longer be distinguished and perceived clearly, the non-linguistic sign can travel further.[266] The signals used by heralds to communicate orders to troops, a puff of smoke, or the showing of a shield are all detectable at a much greater distance.[267]

Such signals do, however, carry with them their own problems. In the case of military signals, the very fact that they are audible or visible for some distance means that one's opponents are also in a position to detect them and decipher the code according to which signal is paired with signifier. This is the problem that Kleomenes faces in his campaign against the Argives. By observation, the Argives, who are encamped near the Spartans, quickly determine the link between the signals used by the Spartan heralds and the responses of the soldiers, and use this knowledge to match their own movements to those

266 The problem of distance, as well as secrecy, is solved in another way while still relying on (written) linguistic signs during the siege of Poteidaia by the Persians. The traitor Timoxeinos, operating within the city, and Artabazos, the Persian general in charge of the siege, communicate with each other by wrapping messages around arrows and shooting them into an agreed-upon place (8.128.1). The plan goes awry when the arrow ceases to function as carrier of signs but resumes its natural function of weapon: Artabazos misses the target and hits one of the citizens instead (8.128.2). For arrows functioning as significant objects themselves, cf. 4.131–132 (arrows as part of message from Scythians to Dareios) and ch. 2.8.

267 Instances of σημαίνω applied to signals in a military context listed in ch. 1.2.1.1 above. The Phoenician traders who travel beyond the Pillars of Herakles signal their arrival to the locals by a puff of smoke (4.196.1). They use other non-linguistic signs (objects: cf. ch. 2.8 below) to communicate with the inhabitants: placing their wares on the beach, they retreat to their ships, while the natives come forward, inspect the goods and leave what they consider to be an appropriate amount of gold next to them. They retreat in turn, the Phoenicians come forward, take the gold and leave the goods if they agree, or leave both if they desire more. Neither cheats the other. A shield is shown at Marathon to the Persian ships as a message to set sail for Athens at once in order to take it before the Athenian army returns (6.115, 6.121–124). A problem revolves around the question of the transmitter of the sign since the sign is transmitted in such a way that the transmitter remains concealed: ἀνεδέχθη μὲν γὰρ ἀσπίς, καὶ τοῦτο οὐκ ἔστι ἄλλως εἰπεῖν· ἐγένετο γάρ· ὃς μέντοι ἦν ὁ ἀναδέξας, οὐκ ἔχω προσωτέρω εἰπεῖν τούτων (6.124.2), "Now a shield was shown, and there is no other way of saying this, for it *did* happen: but who the person was that showed it, I cannot say further than this." Herodotus defends the Alkmaionidai against accusations that it was they who showed the shield. Cf. discussion of other uses of shields in sign communication in ch. 2.8 below.

of the Spartans, mirroring whatever they do (6.77.3). But Kleomenes changes the conventional correspondence between signifier and signified, so that the signal which previously meant breakfast now means "Attack!" and in this way the Argives, who react in accordance with the old code, find themselves surprised and attacked by the Spartans at breakfast (6.78.1–2).[268]

2.7.2 Actions as Encoded Message

Actions constitute a deliberately encoded message in Thrasyboulos' reply to Periandros' question about how best to secure his tyranny. Thrasyboulos' answer is well known: he takes Periandros' messenger into a cornfield and proceeds to dock any ear of corn which stands above the rest until he has rid the whole field of the finest and tallest of the crop (5.92.ζ.2). His reply does not consist of any utterance (ὑποθέμενος ἔπος οὐδέν, 5.92.ζ.3) but lies entirely in a set of actions, which the messenger, accustomed to conveying messages based on linguistic signs, whether spoken or written, is not able to recognize as meaningful signs. As with the Persians when they view the tactics of the Athenians for the first time and consider this destructive madness (6.112.2), the gestures seem senseless:

> ὁ δὲ οὐδέν οἱ ἔφη Θρασύβουλον ὑποθέσθαι, θωμάζειν τε αὐτοῦ παρ' οἷόν μιν ἄνδρα ἀποπέμψειε, ὡς παραπλῆγά τε καὶ τῶν ἑωυτοῦ σινάμωρον.
>
> 5.92.ζ.3
>
> He said that Thrasyboulos had given no advice to him, and said that he was surprised at Periandros for sending him to such a man, because he was a madman and a wanton destroyer of his own property.

Like many of the messengers in the *Histories*, he carries a message without understanding that it is a message or what the message is.[269] Only the intended recipient is in a position firstly to recognize the actions as a set of signs and, secondly, to decode the encoded message, which Periandros readily does:

> Περίανδρος δὲ συνεὶς τὸ ποιηθὲν καὶ νόῳ σχὼν ὥς οἱ ὑπετίθετο Θρασύβουλος τοὺς ὑπερόχους τῶν ἀστῶν φονεύειν, ἐνθαῦτα δὴ πᾶσαν κακότητα ἐξέφαινε ἐς τοὺς πολιήτας.
>
> 5.92.η.1

268 Cf. ch.3.1 below on manipulation involving signs.

269 Messengers and translators are discussed below in ch. 3.2.1.

> Periandros, having understood the action and having grasped in his *noos* that Thrasyboulos was advising him to kill off the prominent among the citizens, from that point on revealed every kind of wickedness against the citizens.[270]

2.7.3 Gestures as Performative Signs

Gestures may produce a change in reality simply by virtue of their performance. The employer of Perdikkas and his brothers contemptuously points to a patch of sunlight on the floor when they ask for their wages. Perdikkas, founder of the future Macedonian dynasty, uses the gesture of drawing a circle around a patch of sunlight and pouring this into his lap three times to claim for himself the "reward" which his master the king has offered him and his brothers (8.137.5). Perdikkas' gesture of claiming the patch of sunlight is nothing less than the claiming of the kingship, and he confirms the symbolic nature of his act by his reply to the king: δεκόμεθα, ὦ βασιλεῦ, τὰ διδοῖς (8.137.5), "We accept, O King, what you give us." His use of the verb δέκομαι at once shows ironic acceptance of the king's "reward" and recognition of it as a meaningful sign (cf. use of δέκομαι below in discussion of 8.114.1–2).[271]

Action of a ritual nature accompanies the swearing of oaths, the effectiveness of which depends not only on linguistic signs (the words spoken by the parties to the oath) but also on ritual activity to ensure irreversibility: as Herodotus himself puts it, ἄνευ γὰρ ἀναγκαίης ἰσχυρῆς συμβάσιες ἰσχυραὶ οὐκ ἐθέλουσι συμμένειν (1.74.4), "Without firm compulsion agreements do not usually remain firm."[272] What could be more irreversible than the sinking of an iron ingot? This is the action to which the inhabitants of Phokaia, who are about to set sail to found a colony on the island of Corsica, attach the words of their oath:[273]

270 The message can thus be regarded as the visual equivalent of an *ainos*, on which cf. ch. 2.4 above. For συνίημι and νόος as terms used as terms relating to the decoding of signs, see ch. 1.3.2 above.

271 Further discussion of this scene in ch. 3.1.3.2 below.

272 Cf. Burkert 1996:173 on the oath as "language validated": "The unseen, with all those superhuman witnesses, gods, and avenging powers, must be bound back again to obvious reality. Beyond the word is action, in the form of ritual to enact what is meant or felt in the linguistic exercise, to give validity to the assertions, imprecations, and curses, and to demonstrate irreversibility." He discusses examples of oath rituals from various cultures, 173–175 (for which cf. also Faraone 1993).

273 An identical ceremony is performed by members of the Delian League in 478/477 BCE (*Constitution of the Athenians* 23.5 and Plutarch *Life of Aristides* 25.1). This is not the only possible interpre-

> ἐποιήσαντο ἰσχυρὰς κατάρας τῷ ὑπολειπομένῳ ἑωυτῶν τοῦ στόλου· πρὸς δὲ ταύτῃσι καὶ μύδρον σιδήρεον κατεπόντωσαν καὶ μοσαν μὴ πρὶν ἐς Φώκαιαν ἥξειν πρὶν ἢ τὸν μύδρον τοῦτον ἀναφανῆναι.
>
> 1.165.3

> They pronounced severe curses on anyone deserting their expedition: in addition to these curses, they also sank an iron ingot and swore not to return to Phokaia before this ingot would appear again.

The pledging of oaths forms an important category in Herodotus' ethnographic descriptions, and in each case he pays attention to the ritual acts which accompany the verbal component of the oath. Ritual connected with oaths made by Greeks is generally not described by Herodotus, except in the case of the oath of the Phocaeans (described above), the oath of the people of Barke with Amasis the Persian (4.201.2–3: cf. ch. 3.1 on the manipulation involved therein), and the oath of Demaratos' mother to her son (6.68).[274] There is good reason in each of these instances for Herodotus to describe the accompanying ritual: the sinking of the iron ingot dramatically demonstrates the resolve of the Phocaeans never to return; Amasis' manipulation of the ritual accompanying the oath by which he tricks the people of Barke into opening their city gates is crucial for Herodotus' story; and the thrusting of the entrails of a bull into the hands of his mother demonstrates the intensity of Demaratos' desire to find out the truth about his parentage and heightens the tone of the account. Otherwise, Herodotus' description of the oaths of Greeks is confined to their contents. The ritual activity connected with oaths is described precisely where it differs from the familiar Greek practice, hence mainly in non-Greek contexts, or where it is particularly striking. Thus Herodotus says of the oaths of Lydians and Persians:

> ὅρκια δὲ ποιέεται ταῦτα τὰ ἔθνεα τά πέρ τε Ἕλληνες, καὶ πρὸς τούτοισι, ἐπεὰν τοὺς βραχίονας ἐπιτάμωνται ἐς τὴν ὁμοχροίην, τὸ αἷμα ἀναλείχουσι ἀλλήλων.
>
> 1.74.6

---

tation of the act: cf. Faraone 1993:79n74, citing Jacobson 1975, who argues that the ritual has to do with the placing of self-curse upon the heads of the participants if they fail to comply.

274 Though this is not formally described by Herodotus as an oath, the fact that she takes the σπλάγχνα of a sacrificed ox in her hands (6.68.1) makes this clear. For parallels involving the handling of animal entrails or genitalia and the importance of touch, see Faraone 1993:66–72 and Burkert 1996:174n83.

> These peoples conclude oaths in the same way as the Greeks, and in addition to this, whenever they make an incision into the surface of the skin on their arms, they lick up each other's blood.

A similar tendency may be observed in his description of sacrifice in general: non-Greek sacrificial practice is described in detail and is a constant category in the ethnographic portions of Herodotus' work, but we learn of Greek sacrificial ritual only inasmuch as it is the implicit model against the background of which Herodotus presents the sacrificial practice of non-Greeks.[275]

Most involve the letting of blood in some way or another: the Lydians and Medes cut their arms to the quick and lick each other's blood (1.74.6), the Arabs cut their hands and then paint seven stones with a bloodied scrap of their clothing (3.8.1), the Scythians mix the blood of the parties to the oath with wine in a large *kylix*, then dip a dagger, arrows, battle-axe, and javelin in the mixture, then pray, then drink from the *kylix*, both the parties themselves and important members of their entourages (4.70).[276] Herodotus' description of the Nasamones' manner of making oaths mentions nothing about blood, but the idea of touch is still important: they swear their oaths while holding on to the tombs of those considered to be the bravest and most just (4.172.3). As with their system of divination, the tomb acts as a sign interface between this world and the realm of the ancestors, who act both as witnesses and guarantors, and, in the case of *mantikê*, as transmitters of signs revelatory of the future.[277] Marking of the body by cutting and the marking of things external to the body (stones and weapons) with blood leave visible traces of the oath, while the blending and ingestion of fluids from both participants effect in physical fashion the binding of the two parties to each other. The actions are symbolic, but this does not mean that they are without effect: just as the words of the oath as speech acts bring about a change in reality, so do the ritual actions which accompany them.

[275] Cf. discussion of this point in Hartog 1988:173–192 and Burkert 1990:19–21.

[276] The dipping of weapons in blood can however be paralleled in a Greek context (though the other party consists of *barbaroi*): Xenophon *Anabasis* 2.2.4: ταῦτα δὲ μοσαν, σφάξαντες ταῦρον καὶ κάπρον καὶ κριὸν εἰς ἀσπίδα, οἱ μὲν Ἕλληνες βάπτοντες ξίφος, οἱ δὲ βάρβαροι λόγχην, "This they swore, slitting the throat of a bull, a goat, and a ram into a shield, the Greeks dipping a sword into it, the barbarians a lance." Cf. Knippschild 2002 on ritual accompaniment to oath ceremonies in Greco-Roman and Near Eastern antiquity.

[277] Cf. discussion of 4.172.4 in ch. 2.4 above.

2.7.4 Laughter and Tears as Signs

Especially interesting are the instances of laughter and tears in the *Histories*: they are exterior indications of interior states, happiness or unhappiness, but just as a single medical symptom may be a sign of a complex internal condition, so too Herodotus uses the laughter and tears of the figures in his work to indicate to his audience a particular pattern of thought and network of associations.

In the case of laughter and smiles, Lateiner has well pointed out that these, for the most part, "suggest not innocent pleasure and benign joy, but arrogance and self-delusion."[278] Laughter in Herodotus generally involves either laughing at the customs of others, often derisively, or the expression of contempt for one's opponents or enemies.[279] The only innocent or good-natured laughter is that of the infant Kypselos, who smiles up at those sent to kill him (5.92.γ.3), possibly that of the soldiers watching the Egyptian master thief (2.121.δ.4) (though he has the last laugh on them: cf. 2.121.δ.6), and that of Kroisos at the sight of Alkmeon stuffing his clothes, his boots, and finally himself with gold from the royal treasury (6.125.5).[280] Kambyses and Xerxes are the two figures whom Herodotus most often depicts as laughing.[281] The laughter of the former is a clear indication of his madness: he laughs as he explains to Prexaspes, whose child he has just used as a target and killed with an arrow straight through the heart, that it is the Persians who are mad and not he, since a madman could not shoot so accurately (3.35.3–4). For Herodotus, the decisive sign is Kambyses' laughter at the rites and customs of the Egyptians. Not only does he stab an incarnation of the Egyptian god Apis and laugh at the Egyptians for worshiping gods who have flesh and blood and may be wounded by swords (3.29.1–2): he also laughs at the cult image of Egyptian Hephaistos and those of the Kabeiroi, even burning the latter (3.37.2–3). His laughter is a highly significant indicator in Herodotus' eyes:

> πανταχῇ ὦν μοι δῆλά ἐστι ὅτι ἐμάνη μεγάλως ὁ Καμβύσης· οὐ γὰρ ἂν ἱροῖσί τε καὶ νομαίοισι ἐπεχείρησε καταγελᾶν. εἰ γάρ τις προθείη πᾶσι ἀνθρώποισι ἐκλέξασθαι κελεύων νόμους τοὺς καλλίστους ἐκ τῶν

278 Lateiner 1987:95. A more extensive discussion of laughter appears in Lateiner 1977.

279 Laughter at customs of others: 3.22.2, 4.79.4, 9.82.2, 9.82.3, and the laughter of Kambyses and Xerxes (references below, n281). Laughter as contempt for one's opponents: 2.118.4, 3.155.2, 4.36.2 (Herodotus himself!), 5.68, 6.67.2, 7.9.1, 8.100.

280 To these should also be added the laughter (or smile) of Kyros (1.90.3) as he listens to Kroisos' complaint against Apollo (*pace* Asheri et al. 2007 *ad loc.*, who see it as an index of *hybris*).

281 Kambyses: 3.29.1, 3.29.2, 3.35.3, 3.37.2, 3.38.1, 3.38.2. Xerxes: 7.103.1, 7.105, 7.209.2, 8.114.2.

> πάντων νόμων, διασκεψάμενοι ἂν ἐλοίατο ἕκαστοι τοὺς ἑωυτῶν· οὕτω νομίζουσι πολλόν τι καλλίστους τοὺς ἑωυτῶν νόμους ἕκαστοι εἶναι. οὐκ ὦν οἰκός ἐστι ἄλλον γε ἢ μαινόμενον ἄνδρα γέλωτα τὰ τοιαῦτα τίθεσθαι.
>
> 3.38.1
>
> It seems clear to me in every way that Kambyses was seriously deranged: he would not otherwise have attempted to ridicule the rites and practices [of others]. For if one were to present all men with the order to choose out of all customs the finest, after examining them, each would choose his own people's laws: to such an extent does every people consider their own laws to be by far the finest. It is not therefore likely that any one other than a madman mocks such things.

Laughter at the customs of others characterizes Xerxes as well, and acts as an effective token of his folly and ultimate failure. He consistently laughs at Demaratos' description of Spartan mettle and his assessment of them as a threat to the Persians (7.103.1, 7.105, 7.209.2), and when the Spartans send heralds to him in accordance with an oracle to demand compensation for the killing of Leonidas at Thermopylai, his reaction is a strange mixture of laughter and silence:

> ὁ δὲ γελάσας τε καὶ κατασχὼν πολλὸν χρόνον, ὥς οἱ ἐτύγχανε παρεστεὼς Μαρδόνιος, δεικνὺς ἐς τοῦτον εἶπε· "Τοιγάρ σφι Μαρδόνιος ὅδε δίκας δώσει τοιαύτας οἵας ἐκείνοισι πρέπει."
>
> 8.114.2
>
> He gave a laugh and kept silent for a long time, and since Mardonios happened to be standing by him, he pointed to him and said, "Mardonios here will give them such compensation as they deserve."

His words turn out to be true, but not in the sense he intends, since the compensation (δίκη) that Mardonios gives the Spartans is his own life, when he is killed at the Battle of Plataiai:

> ἐνθαῦτα ἥ τε δίκη τοῦ φόνου τοῦ Λεωνίδεω κατὰ τὸ χρηστήριον τὸ τοῖσι Σπαρτιήτῃσι ἐκ Μαρδονίου ἐπετελέετο.
>
> 9.64.1
>
> Then the compensation for the killing of Leonidas was brought to fulfillment by Mardonios in accordance with the Spartans' oracle.

Xerxes' laugh and the lengthy silence which precedes his answer to the Spartans alert us to the ominous nature of the words which follow, and the double-edged nature of the answer is played upon in Herodotus' description of the Spartan herald's response: he "accepts" Xerxes reply (ὁ μὲν δὴ δεξάμενος τὸ ῥηθὲν ἀπαλλάσσετο, 8.115.1), just as the oracle instructs them to do (Ξέρξην αἰτέειν δίκας τοῦ Λεωνίδεω φόνου καὶ τὸ διδόμενον ἐξ ἐκείνου δέκεσθαι [8.114.1], "Ask Xerxes for compensation for the killing of Leonidas and accept what is given by him").[282] The verb δέκομαι ("accept, receive"), as we have seen (ch. 2.1), may be used in the sense of recognizing and accepting something as a portent or sign. What Herodotus points out explicitly in the case of Kambyses he indicates silently with respect to Xerxes by means of the mere mention of his laughter.

Tears in Herodotus often represent pain mixed with understanding and insight won through suffering: a particularly striking passage is the one in which the reactions of the defeated Egyptian king Psammenitos and those of his captors are described.[283] Psammenitos is forced to see his daughter enslaved and his son led off to execution, yet he shows no outward signs of grief apart from bowing his head (3.14.2–6). When, however, he sees an elderly companion now reduced to begging, he wails, calls out his companion's name, and beats his own head in lamentation (3.14.7). Asked by Kambyses to explain his behavior, he gives the following reply:

> ὦ παῖ Κύρου, τὰ μὲν οἰκήια ἦν μέζω κακὰ ἢ ὥστε ἀνακλαίειν, τὸ δὲ τοῦ ἑταίρου πένθος ἄξιον ἦν δακρύων, ὃς ἐκ πολλῶν τε καὶ εὐδαιμόνων ἐκπεσὼν ἐς πτωχηίην ἀπῖκται ἐπὶ γήραος οὐδῷ.
>
> 3.14.10

282 Cf. *Odyssey* 20.345–349 for the uncanny laughter induced in the suitors by Athena and which precedes their temporary madness: μνηστῆρσι δὲ Παλλὰς Ἀθήνη | ἄσβεστον γέλω ὦρσε, παρέπλαγξεν δὲ νόημα. | οἱ δ' ἤδη γναθμοῖσι γελώων ἀλλοτρίοισιν, | αἱμοφόρυκτα δὲ δὴ κρέα ἤσθιον· ὄσσε δ' ἄρα σφέων | δακρυόφιν πίμπλαντο, γόον δ' ὠΐετο θυμός, "Pallas Athene stirred up an unextinguishable laughter in the suitors, and made their wits deranged. Now they laughed with jaws not their own and ate meat oozing blood. Then their eyes filled with tears, and their hearts thought of lamentation." Discussion in Levine 1982/3 and Colakis 1986.

283 Cf. Lateiner 1987:95, speaking generally of weeping in Herodotus: "Weeping is a convenient literary shorthand for helpless inaction and suffering. These gestures reveal pain but, more pointedly, painfully won insight." Other instances of weeping: the tears of Kroisos on the pyre as he understands Solon's message and calls on Apollo to save him (1.87.2); the Athenian audience of Phrynikhos' tragedy about the fall of Miletos (6.21.2); the tears of Xerxes on contemplating his army and realizing the brevity of life and human achievement (7.45–46); the tears of the Persian dinner guest at Orkhomenos (9.16.3) who knows what the outcome at Plataiai will be but is helpless to do anything about it.

> Son of Kyros, my own affairs were evils too great to give grief to, but the grief of my companion was worthy of tears, one who having fallen from much good fortune has come to a state of beggary on the threshold of old age.

After this explanation a chain reaction follows: first Kroisos (whose presence Herodotus hastily explains and who is there for good reasons) weeps, then the Persian bystanders, and finally Kambyses himself:

> ὡς δὲ λέγεται ὑπ' Αἰγυπτίων, δακρύειν μὲν Κροῖσον (ἐτετεύχεε γὰρ καὶ οὗτος ἐπισπόμενος Καμβύσῃ ἐπ' Αἴγυπτον), δακρύειν δὲ Περσέων τοὺς παρεόντας, αὐτῷ τε Καμβύσῃ ἐσελθεῖν οἶκτόν τινα καὶ αὐτίκα κελεύειν τόν τέ οἱ παῖδα ἐκ τῶν ἀπολλυμένων σῴζειν καὶ αὐτὸν ἐκ τοῦ προαστίου ἀναστήσαντες ἄγειν παρ' ἑωυτόν.
>
> 3.14.11
>
> According to the Egyptians, Kroisos (for he happened to have followed Kambyses to Egypt) wept, the Persian bystanders wept, and a certain pity came upon Kambyses himself, and he immediately gave orders to rescue Psammenitos' son from those being executed, get him on his feet, and conduct him from the area in front of the city to himself.

All of this happens without words: there is no explanation given by Herodotus for the reactions, only the fact of their tears is recorded, with the verb of weeping twice placed in emphatic position at the beginning of its clause: δακρύειν μέν . . ., δακρύειν δέ . . . Yet behind the simple fact of tears there is a network of connections: each participant "reads" the emotional response of the other, interprets it, and produces his own reaction after comparison, which is then in turn taken up by another.[284] Kroisos makes a connection

[284] The idea of shared grief and pity for others as a catalyst for one's own tears is suggested by the Homeric quotation placed in the mouth of Psammenitos. When Psammenitos describes his companion as "on the threshold of old age" (ἐπὶ γήραος οὐδῷ, 3.14.10) we may think of Priam in *Iliad* 24.487, who attempts to elicit pity from Akhilles by having him bring to mind his own father. Each weeps for his own: Akhilles for Peleus, Priam for Hektor. Their grounds for weeping are separate and, to use Herodotus' terminology, οἰκήια ("their own"), but the two share in common the action of weeping. Yet Akhilles also weeps for Patroklos (502–503): he makes the connection between his own father and Priam, who weeps for his son, then without Priam's prompting makes the further connection between himself and Hektor via Patroklos, and finally releases the body of Hektor. In alluding to this paradigm of pity and shared humanity, Herodotus sets the tone for his own scene. Munson (2005:75n34) compares this scene with Kroisos' communications on the pyre (1.86.4–6) as "structurally analogous"

between Psammenitos and himself and weeps: he, too, was a king in defeat and subject to the "testing" of another;[285] he, too, cried out a name after lengthy silence and was asked by his tormentor the reason for this.[286] When the Persian bystanders see Kroisos weep, as Persians they know his history and the reason for his tears, and they, too, weep in pity in contemplation and comparison of the twin fates of the two men. At the end of the chain Kambyses himself experiences pity as he completes the equation: if Kroisos stands in the same position as Psammenitos, then he is to Psammenitos as his father, Kyros, was to Kroisos. This prompts him to act with mercy, as his father did, and he orders the execution of the son to be stayed.

The tears of the participants in this scene are not just shed but "read." More than being simply the physical expression of a state of distress, these tears act both as signs for others (Kroisos, Persian spectators, and finally Kambyses) through which insight is gained and as signs in a chain of communication between author and audience. Herodotus invites us to draw the connections for ourselves between Kroisos' experience on the pyre set by Kyros with Psammenitos' suffering at the hands of Kambyses, eschewing the use of writing. Just as Herodotus is capable of transmitting and decoding for us the signs that reside in the things men do, so too is he able to leave signs of his own for us to interpret.

---

but lacking the "dimension of understanding or not understanding the hidden message of an utterance. Accordingly, no attention is drawn to language, and the role of intermediary, which in the scene with Croesus is fulfilled by interpreters, is assigned to an *angelos* ('messenger'), with no suggestion of linguistic translation (3.14.8)." On interpreters and translators in the *Histories*, see ch. 3.2.1 below.

285 Cf. 1.86.2, where Kyros puts Kroisos on the pyre along with fourteen Lydian youths either as a victory sacrifice to some god or in fulfillment of a vow or in order to test the truth of Kroisos' reputation for piety and to see if the gods will rescue him, and 3.14.1, where Kambyses inflicts indignities on Psammenitos in order to try his spirit (διεπειρᾶτο αὐτοῦ τῆς ψυχῆς ποιέων τοιάδε).

286 Cf. ἀναστενάξαντα ἐκ πολλῆς ἡσυχίης ἐς τρὶς ὀνομάσαι "Σόλων" (1.86.3), "[Kroisos] groaned out loud after much silence and called out Solon's name three times," and ὁ δὲ Ψαμμήνιτος ὡς εἶδε, ἀνακλαύσας μέγα καὶ καλέσας ὀνομαστὶ τὸν ἑταῖρον ἐπλήξατο τὴν κεφαλήν (3.14.7), "When Psammenitos saw this, he burst out crying loudly, called out his companion's name aloud, and beat his own head." Question by tormenter: καὶ τὸν Κῦρον ἀκούσαντα κελεῦσαι τοὺς ἑρμηνέας ἐπειρέσθαι τὸν Κροῖσον τίνα τοῦτον ἐπικαλέοιτο (1.86.4), "When Kyros heard this he ordered the interpreters to ask Kroisos who this person was whom he was calling," and θωμάσας δὲ ὁ Καμβύσης τὰ ποιεύμενα πέμψας ἄγγελον εἰρώτα αὐτὸν λέγων τάδε . . . (3.14.8), "In astonishment at what was being done, Kambyses sent a messenger and asked him the following . . ."

2.8 Objects as Signs

2.8.1 Transformation of Objects and Their Meaning

Objects in the *Histories* are frequently more than they seem. They may serve one function, while at the same time acting as a bearer of signs which become meaningful when interpreted according to a certain code.[287] Thus in Herodotus' account of the rise of Psammetikhos to power, the latter's bronze helmet (κυνέη) is supposed to serve as protective headgear, but is used by him as a vessel for libations when the high priest of Hephaistos miscounts the number of golden bowls for libation (*phialai*) necessary for all twelve kings of Egypt to perform a libation to the god (2.151). The helmet does not simply become a *phialê*: it becomes a sign vehicle, fulfilling the oracle that whoever of the twelve kings performs a libation in the temple of Hephaistos using a bronze *phialê* will become king of all Egypt (2.147.4).[288] Kurke points out a Dumézilian code at play here, where the *phialê*, associated with the legitimate kingly and priestly function, is usurped by the helmet, symbol of the military function.[289] She also demonstrates that there is another code or language at work here, the "language of metals." Bronze and gold seem to be viewed in terms of a Hesiodic system, where gold is representative of legitimate king-

[287] Discussion in Lateiner 1987:95–100 (list of examples 115–116), Lateiner 1989, and most importantly Dewald 1993.

[288] Further instances of *phialai* in semiotic contexts follow below. A helmet (κυνέη) also plays a role in Amasis' rise to the throne: after one of the rebels whom Amasis has been sent to bring back to the king's service places a helmet on his head and declares that he has done this to make him king (2.162.1), Amasis himself decides to gain power. Cf. Kurke 1995:55–57 on Psammetikhos and the bronze helmet, 57–63 on Amasis.

[289] As Kurke 1995:57 puts it, "Within Herodotus' overdetermined narrative, this act is more than just the fleeting exertion of control over the signification of objects; it is also a prophetic revelation of the tyrant's own nature. The helmet stands as a metonym for the ruler: the instrument of war adapted to kingly rituals." Dumézil's triple function in connection with objects and metals is also seen in the objects that fall from heaven in the native Scythian version of their foundation myth (4.5.2–4), discussed below.

ship and religious authority and the golden age, while bronze represents the age of bronze and *hubris* (*Works and Days* 146–149).

To take another example of an object intended primarily in a military context but converted to quite another use, arrows are used as signifiers by the Scythians in the coded message they send to Dareios in the form of gift-objects (4.131.1), while they also play a role as significant objects in the ritual accompanying the pledging of oaths (4.70; cf. ch. 2.7), and in yet another instance involving the Scythians, arrowheads act as tokens representing individual Scythians in Ariantas' census (4.81.5). These sign-bearers then undergo a physical transformation when they are melted down to form an enormous *kratêr*, which then itself acts as a signifier.[290]

The melting and recasting of an object also accompany change in signification in the case of the golden footbath of Amasis, which is refashioned as an image of a divinity (ἄγαλμα δαίμονος, 2.172.3). When Amasis sees the Egyptians honoring this image, he reveals its humble origin and uses this to make a connection to his own status and identity:

> συγκαλέσας Αἰγυπτίους ἐξέφηνε φὰς ἐκ τοῦ ποδανιπτῆρος τὤγαλμα γεγονέναι, ἐς τὸν πρότερον μὲν τοὺς Αἰγυπτίους ἐνεμέειν τε καὶ ἐνουρέειν καὶ πόδας ἐναπονίζεσθαι, τότε δὲ μεγάλως σέβεσθαι. ἤδη ὦν ἔφη λέγων ὁμοίως αὐτὸς τῷ ποδανιπτῆρι πεπρηγέναι· εἰ γὰρ πρότερον εἶναι δημότης, ἀλλ' ἐν τῷ παρεόντι εἶναι αὐτῶν βασιλεύς· καὶ τιμᾶν τε καὶ προμηθέεσθαι ἑωυτὸν ἐκέλευε.
>
> 2.172.4–5
>
> After assembling the Egyptians, he made a revelation, saying that the statue had been made from a footbath, in which in former times the Egyptians used to vomit and urinate or wash their feet, but which they now greatly revered. And so the same thing, he said, that had happened with the footbath had now happened to him: for if he had previously been a commoner, now he was their king. And he ordered them to honor him and to hold him in respect.

Amasis thus constructs an object which acts as a signifier in two ways, firstly as an iconic representation of a god, which is interpreted as such by the Egyptians and accordingly becomes an object of worship (σέβεσθαι), and secondly as the bearer of an encoded message which has to be revealed (ἐξέφηνε) by Amasis to his subjects.[291]

290 Cf. 2.8.7 below for more on this passage.

291 Cf. Dewald 1993, for whom this is a key passage in her treatment of significant objects in the

2.8.2 Gift-Objects

Gift-objects may also serve bearers of encoded messages, so that the giving of gifts not only is an act of friendship or homage, but becomes a semiotic act, a means of communication which carries a message. Two of the three gift transactions in the *Histories* which involve speaking gifts occur between non-Greek peoples.[292] In both of these cases, one party to the exchange is Persian, and the other party a group from the fringe of the known world, both from the Greek and Persian point of view: the Long-lived Ethiopians, recipients of gifts from Kambyses (3.20–22), live far to the south, while the Scythians, givers of gifts to Dareios (4.131–132), far to the north and east. The remoteness of the peoples, as often in Greek depictions of *barbaroi* and ethnographic satire, seems to go hand in hand with an acuteness of observation which penetrates and reveals the baseness and vanity of the more "civilized" party.[293] In each case, the gifts bridge the gap created by the mutual incomprehension of each other's language, but at the same time equally reveal a gulf of misunderstanding which lies squarely on the side of the Persian king.

Kambyses, wanting to annex the land of the Long-lived Ethiopians, sends spies to the territory, who present the king with gifts of friendship, a purple garment, a necklace and bracelets of gold, a container of myrrh, and a jar of palm wine (3.20.1). The king of the Ethiopians treats the Persian gifts as objects with a particular meaning: the gift of purple cloth is a sign of the trickiness of the Persians (δολερούς, 3.22.1), since their garments are based on deceit, having no natural color of their own but deriving it from the dye in which they are dipped.[294] The gold torque and bracelets are interpreted not as decoration (κόσμος) but as chains designed to enslave and bind (3.22.2): "The king gave a laugh and, thinking that they were shackles, said that they had stronger shackles than these." Gold, being so much in abundance, is precisely the mate-

Histories, and Kurke 1995:59–61 and 1999:93 on this point. The statue (ἄγαλμα) of Hera in the Heraion at Argos also acts as a double signifier when, apart from being a representation of the goddess, it acts as the bearer of a message for Kleomenes (or so he claims) when a flame flares up out of its breast (6.82.2): cf. discussion in ch. 2.1.3 above.

[292] The third is between Euelthon of Cyprus and Pheretime of Cyrene (4.162.4–5), and is discussed further below in this section.

[293] Cf. e.g. Romm 1994:77 on this phenomenon. It is noted and criticized by Plutarch, who accuses Herodotus of using Scythians, Egyptians, and Persians as mouthpieces for his own views (*De malignitate Herodoti* 40, 871d).

[294] Thus in descriptions of the golden age, whether imagined in the past or the future, sheep have wool that is naturally of various hues, so that the deception of dyeing is not necessary, as in Vergil's Golden Age description in *Eclogues* 4.42–45, where the wool will not learn how to falsify (*mentiri*) different colors, but the ram will by himself change the color of his fleece to purple or yellow.

rial from which the Ethiopians make chains for their prisoners, as the messengers are subsequently shown (3.23.4).[295] The container of myrrh is interpreted in the same way as the purple garments (3.22.3): full of deceit, presumably because the myrrh is used to give to the wearer a scent which is not his own. Only the jar of wine receives the king's approbation, but is followed by a scathing remark about the diet of the Persians (3.22.4).[296] The Ethiopian king decodes from the objects a message which Kambyses did not intend to encode. His intended message, as his interpreters, the Fish-eating Ethiopians, relay, is friendship, and the basis for selecting the gifts their high status in the Persian king's eyes:

> Βασιλεὺς ὁ Περσέων Καμβύσης, βουλόμενος φίλος καὶ ξεῖνός τοι γενέσθαι, ἡμέας τε ἀπέπεμψε ἐς λόγους τοι ἐλθεῖν κελεύων καὶ δῶρα ταῦτά τοι διδοῖ τοῖσι καὶ αὐτὸς μάλιστα ἥδεται χρεώμενος.
>
> 3.21.1
>
> Kambyses, king of the Persians, wishing to become your ally and friend, has sent us to come and speak with you, and gives you these gifts in which he himself takes the greatest delight.

The Ethiopian's interpretation nevertheless strikes at the truth: Kambyses simply wishes to take their land:

295 Golden fetters are given by Dareios to Demokedes of Kroton as a "reward" for healing his badly injured foot (3.130.4), a gift which honors and enriches Demokedes inasmuch as the chains are made of gold, but which simultaneously perpetuates his status as the king's slave, merely exchanging the ordinary chains and rags in which he is first brought before him (3.129.3) for shackles of a costlier type. The golden fetters are used by Herodotus as an effective device to introduce the gilded-cage theme that he will develop in his narrative of Demokedes, whose longing for his homeland eventually leads him to ask Atossa, Dareios' wife, to persuade her husband to invade Greece, all so that Demokedes can have an opportunity to return home (3.133–136). Also of interest in this narrative is Dareios' use of objects to persuade Demokedes to reveal his healing powers: when Demokedes pretends that he is not a doctor, Dareios orders whips and goads to be placed in the middle of the room (3.130.2), and Demokedes understands the message and changes his tune. With this can be compared the sack which the Samian exiles show to the Spartan magistrates as a request for help, though they cannot refrain from adding a verbal component to their otherwise silent request (3.46.2).

296 It is interesting that here at least wine is not associated with δόλος. Among another group on the fringe of the Persian world, the Massagetai, who have other stimulants of choice (1.202.2), wine is characterized as a φάρμακον used to trick and rob people of their senses. Cf. the words of Queen Tomyris to Kyros: ἀμπελίνῳ καρπῷ, τῷ περ αὐτοὶ ἐμπιπλάμενοι μαίνεσθε οὕτως ὥστε κατιόντος τοῦ οἴνου ἐς τὸ σῶμα ἐπαναπλέειν ὑμῖν ἔπεα κακά, τοιούτῳ φαρμάκῳ δολώσας ἐκράτησας παιδὸς τοῦ ἐμοῦ, ἀλλ' οὐ μάχῃ κατὰ τὸ καρτερόν (1.212.2), "With the fruit of the vine, with which you fill yourselves and become so frenzied that when the wine goes down into your body evil words float back up, with such a drug did you trick and overpower my son, but not by superior force in battle."

> οὔτε ὁ Περσέων βασιλεὺς δῶρα ὑμέας ἔπεμψε φέροντας προτιμῶν πολλοῦ ἐμοὶ ξεῖνος γενέσθαι, οὔτε ὑμεῖς λέγετε ἀλήθεα (ἥκετε γὰρ κατόπται τῆς ἐμῆς ἀρχῆς) οὔτε ἐκεῖνος ἀνήρ ἐστι δίκαιος· εἰ γὰρ ἦν δίκαιος, οὔτ' ἂν ἐπεθύμησε χώρης ἄλλης ἢ τῆς ἑωυτοῦ, οὔτ' ἂν ἐς δουλοσύνην ἀνθρώπους ἦγε ὑπ' ὧν μηδὲν ἠδίκηται.
>
> 3.21.2
>
> The king of the Persians did not send you here with gifts because he sets great store on becoming my guest-friend, nor are you telling the truth (for you have come here to spy on my kingdom), nor is he a just man. For if he were a just man, he would neither have desired a land other than his own, nor would he try to bring into slavery men at whose hands he has suffered no injustice.

Kambyses' gift does not go unreciprocated. Even before he decodes Kambyses' gifts, the Ethiopian king bids the messengers give Kambyses a bow and relay a verbal message (ἔπεα) to accompany it:

> Βασιλεὺς ὁ Αἰθιόπων συμβουλεύει τῷ Περσέων βασιλέϊ, ἐπεὰν οὕτω εὐπετέως ἕλκωσι [τὰ] τόξα Πέρσαι ἐόντα μεγάθεϊ τοσαῦτα, τότε ἐπ' Αἰθίοπας τοὺς μακροβίους πλήθεϊ ὑπερβαλλόμενον στρατεύεσθαι, μέχρι δὲ τούτου θεοῖσι εἰδέναι χάριν, οἳ οὐκ ἐπὶ νόον τρέπουσι Αἰθιόπων παισὶ γῆν ἄλλην προσκτᾶσθαι τῇ ἑωυτῶν.[297]
>
> 3.21.3
>
> The king of the Ethiopians advises the king of the Persians: whenever Persians will be able to draw a bow of this size with this much ease, at that moment to march against the Long-lived Ethiopians with superior forces, but until that time to be thankful to the gods for not putting it in the minds of the sons of the Ethiopians to seek to add another territory to their own.

His message thus uses three different sign media: the bow itself as significant object, the gestures made by the king (the expressions οὕτως εὐπετέως and τόξα ἐόντα μεγάθεϊ τοσαῦτα are deictic in nature and depend on demonstration for their comprehension), and, accompanying them, the words of his utterance (ἔπεα). The bow then disappears from the narrative, but not for good. It makes an appearance once more when Herodotus describes the

[297] The bow test (which has an obvious Homeric parallel) surfaces again in the account told by Greeks living in Scythia of Herakles' bow (4.9.5): see further below, 2.8.3.

mounting madness of Kambyses. Kambyses sends his brother, Smerdis, back to Persia out of jealousy (φθόνῳ), because he alone of the Persians is able to draw the Ethiopian bow, albeit only two fingers' breadth (3.30.1). It is this very bow that effectively sets off the chain of events which will culminate in Kambyses' murder of his brother, the first of his evils (πρῶτον . . . τῶν κακῶν, 3.30.3),[298] since once Smerdis arrives in Persia, Kambyses has a dream that his brother is sitting on his throne and that his head touches the sky (3.30.2), and so decides to have him assassinated.[299] The bow thus again plays a role as significant object, carefully placed in the narrative to evoke the Ethiopian king's words on giving it and, by extension, his penetrating remarks about the injustice and greed of Kambyses (3.21.2).

While Herodotus in his description of the gifts given to the king of the Ethiopians and given by him to Kambyses does not use any of the vocabulary specifically associated with signs and the transmission and decoding of signs, it is clear that, at least for the Ethiopian, gifts are more than gifts. The gifts of the Scythians show this semiotic potential even more clearly: they are given to Dareios, another Persian monarch bent on conquest, quite deliberately in order to convey a message in terms of a different code, so that their primary function, unlike the gifts and code Dareios is familiar with, is neither to honor nor to flatter nor to convey willingness to submit:

> οἱ Σκυθέων βασιλέες . . . ἔπεμπον κήρυκα δῶρα Δαρείῳ φέροντα ὄρνιθά τε καὶ μῦν καὶ βάτραχον καὶ ὀϊστοὺς πέντε.
>
> 4.131.1

> The kings of the Scythians . . . sent a herald bearing as gifts for Dareios a bird, a mouse, a frog, and five arrows.[300]

The Persians understand that the gifts must be treated as signs standing for something: they ask the messenger what the νόος of the gifts is (4.131.2). The messenger confirms that the gifts do stand for something, but will not reveal what it is: if they are *sophoi*, they will realize what the gifts "say" (λέγει, 4.131.2).[301]

298 The significance of this event is signaled by the πρῶτος motif in Herodotus' expression: cf. the death of the daughter of the Egyptian king Mykerinos as the beginning of the evils Egypt suffered under him (πρῶτον κακῶν ἄρξαι τὴν θυγατέρα ἀποθανοῦσαν αὐτοῦ, 2.129.3), and cf. the Athenian ships sent to aid the Ionians as the ἀρχὴ κακῶν (5.97.3) for Greeks and barbarians.

299 On the problem of interpretation involved in this dream, see above, ch. 2.2.

300 West 1988b discusses these and similar gifts with extremely interesting Central Asian parallels from the modern period.

301 Cf. discussion of this passage and other instances of the term σοφός used in connection with the ability to decode signs in chs. 1.3, 3.1, and 3.2.

The gifts are presented as talking objects, replacing the herald himself, whose function here is to deliver only the gifts, and not any direct message.[302] Despite Dareios' realization that these are gifts of a different kind, his interpretation of them is nevertheless based on the type of gifts and code familiar to him, those of earth and water, tokens of submission:[303]

> Δαρείου μέν νυν ἡ γνώμη ἦν Σκύθας ἑωυτῷ διδόναι σφέας τε αὐτοὺς καὶ γῆν τε καὶ ὕδωρ, εἰκάζων τῇδε, ὡς μῦς μὲν ἐν γῇ γίνεται καρπὸν τὸν αὐτὸν ἀνθρώπῳ σιτεόμενος, βάτραχος δὲ ἐν ὕδατι, ὄρνις δὲ μάλιστα ἔοικε ἵππῳ, τοὺς δὲ ὀϊστοὺς ὡς τὴν ἑωυτῶν ἀλκὴν παραδιδοῦσι.
>
> 4.132.1
>
> Now Dareios' opinion was that the Scythians were handing themselves as well as [the gift of] earth and water over to them, and he reasoned along the following lines, namely that a mouse lives in earth and eats the same food as man, a frog lives in water, a bird is most comparable to a horse, and that by surrendering their arrows to him they were also surrendering their own strength.

Dareios therefore pursues a reading which is based in part on seeing a metonymic connection between signifier and signified (a mouse lives in the earth and so represents the earth, the element with which it is associated; a frog lives in water and so represents water itself).[304] Gobryas, his advisor, draws a connection based largely on metaphor between each sign object and its significance (the Persians must become birds and fly off into the sky, become mice

302 I use the expression "talking (speaking) object" here of an object which relays a message without any accompanying explanation or inscription on it. For talking objects in the sense of objects which contain inscriptions which speak and in which the speaker is sometimes presented as the object itself, cf. 2.106.4 (rock engraving of Sesostris, first person); 2.136.4 (pyramid speaks and refers to itself in first person); 2.141.6 (inscription on statue of Sethos, first person); 3.88.3 (inscription on statue of Dareios on horseback, third person); 4.88.2 (inscription on picture of Dareios crossing Bosporos, third person); 4.91.1–2 (inscription on springs, third person); 5.59–60 (inscriptions on tripods speak in first person); 5.61 (inscription on tripod, third person); 7.228 (three epitaphs to the fallen at Thermopylai, two in third person, one in first); 8.22.1–2 (inscriptions on water sources speak with voice of Themistokles).

303 Other instances of the gift of earth and water: 5.17–21; 5.73.2–3; 6.48–49; 6.94.1; 7.32; 7.131; 7.133.1; 7.163.2; 7.233.1. The Athenians and Spartans play with signs of earth and water by throwing the Persian heralds into the pit at Athens, and a well at Sparta, telling them to take as much earth and water as they wish (7.133.1). Cf. Kuhrt 1988 on the meaning of this gift.

304 The other elements in the Scythians' message, the bird and the arrows, seem to fall rather by the wayside in Dareios' attempt to see in the signifiers the desired gift of earth and water. The connection between bird and horse appears forced, but seems to be made through the property of speed which both share: Corcella in Asheri et al. 2007 *ad loc.* compares *Iliad* 2.763–764, where the horses of Pheretiades are swift as birds.

and sink under the earth, become frogs and jump into the lakes, or be struck by the arrows of the Scythians).[305] He expresses his interpretation in the form of an actual address on the part of the gifts, making them speak (λέγει), just as the Scythian herald advised:

> ἢν μὴ ὄρνιθες γενόμενοι ἀναπτῆσθε ἐς τὸν οὐρανόν, ὦ Πέρσαι, ἢ μύες γενόμενοι κατὰ τῆς γῆς καταδύητε, ἢ βάτραχοι γενόμενοι ἐς τὰς λίμνας ἐσπηδήσητε, οὐκ ἀπονοστήσετε ὀπίσω ὑπὸ τῶνδε τῶν τοξευμάτων βαλλόμενοι.
>
> 4.132.2–3

> If you do not become like birds and fly up into the heavens, O Persians, or become like mice and sink under the earth, or become like frogs and leap into the lakes, you will not return home again, being shot at with these arrows.

The series of gifts given by King Euelthon of Salamis in Cyprus to Pheretime of Cyrene culminate in a gift which is designed to put a stop to her requests for a gift which he will not give. Pheretime asks him for an army as a gift, in order that her son may be restored to power. The gift of an army, as we learn from a later passage in the *Histories*, is a thoroughly typical gift for a Persian to give, even to a woman (this is what Xerxes offers Artaynte instead of the cloak Amestris has given him):

> ἀλλὰ πόλις τε ἐδίδου καὶ χρυσὸν ἄπλετον καὶ στρατόν, τοῦ ἔμελλε οὐδεὶς ἄρξειν ἀλλ' ἢ ἐκείνη· Περσικὸν δὲ κάρτα ὁ στρατὸς δῶρον.
>
> 9.109.3

> But he gave her cites and abundant gold and an army which no one save her would command: the army was a thoroughly Persian gift.

Euelthon refuses her request, but does so indirectly by giving her another gift.[306] The process is repeated a number of times, with Pheretime replying

305 *Contra* Benardete (1969:117–118) and Hartog (1988:55–56), who maintain that Dareios reads the objects as signs and metaphors, but that Gobryas reads them as neither signs nor metaphors at all. This seems a misreading of the passage: both Persians certainly read the objects as signs, but differ in their perceptions of the relationship between signifier and signified. One cannot collapse the distinction between the two.

306 ὁ δὲ Εὐέλθων πᾶν μᾶλλον ἢ στρατιήν οἱ ἐδίδου (4.162.4), "But Euelthon tried to give her everything except an army." The passages recalls Xerxes' attempts to wriggle out of giving Artaynte the gift she wishes: Ξέρξης δὲ παντοῖος ἐγίνετο οὐ βουλόμενος δοῦναι (9.109.3), "Xerxes tried everything to avoid giving [it to her]."

on each occasion that the gift is fine, but finer still would be what she asked for, an army (4.162.4).[307] So far, the gifts of Euelthon only have significance by virtue of the fact that they are not what Pheretime has asked for. His final gift, however, is designed to deliver a message in itself:

> τελευταῖόν οἱ ἐξέπεμψε δῶρον ὁ Εὐέλθων ἄτρακτον χρύσεον καὶ ἠλακάτην, προσῆν δὲ (οἱ) καὶ εἴριον.
>
> 4.162.5
>
> As a final gift Euelthon sent her a spindle of gold and a distaff, and there was wool on it too.

She is unable to recognize the objects as signs and their encoded message until Euelthon spells it out:

> ἐπειπάσης δὲ αὖτις τῆς Φερετίμης τὠυτὸ ἔπος ὁ Εὐέλθων ἔφη τοιούτοισι γυναῖκας δωρέεσθαι ἀλλ' οὐ στρατιῇ.
>
> 4.162.5
>
> When Pheretime once again made the same comment, Euelthon said that these were the sort of gifts which women were given, not an army.

The spindle and distaff, instruments used in the womanly task of spinning, stand metonymically as signifiers for the sphere of female competence, while the material from which they are fashioned, gold, raises them from the status of common objects, marking them as gifts and symbolic objects.[308]

This passage marks the only instance in which a gift acting as signifier is given by one Greek to another, the other instances describing gifts sent between peoples of different cultures, both non-Greek. In these cases, the reactions of the recipients demonstrate fundamental differences between the two parties to the gift-giving: the king of the Ethiopians sees through Kambyses'

[307] Pheretime's hierarchy of priorities is thus the reverse of the one expressed in the famous fragment of Sappho, and thus emphasizes her unusual masculinity even more strongly: o]ἰ μὲν ἰππήων στρότον οἰ δὲ πέσδων | οἰ δὲ νάων φαῖς' ἐπ[ὶ] γᾶν μέλαι[ν]αν | ἔ]μμεναι κάλλιστον, ἔγω δὲ κῆν' ὄτ | τω τις ἔραται (16.1–4), "Some say an army of horseman is the finest thing upon the black earth, others say one of soldiers, others one of ships, but I say it is whatever one loves."

[308] The combination of the everyday object with the rare and costly material is reminiscent of Dareios' gift of golden fetters to Demokedes, mentioned above. In the *Odyssey*, Helen actually uses a golden distaff, which is a gift from Alkandre, wife of Polybos, king of Egyptian Thebes. West 1988a comments drily: "A golden distaff would be inconveniently heavy." The details of the distaff may have influenced the Herodotean description: cf. esp. χρυσέην τ' ἠλακάτην ταλαρόν θ' ὑπόκυκλον ὄπασσεν | ἀργύρεον, χρυσῷ δ' ἐπὶ χείλεα κεκράαντο (*Odyssey* 4.132–133).

gifts and gives a gift in turn which has important consequences for Kambyses, while the gifts of the Scythians to Dareios and his interpretation of them show the latter's fundamental misunderstanding of the Scythian ethos and his own arrogance. Here, too, the gift of Euelthon, and its lack of interpretation by Pheretime (for she does not even realize that it constitutes a message to her), point to an arrogance which later blossoms into a terrible wreaking of vengeance on her enemies (4.202.1) and ends with her being consumed with worms while still alive (4.205). As Herodotus puts it, she did not "plait" her life to completion at all well (οὐ μὲν οὐδὲ ἡ Φερετίμη εὖ τὴν ζόην κατέπλεξε, 4.205): possibly the metaphor, drawn from the realm of handicrafts, reactivates in an ironic fashion the gift of Euelthon and its injunction to Pheretime to confine herself to womanly tasks.[309]

2.8.3 Objects Formed or Touched by the Gods

The golden objects which, according to Scythian tradition, fell from the sky in front of the three proto-Scythian brothers are also marked as symbolic and, in this case, divine by the material from which they are made:

> ἐπὶ τούτων ἀρχόντων ἐκ τοῦ οὐρανοῦ φερόμενα χρύσεα ποιήματα, ἄροτρόν τε καὶ ζυγὸν καὶ σάγαριν καὶ φιάλην, πεσεῖν ἐς τὴν Σκυθικήν, καὶ τῶν ἰδόντα πρῶτον τὸν πρεσβύτατον ἆσσον ἰέναι βουλόμενον αὐτὰ λαβεῖν, τὸν δὲ χρυσὸν ἐπιόντος καίεσθαι. ἀπαλλαχθέντος δὲ τούτου προσιέναι τὸν δεύτερον, καὶ τὸν αὖτις ταὐτὰ ποιέειν. τοὺς μὲν δὴ καιόμενον τὸν χρυσὸν ἀπώσασθαι, τρίτῳ δὲ τῷ νεωτάτῳ ἐπελθόντι κατασβῆναι, καί μιν ἐκεῖνον κομίσαι ἐς ἑωυτοῦ· καὶ τοὺς πρεσβυτέρους ἀδελφεοὺς πρὸς ταῦτα συγγνόντας τὴν βασιληίην πᾶσαν παραδοῦναι τῷ νεωτάτῳ.
>
> 4.5.3–4
>
> During the reign of these men objects made of gold, a plough and yoke, a *sagaris*, and a *phialê*, came out the sky and fell to earth in Scythia, and the eldest of the brothers was the first to see them, and approached them, wanting to take them, but the gold began to burn as he drew forward. When he withdrew, the second brother went

309 The verb καταπλέκω is used metaphorically in one other place in the *Histories*, of Themistokles' artful conclusion of a speech on the eve of the Battle of Salamis (8.83.2). On plaiting, in addition to weaving and sewing, as metaphors for cunning, sometimes in a negative sense, see Detienne and Vernant 1978.

> forward, and he did precisely the same thing. The gold kept them away with its burning, but it extinguished itself when the youngest brother approached it, and he took it away to his own domain: at this, the elder brothers gave way and made over the kingdom in its entirety to the youngest brother.

They also function metonymically as signifiers, each object being drawn from one of the three spheres of society: the plough and yoke, taken together as a pair (τε καί), from agriculture, the *sagaris* (battle-axe) from the military realm, and the *phialê* (for making libations) from the priestly section.[310] Of the three Scythian brothers, only the youngest is able to approach the flaming objects and take them into his possession (4.5.4).[311] His elder brothers recognize this action as a sign (συγγνόντας) and give the entire kingship to him, and since then the Scythian kings (members of clan called the Paralatai, descendants of the youngest brother, Kolaxaïs) have retained control of the sacred gold objects (4.7.1), as if the king is subsuming all the functions of society within his own person.[312]

Significant objects and control over them also play a role in the alternate, Greek version of the origins of the Scythians. According to the Greek inhabitants of the Black Sea region, Herakles founded the Scythian race by having intercourse with a half-woman, half-snake (μειξοπάρθενος, 4.9.1). After giving her three sons, Herakles is finally allowed to leave, but must leave her directions about their upbringing (4.9.4). He leaves one of his bows (Herodotus' source hastily explains that at that time Herakles used to carry two of them) and his belt behind with the following instructions:

310 A passage from Curtius Rufus (7.8.18–19) supports this interpretation, which finds strong parallels in the three functions and divisions of Indo-Iranian society made in Avestan and Vedic liturgy, as Dumézil (e.g. 1976:171–218) has shown. Dumézil is quick to point out, however, that the tripartite division, while undeniably present in this description, does not accord with the picture of Scythian society given by Herodotus in the rest of book 4 (or by other ancient writers). Except for the Enarees and the diviners (see ch. 2.4), there seems to be no priestly caste, and it is the king who performs the most important religious functions.

311 The same motif occurs in Herodotus' account of the beginnings of the Macedonian dynasty: Perdikkas is the youngest of three brothers, who becomes king by appropriating for himself the patch of sunlight (golden, like the heaven-sent objects) which their master has contemptuously given to them in lieu of wages. There is also a *divisio tripartita*: the three Macedonian brothers work in three different sectors of husbandry, one looking after horses, another after cattle, and the third seeing to the lesser animals (8.137.2). This passage is discussed at greater length in ch. 3.1 below.

312 The identity of the Scythian king with the whole society, and especially with his hearth as extension of the king, is shown by the effects of false oaths on the king's person: whenever someone swears falsely by the king's hearth, the king falls ill and can be cured only by finding the perjuror, 4.86.1–2, as discussed in ch. 2.4 above.

ἐπεὰν ἀνδρωθέντας ἴδηαι τοὺς παῖδας, τάδε ποιεῦσα οὐκ ἂν ἁμαρτάνοις· τὸν μὲν ἂν ὁρᾷς αὐτῶν τόδε [τὸ] τόξον ὧδε διατεινόμενον καὶ τῷ ζωστῆρι τῷδε κατὰ τάδε ζωννύμενον, τοῦτον μὲν τῆσδε τῆς χώρης οἰκήτορα ποιεῦ· ὃς δ' ἂν τούτων τῶν ἔργων τῶν ἐντέλλομαι λείπηται, ἔκπεμπε ἐκ τῆς χώρης. καὶ ταῦτα ποιεῦσα αὐτή τε εὐφρανέαι καὶ τὰ ἐντεταλμένα ποιήσεις.

4.9.5

When you see that the boys have grown to manhood, if you do the following you will not go wrong: whichever one of them you see drawing back the bow like this and girding himself with this belt in this way, make this one dwell in this land. Whoever fails these tasks I have laid down, banish him from the land. If you do these things you will enjoy happiness yourself and you will have carried out my behests.[313]

As in the Scythian version of the foundation myth, it is the youngest of the three sons who passes the test, and once again the golden *phialê* figures as a significant object.[314] On the clasp of the belt is a golden *phialê*, presumably a depiction (ζωστῆρα ἔχοντα ἐπ' ἄκρης τῆς συμβολῆς φιάλην χρυσέην, 4.10.1), which the mother then transforms into an actual *phialê* that she hangs from the belt. It is because of this Ur-*phialê* that Scythians wear *phialai* suspended from their belts (4.10.3).[315]

Herakles leaves behind him another trace of his presence in Scythia: this time the object is not preserved in the form of myth (i.e. the story about his bow and belt) or in objects fashioned after an original object belonging to him (the *phialai* hanging from the belts of Scythians in imitation of the *phialê* on Herakles' belt), but in an impression in the landscape:

ἴχνος Ἡρακλέος φαίνουσι ἐν πέτρῃ ἐνεόν, τὸ ἔοικε μὲν βήματι ἀνδρός, ἔστι δὲ τὸ μέγαθος δίπηχυ, παρὰ τὸν Τύρην ποταμόν.

4.82

313 The motif of the bow as test is familiar from the message of the Ethiopian king to Kambyses, discussed above, ch. 2.8.2. Here too the giver of the object uses gesture as well as words to demonstrate the test.

314 As we have seen, it also functions as a significant object in Herodotus' description of Psammetikhos' rise to power (2.151).

315 As Corcella in Asheri et al. 2007 *ad loc.* notes, the depictions of Scythians that have survived show them with the *rhyton*, a different vessel entirely, but Scythian *phialai* have been discovered, one of which (from Kul' Oba, fourth century BCE, Hermitage KO 31, illustration in Asheri et al. 2007, pl. 32) has rings attached to its edge, presumably for suspension, but whether from a belt as opposed to a peg is uncertain.

> They show a footprint of Herakles in a rock along the river Tures, like the footprint of a man in appearance, but two cubits long in size.

The cavity in the rock, once interpreted as an imprint, the negative impression of a positive object, is like the distinctive mark left behind by a signet ring (σφρηγίς) which points to its owner, and demands a τύπος for its ἀντίτυπος, to use the terms of the oracle given to the Spartans in connection with the bones of Orestes (1.67.4).[316] The size alone points to the realm of the divine, and Herakles, wanderer in remote regions both west and east, fits the description.[317]

The landscape itself acts as a surface capable of bearing signs like a wax tablet or piece of clay. In Thessaly, the god Poseidon leaves traces of his presence in the form of a narrow passage or "pipe" (αὐλών) in the ring of mountains that surround the Thessalian plain and through which the Peneios River flows. Without this gap Thessaly would be an inland sea, and indeed formerly was so. The earth-shaking activity of Poseidon (if it is Poseidon who shakes the earth) alone is responsible for creating the gap in the mountains:

> αὐτοὶ μέν νυν Θεσσαλοί φασι Ποσειδέωνα ποιῆσαι τὸν αὐλῶνα δι' οὗ ῥέει ὁ Πηνειός, οἰκότα λέγοντες· ὅστις γὰρ νομίζει Ποσειδέωνα τὴν γῆν σείειν καὶ τὰ διεστεῶτα ὑπὸ σεισμοῦ τοῦ θεοῦ τούτου ἔργα εἶναι καὶ ἂν ἐκεῖνο ἰδὼν φαίη Ποσειδέωνα ποιῆσαι· ἔστι γὰρ σεισμοῦ ἔργον, ὡς ἐμοὶ ἐφαίνετο εἶναι, ἡ διάστασις τῶν ὀρέων.
>
> 7.129.4
>
> Now the Thessalians themselves say that Poseidon made the passage through which the Peneios flows, and what they say is reasonable: for anyone who believes that Poseidon shakes the earth and that separations caused by earthquake are the work of this god would also say upon seeing this that Poseidon had done it.

Just as the presence of Herakles is inferred from an impression of his foot, so in Egypt, in the town of Khemmis, where there is a temple and sanctuary to Perseus, the presence of that hero is deduced from the appearance of one of his sandals, of precisely the same dimensions as Herakles' footprint,

[316] Cf. chs. 1.3.1 and 2.3 above on this passage.

[317] Other examples of unusual size as an indication of the divine discussed in ch. 2.2.3 (dream-figures), and further below in this section (sandal of Perseus). Footprints, not of Herakles himself, but of the cattle of Geryon stolen by him, are found on the opposite side of the world, in Sicily (Diodoros 4.24).

two cubits (all heroes, it seems, take this size shoe). In this instance, the sign does not point back to the remote past but rather to the present:

> οὗτοι οἱ Χεμμῖται λέγουσι τὸν Περσέα πολλάκις μὲν ἀνὰ τὴν γῆν φαίνεσθαι σφίσι, πολλάκις δὲ ἔσω τοῦ ἱροῦ, σανδάλιόν τε αὐτοῦ πεφορημένον εὑρίσκεσθαι, ἐὸν τὸ μέγαθος δίπηχυ, τὸ ἐπεὰν φανῇ, εὐθενέειν ἅπασαν Αἴγυπτον.
>
> 2.91.3
>
> These people of Khemmis say that Perseus often appears to them in the countryside and often within the sacred precinct, and that a sandal worn by him, two cubits in length, is found: they say that whenever it appears, all of Egypt will enjoy prosperity.

Objects closely associated with a hero play a vital role in the account of Demaratos' conception. His mother swears that on the third night after her first night of marriage an apparition (φάσμα, 6.69.1) resembling her husband, Ariston, appeared to her, slept with her, and left the garlands which he was wearing behind him, placing them about her. When her husband returned and questioned her about them, she said that he had given them to her himself after sleeping with her (6.69.2). Ariston then recognizes the hand of the divine (ἔμαθε ὡς θεῖον εἴη τὸ πρῆγμα, 6.69.3) since the garlands were clearly from the nearby shrine of the hero Astrabakos. The garlands, objects originally intended as expressions of devotion in the hero's cult, and the gift of some worshiper, now become signs of the presence of the one himself worshiped.

Presence of the divine is again inferred through presence of an object closely attached to the divine in Herodotus' description of events just before the Battle of Mykale. A herald's staff (κηρυκήιον, 9.100.1) appears on the beach at Mykale. As at 2.91.3, the object makes a sudden appearance, like the epiphany of a divine being (φάνῃ; ἔφανη, 9.100.1).[318] Herodotus does not elaborate on the significance of the object, which is presumably interpreted as the staff of the messenger god Hermes or perhaps the staff of the hero Talthybios, patron of heralds, but he stresses the supernatural nature of the appearance of the object by linking it with a mysterious φήμη, a rumor that "flies into the camp" saying that the Greeks have beaten Mardonios' army in Boiotia. The two signs, one in the form of an object, the other made up of linguistic signs, appear in conjunction:

318 φαίνομαι in connection with the epiphany of a god: 2.91.3; 2.153; 3.27.1, 3; 4.95.5; 4.179.2, 6.106.1.

ἰοῦσι δέ σφι φήμη τε ἐσέπτατο ἐς τὸ στρατόπεδον πᾶν καὶ κηρυκήιον ἐφάνη ἐπὶ τῆς κυματωγῆς κείμενον· ἡ δὲ φήμη διῆλθέ σφι ὧδε, ὡς οἱ Ἕλληνες τὴν Μαρδονίου στρατιὴν νικῷεν ἐν Βοιωτοῖσι μαχόμενοι.

9.100.1

As they were advancing, a rumor flew through the whole camp and a herald's staff appeared lying on the beach: the rumor spread amongst them that the Greeks were victorious in battle against the army of Mardonios in Boiotia.

These signs are *tekmêria* as far as Herodotus is concerned, signs as evidence for the involvement of the divine:[319]

δῆλα δὴ πολλοῖσι τεκμηρίοισί ἐστι τὰ θεῖα[320] τῶν πρηγμάτων, εἰ καὶ τότε τῆς αὐτῆς ἡμέρης συμπιπτούσης τοῦ τε ἐν Πλαταιῇσι καὶ τοῦ ἐν Μυκάλῃ μέλλοντος ἔσεσθαι τρώματος φήμη τοῖσι Ἕλλησι τοῖσι ταύτῃ ἐσαπίκετο, ὥστε θαρσῆσαί τε τὴν στρατιὴν πολλῷ μᾶλλον καὶ ἐθέλειν προθυμότερον κινδυνεύειν.

9.100.2

Divine involvement in [human] affairs is clear on the basis of many *tekmêria*, especially if on that occasion, during the same day, when the defeat [of the Persian] took place at Plataiai and the one in Mykale was about to happen, a rumor reached the Greeks at Mykale, so that the army's spirit picked up considerably and they were all the more eager to undertake danger.

Not only do objects associated with the divine—the things worn, carried, or received by gods or heroes—act as signs for their presence: the bones of heroes themselves make their appearance in Herodotus' narrative. In the

319 For *tekmêria* as signs, see ch. 1.1.3 above.

320 *Pace* Lateiner 1989:200, I see no reason why the adjective θεῖα must here be understood as meaning not "divine" (its normal meaning, as Lateiner himself concedes) "but here only 'beyond human explication, remarkable'." This is one of Herodotus' clearest and most unambiguous statements about the involvement of the divine in human affairs (cf. also 6.27.1–3; 7.137.1–2; 9.65.2), and yet even here Lateiner denies that Herodotus presents this as a possibility (282n36): "9.100.2 seems exceptional, until one notes that the subject is the army's superstition, and its effects, not Herodotus' explanation." Herodotus certainly describes the effect of the φήμη on the army, but there is nothing in his presentation to suggest that he regards it as a mere figment of the army's imagination. More than once he uses the striking image of the φήμη "flying in" (ἐσέπτατο, 9.100.1, 9.101.3), and he does not abdicate narrative responsibility by presenting the occurrence at one remove (e.g. ὡς λέγουσι *vel sim.*).

aftermath of the Battle of Plataiai, the bones of a man five cubits in length are discovered (ἐφάνη, 9.83.2). As with the herald's staff discussed above, Herodotus provides no interpretation of these bones, but the size of the skeleton suggests that it belongs to a hero (a height of four cubits is already sufficiently tall enough to be considered appropriate for a goddess, 1.60.4), and one is led to think of this as evidence for a hero's presence on the side of the Greeks, just as at Marathon, the figure of an enormous man (φάσμα, 6.117.3), whose beard cast a shadow over his entire shield, is said to have been seen by Epizelos, blind ever since that time.[321]

2.8.4 Objects as Bearers of Identity

Authentication of identity may also be established by objects acting as signs. *Sumbola* (6.86.α.5 and β.1), objects decided upon by parties to an agreement and invested with significance, establish the identity of the one who presents them and his claim to certain rights and privileges.[322] The sons of the wealthy Milesian who deposits a large sum with Glaukos the Spartan present their half of the *sumbola* to him several years later. But such tokens derive their meaning only from the will of the parties to the agreement and depend for their validity on the subsequent recognition of the objects' status as a sign. Thus Glaukos, who wishes to keep the deposit for himself, claims that he has no memory of the transaction, so that the signs presented by the Milesian's descendants have no significance for him.[323]

Identity of the individual may be marked by a number of significant objects in close proximity to the individual or, as will be seen later in this chapter, by the body itself. Babylonians carry with them signet rings (σφρηγῖδες) and staffs (σκῆπτρα), each topped with a different emblem which acts as symbols identifying the bearer:

> σφρηγῖδα δὲ ἕκαστος ἔχει καὶ σκῆπτρον χειροποίητον· ἐπ' ἑκάστῳ δὲ σκήπτρῳ ἔπεστι πεποιημένον ἢ μῆλον ἢ ῥόδον ἢ κρίνον ἢ αἰετὸς ἢ ἄλλο τι· ἄνευ γὰρ ἐπισήμου οὔ σφι νόμος ἐστὶ ἔχειν σκῆπτρον.
>
> 1.195.2

> Each man has a signet ring and a finished staff: on top of staff there is represented either a fruit or a rose or a lily or an eagle or some

321 The skeleton of Orestes is even longer: seven cubits (1.68.3).

322 Cf. ch. 1.1.2 above on *sumbolon*.

323 Cf. ch. 2.3 above on this passage.

> other thing, for it is not their custom to have a staff without a distinguishing mark [*episêmon*].

The *sphrêgis*, or signet ring, works in the same way, not only marking out the bearer by its distinctive device, however, but also leaving visible and tangible marks in the form of impressions made in clay or wax, signs which may mark off and define an object or invest a document with the authority of the seal's owner.

Before turning to the ability of the *sphrêgis* to make signs by leaving an impression of itself, let us explore its function as signifier in its own right. Herodotus' description of the Babylonian *nomos* concentrates on the *sphrêgis* and *skêptron* as external markers of identity, each individual having a different and distinctive device, but the story of Polykrates and his ring, which is precisely a *sphrêgis* (3.41.1), brings to the fore the close connection between ring and bearer and the ability of the one to represent the other. For Polykrates, the ring is the one thing he can think of that is most valuable to him in both financial and emotional terms, as his friend and advisor, Amasis, puts it:

> πλείστου ἄξιον καὶ ἐπ' ᾧ σὺ ἀπολομένῳ μάλιστα τὴν ψυχὴν ἀλγήσεις.
>
> 3.40.4
>
> that which is worth most and at the loss of which you will suffer the greatest grief in your heart.[324]

Polykrates, acting on Amasis' advice to undergo a voluntary loss and suffering in order to break the cycle of good fortune which he predicts will bring the envy (φθόνος) of the divine upon him, sails out to the open sea and, with the crew as witness, throws the object into the deep (3.41.2).[325] The apparent

[324] *Contra* van der Veen (1996:6–17), who thinks that Polykrates' choice of object is an attempt to comply with Amasis' instructions only in a superficial way and that he suffers merely annoyance, not genuine distress at its loss. Polykrates' action is thus ineffectual because he does not really mean it. This seems to me to destroy the whole thrust of the story, which is that, try as one might, one cannot escape the envy (φθόνος) of the gods, a repeated theme in the *Histories* beginning with the encounter of Solon and Kroisos (1.32.1; 1.32.9; 1.207.2; 3.40.2; 3.40.3; 3.65.3; 9.16.4). Van der Veen's interpretation rests on what he sees as a significant variation on the words of Amasis' instructions, particularly the use of the verb ἀσᾶσθαι (3.41.1) instead of ἀλγεῖν (3.40.4). The latter, according to van der Veen, refers to grief at a serious loss or life-altering experience, while the former represents an emotion of sadness which can be shaken off at will. Thus is not, however, borne out by Theognis 593 and 657, where it is associated with κακά and appears as the opposite emotion to joy. Even if the poet tells his addressee to put off this feeling, it need not imply (as van der Veen claims) that it is a trivial or easily manipulable emotion.

[325] As Rosenberger (1995:71) notes, Polykrates makes sure to choose the open sea, and not simply

irreversibility of the action[326] suggest a ritual dimension to the act in which Versnel sees the ring as a substitute for Polykrates himself, a *pars pro toto* "sacrifice."[327] On this model, then, the *sphrêgis* becomes much more intimately connected with the wearer than simply being a beloved possession.

That is not, however, the end of Polykrates' ring: a fisherman brings Polykrates an especially large fish as a token of honor, which, when split open, is found to contain the very ring Polykrates had gone to such lengths to get rid of (3.42.1–4). Polykrates interprets the return of the ring as a divine intervention (θεῖον εἶναι τὸ πρῆγμα, 3.42.4), and it is clear that this is not an occasion for celebration for him, in sharp contrast to the mood of the servants, who in a state of joy bring him what they think will be welcome news (ἔφερον κεχαρηκότες παρὰ τὸν Πολυκράτεα, 3.42.4). The gods, so it seems, have picked up the ring which Polykrates made use of as a sign, and now themselves use it as a sign of a different kind, transmitting back to him a message which Amasis, who plays the role of confidante and advisor to Polykrates, is able to decode:

---

the harbor, where it might stand a chance of being salvaged. The crew are witnesses to the proper performance of the act: πάντων ὁρώντων τῶν συμπλόων (3.41.2). I suggest that the detail is there not, as van der Veen (1996:13–14) claims, because it "characterises Polycrates as a man who loves to be in the public eye," but to show the seriousness of Polykrates' intent to rid himself of the object.

326 Cf. Amasis' advice: τοῦτο ἀπόβαλε οὕτω ὅκως μηκέτι ἥξει ἐς ἀνθρώπους (3.40.4), "Cast this away in such a way that it will never more come before the eyes of men." Cf. also the sinking of iron ingots by the people of Phokaia, 1.165.3 (for which cf. ch. 2.7 above).

327 Versnel 1977:25–37, who cites examples of rings as votive offerings, and adduces as a parallel Aelius Aristides' substitution of a ring in place of the finger demanded by the god (*Hieroi Logoi* 2.26–27): "One need not go so far as to bracket Aelius Aristides' sacrifice of the ring completely with Polycrates' action. But at the very least it should be admitted that the two acts have much in common, particularly regarding the motivation of the ritual: in both cases life and luck are at stake, in both cases man offers a valuable possession, i.e. a ring, in order to save his life, in one of them this offering is explicitly described as a substitute." I do not, however, follow Versnel's suggestion in the second part of his article (37–45), in which he maintains that the throwing away of the ring is like the expulsion and drowning (καταποντισμός) of a scapegoat (φαρμακός) which carries away with it the curses and ills of the community. The φαρμακός is an animate creature (whether human or animal), not an inanimate object, at least in the examples cited by Versnel. See further discussion of possible magico-religious aspects of Polykrates' ring by Rosenberger (1995), who compares a magical papyrus (PGM V.305–369) in which instructions are given for the burial of an iron ring and the pronouncement of a spell binding the victim as long as the ring stays buried. But the parallels are not as close as Rosenberger makes out: for one thing, the throwing of a ring into a disused well or the grave of one who has died an untimely death does not serve the same purpose as throwing it into the sea. The choice of a well or grave, both points of contact with the underworld, is important for the activation of the spell by the *nekudaimôn*: cf. Heintz 1998.

> ἐπιλεξάμενος δὲ ὁ Ἄμασις τὸ βυβλίον τὸ παρὰ τοῦ Πολυκράτεος ἧκον, ἔμαθε ὅτι ἐκκομίσαι τε ἀδύνατον εἴη ἀνθρώπῳ ἄνθρωπον ἐκ τοῦ μέλλοντος γίνεσθαι πρήγματος καὶ ὅτι οὐκ εὖ τελευτήσειν μέλλοι Πολυκράτης εὐτυχέων τὰ πάντα, ὃς καὶ τὰ ἀποβάλλοι εὑρίσκοι. πέμψας δέ οἱ κήρυκα ἐς Σάμον διαλύεσθαι ἔφη τὴν ξεινίην.[328]
>
> 3.43.1
>
> When Amasis had read the letter which had come from Polykrates, he realized that it was impossible for one man to remove another man from an action that was going to come about and that Polykrates, though enjoying good fortune in all respects, a man who even found what he cast away, was going to die in a bad way. He sent a messenger to him in Samos and said that he was ending their friendship.

As often in Herodotus, a object used for one purpose or as one kind of signifier becomes used as a different kind of signifier: the ring itself obstinately endures while the meaning invested in it changes.[329]

So much for the *sphrêgis* as signifier in its own right. I now turn to its use as the imprinter of signs. Herodotus describes how Egyptian priests search sacrificial bulls for certain signs (σημήια) and then turn from reading signs to producing them.[330] By means of a set of different signs they mark off the animals as ritually pure and suitable for sacrifice:

> ἣν δὲ τούτων πάντων ᾖ καθαρός, σημαίνεται βύβλῳ περὶ τὰ κέρεα εἱλίσσων καὶ ἔπειτα γῆν σημαντρίδα ἐπιπλάσας ἐπιβάλλει τὸν δακτύλιον· καὶ οὕτω ἀπάγουσι.
>
> 2.38.3
>
> If it is free of these marks, he marks it by winding papyrus around the horns and then he plasters mud for sealing [on the papyrus] and applies his sealing ring: and thus they lead it away.

[328] For Amasis as talented reader of signs, see Dewald 1985 and Kurke 1995:57–61 and 1999:89–100.

[329] For another interpretation of the Polykrates *logos*, see Kurke 1999:101–129, which focuses on the themes of counterfeiting and (perverted) gift exchange.

[330] The signs looked for are those which are the characteristic markings of the god Apis (black, with a white triangle on its forehead, the image of an eagle on its back, double hairs in its tail, and a scarab under its tongue, 3.28.3), and it is these signs that Kambyses ignores and mocks when he strikes the thigh of a manifestation of the god with his sword (3.29.1).

The simple negative impression of such a seal brings with it an immense power: the punishment for sacrificing a bull unmarked (ἀσήμαντον, 2.38.3) by the priest's ring is death.

The power conveyed by the imprint of the *sphrêgis* is also vulnerable to abuse, since it will make its mark not just for its true master but for whoever has possession of it, as is vividly shown in the account of Bagaios, the Persian noble who volunteers to rid Dareios of the troublesome governor Oroites. Bagaios manipulates Oroites' own bodyguards by means of letters to which he applies the king's own *sphrêgis* (3.128.2). The bodyguards show great veneration (σεβομένους μεγάλως, 3.128.4) for the letters themselves, as if their external appearance and the king's seal evoke the presence of the king, as well as for their contents. By reading out a series of letters purporting to be from the king he progressively gets them to lay down their spears, stop their protection of Oroites, and, finally, kill him (3.128.4–5).[331]

2.8.5 Clothing and Ornament

Sign vehicles similarly close to the human body are clothing and ornament, which convey information about both individual and group in terms of *ethnos*, status, and gender. Herodotus devotes attention to the category of dress in his ethnographic descriptions generally and particularly in his catalogue of Xerxes' forces (7.61–99), detailing how the clothing and adornment of a particular group distinguish them from others. As will be explored below in ch. 3.1, he also shows how clothing as a key to identity, status, and gender may easily be manipulated. A woman can be passed off as a goddess if tall enough and provided with the attributes of the goddess (Phye, the tall, good-looking woman whom Peisistratos and Megakles deck out with Athena's panoply, 1.60.4), men can dress up as women in order to break out of jail (the Minyai, 4.146.2–4) or in order to take revenge on those who have tried to handle their womenfolk (5.20.3–5).

2.8.6 Body as Sign-Bearer

The body itself is a potential bearer of signs. Just like a piece of clay or wax, it may be stamped or incised with marks indicating, for example, ownership by another, as Xerxes does to the Thebans who surrender at Thermopylai:

331 Fuller treatment of this passage in ch. 3.1.

> τοὺς δὲ πλέονας αὐτῶν κελεύσαντος Ξέρξεω ἔστιξαν στίγματα βασιλήια, ἀρξάμενοι ἀπὸ τοῦ στρατηγοῦ Λεοντιάδεω.[332]
>
> 7.233.2
>
> At Xerxes' behest, the Persians tattooed the majority of them with the royal *stigmata*, beginning with their general, Leontiades.

Fugitives seeking asylum in the temple of Hephaistos at the Canopic mouth of the Nile mark themselves as the property of the god (ἑωυτὸν διδοὺς τῷ θεῷ, 2.113.2), and thus inviolate, by having "sacred" tattoos (στίγματα ἱρά) placed on themselves. Histiaios uses a slave's head as surface on which to tattoo a secret message to Aristagoras, bidding him wait until his hair grows back before setting out to deliver the message (5.35.3).[333]

The metaphor of the stamping or engraving of a coin is used by Herodotus in his portrayal of Astyages' recognition of Kyros. A number of factors alert Astyages to the true identity of the boy, one of them being the features, which Herodotus describes as the "stamp" or "marking" (χαρακτήρ), of his face:[334]

> ταῦτα λέγοντος τοῦ παιδὸς τὸν Ἀστυάγεα ἐσήιε ἀνάγνωσις αὐτοῦ, καί οἱ ὅ τε χαρακτὴρ τοῦ προσώπου προσφέρεσθαι ἐδόκεε ἐς ἑωυτὸν καὶ ὑπόκρισις ἐλευθεριωτέρη εἶναι, ὅ τε χρόνος τῆς ἐκθέσιος τῇ ἡλικίῃ τοῦ παιδὸς ἐδόκεε συμβαίνειν.
>
> 1.116.1
>
> When the boy said this, recognition of him came upon Astyages, and the stamp of his face seemed to him like his own and his answer rather free-spoken, while the time of the exposure seemed to tally with the boy's age.

Peisistratos and Zopyros both rely on the capacity of the mutilated body to signify when they inflict wounds upon themselves: by so doing, Peisistratos manages to convince the Athenians *dêmos* to provide him with a bodyguard as protection against his enemies, whom he claims have tried to kill him (1.59.4), and Zopyros is able to convince the Babylonians by the marks on his body and his missing ears that he has been maltreated by Dareios and is genuinely deserting to their side (3.154.2). The false Smerdis has no ears because they

[332] As Jones 1987 makes clear, what is meant by στίζω in the ancient world is tattooing, not branding, as it is often translated.

[333] Other examples of the physical concealment of signs in ch. 3.1.

[334] Cf. coin as signifier with Dareios and his coinage below, ch. 2.8.8.

were cut off as the result of an offense against the king (3.69.5), who marks those who commit crimes against him with signs visible to others in the form of mutilations. The presence of these signs, which, read in terms of the Persian penal code, indicate those who have committed a wrong, acts in turn as a sign of a different kind for Otanes: this Smerdis cannot be the brother of Kambyses, since the latter had both ears intact. In this way Otanes, already suspicious on the basis of other signs in pseudo-Smerdis' behavior, is able to confirm the identity of the imposter.[335]

The Persian kings have a penchant for using the human body as signifier. Kambyses has Sesamnes, one of the royal judges, executed for delivering false judgements, and his corpse skinned. He cuts the skin into strips and upholsters a chair with them and then appoints Sesamnes' son, Otanes as a judge, ordering him to sit in the chair and remember in which chair he sits when passing judgment (ἐντειλάμενός οἱ μεμνῆσθαι ἐν τῷ κατίζων θρόνῳ δικάζει, 5.25.2). The strips of human flesh act as signs, carrying a message which by evoking the past warns simultaneously of the future.[336] Xerxes, in order to show his displeasure at Pythios' request that his eldest son be excused from military service, has the young man sliced in half and the two halves placed on either side of the road along which the army marches (7.39.3). The bisected body acts as a grisly warning sign for those who pass between its two bloody halves.[337]

For the Scythians, too, the human body can be used, like any other object, as a signifier. Warriors present the heads of those they have killed in battle to the king as a token enabling them to claim a share of the booty. Without producing these heads, they are not allowed any share of the spoils (4.64.1). The skulls of one's enemies (especially one's personal enemies, defeated in the king's presence), encased in leather or covered with an additional layer

335 Other use of signs in this episode: Otanes is the first to suspect that the *magos* is not Kyros' brother Smerdis. He conjectures (συμβαλόμενος, 3.68.2) this from the fact that he does not spend any time outside the palace complex and that he does not summon any of the Persian nobles into his sight.

336 For the connection between memory (μεμνῆσθαι, 5.25.2) and signs, see the discussion of memorials and monuments, chs. 2.8.7 and 2.8.8 below.

337 This gruesome episode has in fact a number of fascinating parallels in both Greek and Hittite sources, which Faraone (1993:71) has gathered together. I mention only one of them here: Diktys of Crete (1.15) says that Kalkhas bisected a boar and placed one piece on the west and the other on the east. Each soldier was then ordered to march between the halves with drawn sword and swear enmity to Priam. The idea behind the ceremony seems to be to ensure the loyalty of each member of the army by self-imprecation: they call down upon their own heads the fate of the animal (or man, in the case of the Herodotean passage) if they break their oath. The Herodotean passage does not however contain any mention of an oath, and the emphasis is placed rather on Xerxes' cruelty.

of gold, serve as drinking cups and as objects of proud display produced for visitors, demonstrating their nobility and bravery (4.65.2). The Issedones also make objects of the dead, but not, in this instance, of their enemies. They take the skulls of their dead parent and gild them. The skull then represents the parent, becoming an image in the context of worship (ἄγαλμα) and the recipient of great yearly sacrifices (4.26.2).

At the other limit of the earth, the Long-lived Ethiopians also perform a reification of their dead, turning the body into a representation of itself and what it looked like while alive:

> γυψώσαντες ἅπαντα αὐτὸν γραφῇ κοσμέουσι, ἐξομοιοῦντες τὸ εἶδος ἐς τὸ δυνατόν.
>
> 3.24.2
>
> After covering all parts of it with gypsum, they adorn it with a painting, making it look as much like the person in appearance as possible.

In addition, the corpse becomes its own funerary monument when it is encased in a hollowed-out column of transparent crystal, so that the whole becomes a *stêlê*, a marker which, among the Greeks at any rate, is normally an entity separate from the corpse itself:[338]

> ἔπειτα δέ οἱ περιιστᾶσι στήλην ἐξ ὑάλου πεποιημένην κοίλην (ἡ δέ σφι πολλὴ καὶ εὐεργὸς ὀρύσσεται). ἐν μέσῃ δὲ τῇ στήλῃ ἐνεὼν διαφαίνεται ὁ νέκυς, οὔτε ὀδμὴν οὐδεμίαν ἄχαριν παρεχόμενος οὔτε ἄλλο ἀεικὲς οὐδέν· καὶ ἔχει πάντα φανερὰ ὁμοίως αὐτῷ τῷ νέκυϊ. ἐνιαυτὸν μὲν δὴ ἔχουσι τὴν στήλην ἐν τοῖσι οἰκίοισι οἱ μάλιστα προσήκοντες πάντων τε ἀπαρχόμενοι καὶ θυσίας οἱ προσάγοντες· μετὰ δὲ ταῦτα ἐκκομίσαντες ἱστᾶσι περὶ τὴν πόλιν.
>
> 3.24.2–4
>
> Then they place a hollowed-out *stêlê* made of crystal (this is dug up amongst them in large quantities and is easily worked) about the body. The corpse, being in the middle of the *stêlê*, shows through and

[338] Herodotus in his description of Egypt relates how the corpses of oxen act as their own grave markers (σημηίου εἵνεκεν, 2.41.4): they are buried with one or both of their horns protruding above the ground. The wonderful economy of the practice (which has some basis in reality, see Lloyd 1989 *ad loc.*) is rivaled only by the self-cooking oxen of the Scythians: the latter use the bones of oxen as fuel and their stomachs as cauldrons in which to boil their flesh (4.61.1–2).

> does not give off any unpleasant smell or anything else unseemly: and each part shows as clearly as the corpse itself. The closest relatives keep the *stêlê* in their homes for one year, offering it first-fruits of everything and setting sacrifices before it: after this they carry it out and set it up near the city.

Just as Kambyses does with the skin of Sisamnes, the Scythians treat the skin of their enemies as if it is the hide of an animal, scraping and burnishing it with the rib of an ox. From it napkins (χειρόμακτρα, 4.64.2) are made and suspended from the bridles of their horses, acting, like the cups made of skulls, as indicators of the bravery of the one displaying them: whoever has the most of them is judged the bravest (ἀνὴρ ἄριστος, 4.64.2). The entire skin of the enemy may be made into a kind of effigy, an iconic representation which is then mounted on a pole and carried on horseback (4.64.3). As with the corpses of the Ethiopians, the body is made into an icon of itself.

Even the divine is capable of using the human body as signifier: the inhabitants of Amathous on Cyprus decapitate the corpse of Onesilos, who had besieged their city, and suspend his head above the city gates. They intend the head as one kind of sign, an expression of their triumph and revenge over Onesilos (like the breasts of the womenfolk of Pheretime's enemies, which she has displayed at intervals along the city wall of Barke, 4.202.1), but it begins to function in quite another sign system when bees take up residence in it and fill it with honeycombs (5.114.1). The Amathousioi interpret this as a portent, and consult an oracle, which tells them to sacrifice to Onesilos as hero (θύειν ὡς ἥρωι, 5.114.2) annually.

2.8.7 Objects as Indicators of Size and Status

The Scythian use of human skin and skulls as indices, each χειρόμακτρον or skull representing an enemy killed in battle, is paralleled, though not in terms of the use of human flesh, by other passages in Herodotus' ethnographic descriptions where objects act as tallies and markers of status.[339] The women of the Gindanes, a Libyan tribe, wear ankle bracelets which indicate the number of men they have slept with. Whoever has the most of them is considered "best" because she has been loved by the most men (4.176). In Paionia, among the people who live on Lake Prasias in houses built on stilts,

339 Immerwahr (1960:265) remarks on this concern with measurement: "The idea that monuments afford a yardstick for measuring, quite literally, the greatness of persons underlies the mention of monuments in all the ethnographic logoi, especially the Egyptian."

the number of wives a man has is measured by the number of wooden props (and correspondingly, huts) he has. Whenever a man marries, he brings timber from Mount Orbelos and sets up three props for each wife (5.16.2).

The correspondence between the size or number of objects and the status of those associated with them works in an inverted fashion in the case of the criminal code of Sabakos, the Ethiopian ruler over the Egyptians. Instead of inflicting the death penalty for certain crimes, he institutes the following sanction:

> ὅκως τῶν τις Αἰγυπτίων ἁμάρτοι τι, κτείνειν μὲν αὐτῶν οὐδένα ἐθέλειν, τὸν δὲ κατὰ μέγαθος τοῦ ἀδικήματος ἑκάστῳ δικάζειν, ἐπιτάσσοντα χώματα χοῦν πρὸς τῇ ἑωυτῶν πόλι, ὅθεν ἕκαστος ἦν τῶν ἀδικεόντων.
>
> 2.137.3
>
> Whenever an Egyptian committed some offense, he was not prepared to execute any of them, but would assign a punishment to each according to the magnitude of the crime, ordering him to raise earthworks near the city which he came from.

The greater the mound, the greater the crime to which it points. Yet the function of the mound is not primarily to act as a sign: the higher the mound, the greater the benefit to the country, since the higher the elevation of the city, the more it is protected from the Nile's annual flooding.[340]

The mounds left by Dareios and his army on the banks of the river Arteskos function differently, but have nevertheless a semiotic component. These mounds ('hills', κολωνοί μεγάλοι) are composed of hundreds of stones, each stone acting as a token representing one soldier in Dareios' vast host:

> ἀποδέξας χωρίον τῇ στρατιῇ ἐκέλευε πάντα ἄνδρα λίθον ἕνα παρεξιόντα τιθέναι ἐς τὸ ἀποδεδεγμένον τοῦτο χωρίον. ὡς δὲ ταῦτα ἡ στρατιὴ ἐπετέλεσε, ἐνθαῦτα κολωνοὺς μεγάλους τῶν λίθων καταλιπὼν ἀπήλαυνε τὴν στρατιήν.
>
> 4.92
>
> After showing a site to his army he ordered every man to pass by and place one stone on the designated spot. When the army had

[340] Cf. 2.97.1, where Herodotus describes how in the season of flooding the Egyptians cities stand out above the water like islands in the Aegean. Cf. ch. 3.2 on Herodotus' techniques of comparison and analogy.

> accomplished this, leaving great hills of stones behind he marched the army away.

Taken collectively, the stones constitute on the one hand a kind of census, and on the other a monument to the greatness of Dareios' endeavor. Neither purpose, however, is explicitly attributed to Dareios by Herodotus, yet up to this point the narrative of Dareios' campaign against the Scythians has already been punctuated by a number of monuments: that of Mandrokles, architect of the bridge over the Bosporos, which is in both iconic form (a picture depicting the bridge and the progress of Dareios and his army across it, 4.88.1) and the form of written signs (an inscription, relayed by Herodotus at 4.88.2); and that of Dareios himself in the form of a *stêlê* honoring the healthful springs of the Tearos and the fact that they have been visited by so distinguished a visitor (4.91.1–2).[341]

The transformation of signs of one sort into another is even more complete in the description of the bronze *kratêr* of the Scythian king Ariantas, who decides to conduct a census of his people and orders each Scythian on pain of death to bring one arrowhead to him (4.81.5). He then decides to turn the great number of arrowheads into a monument (μνημόσυνον) for himself:

> κομισθῆναί τε δὴ χρῆμα πολλὸν ἀρδίων καί οἱ δόξαι ἐξ αὐτέων μνημόσυνον ποιήσαντι λιπέσθαι· ἐκ τουτέων δέ μιν τὸ χαλκήιον ποιῆσαι τοῦτο καὶ ἀναθεῖναι ἐς τὸν Ἐξαμπαῖον τοῦτον.
>
> 4.81.6

> A great number of arrowheads were brought to him, and he decided to leave behind him a monument made out of them: he made this bronze vessel from them and set it up on the river Exampaios.

A change in sign function is accompanied by a physical change in the sign vehicle as the arrowheads, each representing one individual, are melted down and a new object formed which also has a new semiotic function as monument (μνημόσυνον), recalling and celebrating the one who has set it up.[342] Ariantas'

341 The verb καταλείπω, used of Dareios' leaving behind of the piles as he moves his army onward (4.92), is used in a number of places (but in the middle voice) in the *Histories* for the leaving behind of a monument (the daughter of Kheops, 2.126.1; Rhodopis, 2.135.3; anonymous Persian guest, 9.16.2), discussed below, chs. 2.8.6 and 2.8.7. Cf. Bakker 2002:26 for μνημόσυνα in Herodotus and the fact that "the two phrases *apodexasthai* (*erga megala*) and *mnêmosuna* (*lipesthai*), in fact, are very much in each other's semantic orbit."

342 Immerwahr 1960:265–266: "The idea that a monument may represent its author is for us a

kratêr enacts the metaphor of the body politic, literally fashioning one object from his citizens.

The motif of the monument constructed from the contributions of individuals surfaces in the story Herodotus relays about the daughter of Kheops, but is given a highly unusual and erotic direction. The Egyptian king Kheops, when the funds in his treasury run low, presses his own daughter into prostitution in order to provide him with money. The daughter complies, but asks each of her customers to give her (in addition to her fee) a stone, intending to leave a monument (μνημήιον) behind her:

> τὴν δὲ τά τε ὑπὸ τοῦ πατρὸς ταχθέντα πρήσσεσθαι, ἰδίῃ δὲ καὶ αὐτὴν διανοηθῆναι μνημήιον καταλιπέσθαι, καὶ τοῦ ἐσιόντος πρὸς αὐτὴν ἑκάστου δέεσθαι ὅκως ἂν αὐτῇ ἕνα λίθον [ἐν τοῖσι ἔργοισι] δωρέοιτο· ἐκ τούτων δὲ τῶν λίθων ἔφασαν τὴν πυραμίδα οἰκοδομηθῆναι τὴν ἐν μέσῳ τῶν τριῶν ἑστηκυῖαν, ἔμπροσθε τῆς μεγάλης πυραμίδος.
>
> 2.126.1

> She carried out her father's commands, but privately came up with a plan to leave behind a monument for herself, and demanded of each man who visited her that he present her with one stone: from these stones [the Egyptians] said that the pyramid which is the middle one of the three in front of the great pyramid, was built.

The piquancy of the narrative resides in the fact that each stone represents not one warrior or one royal subject, as in the case of Dareios' mounds of stones or Ariantas' arrowheads, but each man with whom Kheops' daughter has slept, so that the total number of stones indicates the number of times the daughter of Kheops has prostituted herself. But she treats the stones exactly as Dareios and Ariantas regard the stones and arrowheads brought by those under their power, as tokens brought by subjects to their ruler: from what is potentially a record of her shame, she constructs a pyramid which stands besides others (ἐν μέσῳ τῶν τριῶν ἑστηκυῖαν, ἔμπροσθε τῆς μεγάλης πυραμίδος, 2.126.2) and acts as no less proud a monument (even though it is smaller than the others). Collectively, then, the individual tokens function

strange one, since a monument does not tell us anything about the personality of the builder, but merely serves as an *indicator* for measuring that unmeasurable quality, human greatness. Greatness is then simply wealth and power, and these we measure by reckoning up the troubles undergone in the erection of monuments, and by the marvelous size of the surviving structures. The motivation attributed by Herodotus to the great builders is precisely that of arousing in the beholder a feeling of marvel, and thus perpetuating their fame."

together as a new significant object, a μνημήιον which honors her memory for generations to come.

It is interesting that one of two other women in the *Histories* to leave a physical monument behind her is also a prostitute, but this time a professional. Rhodopis, a Greek courtesan operating in Egypt who has amassed for herself a large amount of money, wishes to leave behind a monument to herself. Unlike the daughter of Kheops, her monument does not take the form of a pyramid, since her funds will not run to one (2.135.2). More important is the desire to leave behind a monument of a completely different kind:

> ἐπεθύμησε γὰρ Ῥοδῶπις μνημήιον ἑωυτῆς ἐν τῇ Ἑλλάδι καταλιπέσθαι, ποίημα ποιησαμένη τοῦτο τὸ μὴ τυγχάνοι ἄλλῳ ἐξευρημένον καὶ ἀνακείμενον ἐν ἱρῷ, τοῦτο ἀναθεῖναι ἐς Δελφοὺς μνημόσυνον ἑωυτῆς.
>
> 2.135.3
>
> For Rhodopis conceived a desire to leave a monument to herself in Greece, to create a work which had not chanced to be thought of and dedicated in a temple by anyone else, and to set up this work in Delphi as a monument to herself.

No matter that Rhodopis' μνημήιον is only a collection of iron cooking spits big enough to spear an ox (ὀβελοὶ βούποροι, 2.135.4): the novelty of her monument ensures that her memory will be perpetuated, and Herodotus, as with his descriptions of all the other monuments in the *Histories*, subsumes and weaves her monument into his text, making the objects speak.[343]

2.8.8 Objects as Memorials and Monuments

The semiotic ability of objects to point back to the past and glorify the one associated with the object lies at the heart of the memorial (μνημόσυνον, μνημήιον, μνῆμα). It is an ability that any object of any type and size may assume, ranging from the pyramids and colossal statues of the Egyptian kings to the iron spits of Rhodopis. Common to all these monuments is the desire of

343 There is also a polemical thrust behind Herodotus' account: he wishes to challenge the interpretation of certain people who claim that a small pyramid is the pyramid of Rhodopis (2.134.1). He not only disputes this reading on the basis of iron spits, from which he is able to calculate the extent of Rhodopis' capital assets (the offerings represent a tithe) and finds them inadequate to pay for a pyramid, but explains to us where her true monument is to found: in the spits themselves! Lloyd in Asheri et al. 2007 *ad loc.* notes that a cache of these spits, each measuring 1.2 m., was found in the Heraion at Argos.

the builder (in both literal and figurative senses) to leave a perceptible trace of himself or herself on the surface of the world, and in so doing to surpass the achievements of others.[344] This competitive element, seen already in Rhodopis' desire for an unprecedented type of monument, one not to be found in any other temple precinct (τὸ μὴ τυγχάνοι ἄλλῳ ἐξευρημένον καὶ ἀνακείμενον ἐν ἱρῷ, 2.135.3), is also evidenced in Aryandes' desire to issue a new type of coin, in silver, rivaling Dareios' famous gold coin. Dareios' reasons for issuing such a coin are presented as a desire to leave behind a monument to himself which no other king has ever wrought (ἐπιθυμέοντα μνημόσυνον ἑωυτοῦ λιπέσθαι τοῦτο τὸ μὴ ἄλλῳ εἴη βασιλέϊ κατεργασμένον, 4.166.1).[345] Aryandes' action is on the one hand pure imitation (ἐμιμέετο),[346] since his coin is modeled on Dareios', but on the other hand he creates a new coin which is issued by his authority and to which his name becomes attached:

> πυθόμενος γὰρ καὶ ἰδὼν Δαρεῖον ἐπιθυμέοντα μνημόσυνον ἑωυτοῦ λιπέσθαι τοῦτο τὸ μὴ ἄλλῳ εἴη βασιλέϊ κατεργασμένον, ἐμιμέετο τοῦτον, ἐς οὗ ἔλαβε τὸν μισθόν. Δαρεῖος μὲν γὰρ χρυσίον καθαρώτατον ἀποψήσας ἐς τὸ δυνατώτατον νόμισμα ἐκόψατο, Ἀρυάνδης δὲ ἄρχων Αἰγύπτου ἀργύριον τώυτὸ τοῦτο ἐποίεε· καὶ νῦν ἐστὶ ἀργύριον καθαρώτατον τὸ Ἀρυανδικόν.
>
> 4.166.1–2
>
> Having learned and seen that Dareios was keen to leave a monument to himself which no other king had effected, Aryandes imitated him, until he paid the price for it. Dareios had struck a coinage of gold which he had refined to the highest possible degree, and Aryandes, when he was in charge of Egypt, did the same thing with silver coinage: even now the Aryandic is the purest silver coin.

344 This also reflects on Herodotus' own achievements and glory: see ch. 3.2 below.

345 Immerwahr 1960:266, surveying the use of the words ἔργον and μνημόσυνον in the *Histories*, remarks that "all *mnêmosyna* share the feature that the utilitarian purpose of the *ergon* is secondary, or even disregarded. Thus, in IV, 166, 1 Darius' gold coinage is considered not under its practical aspect, but merely as a memorial sought by the king. The most famous instance of the disregard for the practical is the Mount Athos canal (VII, 24), which Herodotus considers merely as a memorial to Xerxes' pride (μεγαλοφροσύνη). The motivation of the builder is again to create that very effect in the spectator which Herodotus attributes to him."

346 For imitation as a linking and explanatory device in Herodotus, cf. e.g. 2.104.4 (Kolkhoi imitate Egyptians in matter of circumcision); 5.67.1 and 5.69.1 (Kleisthenes of Sikyon and Kleisthenes of Athens; cf. ch. 2.6.1 above); 9.34.1 (Teisamenos imitates Melampous; cf. ch. 2.4 above).

Aryandes achieves his immortal monument at the cost of his own life, because he trespasses on the prerogative of the king, who has the exclusive right to strike and mark coinage, just as he alone has the right to mark and mutilate his slaves.[347] Anyone else who does so is either suspected of treason and executed, as are Aryandes and Intaphrenes, who usurps the king's right by disfiguring the servants of Dareios when they refuse to let him in for an audience while the king is with a woman (3.118.1–119.2).

The desire of the Egyptian Asykhis to outdo (ὑπερβαλέσθαι) his predecessors, a frequent motif in such descriptions, as we have seen above, leads him to erect a pyramid made of mud bricks instead of stone, and so that the monument may indicate his greatness not just by its mere presence, he endows it with a voice in the form of a talking inscription in which it proclaims its own superiority (and by extension, that of its maker):

> "μή με κατονοσθῇς πρὸς τὰς λιθίνας πυραμίδας· προέχω γὰρ αὐτέων τοσοῦτο ὅσον ὁ Ζεὺς τῶν ἄλλων θεῶν. κοντῷ γὰρ ὑποτύπτοντες ἐς λίμνην, ὅ τι πρόσσχοιτο τοῦ πηλοῦ τῷ κοντῷ, τοῦτο συλλέγοντες πλίνθους εἴρυσαν καί με τρόπῳ τοιούτῳ ἐξεποίησαν."
>
> 2.136.4

> "Do not compare me slightingly to the pyramids made of stone: for I am as superior to them as Zeus is to the rest of the gods. For by pushing down with a pole into a lake and collecting whatever mud attached to the pole they turned this into bricks and constructed me in this fashion."[348]

Monuments, being signs, require, or at least attract, interpretation, as Herodotus has already shown in the case of the μνημήιον of Rhodopis and in a number of other instances where he corrects the readings of others. Those who interpret (εἰκάζουσι, 2.106.5) the figure of a man carved in rock as a representation (εἰκών, 2.106.5) of Memnon are "far short of the truth" (πολλὸν τῆς

347 Kurke (1999:69) points out how the language of metals can also be seen here: "Refined gold signifies Darius' own rightful sovereignty, while Aryandes' silver imitation precisely reenacts the originary *hubris* of the silver race. . . . So here, the logic of the Hesiodic myth makes Darius' conclusion eminently comprehensible: Aryandes' silver coinage in immediately construed by Darius (and by our narrator) as a violent, unlawful bid for sovereignty—as an act of insurrection."

348 Cf. the speaking dedicatory epigram, which might be termed a μνημόσυνον, of Mandrokles that accompanies his painting (μνημόσυνον σχεδίης, 4.88.2) of his bridge constructed for Dareios across the Bosporos, which itself could be called a μνημόσυνον: Herodotus speaks of *mnêmosuna* (plural) in the conclusion to the description (ταῦτα μέν νυν τοῦ ζεύξαντος τὴν γέφυραν μνημόσυνα ἐγένετο, 4.88.2).

ἀληθείης ἀπολελειμμένοι, 2.106.5): it is in fact Sesostris. Herodotus is also able to interpret the *stêlai* which Sesostris left behind him along the route he followed in returning to Egypt from his campaign against those living in the area of the Red Sea and the Persian Gulf and which commemorate his own prowess and his enemies' weakness. According to Herodotus, the *stêlai* fall into two types, the one containing only an inscription, and the other an inscription together with a representation of a woman's genitalia. Herodotus produces a reading of the two types. In those countries where Sesostris encountered spirited resistance, he erected *stêlai* with an inscription with his name, country, and the fact that he had subdued them by his might; in those countries where no resistance was given, he put up *stêlai* of the second type, having the same inscription as those erected in the countries of brave men, but in addition the depiction of a woman's genitalia, which Herodotus interprets as a contemptuous sneer at the cowardice of his opponents (2.102.4–5). Herodotus thus interprets the *stêlai* according to a code in which the exposure of the female genitalia indicates contempt, as it does, for example, in the festival of Artemis at Boubastis, where female participants traveling to the festival on barges display themselves in ritual obscenity to those on the shore, to the accompaniment of mocking remarks (2.60.2).[349]

Those who say that that the large wooden cow in the city of Saïs is in fact the coffin of Mykerinos' daughter, that the twenty wooden images represent his concubines, and that their lack of hands commemorates the fact that Mykerinos' wife chopped off the hands of the models for these statues for allowing Mykerinos to sleep with his daughter are talking nonsense, says Herodotus (2.131.3). According to him, the hands of the images have merely fallen off because of the passage of time, and lie there at their feet for anyone to see (2.131.3). In other words, they simply do not act as signifiers of the message these people believe to be encoded in the statues.

***

It would be possible to add many more examples of objects used as signs in Herodotus' work: the survey in this chapter at least shows how objects are invested with meaning, the manifold messages with which they are encoded, and the ways in which they may be decoded. What is most important is that it is Herodotus himself who has selected and placed these objects in his narrative. Consider, for example, how objects form the center of certain narratives (e.g. Polykrates' ring, the gifts of the Scythians), and how the reactions of figures in the work to, and their interpretations of, these objects exercise a

349 Cf. examples of the use of body as sign vehicle, above 2.8.6.

powerful influence on the direction of the narrative and serve to reveal key elements in the character of the participants: Polykrates' ring will not be got rid of but stays there, "objet chargé d'une malédiction";[350] the bow sent as a gift by the Ethiopian king causes the falling-out between Kambyses and his brother, Smerdis; the gifts of the Scythians demonstrate in concise and direct fashion the gulf that lies between Dareios' understanding of the Scythian *nomoi* and Gobryas' realistic assessment of the situation.

350 The expression is Legrand's (1932–54 *ad loc.*).

Part 3

The Use and Abuse of Signs

3.1 The Manipulation of Signs in Herodotus' *Histories*

3.1.1 Introduction

Herodotus' *Histories* contain many examples of figures who by a certain ingenuity and cunning manage to turn an unfavorable situation to their own advantage.[1] These figures have in common an ability to think quickly and to outwit others, and they make use of techniques which, when evaluated in strictly ethical terms, are unscrupulous, deceitful, and dishonest. They are figures of the trickster type, familiar to audiences not merely of Herodotus but of Greek literature in general. Among their earliest manifestations are the Homeric Odysseus and Penelope and the Hermes of the Homeric hymn. In the case of the *Histories*, they have been examined by Camerer (1965), Lateiner (1990), Dewald (1993), and in particular Bencsik (1994), and as a general phenomenon in Greek literature by, for example, Detienne and Vernant (1978) and Pratt (1993). With the exception of Dewald's important study of significant objects in the *Histories*, the fact that to a large degree the trickster's skill lies in the use and abuse of signs of various types has not been explored.[2] Out of the sixty-

1 A full list of these instances of trickery in the *Histories* is given in Appendix 1 at the end of the book.

2 Dewald in her discussion of significant objects in the *Histories* makes the connection between the trickster figure and the ability to read objects (1993:59n8). She speaks in several places of the "manipulation of significant objects" by figures in the *Histories* (59, 63–65, 67, 70). Bencsik 1994 groups together instances of oath-breaking (55–58), the deceptive use of clothing (46–49), and secret messages (59–62), but does not consider as a common denominator between these instances the use and abuse of signs. Lateiner (1990), though sensitive in previous work to semiotic aspects in the *Histories* (cf. Lateiner 1987 on non-verbal communication and the useful appendices there), does not consider the manipulation of signs as a factor in his article on deceptions. He links instances of deception in Herodotus with what he terms "delusions," the shared "belief in a natural or supernatural event without anyone's being the richer for it" (1990:230), two categories which may be viewed together only if one believes, as Lateiner does, that Herodotus is a "skeptical empiricist" who "usually shows little sympathy for belief in supernatural interference in earthly affairs" (237) and thus in general presents such supernatural phenomena as the realm of "bogus gods, false priests, and sham messengers of the

nine instances of trickery I have identified in the *Histories*, I find that thirty-three involve a manipulation of signs (see Appendix). By the latter expression I mean an attempt in various ways to interfere with or hijack the process of signification and, in so doing, to achieve a result that is favorable to the manipulator's own ends. Trickery will naturally often involve the use of signs, but this may be only incidental to the essence of the trick, for example when persuasive or lying speech is used, such as when Kleomenes tricks the Argives he has surrounded in a wood into coming out of hiding. He calls each man by name, claiming he has received ransom for him; when the man emerges, he is killed (6.79.1–2). Contrast this instance of trickery with one which immediately precedes it in Herodotus' narrative, where the Argives penetrate the Spartan system of military signals, so that they are able to anticipate Spartan actions (6.77.3). Once the Spartans find this out, however, they change their code, confound their enemy, and kill a large number of them (6.78.1–2). Here the trick consists precisely in meddling with and manipulating the system of signs.

In what follows we will explore how this manipulation of signs is achieved and how Herodotus presents the manipulators. It will be suggested that Herodotus' interest in and admiration of these manipulators of signs is intimately connected with his narrative persona as a master presenter and interpreter of signs, and that this is part of his distinctive and authoritative "voiceprint." There has been a tendency in some recent scholarship to see in Herodotus an overly pessimistic, postmodern figure who broods over the indeterminacy of meaning and the myriad possibilities for disconnection between signifier and signified.[3] A re-appreciation of instances of interpretation, taking into account the status of the interpreter (professional vs. lay interpreter,

divine" (235). For a different view of Herodotus and the divine, see Harrison 2000 and Scullion 2006. The present study looks beyond the field of significant objects to other sign systems, explores the means of manipulation in more detail, and comes to different conclusions about the role of the manipulation of signs in the *Histories*.

3 Cf. e.g. Lateiner 1987:100 on the limitations of human knowledge and ability in the *Histories* when it comes to signs and symbols, and Dewald 1993:63–64 on the problems faced by figures in the *Histories* in the use and abuse of significant objects. Braund stresses the "problematics of reciprocity" and cross-cultural communication in the work (1998:169, 172), yet is careful to emphasize that the *Histories* equally show the possibility of overcoming these difficulties, in particular with the help of Herodotus himself (177): "In exploring the difficulties of forming relationships with the 'other,' Herodotus' *Histories* present readers with failures and disasters, arising primarily from ignorance, over-confidence, and cultural chauvinism. There is a definite element of pessimism in the *Histories*. . . . But there is also hope, for the author claims for himself the ability to rise above commonplace failings and offers to provide his readers with a better understanding of themselves, of others, and of reciprocity." On Herodotus as master reader of signs, see ch. 3.2.

Greek vs. non-Greek) as well as the type of sign communication (e.g. oracle, dream, portent) suggests that Herodotus celebrates the triumph of human ingenuity (including his own) in both the use and abuse of signs.

At each step in the chain of communication by signs there is a certain window of opportunity for interference and manipulation, and the Herodotean manipulators of signs examined in this book make full use of these moments. For this reason we will use the process of sign communication as a framework to structure our investigation in this chapter. The vast majority of Herodotean manipulators take advantage of the process of encoding and transmission, while there are by my reckoning only five instances where sign manipulation takes place during the process of reception and decoding. The instances we will discuss below have been chosen to illustrate particular types of sign manipulation and are drawn from the various sign systems found in the *Histories.*

3.1.2 Encoding and Transmission

3.1.2.1 Oracles

Let us begin with the process of encoding and transmitting signs and, in particular, the manipulation of signs through appropriation of the means of sign production. This type of manipulation involves simply seizing the source of sign transmission and making it produce signs favorable to one's own objectives, rather like rebels whose first move is to capture the local radio or television station.[4] It is a tactic (characterized as a scheme or μηχανή at 5.90.1 and 6.123.1) used by Kleisthenes and the Alkmaionidai, who bribe the Pythia so that she will produce oracular responses enjoining the Spartans to liberate Athens and expel the Peisistratidai (5.63.1). For the Spartans, the Pythia simply relays the words of the god and they never suspect that she may be being used to transmit the words of men. Their respect for the oracle is so strong that it overcomes their ties to the Peisistratidai, their ξεῖνοι. As Herodotus puts it (5.63.2), "They considered the affairs of the god of more importance [πρεσβύτερα] than those of men." The Spartans as a whole are presented by Herodotus as not particularly talented in the field of sign interpretation, though individuals among them such as Likhas (1.67.2–1.68.6), Kleomenes, and his daughter, Gorgo (7.239.2–4, discussed below), do demonstrate this ability in full measure. Kleomenes, in his own right no mean manipulator of

4 This comparison is used by Steiner (1994:152n65) in talking of Kyros' appropriation of Astyages' royal writing (1.125.2), discussed below in connection with Bagaios' scheme for killing Oroites (3.128.2–5).

signs, is able to resist Aristagoras' attempt to manipulate him by means of the signs of a map, thanks to the intercession of Gorgo (5.49–50). He forces Aristagoras to reveal unwittingly the real relationship between the signifiers of the map (marks representing the coast of Asia Minor, Sardis, and Susa and their positions relative to each other) and the signified, the real cities and the real distances between them (three months from the sea to Susa!) (5.50.1–2). Aristagoras has to leave because he can neither control nor mask the true connection between signifier and signified any longer (οὐδέ οἱ ἐξεγένετο ἐπὶ πλέον ἔτι σημῆναι, 5.51.3), despite his considerable skills (τἆλλα ἐὼν σοφὸς καὶ διαβάλλων ἐκεῖνον εὖ).[5] It is one of the few moments when Herodotus expressly talks of the failure of an attempt to manipulate signs, using a wrestling metaphor to describe Aristogoras as being "thrown down" in this plan: ὁ δὲ Ἀρισταγόρης . . . ἐν τούτῳ ἐσφάλη (5.50.2).[6]

Athenian audiences do not emerge particularly well either, as shown by Peisistratos' notorious deception of them using the statuesque Phye (1.60.4, discussed below), and Herodotus' remark concerning Aristagoras' success in deceiving the Athenians:

> πολλοὺς γὰρ οἶκε εἶναι εὐπετέστερον διαβάλλειν ἢ ἕνα, εἰ Κλεομένεα μὲν τὸν Λακεδαιμόνιον μοῦνον οὐκ οἷός τε ἐγένετο διαβάλλειν, τρεῖς δὲ μυριάδας Ἀθηναίων ἐποίησε τοῦτο.
>
> 5.97.2
>
> It seems that it is easier to mislead many people than it is to mislead a single person, if Aristagoras was unable to deceive Kleomenes the Spartan when he was on his own, but managed it in the case of thirty thousand Athenians.

The commander of the second Spartan campaign against the Peisistratidai is none other than Kleomenes, who himself resorts to precisely the same kind of manipulation when trying to depose Demaratos from the other kingship. Through the services of Kobon, an influential citizen of Delphi, he is able to corrupt the Pythia, who, when doubt is thrown on Demaratos' legitimacy and the oracle is approached to resolve the issue, gives the reply that Demaratos is not the son of Ariston (6.66.1–3).

[5] For *sophiê* in connection with sign manipulation and trickery, see further below. διαβάλλω as a verb of deception is used at 3.1.4 (Amasis deceives Kambyses by passing off an Egyptian noblewoman as his daughter); 5.97.2 (cited above); 5.107 (Histiaios deceives Dareios); 8.110.1 (Themistokles talks the Athenians into not immediately pursuing Xerxes); 9.116.2, in middle voice (Artayktes tricks Xerxes into giving him the sanctuary of Protesilaos, discussed below).

[6] Other failed manipulations of signs: 7.6.3 (Onomakritos); 9.120.2–4 (Artayktes).

The Alkmaionidai and Kleomenes achieve their ends by seizing control of the source of signs in the form of the Pythia, but there are other ways of manipulating oracular signs at their source. In the case of the oracles of Musaios and Bakis, the utterances are gathered together into a collection, parts of which are then recited by a collector and purveyor of oracles (χρησμολόγος) when consulted.[7] Should the collection fall into the hands of an individual, that person is in a position to control access to information by placing them in a restricted location, and by controlling their retransmission and, as Nagy has described, their performance.[8] This is what the Peisistratidai do. Herodotus reports that Kleomenes got hold of (ἐκτήσατο, 5.90.2) a collection of oracles which were previously in the possession of the Peisistratidai (ἔκτηντο, 5.90.2) and which they had left in the temple on the Akropolis in their haste to depart (5.90.2).[9]

Herodotus' account also demonstrates in another way the power conferred by possession of these oracular texts. When the Spartans discover that the oracles contain predictions that they will suffer many dire things at the hands of the Athenians, this makes them even more determined to restore the Peisistratidai (5.90.2). It is as if the Athenians' possession of these oracles grants them a knowledge of the future, a kind of secret weapon of which they have now been disarmed, luckily for the Spartans.[10] Hippias' previous possession of the oracles and his expert knowledge of their contents (τοὺς χρησμοὺς ἀτρεκέστατα ἀνδρῶν ἐξεπιστάμενος, 5.93.2)[11] also constitute a weapon which he is able to hurl at Sokles and the Corinthians, who have just talked the allies of the Spartans out of participating in an attempt to restore him to power. In what is effectively a curse as well as a prediction, he threatens

7 Cf. ch. 2.3 above on the figure of the χρησμολόγος.

8 Nagy 1990b:158–159, and esp. 169–170: "As long as private interests control the public medium, there is the ever-present danger of premeditated selective control over the content of poetry, leading to stealthy distortions or perversions of the poetic truth." Harrison (2000:141n69) also points out the "powerful political prerogative" that such possession gives, and that the Spartan kings had the privilege and responsibility of keeping collections of prophecies (6.57.4). On oral performance and oracles, see also Maurizio 1997.

9 Nagy points out that the use of the verb κτῆμαι suggests private possession, as does the collection's location in a temple (1990b:159): "the writing down of the oracular utterances makes it possible for the tyrants to possess this poetry as their private property. But this poetry is private property only because the tyrants, as Herodotus implies with the details about the storage of poetry on the akropolis, have the power *not* to make all such poetry public property, by withholding public performance."

10 Cf. 1.20, where, as Harrison (2000:142n69) notes, "Periander forewarns his friend Thrasybulus of Miletus of an oracle given to Alyattes almost as if it were an industrial secret."

11 Peisistratos is also credited with expert knowledge of oracles in some sources: scholia to Aristophanes *Peace* 1071, Suda β 47 s.v. Βάκις, where he is given the epithet "Bakis" and called χρησμολόγος.

that there will be a time when the Corinthians will long for the Peisistratidai (5.93.1).[12]

Oracular manipulation of a further kind is revealed when Onomakritos, arranger (διαθέτης) of the oracles of Musaios and χρησμολόγος, is caught inserting a spurious oracle into the collection:

> ἐξηλάσθη γὰρ ὑπὸ Ἱππάρχου τοῦ Πεισιστράτου ὁ Ὀνομάκριτος ἐξ Ἀθηνέων, ἐπ' αὐτοφώρῳ ἁλοὺς ὑπὸ Λάσου τοῦ Ἑρμιονέος ἐμποιέων ἐς τὰ Μουσαίου χρησμὸν ὡς αἱ ἐπὶ Λήμνῳ ἐπικείμεναι νῆσοι ἀφανιοίατο κατὰ τῆς θαλάσσης· διὸ ἐξήλασέ μιν ὁ Ἵππαρχος, πρότερον χρεώμενος τὰ μάλιστα.
>
> 7.6.3
>
> Onomakritos was expelled from Athens by Hipparkhos, son of Peisistratos, when he was caught by Lasos of Hermione in the act of inserting into the oracles of Mousaios an oracle to the effect that the islands of Lemnos would disappear under the sea: it was for this reason that Hipparkhos expelled him, although he had made extensive use of his services before.

The possibility for manipulation is already present in his function of arranger (διαθέτης) of the collection, and, as will be seen below, it is by skillful arrangement, selection, and omission of oracular material that he will attempt to convince Xerxes to invade Greece. But his manipulation here lies in adding wholly new χρησμοί to the corpus of traditional material, in taking over control at the source and manufacturing signs. While the Alkmaionidai and Kleomenes must convince the Pythia to produce the message they need, Onomakritos needs no intermediary and as poet-performer can himself clothe the message in its appropriate form.[13] His patrons, the Peisistratidai, who are themselves, as has been seen, potential manipulators, expel him from the city, since he has usurped their control.

[12] Herodotean tyrants are generally good sign manipulators and readers of signs: cf. Thrasyboulos (1.20–22.1, 5.92.ζ.1–η.1); Peisistratos (1.59.4, 1.60.4); Periandros (3.51.2, 5.92.ζ.1–η.4); Kleisthenes of Sikyon (5.68.1–2). Cf. Steiner 1994, Gray 1996 (on the Bakkhiadai), Brandt 1998 (relationship between Delphi and Greek tyrants).

[13] Cf. Nagy (1990b:170) and Dillery (2005:189–191) on this passage, who think it more likely that Onomakritos was caught by Lasos while reciting the spurious oracle in the midst of a performance, rather than while writing it into the collection. Following Privitera (1965:48) and Nagy (1990b: 172–173), Dillery envisages the occasion as a competition between the two. He points out that there is a tradition (Athenaeus 8.338b–c, Hesychius s.v. λασίσματα) that presents Lasos as a well-known expert in manipulating language, and that he is thus a worthy opponent for Onomakritos.

He is shown to be equally adept at performing manipulation by means of the selective transmission of oracles. As arranger of the oracles of Mousaios (7.6.3), he legitimately practices selection in admitting or rejecting oracles: now he illegitimately transfers the process to the selective transmission of parts of an oracle. He is brought to the court of Xerxes by the exiled Peisistratidai, the very same people who expelled him from Athens. There he recites to Xerxes from his collection of oracles, suppressing any prediction unfavorable to the Persians and relating only those parts favorable to their endeavors:

> εἰ μέν τι ἐνέοι σφάλμα φέρον τῷ βαρβάρῳ, τῶν μὲν ἔλεγε οὐδέν, ὁ δὲ τὰ εὐτυχέστατα ἐκλεγόμενος ἔλεγε, τόν τε Ἑλλήσποντον ὡς ζευχθῆναι χρεὸν εἴη ὑπ' ἀνδρὸς Πέρσεω, τήν τε ἔλασιν ἐξηγεόμενος.
>
> 7.6.4
>
> Whenever there was something in [an oracle] spelling disaster for the Persians, of this he would make no mention, but would select the most optimistic parts and recite those, [for example] that the Hellespont would be yoked by a Persian, explaining this as the invasion.

Onomakritos' manipulation lies not in the interpretation of words but rather in his control of them: by acting as a secondary transmitter with a filter that allows through only the positive and not the negative, he produces a reaction in the king in favor of invasion, which is in the interests of Onomakritos' masters, the Peisistratidai, and ultimately himself.[14]

3.1.2.2 Dareios and the horse's whinny

The device of a sign artificially created and, like Onomakritos' forged oracle about the islands near Lemnos, designed to be indistinguishable from a sign produced according to legitimate and recognized means, is also seen in the account of Dareios' rise to the throne. The seven Persian conspirators agree amongst themselves to leave the selection of a king from their number to the random appearance of a sign: the one whose horse is the first to whinny at dawn will be king (3.84.3). Dareios, with the help of his cunning groom Oibares (described as ἀνὴρ σοφός, 3.85.1), is able to produce this sign artificially.[15]

14 For both instances of manipulation cf. the *theôros* (official sacred messenger) in Theognis 805–810, who must be straighter than a carpenter's rule and not add anything (οὐτέ τι . . . προσθείς, 807) to what the Pythia indicates (σημήνῃ, 808). Discussion in Nagy 1990b:165–166 and Dillery 2005.

15 Herodotus' narrative and the exchanges between Dareios and Oibares are full of the vocabulary often found in descriptions of trickery: see observations in Appendix.

During the night, Oibares brings Dareios' stallion's favorite mare near him and eventually allows him to mount her in the place where the test is to happen in the morning (3.85.3). At dawn, when the horses are led forth to this place, Dareios' horse catches a trace of the mare's scent and whinnies (3.86.1). As an ironic contrast to this wholly manipulated sign comes a sign of a different kind, one impossible to produce by any human means:

> ἅμα δὲ τῷ ἵππῳ τοῦτο ποιήσαντι ἀστραπὴ ἐξ αἰθρίης καὶ βροντὴ ἐγένετο.
>
> 3.86.2
>
> As soon as the horse did this, there was a lightning flash from a clear sky and a clap of thunder.[16]

It is read by the other Persian nobles as a confirmation and fulfillment (ἐτελωσέ μιν) of the first sign, as is made clear by their immediate reaction:

> ἐπιγενόμενα δὲ ταῦτα τῷ Δαρείῳ ἐτελέωσέ μιν ὥσπερ ἐκ συνθέτου τευ γενόμενα· οἱ δὲ καταθορόντες ἀπὸ τῶν ἵππων προσεκύνεον τὸν Δαρεῖον.
>
> 3.86.2
>
> These supervening events confirmed Dareios [as king], as if they had happened by some sort of arrangement: the others leapt down from their horses and prostrated themselves before Dareios.

Herodotus comments that the second sign followed upon the first "as if by some kind of arrangement" (ὥσπερ ἐκ συνθέτου τευ), and the word σύνθετος itself mirrors the verb συντίθεμαι, used to describe the agreement (συνεθήκαντο, 3.86.1) of the Persian nobles about the sign of the whinnying horse. The idea of agreement and arrangement suggests also the notion of agreement and convention as the basis of the link behind signifier and signified and what determines the meaning of a sign. Dareios' success and the fact that the heavens seem to wink at his deception show that the circumstances of the sign's production do not matter, merely the fact of its appearance. What is completely artificially produced may so resemble the natural as to be indistinguishable from it.[17]

[16] Cf. the double portent which Zeus sends to Odysseus in the form of a thunderclap from a clear sky and the φήμη uttered by a woman grinding corn (*Odyssey* 20.102–121). See also the story of Zopyros (3.153.1–158.2), discussed below, which also involves a double portent in which one of the portents is a φήμη.

[17] Harrison 2000:99 groups this passage together with 7.43.1 (thunder as Xerxes approaches

It has been suggested on the basis of Vedic parallels that an actual (though unattested) Iranian kingship ritual could lie behind the Herodotean account.[18] The parallels are particularly instructive in that a key part of these rituals is the carefully stage-managed production of what is "supposed" to be a naturally occurring sign. In the ritual called the *aśvamedha*, designed to renew the king's power, a horse is let loose and left to roam on its own, returning after a year, at which time it is sacrificed. But the horse is carefully observed all the time and made to return, so that the same fiction of the arbitrarily arising sign is present.[19] The *vājapeya* ritual also involves horses, but this time in a chariot race, in which the king competes against competitors from other social classes and always wins.[20] In part of the *rājasūya* ritual, the consecration of the king is confirmed by a particular throw of dice in a game played by the king and certain of his subjects. Again, we have here the production of what appears to be a sign impossible for humans to control and thus presumably indicative of the will of the gods. But the game is rigged, and the king who throws the dice always throws the winning combination and is confirmed as true king.[21] Herodotus may thus have been reacting to a similar combination of the arbitrary and manipulated in Persian kingship ritual, reflected and refracted in the myth of Dareios' ascent to the throne.

3.1.2.3 Manipulation of oaths

Dareios finds a way to preserve the outward integrity of the sign, and this concern for the formality of the sign system even while subverting it, thus enabling the manipulator to obtain his own aims, is especially seen in an important subcategory of verbal signs in the *Histories*, namely, oaths. By the very utterance of certain words framed in a certain format a binding effect is produced on both those who swear and those who receive the oath.[22] The

---

Troy) and 8.64 (earthquake heralding beginning of battle at Salamis): "The implication of some significance to natural phenomena is often no more than a matter of narrative timing."

18 Most recently Dumézil 1984 on the Vedic rituals of the *vājapeya* and *aśvamedha* as parallels. Cook (1983:54–55) collects other suggestions about possible ritual backgrounds.

19 Dumézil does not make this point about arbitrarily occurring signs. He does, however, draw attention to the importance of neighing and whinnying in the Vedic ritual (1984:144–145), which is a vital component in the Herodotean story.

20 See Dumézil 1984:146–147, who describes it as "[une] course truquée."

21 I owe this observation about the manipulation of the arbitrarily occurring sign of the dice game to an unpublished paper by Stephanie Jamison. The "dice" are in fact identical nuts from the *vibhītaka* tree (or imitations thereof). The aim appears to be to produce a throw containing a certain number of nuts divisible by the number four. See Heesterman 1957:143–157, who collects and compares the relevant Vedic texts.

22 See later discussion of speech acts in connection with 3.128.2–5. Metaphors of binding and

oath-making may be accompanied by tangible and physical signs: cutting of the body, for example, as described by Herodotus in the ethnographic chapters of his work.[23] But, as Burkert (1996:170) reminds us, the institution of the oath is inevitably accompanied by that of the false oath.

The Persian general Amasis, after nine months of besieging the city of Barke in Libya, is able to take the city by the simple stratagem of an oath. Herodotus introduces his account with an expression that invariably acts as a sign to the audience that a manipulation is about to occur (what Bencsik terms a *Signalsatz*): "Amasis contrives the following" (Ἄμασις . . . μηχανᾶται τοιάδε, 4.201.1).[24] Amasis invites the inhabitants of Barke to swear to an agreement that they will resume paying tribute to the king and that, for their part, the Persians will not visit them with any consequences for their previous disobedience (4.201.2). As with many oaths, the verbal signs of this oath are combined with a visual symbol to ensure irreversibility: the conditions agreed to will be binding "as long as this earth is as it is" (ἔστ' ἂν ἡ γῆ αὕτη οὕτως ἔχῃ, 4.201.2).[25] The seeming impossibility of the ground under their feet ever vanishing acts as a guarantee of the oath, and the people of Barke agree to the terms. But, unknown to them, they are standing on only the thinnest layer of earth, since Amasis has had a ditch dug and then covered with boards and a thin layer of soil to simulate the appearance of real earth (4.201.1), just as Xerxes' Persians fool their horses into crossing the bridge over the Hellespont by strewing the bridge's planks with earth, thus convincing the horses that they are on solid ground (7.36.5).[26] Once the oath is sworn, and the city gates have been opened, Amasis quite literally removes the oath's foundation by pulling up the boards and revealing the gaping hole over which they have been standing, and then orders his soldiers to seize the city (4.201.3). Herodotus in fact mirrors this removal of the foundation by a play on words: he says that Amasis and his men break up the planking "in order that their oath might

---

possession in the context of oaths appear at 1.29.2 (ὁρκίοισι . . . μεγάλοισι κατείχοντο) and 3.19.2 (ὁρκίοισι . . . μεγάλοισι ἐνδεδέσθαι).

23 1.74.6 (the Lydians and Medes cut their arms to the quick and lick each other's blood); 3.8.1 (Arabs); 4.70 (Scythians); cf. ch. 2.7.3 above on this performative aspect. Cf. the expression ὅρκιον τάμνειν: 4.70 (in the middle voice); 4.201.2; 4.201.3; 7.132.2; 9.26.4. On expressions of binding and cutting and connections with Near Eastern rituals, see Faraone 1993, esp. 76, and Knippschild 2002, index s.v. *Blutsbruderschaft*.

24 Bencsik 1994:11. See Appendix for examples of μηχανάομαι used in connection with tricksters.

25 "This earth" (ἡ γῆ αὕτη) is deictic: the parties to the oath point to the earth under their feet as part of the ritual of swearing. On touching the earth while swearing an oath, see Knippschild 2002:85. For another extreme of irreversibility, compare the oath of the people of Phokaia (1.165.3), who throw an ingot of iron into the harbor, and swear not to return before this ingot resurfaces: cf. ch. 2.7.3 above and discussion in Steiner 1994:68.

26 Cf. also the Phocian tactic at 8.28, where earth is spread over a ditch filled with pots.

remain firm" (ἵνα ἐμπεδορκέοιεν, 4.201.3). The irony of keeping an oath "on steady ground" (ἔμπεδος = ἐν πέδῳ) by removing the ground on which it was sworn is surely intended by Herodotus, and draws attention to his own role as a talented shaper and presenter of signs.[27] Through his physical manipulation of the earth Amasis thus manipulates the sign system by which the oath is constituted by removing the agreed-upon symbol of the oath's validity and artificially creating the conditions which render it inapplicable.

The oath extracted by Etearkhos from Themison (4.154.2–4) demonstrates two kinds of manipulation, one involving manipulation by means of oath, the other manipulation of the oath itself. The Cretan ruler Etearkhos, hard pressed by his "all-scheming" (πᾶν ... μηχανωμένη, 4.154.2) second wife to get rid of his daughter, tricks a visiting merchant from Thera, Themison, into agreeing to throw her into the sea (4.154.4). He is able to do so by using the device of the open-ended oath, in which one party requests the other to swear to do whatever he requests him to do (4.154.3), revealing the request only after the oath is sworn. The scheme is seen elsewhere in the *Histories* (further examples below), but only here does the deceived respond with a deception of his own. Once Themison realizes that he has sworn to drown Etearkhos' daughter, he protests and dissolves his guest-friendship with Etearkhos, but nevertheless takes her on board his ship, sails out to sea, and throws her into the water—after having tied a rope about her middle. The girl is submerged and then hoisted back on board. In this way Themison replies to Etearkhos' manipulation with a countermanipulation, relying on a very literal use of the verb καταποντῶσαι ("submerge in the sea") and fulfilling the terms of the oath, if not Etearkhos' intention.

The open-ended oath is also used by the Spartan king Ariston, who obtains his friend's wife by these means. Herodotus introduces his account with the usual vocabulary of trickery:

> μηχανᾶται δὴ τοιάδε· αὐτός τε τῷ ἑταίρῳ, τοῦ ἦν ἡ γυνὴ αὕτη, ὑποδέκεται δωτίνην δώσειν τῶν ἑωυτοῦ πάντων ἕν, τὸ ἂν αὐτὸς ἐκεῖνος ἕληται, καὶ τὸν ἑταῖρον ἑωυτῷ ἐκέλευε ὡσαύτως τὴν ὁμοίην διδόναι.
>
> 6.62.1

27 A similar play between ἔμπεδος in the meaning of "steadfast, connected to the ground" (as applied to physical objects) and ἔμπεδος in the meaning of "secure, certain" (as applied to words or signs) is already present in the *Odyssey*. At 23.202–204, Odysseus says he does not know whether the bed which he built is still ἔμπεδον or whether someone has cut it from the massive trunk of the olive tree of which it is such an integral part. The signs (σήματα) that Odysseus gives Penelope in relating the unique details of their bed are described as ἔμπεδα, which refers to their certainty, but also reminds us of the bed: ὣς φάτο· τῆς δ' αὐτοῦ λύτο γούνατα καὶ φίλον ἦτορ, | σήματ' ἀναγνούσῃ τά οἱ ἔμπεδα πέφραδ' Ὀδυσσεύς (*Odyssey* 22.205–206).

> [Ariston] contrived the following: he undertook to give his companion, who was the husband of this woman, any one item of his entire property he chose as a gift, and he bade his companion grant precisely the same to him.

The conclusion contains the language of compulsion and deceit:

> ἀναγκαζόμενος μέντοι τῷ τε ὅρκῳ καὶ τῆς ἀπάτης τῇ παραγωγῇ ἀπιεῖ ἀπάγεσθαι.
>
> 6.62.2
>
> [The companion], forced however by his oath and by the misleading deception, went off to fetch [his wife].

In another case involving erotic passion (ἔρως), invariably a destructive emotion in the *Histories*, the device of the open-ended oath figures not just once, but twice.[28] Xerxes promises his mistress, Artaynte, any gift she likes. She asks for the multicolored cloak which he is wearing (the gift of his wife, Amestris), and though Xerxes tries to wriggle out of the request (9.109.3), he is forced to give her the cloak, which then confirms his wife's suspicions of his infidelity when she sees Artaynte wearing it. Amestris is the master manipulator of signs in this scene: her weaving of the highly variegated cloak (ἐξυφήνασα Ἄμηστρις . . . φᾶρος μέγα τε καὶ ποικίλον καὶ θέης ἄξιον, 9.109.1) seems to go hand in hand with her cunning in weaving a plan in which to ensnare her husband and to destroy her rival.[29] The cloak itself becomes invested with meaning when it acts as a clear sign of Xerxes' betrayal. It is Amestris who makes use of the second open-ended promise in this story as a manipulative device to extract from Xerxes an undertaking to send her the wife of Masistes (and mother of Artaynte), whom she regards as her true rival (9.110.1). Herodotus gives the device a particularly Persian flavor by explaining

[28] Disastrous ἔρως: 1.8.1 (Kandaules and his wife); 2.131.1 (Mykerinos and his daughter); 3.31.2 (Kambyses and his sister); 6.62.1 (Ariston and his friend's wife); 9.108.1–2 (Xerxes and the wife and daughter of Masistes). Hall (1989:208), cited by Harrison (2000:238n34), comments that in Herodotus "the transgressive desire denoted by the term *eros* is attributed only to tyrants and kings."

[29] For weaving as a metaphor for cunning and duplicity cf. e.g. the expression μῆτιν ὑφαίνειν (e.g. *Iliad* 7.324, *Odyssey* 4.739); δολοπλόκος as epithet of Aphrodite in Sappho 1.2; and Klytemnestra's work of weaving (ὕφασμα, Euripides *Orestes* 25) in which she catches Agamemnon. The adjective ποικίλος, which refers literally to the variegated embroidery or inlay work, may also act metaphorically to characterize the artfulness of the craftsman. Pratt (1993:70) discusses the link between τέχνη and deception, and ποικιλία at 82–85, as do Detienne and Vernant (1978:19–20 and 279–318). For the poetic implications of weaving and embroidery, see also Nagy 1996a:64–66. Cf. also καταπλέκω in Herodotus at 4.205 and 8.83.2; cf. ch. 2.8.2 above.

that this occurred at the king's birthday feast, an occasion on which Persian *nomos* demands that the king grant any favor asked of him (9.110.2–111.1). Her use of signs does not end here: she has the wife of Masistes horribly mutilated, slicing off her breasts, nose, ears, and lips, and cutting out her tongue (9.112), matched only by the mutilations inflicted by Pheretime on her enemies (4.202.1).

3.1.2.4 Body used as signifier in manipulation

Mutilation of the body may be regarded as a semiotic act, especially in a Persian setting, where the mutilations act as a kind of text of the victims' offenses against the king.[30] Peisistratos' first attempt to seize power is based precisely on this semiotic potential of mutilation. In order to obtain a bodyguard from the *dêmos*, Peisistratos inflicts wounds on himself (and his mules), then runs into the *agora*, claiming that his enemies have tried to kill him (1.59.4). The scheme is successful: with the armed men voted him by the *dêmos* he seizes the akropolis and becomes ruler of Athens.[31] Peisistratos' body becomes in effect a text, with the wounds as bearers of meaning which the gullible Athenian populace is ready to interpret, at Peisistratos' prompting, as sure signs of his mistreatment at the hands of his enemies. As with Dareios' trick, Peisistratos' ruse succeeds because the possibility that such a sign may have been produced artificially does not even occur to the recipient.[32]

The most extreme manifestation of this is the tactic of the Persian Zopyros, who is so determined to win the honor of being the captor of Babylon that he mutilates himself, slicing off his nose and ears, in order that the Babylonians will believe he is a genuine defector from the Persian side and will admit him into the city, where he will be able to sabotage their defenses (3.154.2). Zopyros' self-inflicted mutilations are read against a specifically Persian code, in which wrongdoers and those who have offended against the king are inscribed with indelible signs of their offenses, ever-present and

30 Other instances of the Persian use of the human body as signifier: 3.69.3–6 (the earlessness of the false Smerdis, the result of an earlier transgression against the king, tips Otanes off); 5.25.1–2 (Kambyses has judge's throne upholstered with the skin of Sesamnes to act as a reminder to the latter's son, Otanes, of his father's transgressions and punishment); 7.39.3 (two halves of bisected body of Pythios' son act as a warning sign to the Persian army as they march between them). Cf. ch. 2.8.6 above.

31 Note characteristic trickster vocabulary: μηχανᾶται τοιάδε (1.59.3), ὁ δὲ δῆμος ὁ τῶν Ἀθηναίων ἐξαπατηθείς . . . (1.59.5).

32 As with Dareios, here too luck is combined with cunning: cf. the favorable oracle which Peisistratos receives through Amphilytos and which he interprets and acts on immediately; see Lavelle 1991.

ever-speaking tokens of their crimes.[33] His ability at manipulating signs goes hand in hand with an ability to recognize them, since the realization that Babylon is susceptible to capture is suggested to him by a combination of signs (3.153.1–2). The first sign comes in the form of a φήμη, a chance utterance pronounced by a Babylonian soldier and intended as a taunt: "What are you sitting here for, Persians? Why don't you go home? You'll capture us when mules give birth!" (3.151.2). This Zopyros subsequently interprets as having a deeper and divinely inspired meaning (σύν . . . θεῷ, 3.153.2). The second sign comes in the form of a *teras*: a mule does in fact give birth some months later.[34] Zopyros is able to read the two signs against each other, and his combined reading is a secret weapon which he guards jealously:

> ὡς δέ οἱ ἐξηγγέλθη καὶ ὑπὸ ἀπιστίης αὐτὸς ὁ Ζώπυρος εἶδε τὸ βρέφος, ἀπείπας τοῖσι ἰδοῦσι μηδενὶ φράζειν τὸ γεγονὸς ἐβουλεύετο.
>
> 3.153.1
>
> And after it had been reported to Zopyros and he, not believing it, had seen the offspring for himself, he forbade those who had seen it to report the event to anyone and began to think up a plan.

3.1.2.5 Clothing as signifier

We have seen how the body can act as a surface on which signs in the form of wounds and mutilations may literally be inscribed. That which surrounds the body, clothing, may also act as a signifier, providing information about ethnicity, status, sex, and identity, as is evident from Herodotus' ethnographic excursuses in which dress is an important category in describing a people.[35]

33 Dareios in the Behistun Inscription (§32) describes this punishment being given to the rebel Fravartiß, who is then displayed so that all the people may see him. The conventional meaning of these signs within the Persian penal system is precisely what Otanes and his daughter rely on in determining the identity of the false Smerdis. When Otanes' daughter discovers that the pseudo-Smerdis has no ears, this is testimony to a previous offense against the king and serves as incontrovertible proof that he is not Smerdis, the brother of Kambyses (3.69). Xenophon (*Anabasis* 1.9.13) describes this system of punishment being used by Kyros the Younger, saying that on the roads it was often possible to see people without legs, hands, and eyes. On the motifs of the Zopyros story and of other stories of the Persian court, see West 2003.

34 Bencsik 1994:39 comments that the appearance of a *teras* in connection with a σοφὸς ἀνήρ is common in the *Histories:* 1.59.1 (Peisistratos); 3.76.3 and 3.86.2 (Dareios); 2.162.1 (Amasis); 8.64.2 (Themistokles). For the double portent, which has a Homeric pedigree, see ch. 3.1.2.2 above on Dareios' scheme. On the prodigy of a mule giving birth, cf. the parallels gathered in Pease 1920–1923 on Cicero *De divinatione* 1.36.

35 E.g. 1.135.1, 1.202.3, 2.37.3, 4.78.4, 4.106, 4.111.1, 4.168.1, 4.189–190. On clothing as an extension of the body and the person, cf. the practice of touching or kissing the garment of a person:

As a marker and bearer of signs, clothing may also be manipulated for specific ends and made to convey a deceptive message.[36] Peisistratos makes use of this when he installs himself as tyrant for a second time with the help of Megakles. He finds a particularly tall and striking village girl named Phye, dresses her up in the panoply of the goddess Athena, places her on a chariot, and then sends messengers ahead to announce that the goddess herself is bringing Peisistratos back from exile (1.60.4). To the vast discredit of the Athenians, who pride themselves on being first among Greeks in intelligence, the scheme actually works:

> μηχανῶνται δὴ ἐπὶ τῇ κατόδῳ πρῆγμα εὐηθέστατον, ὡς ἐγὼ εὑρίσκω, μακρῷ (ἐπεί γε ἀπεκρίθη ἐκ παλαιτέρου τοῦ βαρβάρου ἔθνεος τὸ Ἑλληνικὸν ἐὸν καὶ δεξιώτερον καὶ εὐηθίης ἠλιθίου ἀπηλλαγμένον μᾶλλον), εἰ καὶ τότε γε οὗτοι ἐν Ἀθηναίοισι τοῖσι πρώτοισι λεγομένοισι εἶναι Ἑλλήνων σοφίην μηχανῶνται τοιάδε.
>
> 1.60.3
>
> For Peisistratos' return from exile [Peisistratos and Megakles] engineered by far the most simpleminded scheme, as I find (since long ago Greeks have been set apart from the barbarians in terms of being cleverer and more removed from foolish simplemindedness), if they were then able to contrive such a scheme amongst the Athenians, reputed to be first among the Greeks in *sophiê*.

The episode and Herodotus' comments on it illustrate an important feature of Greek descriptions of trickery and the manipulation of signs, namely that the cleverness of the scheme reflects not only on the perpetrator but equally on those it is designed to deceive. As Pratt puts it:

> Because of the close association of lying and deceiving with a certain kind of intelligence, the failure to recognize a lie or the succumbing to an act of deception may be seen as failure of intelligence.[37]

Near Eastern examples and discussion in Knippschild 2002:72–75.

36 Bencsik (1994:48) notes a further role played by clothing at 1.155.4, where a change in dress produces a change in the character of the bearer. Kroisos advises Kyros to make the Lydians wear long tunics (κιθῶνες) and high, soft boots (κόθορνοι) so that they will become women instead of men (γυναῖκας ἀντ' ἀνδρῶν ὄψεαι γεγονότας) and will pose no threat of rebellion. Cf. the idea that soft lands make for soft people in Kyros' speech at the end of the *Histories* (φιλέειν γὰρ ἐκ τῶν μαλακῶν χώρων μαλακοὺς ἄνδρας γίνεσθαι, 9.122.3), and see Dewald 1997 on this passage as a link back to the first book and a device for closure.

37 Pratt 1993:60. For Herodotus and epiphanies, see Harrison 2000:90–92, making the point that Herodotus' skepticism here should not be interpreted as indicative of a general skepticism about the possibility of divine epiphany.

Clothing as conveyor of information about identity and gender plays a role in two other passages in the *Histories*.[38] In the first, the wives of the Minyai, a people descended from the Argonauts and Lemnian women and now settled in Sparta, use dress as a means to free their husbands from prison. While on a prison visit to their husbands, the wives swap clothes with their husbands and the husbands are thus able to escape by assuming a female identity (4.146.2–4).[39] The same technique is used by Alexandros, son of the Macedonian ruler Amyntes, but in a deadly fashion. In order to prevent his Persian guests from imposing themselves sexually on the Macedonian women whom they have insisted be present at the symposion, Alexandros removes the women on the pretext that they must have a bath before proceeding any further, and then secretly dresses the same number of smooth-skinned Macedonian men in feminine attire and sends them into the dining room (5.20). When the Persians begin to paw them, they draw out daggers and kill them. The manipulation of these visual signs is accompanied by a manipulation of verbal signs, since when Alexandros invites the Persians to enjoy the women, he uses language that works on two different levels. He tells them that the Macedonians are lavishing their mothers and sisters upon them, "so that you may know completely that you are being honored by us with the things which you deserve" (ὡς παντελέως μάθητε τιμώμενοι πρὸς ἡμέων τῶν πέρ ἐστε ἄξιοι, 5.20.4), and asks them to "tell the king who sent you that a Greek, ruler of the Macedonians, entertained you well with both food and bed" (5.20.4). The phrase "with the things you deserve" amounts to a code that works on two planes: a surface level, on which the words are a conventional expression of flattery and subjection, and a hidden, deeper level, on which the phrase is a sinister forewarning of the punishment Alexandros is about to inflict on them for their insulting behavior.

3.1.2.6 Manipulation and coded utterances

Manipulation by coded utterance is used on a more extensive scale by the Persian Artayktes. Appointed commander of the Hellespontine region by Xerxes, he decides to get his hands on the sanctuary of the hero Protesilaos, the first Greek casualty in the Trojan War (*Iliad* 2.698–702), and on the consider-

[38] Cf. also 3.1.3 (daughter of Apries dressed to look like daughter of Amasis in order to fool Kambyses); 7.15.3 (Artabanos wears Xerxes' clothing in order that the same dream appear to him). Lateiner (1990:233) mentions as an instance of deception by dress 8.24–25, where Xerxes attempts to pass off four thousand of his own dead at Thermopylai as Spartans, though Herodotus does not talk of the use of clothing in this deception.

[39] The scheme is described by Herodotus as a δόλος (4.146.4).

able property attached to it. He does so by a request to Xerxes, framed in such a way as to enable him, on the surface at least, to preserve some semblance of a claim to the sanctuary and its contents.

> δέσποτα, ἔστι οἶκος ἀνδρὸς Ἕλληνος ἐνθαῦτα, ὃς ἐπὶ γῆν τὴν σὴν στρατευσάμενος δίκης κυρήσας ἀπέθανε. τούτου μοι δὸς τὸν οἶκον, ἵνα καί τις μάθῃ ἐπὶ γῆν τὴν σὴν μὴ στρατεύεσθαι.
>
> 9.116.3

> Master, there is a house of a Greek here who marched against your land, got his due, and died. Grant me this man's house, so that in the future people may learn not to invade your land.

Artayktes' words, taken on a surface level, appear to Xerxes as a reasonable request, but read on another level they reveal what Artayktes is really asking for. The "house" (οἶκος) that Artayktes mentions has two referents, one unmarked ("house") and one marked ("house" in the sense of *hêrôon*), and, as Herodotus points out, Artayktes' use of the term "your land" turns on the fact that the Persians regard all of Asia as the king's property (9.116.3).[40] The coded utterance is in ainetic form, a variety of speech which uses precisely this ability of words to function on two levels, a surface level and a deeper level which is concealed yet open to those with the necessary *noos* to decode them.[41] In this way, the message of the *ainos* is decoded only by those whom it is designed to advise, help, warn, or admonish. Artayktes' appropriation of this kind of encoding, however, is motivated solely by gain and the desire for personal profit, and he does not of course want Xerxes to understand the true meaning behind the term *oikos* and the real identification of this man, nor does Xerxes show himself worthy of understanding the message. Artayktes' manipulation of the *ainos* parallels and foreshadows his manipulation of the *teras* of the *tarikhoi*: his manipulations always contain the truth, which in the case of his second manipulation he is unable to control for his own purposes.

40 Also mentioned by Herodotus at 1.4.4: cf. note below on the sense of coming full circle and closure in the last chapters of book 9. For the sanctuary of a hero conceived of as a dwelling, compare, for example, Oedipus' description of himself as a οἰκητήρ 'inhabitant' (Sophocles *Oedipus Coloneus* 627) of the place where his tomb will eventually be. Here too the reference is in coded form: κοὔποτ' Οἰδίπουν ἐρεῖς | ἀχρεῖον οἰκητῆρα δέξασθαι τόπων | τῶν ἐνθάδ', εἴπερ μὴ ψεύδουσί με (626–628). Discussion of the Herodotean passage and its connection with hero cult in Nagy 1990b:268–269 and Nagy 2001. On the hero's "possession" of his tomb and the use of the terms κατέχειν ('possess') and ἔχειν ('hold') in this regard, which may also indicate ownership of land, see the comments of Henrichs (1993:175). Henrichs (1976:278) (with references) discusses instances of οἶκος in the sense of temple.

41 Cf. ch. 2.5 above on the *ainos*.

3.1.2.7 Concealment of signs

What has been described above is a cloaking device in which a deeper meaning is overlaid by a surface meaning. The cover is provided by the sign itself in that the signifier (e.g. the word οἶκος, 'house', in Artayktes' request to Xerxes) has two meanings, one of which, the signified, conceals the other, the referent. The concealment of signs may also be achieved by physical means (steganography), a technique which does not rely on the sign's own polysemic ability, but merely on its removal from the human gaze. Herodotus presents three clever variations on this principle, all involving the concealment of written signs from the watchful eyes of Median and Persian guardians of the royal roads.[42] Harpagos, who is plotting to depose the Median ruler Astyages and put Kyros the Persian on the throne, gets his message through in an ingenious fashion:

> ὁ δὲ ἐπιτεχνᾶται τοιόνδε. λαγὸν μηχανησάμενος καὶ ἀνασχίσας τούτου τὴν γαστέρα καὶ οὐδὲν ἀποτίλας, ὡς δὲ εἶχε, οὕτω ἐσέθηκε βυβλίον, γράψας τά οἱ ἐδόκεε.[43]
>
> 1.123.4
>
> He contrived the following: he prepared a hare and made a slit in its belly, and without pulling any of its fur off, but [leaving it] just as it was, he inserted into it a letter, having written down what he wanted to say.

The hare becomes a literal bearer of signs and is allowed to pass without suspicion owing to its status as a gift-object.[44] (Harpagos disguises his messenger as a huntsman, giving him nets for the sake of verisimilitude: 1.123.4.) The hare thus hides the message it carries, both physically and in the sense that its external appearance as a gift masks its actual function. In a second passage, Histiaios uses not an animal, but a human as sign-bearer to convey his secret

42 1.123.3: Harpagos cannot send message because the roads are watched (ἅτε τῶν ὁδῶν φυλασσομένων); cf. 5.35.3: Histiaios tries to send a message (σημῆναι) to Aristagoras but cannot because the roads are watched (φυλασσομένων τῶν ὁδῶν), and 7.239.3: Demaratos cannot send a message from Sousa (σημῆναι) because of the danger that it might be intercepted.

43 Note the verbs characteristic of trickery and manipulation: ἐπιτεχνάομαι and μηχανάομαι. Powell maintains that here and at 1.94.6 μηχανάομαι means simply "procure," but the notion of resourcefulness and craft is still surely present.

44 For other sign-bearing hares, cf. 4.134.1–2 (Scythians' pursuit of a hare in preference to fighting the Persians convinces Dareios to abandon his campaign) and 7.57.1 (a mare gives birth to a hare: see ch. 2.1.6 above). For animals in the *Histories* as narrative omens or signs, see also ch. 2.5 above and Munson 2001a:247–251. On gift-objects see ch. 2.8.2 above.

message to Aristagoras. The slave, instead of simply secreting the text on his person or in some object, becomes the text himself when Histiaios tattoos the message onto his shaven head and dispatches him once his hair has grown back and covers the letters (5.35.3).[45]

Finally, Demaratos, deprived of his right to the Spartan kingship and now a member of Xerxes' entourage, uses perhaps the ultimate method of concealment, a sign-bearing surface which bears no signs. He sends a message to his compatriots in Sparta warning them of the imminent Persian invasion and, in order to avoid its interception by Persian spies, devises the scheme (μηχανᾶται τοιάδε, 7.239.3) of writing not on the wax surface of the writing tablet, but directly on the wooden surface of the tablet itself, which he then covers with a layer of wax. The tablet thus presents the aspect of a *tabula rasa* and reaches its destination unhindered. But there remains the crucial step of detection and decoding by the recipient. Harpagos (1.123.4) and Histiaios (5.35.1) at least give instructions to their respective messengers so that the recipient will know where to look for the message, but this is not the case with Demaratos' dispatch. As will be suggested below, this is for reasons other than concern about the safe passage of the message. When the Spartans receive the tablet, they see only an empty surface, bereft of any signs, and as Herodotus says, they are unable to "put it together" (οὐκ εἶχον συμβαλέσθαι, 7.239.4).[46] They can find no signifier to join together with any signified, and are rescued from their aporia only by Gorgo, daughter of Kleomenes, who is able to find meaning in the absence of signs and interprets the lack of signs as a kind of sign itself:[47]

> Γοργὼ ὑπέθετο ἐπιφρασθεῖσα αὐτή, τὸν κηρὸν ἐκκνᾶν κελεύουσα, καὶ εὑρήσειν σφέας γράμματα ἐν τῷ ξύλῳ.[48]
>
> 7.239.4

45 The ultimate example of the human skin as text is the Cretan lawgiver Epimenides, whose skin was found to be tattooed with letters (γράμματα, Suda ε 2471 τὸ Ἐπιμενίδειον δέρμα). The theme of secrecy is also present, since the Suda explains that the expression τὸ Ἐπιμενίδειον δέρμα ("the skin of Epimenides") is used of things that are mysterious or hidden (ἐπὶ τῶν ἀποθέτων). See Svenbro 1993:137 and Dillery 2005.

46 On συμβάλλεσθαι in contexts of sign decoding, see ch. 1.3.1 above.

47 Cf. the blank shield of Amphiaraos in Aeschylus *Seven Against Thebes* 591–592, which acts as a sign though, unlike the shields of the other six warriors, it bears no actual *sêma*. Steiner 1994:56 discusses the passage, but does not draw a connection between it and Demaratos' *tabula rasa*. For Zeitlin (1982:115), "the sightless surface of Amphiaraos' shield is itself a sign of the seer, the mantic emblem of blindness and insight."

48 As Dewald (1993:58) puts it, "A certain skill at reading objects seems to run in the family." Gorgo has already proved herself a precocious reader of signs: as a child, she prevents her father from being corrupted by a smooth-talking Aristagoras and his map (5.51.2). The use of ἐπιφράζομαι as a verb of decoding is also seen at 4.200.2 (blacksmith of Barke detects siege-tunnels), discussed below.

> Gorgo herself came up with a suggestion: if they rubbed off the wax they would find the letters on the wooden surface.

The issue is to *find* the signifier in the first place and recognize that there is one. Similarly, in the episode of Thrasyboulos' famous non-verbal message to Periandros in which he strolls through a field of wheat, cutting down those stalks that project above the others, the messenger does not recognize that this constitutes a message (5.92.ζ.1–3), but Periandros, using his *noos* (νόῳ σχών, 5.92.η.1), correctly realizes that the actions function as signifiers and decodes the message.[49] As we observed earlier about the manipulator and his audience, the manipulation reflects equally on the competency of those who are manipulated. Herodotus presents us with two possible motives behind Demaratos' communication, either good will or *Schadenfreude*:

> Δημάρητος γὰρ ὁ Ἀρίστωνος φυγὼν ἐς Μήδους, ὡς μὲν ἐγὼ δοκέω καὶ τὸ οἰκὸς ἐμοὶ συμμάχεται, οὐκ ἦν εὔνοος Λακεδαιμονίοισι, πάρεστι δὲ εἰκάζειν εἴτε εὐνοίῃ ταῦτα ἐποίησε εἴτε καὶ καταχαίρων.
>
> 7.239.2
>
> For Demaratos, since he had fled to the Persians, was not in my opinion—and likelihood is on my side—well-disposed towards the Spartans, and one may conjecture whether he performed these actions out of good will or in fact with a sense of pleasure.

There is after all good reason for Demaratos to dislike the Spartans, since they have wrongfully deprived him of his kingship. Viewed in this light, Demaratos' μηχανή is more than a method of getting his message past the Persians: it is a means to mock and test the Spartans, an additional barb to the already disturbing contents of his message. The Spartans come very close to failure and are saved only by the intervention of a talented individual who is able to match Demaratos' skill in encoding with her skill in decoding.[50]

49 Cf. ch. 1.3.2 above on *noos* and sign interpretation.

50 Steiner (1994:151) overlooks Demaratos' testing of the Spartans and the role of Gorgo: "The Spartans, with their notorious mistrust of writing and rejection of *grammata* for all but the most restricted of uses, are ideally suited to discover the meaning of the *pinax*. For them an empty tablet is a token, no less significant an object than the text that lies beneath." As I read Herodotus' passage, the Spartans are anything but "suited" to interpret the *pinax* (actually a δελτίον, 7.239.3). There is more to this story than "the familiar pattern of the clever Greek who outwits the foreigner" (150), since it is the Spartans too that Demaratos outwits. The pattern observable here is rather one in which signs are used to ensure that the message is decoded by a worthy audience (cf. ch. 2.5 above on the *ainos* and ainetic mode in Herodotus).

3.1.2.8 Written signs and manipulation

Writing as a means of deception and manipulating others takes center stage in Herodotus' account of Bagaios, the Persian who kills the troublesome governor Oroites on Dareios' behalf. The theme of concealment is present here again, but in a different sense from that in the examples considered above, in which writing is concealed. In the present instance (unconcealed) writing itself forms part of the plan of concealment. Dareios wants the capture or killing of Oroites to be carried out not by brute force (*biê*), but by intelligence (*sophiê*, 3.127.2), and Bagaios undertakes to do so on these terms. His method is to test the loyalty of Oroites' bodyguards to the king through a series of letters purporting to be from the king. The bodyguards react to two types of signs: firstly, the letters themselves, physical objects sealed with the king' *sphrêgis*, act as tokens of the king's presence, so that the bodyguards pay them the devotion (σεβομένους) they pay to the king himself, and, secondly, the contents of the letters (τὰ λεγόμενα) are signs purporting to convey the king's voice and will, which produce even more reverence in the bodyguards:

> ὁρέων δέ σφεας τά τε βυβλία σεβομένους μεγάλως καὶ τὰ λεγόμενα ἐκ τῶν βυβλίων ἔτι μεζόνως, διδοῖ ἄλλο ἐν τῷ ἐνῆν ἔπεα τάδε· "Ὦ Πέρσαι, βασιλεὺς Δαρεῖος ἀπαγορεύει ὑμῖν μὴ δορυφορέειν Ὀροίτην."[51]
>
> 3.128.4

> When he saw them revering the letters greatly and the contents of the letters even more so, he handed over another one which contained the following words: "O Persians, Dareios the king orders you not to act as bodyguards for Oroites."

Encouraged by this reaction, Bagaios has another letter read out, which orders them to cease protecting Oroites, and when they throw down their spears, he produces a final letter in which the king orders them to kill Oroites (3.128.5). Once again, the reaction is instantaneous, and the bodyguards promptly draw their Persian daggers and kill the very person it is their function to protect. There are a number of interesting features in this account: most striking is the manner in which signs, functioning here as speech acts, are translated directly into action.[52] True, the signs must be converted from

51 On the function of *epea* in Herodotus as authoritative utterances, see Hollmann 2000. On other *sphrêgides* in the *Histories*, cf. ch. 2.8.4 above. Further references on the concept of the *sphragis* in Edmunds 1997.

52 On the concept of the speech act see Austin 1962; cf. Bierl 2009:36–44 on speech acts and ancient Greek literary genres.

written to auditory form via mediation of the *grammatistês*, or scribe, a figure whose sole function here is essentially to act as a transcription and playback machine:

> τῶν βυβλίων ἓν ἕκαστον περιαιρεόμενος ἐδίδου τῷ γραμματιστῇ τῷ βασιληίῳ ἐπιλέγεσθαι (γραμματιστὰς δὲ βασιληίους οἱ πάντες ὕπαρχοι ἔχουσι).[53]
>
> 3.128.3
>
> He undid the letters one by one and handed them over to the royal *grammatistês* to read out loud (for all the governors have royal *grammatistai*).

But once the *grammatistês* pronounces the last syllable, the words produce an instantaneous effect on the bodyguards, and they act like automata. Herodotus' description focuses on this immediacy of action and unquestioning obedience. No moment of reflection intervenes between the guards' perception of the words and their performance of the commands:

> οἱ δὲ ἀκούσαντες τούτων μετῆκάν οἱ τὰς αἰχμάς. ἰδὼν δὲ τοῦτό σφεας ὁ Βαγαῖος πειθομένους τῷ βυβλίῳ, ἐνθαῦτα δὴ θαρσήσας τὸ τελευταῖον τῶν βυβλίων διδοῖ τῷ γραμματιστῇ, ἐν τῷ ἐγέγραπτο· "Βασιλεὺς Δαρεῖος Πέρσῃσι τοῖσι ἐν Σάρδισι ἐντέλλεται κτείνειν Ὀροίτην." οἱ δὲ δορυφόροι ὡς ἤκουσαν ταῦτα, σπασάμενοι τοὺς ἀκινάκας κτείνουσι παραυτίκα μιν.
>
> 3.128.4–5
>
> Upon hearing this, they threw down their spears. When Bagaios saw them obeying the letter, he took heart and gave the last of the letters to the *grammatistês*, in which had been written: "King Dareios orders the Persians of Sardis to kill Oroites." When the bodyguards heard this, they drew their daggers and killed him forthwith.

Bagaios appropriates the authenticating frame needed to invest an utterance not simply with meaning but with a stimulus to action: he is able to stamp the utterances with the king's seal and also has the ability to present the commands in the correct format, in terms of both physical form (βύβλια) and style ("Dareios

[53] Just as the *grammatistai* act as machines converting signs from one medium to another, translators (ἑρμηνεῖς) in Herodotus transfer signs from one language to another: cf. ch. 3.2 below on these figures in the *Histories*.

the king orders ...").[54] The Persian system of administration, with its extreme reliance on writing as a means of conveying commands and its hierarchy of command filtering down from the king as ultimate authority, produces an environment where judicious manipulation may have enormous consequences and where the sign is mightier than the sword, or *sophiê* outdoes *biê*.[55]

3.1.2.9 Military signals and manipulation

The capacity of signs to act as stimuli productive of an automatic response is also at the base of military signals, sets of signs which are assigned a conventionally determined meaning, and by which commanders pass along orders (σημαίνω) to their troops to advance, retreat, and, as will be seen, eat.[56] The signs and the code according to which they are interpreted are naturally intended only for their users, but are susceptible to discovery by the opposing side, who may then use the information to their own advantage. This is what happens when Kleomenes leads his campaign against the Argives. The two armies take up a position near each other. The Argives, wary of being taken by deception (δόλῳ, 6.77.1), attempt to guard against this by noting whatever the Spartan soldiers do whenever the Spartan herald gives a signal (προσημαίνοι, 6.77.3) and performing exactly the same action. But Kleomenes detects this, and counters with a manipulation of his own: he takes advantage of the purely conventional connection between signifier and signified and changes the code of the system, so that the signal for taking a meal now constitutes a command to arm and to attack (6.78.1).[57] When this signal is given by the Spartan herald,

54 The expression "authenticating frame" comes from Steiner 1994:40, where it appears in a discussion of Phaidra's use of writing tablets to incriminate Hippolytos. Those tablets, too, are sealed with an authenticating seal, Phaidra's ring (Euripides *Hippolytus* 862).

55 Kyros is the first to exploit this reliance on writing when he unrolls a scroll in front of an assembly of the Persians and reads out what purports to be an edict from Astyages appointing him general of the Persians (1.125.2). Herodotus frames the tactic with words which draw attention to Kyros' *sophiê*: ὁ Κῦρος ἐφρόντιζε ὅτεῳ τρόπῳ σοφωτάτῳ Πέρσας ἀναπείσει ἀπίστασθαι (1.125.1). *Grammatistai*, who in the story of Bagaios demonstrate the machine-like nature of the imperial system of command and who faithfully render messages from one medium into another, are not a feature of this account: as Herodotus presents it, Kyros performs the action of writing, unfolding, and reading himself. The stress in this passage falls rather on Kyros' winning over the Persians by using a different sign system in the form of a practical demonstration of first the hard life and then the easy life (1.126.1–6).

56 See ch. 1.2.1.1 above for similar instances of σημαίνω.

57 The motif of trick and countertrick is also found at 4.200.2: Pheretime and the Persians under Amasis attempt to take the city of Barke by tunneling underneath the walls, but one of the inhabitants, a blacksmith, detects the attempts by the judicious interpretation of signs (ἐπιφράζομαι; also used of Gorgo's reading of the blank tablet [7.239.4], described above). Those parts of the wall which are being undermined by the enemy produce an echoing sound

the Argives, following the old code, sit down to eat, but the Spartans, in accordance with the new code, attack, killing a large number of them (6.78.2).

3.1.3 Manipulation of Signs During the Process of Reception and Decoding

So far we have looked at the manipulation of signs with respect to their production and encoding: how signs may be produced artificially and how they may be appropriated or hijacked.[58] Let us next consider manipulation of signs at a different point in the chain of communication: the decoding stage, when the sign or complex of signs is interpreted by the recipient.

3.1.3.1 Mykerinos and the oracle

The manipulator may by interpretation twist a set of signs in such a way as to serve his own interests, as when Mykerinos the Egyptian king receives an oracle which tells him he has six years left to live (2.133.1). Mykerinos is enraged by the oracular utterance and determined to disprove it. He does so by manipulating the meanings of the terms 'day' and 'night', taking 'day' as meaning a period of light, and 'night' as the absence of light. In this way he is able to turn nights into days: at nightfall, he lights lanterns and spends his nights in drinking and dissipation, wandering through the marshes and frequenting places of enjoyment (2.133.4). By this machination (ταῦτα δὲ ἐμηχανᾶτο, 2.133.5) he is able to double the number of "days" and makes twelve years out of six. His manipulation cannot of course make his life longer in any real sense, but he is able to show in a limited fashion that the oracle has not been fulfilled (ψευδόμενον, 2.133.5).[59]

---

in the bronze shield which the blacksmith taps against it (4.200.3). The inhabitants then dig opposing tunnels (ἀντορύσσοντες) in those places and kill the Persian sappers. This countertrick is answered by Amasis' manipulation of an oath (4.201.1–3, discussed above), which also involves digging of a sort. Cf. also 2.121 for the sequence of trick and countertrick between the master thief and Rhampsanitos.

[58] Another example of artificial sign production and appropriation, which here finds expression in physical terms, is Amasis the Egyptian's recasting of the golden footbath (ποδανιπτήρ), formerly used for the washing of feet and for vomiting and urinating into, as a cult statue (ἄγαλμα), which the Egyptians now worship and revere (2.172.3–5): see ch. 2.8.1 above.

[59] Another Egyptian king, Amasis, also manages to outwit certain oracles, though he does not rely on manipulation, only the incompetence of some μαντήια. When still a private citizen, he used to steal. If challenged, he would go to the nearest μαντήιον to ask whether he had stolen someone's property or not. Some correctly indicted him, while others acquitted him. After becoming king, he honored those oracles that detected his thefts as ἀψευδέα μαντήια and those that did not as ψευδέα (2.174.1–2).

3.1.3.2 Perdikkas and the sun

Manipulation at the stage of decoding may also take place when already existing signs are viewed and interpreted according to a different sign system. This is how Perdikkas, founder of the Macedonian dynasty, seizes power. He and his two brothers, Gauanas and Aeropos, work as hired hands for the king of Lebaia (8.137.2). Because of what the king considers to be a disturbing *teras* (when the king's wife bakes bread for the laborers, the loaf destined for Perdikkas always turns out to be double its original size), he decides to dispense with the brothers' services (8.137.3). When they ask for their wages, the king points to a patch of sunlight on the floor:

> ὁ βασιλεὺς ... εἶπε, θεοβλαβὴς γενόμενος· "Μισθὸν δὲ ὑμῖν ἐγὼ ὑμέων ἄξιον τόνδε ἀποδίδωμι," δείξας τὸν ἥλιον.
>
> 8.137.4
>
> The king . . . , struck with a divinely-induced madness, said: "I give you this wage, which is what you deserve," and pointed to the [patch of] sunlight.

The elder brothers are dumbfounded (ἐκπεπληγμένοι, 8.137.5), but Perdikkas knows what to do:

> ὁ δὲ παῖς, ἐτύγχανε γὰρ ἔχων μάχαιραν, εἴπας τάδε· "Δεκόμεθα, ὦ βασιλεῦ, τὰ διδοῖς," περιγράφει τῇ μαχαίρῃ ἐς τὸ ἔδαφος τοῦ οἴκου τὸν ἥλιον, περιγράψας δέ, ἐς τὸν κόλπον τρὶς ἀρυσάμενος τοῦ ἡλίου, ἀπαλλάσσετο αὐτός τε καὶ οἱ μετ' ἐκείνου.
>
> 8.137.5
>
> But the boy, who happened to have a knife, said the following: "We accept, O King, what you give us," and traced [the outline of] the sun on the floor with his knife, and, after outlining it, poured the sun into his lap three times and left, both he and his brothers.

What the king intends as a gesture of contempt, Perdikkas converts into a sign of a different kind. His reply plays on two meanings of the verb δέκομαι, the first in the general sense of accepting wages or presents, the second in the more specific sense of the recognition and acceptance of a portent.[60] The word

60 Examples in the *Histories* of the use of δέκομαι as technical term in the context of sign recognition: 1.63.1, 4.15.3, 7.178.2, 8.115.1, 9.91.2. Burkert (1996:159) also draws attention to Perdikkas' appropriation and reworking of the sign and to the special meaning of δέκομαι: "Through this

which the king uses in a slighting and ironic sense of the brothers' wages, "worthy" (ἄξιον), is effectively taken up and used by Perdikkas in a sense favorable to himself.[61] The giving of a patch of sunlight is decoded not as a contemptuous gift of something worth nothing (sun as an element, like air, common to all and hence worthless) but the bestowal of something valuable (sun as gold and symbol of kingship). When one of the king's advisors conveys (σημαίνει) to the king that Perdikkas' strange action has meaning (σὺν νόῳ) and what this meaning is (8.138.1), he orders his men to pursue the brothers and kill them. The verb σημαίνω, here used to describe the transmission of a decoded message (cf. ch. 1.2.1.2 above), underscores the advisor's point that Perdikkas' actions and words constitute a meaningful set of signs that cannot be ignored. The term σὺν νόῳ stresses the importance of *noos*, used elsewhere in the *Histories* in sign-related contexts both in the sense of the message behind the encoded form (e.g. 4.131.2) and the ability to encode and decode signs (see ch. 1.3.2 above). These two aspects of *noos* are related: as we have seen, one must have *noos* to detect the *noos* of the message.

Perdikkas' appropriation and re-interpretation of signs make the situation true in some magical way and confer on him a power which makes the king uneasy; the gesture of pouring the sun into his lap three times has the solemnity of ritual. The manipulation of signs on a human level (Perdikkas' mixture of speech and action) actually ends up working in harmony with a set of signs originating on the divine level. There is first the *teras* of the loaf of bread, then another incident which may equally be regarded as showing the hand of the divine: when the brothers are pursued by the king's horsemen, they cross a river which mysteriously rises after their crossing and prevents their pursuers from riding across after them. This river, Herodotus tells us, is sacrificed to as "savior" (σωτῆρι) by the descendants of the brothers, the royal house of Makedonia (8.138.2). The situation is in this respect comparable to the manipulation of Dareios and Oibares (3.86.2), where the divine, "as if by arrangement" (ὥσπερ ἐκ συνθέτου), confirms with its own method of signification a sign (the whinnying of the horse) produced by human agency.

---

acceptance, the king's arrogant utterance, by which he meant to give the boy nothing, turned into a sign of power, connecting Perdikkas and his offspring forever to the grand light that dominates the sky, the royal star of Macedonia. By accepting the sign of cosmic rank, Perdikkas received what it stood for: royalty."

61 Compare his descendant Alexandros' use of the same word in his reply to his Persian guests (5.20.4), discussed above.

3.1.3.3 Artayktes' second manipulation

We continue this theme of the human manipulation of signs and interaction with signs of divine origin by returning to Artayktes the Persian. The latter, successful in his efforts to gain control of the sanctuary of Protesilaos by means of the manipulation of language, incurs the wrath of the inhabitants of Elaious when he appropriates all the goods kept in the shrine, turns the sacred enclosure over to cultivation and pasturing, and sleeps with women in the sanctuary (9.116.3). He is eventually captured by the Athenians, and while being kept under guard, observes the strange spectacle of preserved fish (τάριχοι) over a fire suddenly coming to life and flopping about over the flames. Artayktes immediately takes it upon himself to provide an interpretation of this *teras*:

> Ξεῖνε Ἀθηναῖε, μηδὲν φοβέο τὸ τέρας τοῦτο· οὐ γὰρ σοὶ πέφηνε, ἀλλ' ἐμοὶ σημαίνει ὁ ἐν Ἐλαιοῦντι Πρωτεσίλεως ὅτι καὶ τεθνεὼς καὶ τάριχος ἐὼν δύναμιν πρὸς θεῶν ἔχει τὸν ἀδικέοντα τίνεσθαι.
>
> 9.120.2

> Athenian, do not be alarmed at this *teras*: for it is not to you that it has appeared, but it is to me that Protesilaos who lies in Elaious is sending a sign that even though he is dead and a *tarikhos*, he has power from the gods to take vengeance on the one who does him wrong.

Not only does Artayktes appropriate the portent, putting himself forward as recipient (ἐμοὶ σημαίνει), he constructs a reading based on the double meaning of the term *tarikhos* ('preserved'), which may refer to fish preserved by salting (cf. 2.77.4–5, 4.53.3), but also to a corpse treated with preservatives (e.g., 2.86–90 *passim*).[62] The portent is in itself remarkable, but even more remarkable is the fact that Artayktes chooses to interpret it the way he does, since it only seems to aggravate his already precarious position. He offers exorbitant restitution:

> νῦν ὦν ἄποινά μοι τάδε ἐθέλω ἐπιθεῖναι, ἀντὶ μὲν χρημάτων τῶν ἔλαβον ἐκ τοῦ ἱροῦ ἑκατὸν τάλαντα καταθεῖναι τῷ θεῷ, ἀντὶ δ' ἐμεωυτοῦ καὶ τοῦ παιδὸς ἀποδώσω τάλαντα διηκόσια Ἀθηναίοισι περιγενόμενος.
>
> 9.120.3

62 On the *tarikhos*, with interesting late antique parallels, see Nagy 1990b:269–273 and Nagy 2001: xvii–xviii.

> I wish to present the following as my ransom: in recompense for the money which I took from the shrine, I will deposit one hundred talents for the god, and in exchange for myself and my son I shall give two hundred talents to the Athenians, if I survive.

The people of Elaious will have none of it, nor will the Athenian commander, Xanthippos (Perikles' father), who orders him to be impaled on the spot where Xerxes began his bridge across the Hellespont (9.120.4). It seems that Artayktes produces his interpretation either under the influence of some kind of *atê*, a divinely induced destructive folly, becoming like Perdikkas' boss θεοβλαβής (8.137.4, discussed above), or as a conscious tactic, an acknowledgment of guilt designed to obtain clemency and absolution on easy terms. I would argue that the narrative presents both possibilities. Artayktes' reading of the omen, though he may not have believed it himself and though it is an appropriation and manipulation of the divine sign, turns out to be correct in an ironic fashion: the dead Protesilaos may indeed be said to have come alive like the writhing *tarikhoi* and to have "power from the gods to avenge himself against the one who has done him injustice," since the townspeople of Elaious, who clamor for Artayktes' execution, are described as taking vengeance on Protesilaos' behalf (9.120.4).[63] Artayktes may have thought himself in control through his interpretation, but his very interpretation can be seen as part of Protesilaos' plan of revenge. There is a suitable symmetry in the fact that Artayktes should be punished by the fruits of his own manipulation, just as in the case of the ultimate revenge (μεγίστη τίσις) of the eunuch Hermotimos,

[63] Dewald (1997:71 and n22) sees, as do I, Artayktes' interpretation of the jumping fish as a tactic, but is unwilling to grant that his interpretation seems in some sense to be validated ultimately by the narrative: "The divine portent that . . . Artayctes claims to see . . . is . . . mildly comical, and the narrative does not support Artayctes' own desperately self-interested claims to have seen a portent." Similarly Darbo-Peschanski 1987:57, cited by Dewald: "L'enquêteur laisse à Artayctès lui-même la responsabilité d'interpréter son sort comme une vengeance des dieux." Nagy (2001:xviii) shows that the sign of the *tarikhos* works far beyond Artayktes' attempts to control it: "Ironically, when the dead Protesilaos 'gives a sign', *sēmainei*, to the living, the Greek hero's 'meaning' seems at first sight to depend on whether the word *tarikhos* is to be understood in the everyday Greek sense of 'preserved fish' or in the hieratic non-Greek sense of 'mummy' (Herodotus 9.120.2). But there is a third sense, both hieratic and Greek, and it depends on the meaning of the word *sēmainei*: [what follows is Nagy 1990a:271] In the image of a dead fish that mystically comes back to life, we see a convergence of the everyday and the hieratic senses of 'preservation'. This image [in the story of Herodotus], where Protesilaos *sēmainei* 'indicates' (9.120.2) the power that he has from the gods to exact retribution from the wrongdoer, amounts to a *sēma* or sign of the revenant, the spirit that returns from the dead. The hero Protesilaos himself is represented as giving the *sēma*, the 'sign' of his power as a revenant [from the heroic past]."

who forces Panionios, the man responsible for castrating him, to castrate his own sons and in turn be castrated by them (8.105–106).[64]

As in the accounts of Dareios and Perdikkas, human manipulation of signs actually receives confirmation from the divine. The difference in this case, of course, is that the manipulator does not enjoy the fruits of his manipulation. Artayktes is impaled by order of Xanthippos, and his son stoned to death in front of his eyes (9.120.4), a punishment striking not just in its form (impalement is generally perpetrated by non-Greeks) but highly significant in terms of its location, precisely where Xerxes yoked the Hellespont.[65] He is the only manipulator to come to so awful an end, and the only one to be characterized in such strongly negative terms by Herodotus, who calls him "clever and wicked" (δεινὸς δὲ καὶ ἀτάσθαλος, 9.116.1). To be δεινός is a quality in itself not necessarily negative,[66] but ἀτασθαλίη is never presented as anything but extreme turpitude, involving *hubris*, excess, and transgression. Themistokles, for example, calls Xerxes ἀνόσιόν τε καὶ ἀτάσθαλον ("impious and wicked," 8.109.3) because of his destruction of the shrines and images of the gods.[67] Artayktes' ἀτασθαλίη, like that of Xerxes, lies not in his manipulation, but in his desecration of divine property:[68]

> ἐς τοῦ Πρωτεσίλεω τὸ ἱρὸν ἐς Ἐλαιοῦντα ἀγινεόμενος γυναῖκας ἀθέμιστα ἔργα ἔρδεσκε.
>
> 7.33
>
> He had women brought to Elaious, into the sanctuary of Protesilaos, and committed sacrilegious deeds.

64 Braund (1998:166–167) makes the point that it is Hermotimos, not Herodotus, who claims the support of the gods (8.106.3) in carrying out his extreme vengeance: "[W]e cannot be entirely at ease with Hermotimos' reciprocal vengeance or his protestations of justice."

65 Cf. Harrison 2000:120n60, citing the following passages of the hanging up of the body, alive or dead, by barbarians, especially Persians: 2.121.γ.2; 3.125.4; 4.103.2; 6.30.1; 7.194.1–2; 7.238.1; 9.78.3. See more generally Hall 1989:25–27, 103–105, 158–159 on punishment and barbarians. The significance of the site of the punishment, as well as the positioning of this episode at the end of *Histories*, is discussed in Boedeker 1988, Dewald 1997, esp. 67 and 71, and Gray 2002: 313–314.

66 Camerer (1965:50n50) notes the closeness and ethical neutrality of the terms δεινός and σοφός (cf. Megabazos' characterization of Histiaios as ἀνδρὶ Ἕλληνι δεινῷ τε καὶ σοφῷ, 5.23.2): "δεινός kommt in der Bedeutung σοφός sehr nahe. Es bezeichnet eine Art intellektuelle Gewandtheit und ist an sich ein ethisch neutraler Begriff."

67 The term ἀτασθαλίη has strong associations with the Homeric poems, where it is also linked to greed, ritual transgression, and desecration: cf. the ἀτασθαλίη of Odysseus' companions (eating of cattle of Sun, *Odyssey* 1.7) and that of the suitors (e.g. *Odyssey* 24.458). Cf. Mikalson 2002:193–194 on *atasthaliê* and *hubris* in the *Histories*.

68 As Bencsik 1994:84 comments: "*Frevel* und *Skrupellosigkeit* in Hdt.s Historien müssen sorgfältig geschieden werden."

3.1.4 Herodotus' Presentation of Sign Manipulation and Manipulators

Apart from this example, however, Herodotus does not comment on the morality or immorality of manipulators or their actions. Rather, actions are presented in such a way as to invite evaluation in terms of the perpetrator's (or victim's) resourcefulness, intelligence, and ingenuity, and questions of morality are not allowed to overshadow the achievement itself.[69] Key terms in Herodotus' descriptions are μηχανή, τέχνη, and σοφίη, which have the narrative function of indicating to the audience an upcoming action of ingenious deception, and also signal that the action is to be looked at in the way I have just described.[70] These terms are in themselves ambivalent, having in certain contexts positive connotations, but in others negative ones. Solon the sage may be credited with *sophiê* (1.30.2), while Dareios' cunning groom can equally be called an ἀνὴρ σοφός (3.85.1). Herodotus can use the verb μηχανάομαι to refer to Kyros and his benefactions for the Persians (ἀγαθά σφι πάντα ἐμηχανήσατο, 3.89.3), but equally of Psammenitos and how he paid for his evil deeds (νῦν δὲ μηχανώμενος κακὰ ὁ Ψαμμήνιτος ἔλαβε τὸν μίσθον, 3.15.4). Respectable trades and crafts may be referred to as τέχναι (e.g. office of herald, playing the aulos, cookery [6.60]), but Demokedes' false avowal that he knows nothing of medicine is described using the verb τεχνάζω (3.130.2).[71]

If we are asked to admire the manipulators of signs, this would not be to say that their actions and their consequences are somehow morally neutral. It is clear that the perpetrator is in some way bending the rules, and it is at least partly in this that the interest and astonishment induced in the audience

69 Cf. Harrison 2000:109n24 on the oath of Themison: "There is interestingly no implication that oaths should not be used for unjust ends: the narrative is rather shaped around Themison's ingenious fulfilment of the oath."

70 Bencsik 1994:11: "Der vorausdeutende 'Signalsatz' hat als Bindegelied zwischen der Nennung des Motivs und der Schilderung der List die literarische Funktion, beim Leser/Hörer eine Erwartungshaltung und somit Spannung zu erzeugen." See Appendix for instances of these words in connection with trickery and manipulation of signs.

71 The positive and negative sides of these terms are really intertwined and interconnected. Pratt (1993:70), in talking of Archaic poetry and depictions of τέχνη, speaks of this interconnectedness: "Figures in archaic poetry who are characterized by the kind of practical knowledge that gives rise to *technai* are virtually always also presented as exemplary liars or deceivers. Hephaestus can create both the shield of Achilles and the nets that ensnare Ares and Aphrodite, Athene can weave both a complex tapestry and a plot, Hermes can shape both a lyre and a lie." In the case of *sophiê* in the *Histories* Bencsik (1994:5) also shows clearly that both strands of meaning ('wisdom' vs. 'cunning') are inseparably intertwined.

can be said to lie.[72] If there were no transgression to speak of, the manipulation would not be thrown into relief and the manipulator's skill would have no suitable arena in which to be appreciated.[73] "Bending" rather than "breaking" the rules is the appropriate term because the manipulation of signs derives its effectiveness precisely from working *within* a sign system and following its rules, even if only in the most tenuous and superficial fashion. This should be distinguished from the lie built simply on a false premise, saying that something is so which is not, and from other transgressions which make no attempt to operate within a system. The distinction is clear when one looks back at the examples discussed above. Persian Amasis does not simply break his oath but goes to elaborate lengths to show that the oath has no foundation and is thus invalid (4.201.3). Themison preserves intact the fabric of the oath and fulfills it (ἀποσιεύμενος τὴν ἐξόρκωσιν, 4.154.4), but without drowning the daughter of Etearkhos. The oath of Leotykhides, however, who swears that Demaratos is not the legitimate child of Ariston, is simply based on a lie (6.65.3). Artayktes' claim to the shrine of Protesilaos (9.116.3) has a logic to it and is predicated on a mythological basis and the Persian title to all of Asia.

72 Instances of trickery and manipulation may be the object of wonder (θῶμα) as much as any deed of bravery or great building. Bencsik 1994:145–148 discusses σοφίσματα in Herodotus as part of the category of "great and wondrous works" (ἔργα μεγάλα τε καὶ θωμαστά) mentioned in the proem to the work, and cf. Bakker 2002:28 on Herodotus' *apodexis* itself as a *mega ergon*. Though the epithets θωμαστός or θωμάσιος ('wondrous, amazing') may not be expressly applied to these actions, the attention devoted to them in the text and their striking qualities entitle them to inclusion in this category. Astonishment as a reaction in witnesses to acts of cunning is described several times in Herodotus' narrative, for example in the story of the Egyptian master thief (ἐκπεπλῆχθαι, 2.121.γ.1, 2.121.ζ.1; θωμάσαι, 2.121.ζ.2). Pratt (1993:73) has well described the relationship between trickster and audience, where "audience" may refer not just to the original audience of a trick, but may include subsequent audiences as well: "Archaic literature often seems to ask us to admire lies and acts of deception from precisely this perspective, from the perspective of an outsider, of an audience to the lie who admires it purely as a manifestation of the artist's imagination and intelligence—as a kind of performance, a form of entertainment." Cf. Munson 2001a on *thôma*, esp. 232: "[Expressions of *thôma*] tend to announce special semiotic challenges and occasionally mark the highest philosophical level of the inquiry." Cf. also 251, with reference to animal stories: "Familiarity with the cultural conventions on which these different types of animal stories are based allows Herodotus' listeners to integrate into an ethical structure individual events that do not in themselves need to signify anything beyond their literal meaning. Herodotus' narration does its share to make these events fulfill the function of narrative omens or signs. The word the discourse uses to celebrate them, *thôma*, is a *sign of signs*."

73 Cf. Pratt 1993:71: "Tricksters can certainly speak *aletheia* if they wish to—it is not a lack of ability that prevents their speaking the truth—but tricksters are characterized by the speaking of lies and misleading statements, because only through these can their *techne* be revealed."

3.1.4.1 Herodotus' interest in sign manipulation and manipulators

Why is Herodotus interested in the manipulation and the manipulators of signs? Perhaps because this kind of manipulation involves the spectacular victory of intelligence over mere force, or at least the harnessing of brute force to cunning intelligence, an opposition that is central to much of Greek literature and thought, as Detienne and Vernant's 1978 study of *mêtis* has demonstrated. In terms used by Herodotean figures, this is the triumph of *sophiê* over *biê*. In several instances in the *Histories* a sharp distinction between *biê* and *sophiê* is drawn, where it is clear that the path of *sophiê*, often involving the manipulation of signs, is assigned a higher value than the use of *biê* alone. These are the terms in which Dareios presents the assignment to kill Oroites (σοφίῃ καὶ μὴ βίῃ, 3.127.2), and the stratagem of the Persian general Amasis is framed in a similar way, as a choice between δόλος and τὸ ἰσχυρόν (4.201.1).[74] Both Camerer (1965) and Bencsik (1994) have concentrated on the political importance of this cunning intelligence, *praktische Klugheit*, and its connection with the seizure and maintenance of power (*Schelmentum und Macht* is the title of Bencsik's work). As Dewald (1993:70) puts it, "The person who knows how to read objects in the world, and extract from them the meanings they hold in context, succeeds in uncovering something significant and does so by using the same kind of canny general attentiveness that Herodotus himself displays as an investigator."[75]

The latter part of Dewald's statement brings us to another vital factor behind Herodotus' interest in these manipulations: the relationship between trickster, audience, and Herodotus. The actions of the trickster call forth a certain reaction in the audience, a feeling of wonder, admiration, and amusement. The admiration of the manipulator's *sophiê* and *tekhnê* is experienced by two kinds of audience: the first being the immediate audience of the trick, and the second being the audience of Herodotus' work. In this way Herodotus as narrator and conveyor of manipulations receives a share of the audience's admiration, and the manipulator's *tekhnê* and *sophiê* become in a sense Herodotus' too. This is not, however, to say that Herodotus himself is a manipulator of signs or a trickster,[76] but he certainly presents himself as a

[74] Compare also 3.65.6, where the opposition is between δόλος and σθένος.

[75] Cf. also Kurke 1999:115 on the maintenance of power and ability to read signs: "Throughout the *Histories*, part of the dynastic survival kit is the ability to interpret ambiguous signifying systems (both objects and spoken/written messages)."

[76] Cf. the critical remarks of Harrison (2000:1): "Herodotus has been growing increasingly ingenious in recent years. . . . [H]e has emerged as a figure almost sinisterly clever, creating patterns of reciprocity, setting up expectations which he then subverts, manipulating his char-

master reader of signs, as will be explored in the final chapter. Louise Pratt has observed this identification of artist and trickster with regard to Archaic poets and the tricksters depicted in their works:

> Poetic fictions become a revelation of the artist's *techne*, *sophia* and *metis*. By calling attention to them or suggesting an affinity between the bard and an Odysseus or a Hermes, the poets make the creative intelligence of the trickster an essential component of their art.[77]

Just as in the case of the Archaic poets, Herodotus' depiction of manipulation is a demonstration of his own skill, and this is an aspect of his distinctive narrative persona.

3.1.4.2 Success of sign manipulation and sign interpretation in general

As we have seen with the examples of Dareios, Perdikkas, and the portent of the jumping fish, there is a very real sense in which an instance of manipulation may turn out to be a legitimate and successful use of signs. In fact, almost all of the manipulations of signs in the *Histories* are successful, a point worth emphasizing in light of the tendency of Dewald and Lateiner to overemphasize in general the problems of correctly fitting signifier and signified together. According to the former, the symbolic use of objects "very often backfires" on those who exploit them (1993:63–64). This does not seem to me to be the case. There are, to be sure, instances of failed manipulation—Aristagoras and his map (5.50.2), Onomakritos' attempt to add to the oracles of Musaios (7.6.2), Artayktes' interpretation of the portent of the jumping fish (9.120.1–4)—but they are not frequent enough to justify this conclusion, which is connected with Dewald's assertion (1993:63) that "objects in Herodotus often mislead because it is inherent in the nature of things that they do so." For example, she interprets Amasis' manipulation of the terms of the oath at Barke as superficially successful, but ultimately a failure: "his army flees in panic at Cyrene, and Pheretime, the queen of Cyrene, who has called in the Persians in the first place, dies a horribly lingering death, living but 'boiling over,' Herodotus

acters and their preoccupations like puppets."

77 Pratt 1993:71. Cf. Winkler 1990:129–161, who makes a connection between Penelope's cunning and Homer's. Pratt also stresses the connection with the agonistic nature of poetry: "The ability to deceive and lie becomes particularly desirable in a competitive context, because a successful act of deception vividly represents the superiority of one intelligence to another. In a system in which one poet competes against another, one way to reveal one's craft is to parade one's inventions, one's improvements on the accounts of one's predecessors. " On Herodotus' polemical stance, see now esp. Thomas 2000:214–221.

says, with maggots (4.205)." But Herodotus does not actually link the failure of Amasis' campaign to his false oath, and makes it clear that Pheretime's death is because of her excesses in taking vengeance for the death of her husband and because such excesses excite divine envy (ὡς ἄρα ἀνθρώποισι αἱ λίην ἰσχυραὶ τιμωρίαι πρὸς θεῶν ἐπίφθονοι γίνονται, 4.205). Like Dewald, Lateiner (1987:100) also tends to problematize the interpretation of signs in the *Histories*:

> The distance between the signifying message, the signifier, and what it is meant to signify, the signified, encourages the original recipient—and the reader—to err, to misinterpret. Indeed the reader is forced to participate in history as it happens, and Herodotus warns us not to relax in comfortable hindsight. Human knowledge, always partial and provisional in Herodotus, shows its limitations most clearly when forced to deal with signs and symbols. Men ignore them, misread them, and suffer.

As we will see from the conclusions of the following chapter, however, the evidence suggests that the interpreters of signs, with some interesting exceptions, generally overcome the problem of the distance between signifier and signified.

3.2 Conclusion

3.2.1 The Success or Otherwise of Sign Interpreters

Our investigation of signs and sign interpretation in the *Histories* suggests that the interpreters of signs, with some interesting exceptions, generally overcome the problem of the distance between signifier and signified. Among these exceptions are professional interpreters of signs in the *Histories*: either they produce an incorrect interpretation, or their interpretation is not heeded or comes too late.[78] But this is often a matter of their ethnicity or that of their masters and clients: the *magoi* and *oneiropoloi* of the Persians produce readings which flatter the king and look to their own security. A major exception to this group are the *manties*, who are all Greek: generally, a Greek army in the *Histories* will not fight unless the omens are favorable, and when Herodotus describes the omens as favorable, the outcome of the battle is usually favorable too.[79]

The *hermeneis*, like Hermes, the god they are named for, go as messengers between different worlds. They are translators, but they are far from hermeneuts: as we see them in the *Histories*, all they are capable of doing is

78 Noted by Darbo-Peschanski (1987:81). Incorrect interpretations by professionals: 1.107.1, 1.108.1, 1.128.2 (dream interpreted by *magoi* and *oneiropoloi*); 7.19.1 (dream interpreted by *magoi*); 7.37.2 (*teras* interpreted by *magoi*); 7.113.2 (divinatory sacrifice interpreted by *magoi*); 7.142.3–7.143 (oracle interpreted by Greek *khrêsmologoi*). Interpretation by professionals unheeded: 5.56.2 (dream interpreted by Greek *oneiropoloi*); 9.37.1 (divinatory sacrifice for non-Greeks by Hegesistratos). Interpretation by professional arrives too late: 1.78 (*teras* interpreted by Telmessians). Cf. Mikalson 2002:195n18.

79 Interpretations by *manties*: 7.219.1 (divinatory sacrifice by Megistias: correct); 9.37.1 (divinatory sacrifice for non-Greeks by Hegesistratos: correct, but ignored); 9.92.2 (divinatory sacrifice by Deiphonos: correct). On the high correlation between prediction of outcome and actual outcome, note Jameson's (1991:198) instructive remark: "Modern commentators, after a period when sceptical rationalism prevailed, have tended to be impressed by the Greeks' faith, their strict adherence to the signals they received through sacrifices and the rarity of cases in which the gods' advice was ignored or proved false. However, examples of successful action *contrary* to negative signs are not likely to be reported in our sources."

transferring messages from one code to another. That this does not involve the decoding of any secondary or deeper meaning is shown by the *hermeneis* who go between Kroisos and Kyros while the former is on the pyre. Kroisos sighs, groans, and speaks Solon's name three times (1.86.3). Kyros sends his interpreters (τοὺς ἑρμηνέας, 1.86.4) to ask whose name Kroisos is invoking. When the latter eventually replies, "He whom I instead of large sums of money would have had speak to all rulers," his words are "signless" for them (ἄσημα ἔφραζε, 1.86.4). They can translate the surface meaning of his words (from Lydian into Persian, presumably), but not their deeper meaning. When they transmit Kroisos' further explanation, with its appeal to humanity (τὸ ἀνθρώπινον, 1.86.5), to Kyros, it immediately produces in him a process of intense reflection and the realization that this is another human being, one no less fortunate than himself, that he is consigning to the flames (μεταγνόντα τε καὶ ἐννώσαντα ὅτι καὶ αὐτὸς ἄνθρωπος ἐὼν ἄλλον ἄνθρωπον, γενόμενον ἑωυτοῦ εὐδαιμονίῃ οὐκ ἐλάσσω, ζώοντα πυρὶ διδοίη, 1.86.6). This is in turn translated into clemency and an attempt to put out the flames. The presence of the *hermeneis* stresses the initial distance in language and comprehension that lies between Kroisos and Kyros, but also ultimately emphasizes the meeting of the minds of the two men across this gap: *they* can understand each other, but their interpreters cannot.[80] Elsewhere in the *Histories*, the *hermeneis* appear rarely and only in situations where the narrative is concerned to draw attention to the distance in language and culture that separates two or more parties, certainly not on every occasion when they must have been needed. Thus, in Dareios' famous experiment with the *nomoi* of the Greeks and the Kallatiai, an interpreter is there to translate the response of the Indian tribe to the Greeks, a detail which effectively underscores the vast gulf that separates the two groups when it comes to treatment of the remains of their dead (3.38.4).[81] Once more at Dareios' court, interpreters ask Syloson of Samos who he is and how he is a benefactor of King Dareios (3.140.3). The presence of interpreters, mentioned in a Persian setting only here and at 3.38.4, although much business must have of necessity been transacted through them, perhaps shows the

[80] Much the same contrast between unknowing messenger and knowing recipient is made in the account of Thraryboulos' famous non-verbal message to Periandros (5.92.ζ.2–η.1): Periandros' messenger faithfully conveys to Periandros what Thrasyboulos did (namely, cut down all the ears of grain that stand taller than the rest), but to him it is no message, since he does not recognize the actions of Thrasyboulos as being signifiers. Periandros sees that there is a message and grasps it immediately: the one tyrant understands the other perfectly.

[81] Cf. 4.24, where the vastness of Scythia and the remoteness of the tribe known as the Argippaioi are emphasized by the fact that other Scythians who interact with them need seven sets of interpreters and seven languages to communicate.

vast distance between the insignificant Greek and the powerful Persian ruler, who are in fact linked by an action that happened many years before in Egypt, when Syloson gave his cape under no compulsion to an admiring Dareios, who was not yet king (3.139.2–3).

Lay interpreters, individuals, or communities who must decode for themselves the signs with which they are confronted are depicted more frequently by Herodotus and enjoy greater success than professionals.[82] Their success depends in part on the sign type: in the case of oracles, the vast majority are in fact deciphered correctly by their recipients, despite the notorious and fatal ambiguity of the oracle given to Kroisos, for example, which admittedly looms large in the narrative and functions together with other oracles as a structuring device for Herodotus' extended *logos* on Kroisos' rise and fall.[83] Of the some sixty-four oracles referred to in the *Histories*, only eleven appear to be misinterpreted.[84] Of the more than twenty-five portents described by Herodotus, only three go completely ignored and unrecognized by the persons in whose vicinity they occur.[85] The dreams of the *Histories*, however, present a different picture. Out of eighteen, only three have favorable outcomes or happy endings, while in the case of another three, the content is not mentioned, only the dreamer's ensuing actions in carrying out the directives of the dream, nor is it possible to judge the effectiveness of the dreamer's actions.[86] All other dreams are ignored, misinterpreted, or followed by the dreamer to his doom.[87]

82 For Vernant (1974:18–22), the use of reason and logic, rather than priestly knowledge, by laypersons or communities to interpret oracles is connected with the rise of writing, which "fixes" oracles and places them at the disposal of all, so that a professional competency is no longer needed to interpret them.

83 On oracles and interpretations of signs as a stuctural technique in the narrative of the *Histories*, see e.g. Darbo-Peschanski 1987:74–75, Mikalson 2002:196.

84 Failures in interpretation of oracles: 1.53, 1.55, 1.85.2 (oracles to Kroisos); 1.66.2 (oracle to Spartans about Arcadia and Tegea); 2.152.3 (oracle of Bouto to Psammetikhos); 3.57.3–4 (oracle to Siphnians); 3.64.4 (oracle of Bouto to Kambyses); 4.163.2 (oracle to Arkesilaos III); 6.76.1 (oracle to Kleomenes); 8.20.2 (Euboians do not pay attention to oracle of Bakis); 9.33.2 (oracle to Teisamenos). Saïd (2002:122) notes: "Deceptive oracles do not always have a tragic outcome in the *Histories*."

85 Unrecognized portents: 4.79.1 (Skyles' town house struck by lightning); 7.57.1–2 (portent of mare giving birth to hare, portent of mule giving birth to mule with double set of genitalia).

86 Successful interpretations and outcomes of dreams: 2.139 (dream of Sabakos); 2.141 (dream of Sethon); 6.131 (dream of Agariste, mother of Perikles). Unclear: 3.149 (Otanes resettles Samos after dream and illness); 6.118.1 (Datis restores statue of Apollo after dream); 8.54 (Xerxes makes offerings on Athenian akropolis possibly because of dream). Cf. Mikalson (2002:195), who makes a distinction between Herodotean oracles, *manties*, and omens on the one hand, whose warnings can allow one to escape disaster, and Herodotean dreams, which "announce . . . an inescapable future."

87 1.34 (Kroisos and Atys); 1.107 (Astyages and Mandane); 1.108 (Astyages and Mandanes: second

This may be a function of the status of these dreamers, who form something of an exclusive club: only Persian kings, their relatives, and high officials, as well as Greek tyrants, dream in the *Histories*—figures whose high positions and arrogance make them vulnerable to the classic concatenation of excess, *hubris*, and disaster familiar to readers of Herodotus (e.g. 3.80.4, 7.10.ε) and of Greek literature in general (cf. e.g. Aeschylus *Persae* 821–822, Sophocles *Oedipus Rex* 872–879). Apart from these instances of misinterpretation, there are plentiful examples to be found in the work of triumphs and successes in the field of interpretation, including those of Herodotus himself.[88] In short, successes and failures of sign interpretation in the *Histories* are not so much a function of the nature of signs, the distance between signifier and signified, as they are caused by the qualities of the interpreter (his or her *hubris*, excess, etc.). Those who are not subject to these disadvantages are, more often than not, able to bridge the distance between signifier and signified and even exploit it to their advantage.

3.2.2 Herodotus and Signs

Where does Herodotus' interest in signs come from? Is it a feature of Herodotus himself, to be located in the personality of the historical Herodotus, or do its roots lie elsewhere, in a tradition or traditions which Herodotus draws upon? A strong interest in signs is found in a number of areas and genres of Greek

---

dream); 1.209 (Kyros' dream of Dareios); 3.30 (Kambyses' dream of Smerdis); 3.124 (dream of Polykrates' daughter); 5.55f. (dream of Hipparkhos); 6.107 (dream of Hippias); 7.12 (first dream of Xerxes); 7.14 (second dream of Xerxes); 7.17 (same dream appears to Artabanos); 7.19 (Xerxes' third dream).

88 As a sample, consider the following list of individuals, both non-Greek and Greek, male and female, tyrant, despot, and citizen, who make successful use of signs, whether as encoder or decoder, "straight" user or manipulator: Kyros (1.125.1–2, 1.126, 1.141.1–2); Harpagos (1.123.4); Dareios and Oibares (3.85.1–3.86.2); Otanes (3.68–69); Bagaios (3.127.2–3.128.5); Gobryas (4.132.2–3), Zopyros (3.153–158); Amasis (the Persian, 4.201.1–3); Artaphrenes (6.1.2); Artayktes (9.116.3); Amestris (9.109–112); Amasis (the Egyptian, 2.172.3–5); Mykerinos (2.133.4–5); Sabakos (2.139.1–3); Psammetikhos (2.2.1–5, 2.151–2); Kheops' daughter (4.126.1); Ariantas (4.81.5–6); the king of the Long-lived Ethiopians (3.21.2–22.4); Solon (1.30.3–32.9); Thrasyboulos (1.20–22.1, 5.92.ζ.1–η.1); Peisistratos (1.59.4, 1.60.4); Periandros (3.51.2, 5.92.ζ.1–η.4); Lykophron (3.50.1–3); Kleisthenes of Sikyon (5.68.1–2); Kleisthenes of Athens (5.69.1–2); Perdikkas (8.137.5); Alexandros (5.20.3–5); Tellias (8.27.3–4); Megistias (7.219.1); Histiaios (5.35.3); Themistokles (7.143.1–3, 8.22.1–3); Likhas (1.68.3–4); Khilon (1.59.1–2); Kleomenes (6.66.1–3, 6.77.3–78.2, 6.82.2); Demaratos (7.239.2–4); Gorgo (7.239.2–4). One should also consider successful interpretations made by groups: the Thebans (5.79.1–81.3); the Paiones (5.1.2–3); and the Athenians (7.189.1–3, though cf. 1.60.3–5, discussed above), for example. On Herodotus as interpreter, see below.

literature, both antedating and contemporary with Herodotus. In what follows I briefly survey Herodotus' points of contact with these tradition.

Signs and their interpretation feature prominently already in the *Iliad* and *Odyssey*, where prophecy, portent, dream, *ainos*, gesture and behavior as signifiers (e.g. crazed laughter of suitors, *Odyssey* 20.346), the body as sign vehicle (e.g. Odysseus' scar, *Odyssey* 19.393, 21.221, 23.73), and name-play all appear and have an important role.[89] Herodotus is directly influenced by the form and vocabulary of the Homeric dream;[90] and the double portent seen when the whinnying of Dareios' horse is answered by a simultaneous bolt of lightning and thunderclap from a clear sky (3.86.2) recalls the double portent which Zeus sends to Odysseus in the form of a thunderclap from a clear sky and the φήμη uttered by a woman grinding grain (*Odyssey* 20.102–121).[91]

The Athenian tragedies of the fifth century and their plots, studded with oracles, dreams, portents, and tokens of recognition, may also have had their influence on Herodotus and at least provide evidence for the prominence of certain types of signs in a genre other than epic.[92] The attempt to comply with the conditions of an oracle or a dream and avoid its fulfillment—while nevertheless being drawn into circumstances that will lead to the occurrence of the very thing one seeks to avoid—links, for example, the fates of Oedipus and of Kroisos, Atys, and Adrastos. The matching of three sets of signifier and signified made by Elektra in Aeschylus *Libation Bearers* as she considers first the lock of hair found by her father's tomb (which she describes as εὐξύμβολον, 170, "easy to interpret"), then the nearby footprints (which she describes as a τεκμήριον, 205), and finally the tapestry with its designs (232) remind one of signifiers in the *Histories* and the kind of interpretation I have been examining in this work.[93]

89 See appendix I in Lateiner 1987 for categories and illustrative lists of non-verbal communication in Homer (including objects, tokens, and clothes) and cf. Nagy 1990a:202–222 on *sêma* and *noêsis* in the Homeric poems. Recent discussion of the general relationship between Homer and Herodotus and shared mythical patterns in Boedeker 2002.

90 See ch. 2.2 above.

91 The woman's utterance is referred to as a φήμη at 20.100 and 105, and then as a κλεηδών at 120. It is interesting that in Herodotus' description of the double portent at Mykale, the rumor is also referred to first as a φήμη and then as a κληδών (9.100.1).

92 On Herodotus and tragedy, see, for example, Fohl 1913, Egermann 1968, Stahl 1968, Snell 1973, Chiasson 1979, Saïd 2002. For a semiotic reading of a tragedy, cf. Zeitlin 1982 on Aeschylus *Seven against Thebes*.

93 For the term εὐξύμβολον, compare Herodotus' description of a portent as εὐσύμβλητον (7.57.1) and cf. ch. 1.1.3 above on the τεκμήριον in the *Histories*; footprint as an indicator of identity at 4.82.1 (Herakles); garment as significant object (cloak that Amestris weaves for Xerxes, 9.109.1; discussed in ch. 3.1.2.3).

Much in Herodotus' confident persona is reminiscent of the figure of the Archaic poet who proudly declares his own ability (*sophia*), sings of his superiority over his competitors, demonstrates his knowledge of alternate versions, and addresses himself to those who are *sophoi* and discriminating enough to decode his message, just as the Scythian messenger tells the Persians they will get the *noos* behind the Scythians' gifts if they are *sophoi* (4.131.2).[94] The poet may assume the pose of prophet or spokesman, relaying the words of the Muses, just as Herodotus presents himself as one who "indicates" authoritatively from a superior vantage point (σημαίνω: cf. ch. 1.2.1.2 above).[95] For Nagy, Herodotus is in fact master of a prose tradition that is comparable and parallel to the master-of-song tradition, the *aoidos*, so that "the prose of Herodotus, like the poetry and song of the *ainos*, is a speech act of authority."[96]

Among the fragmentary traces of the works of Herodotus' predecessors and contemporaries in the field of history there are also indications of an interest in signs and the interpretation of signs. A fragment of Kharon of Lampsakos (whom Fowler believes to be a contemporary, not a successor of Herodotus) has a fascinating description of a manipulation of signs that reminds one strongly of Herodotean accounts of tricksters and horses.[97] Having learned that the people of Kardia have trained their horses to rear up and dance to certain tunes on the *aulos*, even beating out the time with their forelegs, Naris, leader of the Bisaltai, who have previously been unsuccessful in the field again the Kardianoi, gets hold of an *aulos*-player from Kardia and has her teach the appropriate *aulos* melodies to other *aulos*-players. These

94 On the σοφία of the poet and his superiority as well as the idea of the utterance directed at the σοφοί, cf. Pindar *Olympian* 2.83–88: πολλά μοι ὑπ' | ἀγκῶνος ὠκέα βέλη | ἔνδον ἐντὶ φαρέτρας | φωνάεντα συνετοῖσιν·| ἐς δὲ τὸ πὰν ἑρμανέων | χατίζει. σοφὸς ὁ πολλὰ εἰδὼς φυᾷ· | μαθόντες δὲ λάβροι | παγγλωσίᾳ κόρακες ὣς ἄκραντα γαρύετον | Διὸς πρὸς ὄρνιχα θεῖον, "Many are the swift darts in the quiver under my arm, and they speak to those who can understand: but for the whole they need interpreters. *Sophos* is the man who knows many things by nature: but those who learn are garrulously boisterous like a pair of crows who sing empty words against the divine bird of Zeus." Cf. also Theognis 681–682, where the poet delivers an encoded message, an *ainos*, which only those who are *agathoi* and *sophoi* will recognize: ταῦτά μοι ἠνίχθω κεκρυμμένα τοῖς ἀγαθοῖσι· | γινώσκοι δ' ἄν τις καὶ κακός, ἂν σοφὸς ᾖ, "Let these things become an enigma, kept hidden for the *agathoi*: but even one who is *kakos* could understand them, if he is *sophos*."

95 Cf. Pindar fr. 150 SM: μαντεύεο Μοῖσα προφατεύσω δ' ἐγώ, "Prophesy, Muse, and I will be your spokesman"; Bakkhylides *Epinician* 8.3: Μουσᾶν γε ἰοβλεφάρων θεῖος προφάτας, "divine spokesman of the violet-eyed Muses." On this point cf. Nagy 1990b:164–165.

96 Nagy 1990b:13.

97 FGH 262 F1. On Kharon's date, see Fowler 1996:67. For Herodotean horses trained or used in a manipulation, cf. the horse of Artybios the Persian, trained to rear up and attack with its forelegs, whose μηχαναί (5.111.4) are overcome by Onesilos' squire (5.111–112), and also the story of Dareios and his groom Oibares (3.85–87), discussed in ch. 3.1.2.2 above.

aulos-players then form part of a new military campaign against Kardia, and at a critical moment play the *aulêmata* they have learned, inducing the horses of the enemy to rear up and dance and thus throw their riders. Here is a hijacking and manipulation of sign system of a type familiar to Herodotean readers (cf. the Argives' cracking of the Spartan code of military signals and the Spartans' countermanipulation, 6.77–78, discussed in chs. 2.7.1 and 3.1.2.9 above). There is another familiar pattern in the introduction to this story: Naris conceives the idea of an attack on Kardia after he hears about an oracle while in enslavement in Kardia. The oracle tells the people of Kardia that the Bisaltai will attack them. The knowledge of one set of signs gives Naris the impulse to use another set of signs to attack his enemy by cunning, much as Herodotus' Zopyros conceives of his plan of deceptive self-mutilation after putting together the chance remark of a Babylonian soldier (3.151.2) and the *teras* of a mule giving birth (3.153.1; above, ch. 3.1.2.4).

The controlling, self-confident, and assertive narrative voice, disdainful of predecessors, is not unique to Herodotus, but is already present in Hekataios of Miletos,[98] and seems to be *de rigueur* for early writers, including the Presocratics and the medical writers. Among the Presocratics the figure of Herakleitos of Ephesos is notable for his use of sign vocabulary familiar to us from Herodotus: there is his famous remark about the Delphic oracle: ὁ ἄναξ οὗ τὸ μαντεῖόν ἐστι τὸ ἐν Δελφοῖς οὔτε λέγει οὔτε κρύπτει, ἀλλὰ σημαίνει (DK 22 B 93), "The lord whose oracle is in Delphi neither speaks nor conceals, but indicates with signs." In another fragment (κακοὶ μάρτυρες ἀνθρώποισιν ὀφθαλμοὶ καὶ ὦτα βαρβάρους ψυχὰς ἐχόντων [DK 22 B 107], "The eyes and ears of those who have barbarian [i.e. imperfectly understanding and speaking] souls are bad witnesses"), Herakleitos stresses the importance of correct interpretation and reading of the signs of language (and his *Logos*), which produce only babbling for those who do not know how to see and hear properly, just as in the *Histories* Kroisos' words on the pyre are ἄσημα for the interpreters, who translate them literally but are ignorant of what they refer to (1.86.4).[99] Another fragment of Herakleitos contains an instance of the verb

98 FGH 1 F 1: Ἑκαταῖος Μιλήσιος ὧδε μυθεῖται· τάδε γράφω, ὥς μοι δοκεῖ ἀληθέα εἶναι· οἱ γὰρ Ἑλλήνων λόγοι πολλοί τε καὶ γελοῖοι, ὡς ἐμοὶ φαίνονται, εἰσίν. "Hekataios of Miletos speaks thus: I write the following things as they seem true to me: for the accounts of the Greeks are many and, as it seems to me, ridiculous."

99 Following the interpretation of Kahn (1979:107), who groups together with this fragments DK B 55 (ὅσων ὄψις ἀκοὴ μάθησις, ταῦτα ἐγὼ προτιμέω, "I give preference those things which it is possible to see, hear, and perceive") and 101a (ὀφθαλμοὶ τῶν των ἀκριβέστεροι μάρτυρες, "Eyes are more accurate witnesses than the ears": cf. *Histories* 1.8.2: ὦτα γὰρ τυγχάνει ἀνθρώποισι ἐόντα ἀπιστότερα ὀφθαλμῶν, "Ears are less trustworthy for humans than eyes"). Kahn explains

συμβάλλομαι, rarely found in the middle in authors besides Herodotus and the medical writers: μὴ εἰκῆ περὶ τῶν μεγίστων συμβαλλώμεθα (DK 22 B 47), "Let us not conjecture carelessly about the most serious things."[100] The context of the fragment is not clear.[101] Like Herodotus, he also uses the verb φράζω for the transmission of an interpretation, and he projects the same air of competency, knowledge, and control:

> γινομένων γὰρ πάντων κατὰ τὸν λόγον τόνδε ἀπείροισιν ἐοίκασι πειρώμενοι καὶ ἐπέων καὶ ἔργων τοιούτων ὁκοίων ἐγὼ διηγεῦμαι, κατὰ φύσιν διαιρέων ἕκαστον καὶ φράζων ὅκως ἔχει. τοὺς δὲ ἄλλους ἀνθρώπους λανθάνει ὁκόσα ἐγερθέντες ποιοῦσιν ὅκωσπερ ὁκόσα εὕδοντες ἐπιλανθάνονται.[102]
>
> DK 22 B 1
>
> For although all things happen according to this *Logos* men are like people of no experience, even when they experience such words and deeds as I explain, when I distinguish each thing according to its constitution and show how it is; but the rest of men fail to notice what they do after they wake up, just as they forget what they do when asleep.[103]

---

them as follows: "The world order speaks to men as a kind of language they must learn to comprehend. Just as the meaning of what is said is actually 'given' in the sounds which the foreigner hears, but cannot understand, so the direct experience of the nature of things will be like the babbling of an unknown tongue for the soul that does not know how to listen. . . . The new concept of the psyche is expressed in terms of the power of articulate speech: rationality is understood as the capacity to participate in the life of language, 'knowing how to listen and how to speak.'"

100 Hohti (1977:5) suggests that the use of the middle form in this sense may be peculiarly Ionic. Its occurrence in the Hippocratic Corpus (see below), a source not considered by Hohti in his investigation, would seem to confirm his theory and mark this form as associated with the Ionian intellectual movement.

101 Kahn (1979:106) groups it together with DK A 23 (=Kahn XI) and DK B 74 (=Kahn XIII), which both reject taking poets and storytellers as witnesses for things unknown and acting and speaking "like children of our parents." He views the three fragments as expressing "a critical attitude towards traditional or current practice and belief."

102 Cf. Parmenides' description of the goddess' revelation to him, in which φράζω also conveys a tone of omniscience and control: τὴν δή τοι φράζω παναπευθέα ἔμμεν ἀταρπόν· | οὔτε γὰρ ἂν γνοίης τό γε μὴ ἐὸν (οὐ γὰρ ἀνυστόν) | οὔτε φράσαις (DK 28 B 2.12–14), "This path [i.e. the way 'that it is not' and 'that it ought not to be'], I [will] show to you, is completely inscrutable: for you could not know what is not (for it is unaccomplishable), nor could you communicate it [to another]."

103 Translation of Kirk and Raven (1963:187). I have substituted "show" for "declare" as a translation of φράζων.

A fragment of Alkmaion of Kroton seems to contrast the gods' ability for exact knowledge with man's need to work on the basis of indications and signs: περὶ τῶν ἀφανέων, περὶ τῶν θνητῶν σαφήνειαν μὲν θεοὶ ἔχοντι, ὡς δὲ ἀνθρώποις τεκμαίρεσθαι (DK 24 B 1), "Concerning invisible things, concerning mortal affairs, the gods possess clarity, but it is for men to proceed on the basis of *tekmêria*."

The writers of the Hippocratic Corpus provide important parallels for Herodotus' arguments based on signs and analogy, using external signs to deduce information about internal conditions.[104] Visible signs may reveal the invisible, as Anaxagoras of Klazomenai famously puts it: ὄψις ἀδήλων τὰ φαινόμενα (DK 59 B 21a), "Appearances are the vision of unseen things."[105] Where a disease has a seat that is not susceptible to vision, the practitioner must also make use of signs perceptible by touch, sound, or smell (*On the Art* 9).[106] The corpus is rich in instances of σημεῖα, μαρτύρια, and τεκμήρια, often in combinations found in the *Histories*: the writer of *On Ancient Medicine*, for example, uses the expression τοῦτό μοι μέγιστον τεκμήριον (17).[107] Highly instructive is a passage from the writer of *Prorrhetic II* in which he says he will not work by divination (οὐ μαντεύσομαι, 1) but describe the signs (σημεῖα) according to which one should conjecture (τεκμαίρεσθαι) which people will recover, which will die, and the speed with which they will recover or die. The author of another treatise, in which he attempts to prove that all winds are ultimately the result of water, even uses συμβάλλομαι in the same fashion as Herodotus:[108]

> τὰ δὲ πνεύματα ἡμῖν ἐστι πάντα ἀφ' ὕδατος· τούτου δὲ πέρι πάρα συμβάλλεσθαι, ὅτι οὕτως ἔχει, ἀπὸ γὰρ τῶν ποταμῶν πάντων πνεύματα χωρέει ἑκάστοτε καὶ τῶν νεφέων, τὰ δὲ νέφεα ἐστὶν ὕδωρ ξυνεχὲς ἐν ἠέρι.
>
> *On Seed, the Nature of the Child, Diseases IV* 25

104 On signs and semiosis in Greek medicine, see Manetti 1993:36–52; Thomas 2000. Signs used in the *Histories* to draw inferences: Corcella 1984; Darbo-Peschanski 1987:137–157; Manetti 1993.

105 Cf. *Histories* 2.33.2: καὶ ὡς ἐγὼ συμβάλλομαι τοῖσι ἐμφανέσι τὰ μὴ γινωσκόμενα τεκμαιρόμενος, "As I conjecture on the basis of *tekmêria*, putting together things unseen with things apparent."

106 Cf. Manetti 1993:41–43.

107 Cf. e.g. *Histories* 2.104.4: μέγα μοι καὶ τόδε τεκμήριον.

108 Cf. also *On Sensations* 1: ὅσα δὲ τοὺς χειροτέχνας εἰκὸς ἐπίστασθαι καὶ προσφέρειν καὶ διαχειρίζειν, περὶ δὲ τούτων καὶ τῶν λεγομένων καὶ τῶν ποιευμένων οἷόν τε εἶναι τὸν ἰδιώτην γνώμῃ τινὶ ξυμβάλλεσθαι, "As for those things which it is reasonable for practitioners to know, apply, and manage, concerning these ideas and actions the layman [ought] to be able to come up with a conjecture using his judgment." Kühn and Fleischer 1989 (s.v. συμβάλλω III.2) list a total of seven instances in the corpus.

> All winds come about from water: on this point one may conjecture that it is so, for in every case winds proceed from all rivers and from clouds, and clouds are water held together in the air.

The common persona of the writers, polemical, defiant, and self-confident (cf. for example the beginning of *On Ancient Medicine*[109] or *On the Sacred Disease*), also reminds one of Herodotus. In particular, their use of the performative future of φράζω to introduce an explanation of phenomena, seen also in the fragments of Herakleitos discussed above, strikes a reader of the *Histories* as familiar (see ch. 1.2.2.2 above). The author of *Airs, Winds, and Places* is particularly fond of this construction, using it six times in all, e.g., ὅκως δὲ χρὴ ἕκαστα τῶν προειρημένων σκοπέειν καὶ βασανίζειν, ἐγὼ φράσω σαφέως (3), "I will clearly show how one should observe and test each of the above-mentioned things."

Herodotus' interest in signs and the particular narrative persona that he cultivates in this regard thus find parallels in a number of areas. The technical terminology of Herodotus explored in Part 1 of this book clearly and unmistakably shows him quite at home in the fifth-century Ionian scientific tradition, but he is simultaneously part of a tradition rich in sign interpretation and manipulation that extends back to the Archaic period.[110] Yet he is neither archaism nor archaizer, but fully a creature of his time.[111] Here I think Nagy's formulation of Herodotus as the "master of speech," referred to above, is useful. He argues that the figure of the poet, the "master of song," who delivers praise (*kleos*) and, together with this praise, warning and advice, *ainos*, stands not as a source for what he sees as Herodotus' similar concern with *kleos* and *ainos*, but actually represents a parallel tradition in which the "master of song" stands alongside the "master of speech."[112] Thus the similarities between Herodotus' persona and the poetic persona have a natural and organic cause.

[109] *On Ancient Medicine* 1: ὁκόσοι ἐπεχείρησαν περὶ ἰητρικῆς λέγειν ἢ γράφειν . . . καταφανέες εἰσὶν ἁμαρτάνοντες, "All those who have tried to speak or write about medicine . . . are manifestly wrong."

[110] On Herodotus and the Ionian scientific tradition and the medical writers, see Barth 1964, Müller 1981, Manetti 1993:36–52, Thomas 2000, Raaflaub 2002.

[111] I am attempting to avoid the fate Herodotus is sometimes subjected to, as described by Bakker (2002:11) in his investigation of the term *apodexis*: "Herodotus could hardly have been pulled in two more different directions. Against Thomas' modern scientific Herodotus, firmly rooted in contemporary intellectual debate, we have Nagy's conception of a prose storyteller who subsumes the preceding epic tradition."

[112] Nagy 1987 and 1990b, esp. 215–225. Nagy suggests that this title in fact corresponds to the Greek term *logios* (cf. e.g. *Histories* 1.1.1; Pindar *Pythian* 1.94; *Nemean* 6.45), which he understands as corresponding to *aoidos*, "master of song" (here Pindar *Pythian* 1.94, καὶ λογίοις καὶ ἀοιδοῖς, which groups the two, is a key passage). For criticism of the use of *logios* in this sense,

It is clear by now whence I derive part of the title of my work. The appellation of "master" (or a variation on this) has been applied a number of times to Herodotus in recent scholarship.[113] This is in fact a reflection of the impact Herodotus' distinctive narrative persona has had on his readers. This persona, or "voiceprint," is marked by its confidence, control, and authority: Dewald has termed it the "expert's persona" (2002:268, 288).[114] Apart from presenting the semiotic activities of others, Herodotus himself acts as transmitter and reader of signs, providing interpretations of oracles, dreams, portents, human behavior, and objects alike, transmitting these to his audience.[115] It is he who is able to give an interpretation of the oracle given to the Siphnians which they themselves could not understand (3.58.1).[116] He becomes in effect the φράδμων ἀνήρ (3.57.4) that the Pythia calls for, supplying his audience with the key to the "wooden ambush" and "red herald" by explaining that in previous times ships used to have prows colored with ochre. It is also Herodotus in his own right who decodes the "easily interpretable" (εὐσύμβλητον, 7.57.1) portent of a mare giving birth to a hare, a *teras* that Xerxes on his way to cross the Hellespont ignores. He provides an interpretation of how the dream of Polykrates' daughter corresponds to the circumstances of his death (3.125.4), and gives a detailed reconstruction through the eyes of Likhas (κατὰ τοιόνδε τι

see Luraghi 2009, who concludes (456): "It is true that essentially most of the positive qualities of being λόγιος apply to Herodotus himself: his statements about the gods and human destiny imply a claim to wisdom, and the *Histories* as a whole are a hugely impressive display of knowledge. And yet, it would be wrong to say that he intended to depict himself as a λόγιος. In critically comparing and scrutinizing the traditions of different peoples, he acts as a practitioner of a knowledge that is emphatically non-local and therefore impartial and superior. The authority he claims for himself is based on ἱστορίη, a more comprehensive and complex practice that puts him on a different and higher level than any group of λόγιοι."

113 Apart from Nagy's use of the term, cf. Hartog's aretalogy (1988:370): "He is the master of seeing, the master of knowing, the master of believing, through his use of all the figures and procedures of a rhetoric of otherness set in motion by the deployment of all the indicators as to the source of the utterance. It is he who names, who lists, who classifies, who counts, who measures, who surveys, who sets things in order, who marks out limits, who distributes praise and blame, who knows more than he lets on, who remembers: he knows. He makes things seen, he makes known, he makes us believe."

114 The term "voiceprint" is taken from Fowler (1996:70). On the narrative persona of Herodotus, see Dewald 1987 and 2002, Marincola 1987, Lateiner 1989, and in particular Thomas 2000: 214–227 on the polemical character of this persona.

115 Cf. Munson (2005:30–63) on the figure of what she terms "Herodotus the *hermêneus*." She examines passages where "Herodotus asserts his authority as interpreter by translating foreign words" and instances of what she terms "metanarrative glosses."

116 On Herodotus as interpreter of oracles, cf. Darbo-Peschanski 1987:81: "C'est alors que l'enquêteur apparait comme un chresmologue, mais du passé, herméneute paradoxal de prévisions portant sur des faits révolus et dont l'interprétation prend, par là même, la force de l'évidence."

εἰκάζων, 1.68.4) of just how the oracle about the bones of Orestes relates to the surroundings of the bones the latter discovers (1.67.4–1.68.4). As transmitter and decoder he frequently uses in the first-person singular verbs specifically connected with the transmission of signs.[117] He retains a tight control over names, boasting of his knowledge and ability to name many of them, singling out some, while refusing at times to transmit others,[118] thus depriving their bearers of the *kleos* which he considers it his duty to provide to those who have shown ἔργα μεγάλα τε καὶ θωμαστά.[119] Also highly characteristic of this approach is the argument based on signs, phenomena in the real world that are taken as manifestations of the unseen.[120] With this capability Herodotus is able to investigate the past, to arbitrate, to deliver praise (*kleos*) and blame where it is due, and together with this, to deliver warning and advice (*ainos*). A persona thus emerges of one who is involved in every aspect of the transmission and interpretation of signs, one who both admires and celebrates the ingenuity of figures engaging in this activity within the *Histories* and who proudly draws attention to his own capability: a master of signs.

[117] On Herodotus' first-person use of the verbs σημαίνω, φράζω, συμβάλλομαι, see chs 1.2.1.2, 1.2.2.2, 1.3.1.1. On Herodotus' use of the first person in general, see Thomas 2000:235–248; Dewald 1987; Marincola 1987; Lateiner 1989. Herodotus as narrator and the verb σημαίνω: Hartog 1988:355n140, 366, 377; Nagy 1990b:233, 259.

[118] Herodotus relays e.g. the names of the *aristoi* at the battles of Marathon (6.114), Artemision (8.17), Thermopylai (7.224–228), Salamis (8.93), Plataiai (9.71–75): cf. in general ch. 2.6 above. Deliberate withholding of names and hence denial of fame and glory is shown in his omission of the names of the three Greeks wanting to become "marked" (ἐπίσημοι) for their *sophiê* and their theories about the flooding of the Nile in summer (2.20.1), discussed in ch. 1.2.1.2 and ch. 2.6.2 above.

[119] On Herodotus as subsumer of the authority of poetic memory and the Muses, see Darbo-Peschanski 1987:162; Bakker 2002:28. In his discussion of *apodexis* in the *Histories*, Bakker notes that "*apodexis* is not only the *accomplishment* of great deeds, but also their *recording*, which cannot fail to become a great accomplishment itself, a *mega ergon*, in the process."

[120] Key words in Herodotus' arguments and proofs using signs are τεκμήριον, μαρτύριον, and the verbal forms μαρτυρέει μοι, as well as τεκμαίρομαι, συμβάλλομαι, and εἰκάζω. On the use of signs in reasoning, see Darbo-Peschanski 1987:139–144; Manetti 1993; Thomas 2000:168–212.

Appendix

Instances of Trickery in Herodotus' *Histories*

Appendix: Instances of Trickery in Herodotus' *Histories*

Trick	*Trickster Vocabulary*	*Manipulation of signs?*	*Successful?*	*Sign Type*	*Stage of Signification Process*
1.21.1–22.3 Thrasyboulos tricks Alyattes into thinking Miletos has plenty of food	μηχανᾶται 1.21.1	no	yes		
1.59.3–6 Peisistratos mutilates himself as if attacked	μηχανᾶται τοιάδε 1.59.3 ὁ δὲ δῆμος . . . ἐξαπατηθείς 1.59.5	yes	yes	object (body as signfier)	transmission
1.60.3–5 Phye and Peisistratos	μηχανῶνται 1.60.3	yes	yes	object (body and clothing as signifiers)	transmission
1.80.2 Kyros' trick of using camels against Lydian cavalry		no	yes		
1.96.2–98.2 Deiokes' ruse to get power	ἀνὴρ σοφός 1.96.2	no	yes		
1.123.4 Harpagos and message in the hare	ἐπιτεχνᾶται τοιόνδε 1.123.3	yes	yes	object (gift)	transmission
1.125.1–6 Kyros' rise to power: forges letter from Astyages	ἐφρόντιζε ὅτεῳ τρόπῳ σοφωτάτῳ Πέρσας ἀναπείσει ἀπίστασθαι 1.125.1	yes	yes	object (seal, writing)	transmission
1.187.1–5 Babylonian Nitokris and the trick grave	ἀπάτην τοιήνδε τινὰ ἐμηχανήσατο 1.187.1	no	yes		
1.191.1–6 Kyros takes Babylon by trick of diverting river		no	yes		

1.207.6–7 Kroisos' advice to Kyros to trick Massagetai with wine	τοιούτῳ φαρμάκῳ δολώσας 1.212.2 (Tomyris)	no	yes		
2.100.2–4 Egyptian Nitokris and flooding chamber	δόλῳ διαφθεῖραι 2.100.2	no	yes		
2.121.α.1 Architect of Rhampsinitos' treasury	τὸν δὲ ἐργαζόμενον ἐπιβουλεύοντα τάδε μηχανᾶσθαι 2.121.α.1	no	yes		
2.121.δ.1–6 Master thief tricks guards to retrieve his brother's body	ἐπιτεχνήσασθαι τοιάδε 2.121.δ.1	no	yes		
2.121.ε.1–3 Rhampsinitos devises way to trick master thief		no	yes		
2.121.ε.3–5 Master thief outwits Rhampsinitos again	πολυτροπίῃ 2.121.ε.3, πολυφροσύνῃ, τόλμῃ 2.121.ζ.1	no	yes		
2.133.1–5 Mykerinos and the oracle: Mykerinos makes 6 years into 12 by making nights into days with light	ταῦτα δὲ ἐμηχανᾶτο 2.133.5	yes	?	oracle	reception
2.162.1 Soldier places helmet on Amasis' head, declares him king		yes	yes	object, gesture	transmission
2.172.1–5 Amasis and golden *podaniptêr*	μετὰ δὲ σοφίῃ αὐτοὺς ὁ Ἄμασις, οὐκ ἀγνωμοσύνῃ, προσηγάγετο 2.172.2	yes	yes	object	transmission

Trick	*Trickster Vocabulary*	*Manipulation of signs?*	*Successful?*	*Sign Type*	*Stage of Signification Process*
3.1.3–5 Amasis tricks Kambyses by passing off Apries' daughter as his own	διαβεβλημένος 3.1.4	no	yes		
3.4.1–2 Phanes outsmarts Amasis' guards by getting them drunk	σοφίῃ γάρ μιν περιῆλθε ὁ Φάνης 3.4.2	no	yes		
3.16.6 Amasis' final trick: has someone else's corpse placed in his tomb to foil Kambyses		no	yes		
3.61 Pseudo-Smerdis		yes	yes (but see next entry)	object (body), name	transmission
3.69.3 Otanes uses absence of ears to identify pseudo-Smerdis		no	yes		
3.85.1–3.86.2 Dareios and groom artificially produce agreed-upon sign: horse neighs	σοφίην, μηχανῶ 3.85.1 φάρμακα, σόφισμα, μηχανᾶσθαι 3.85.2	yes	yes	portent	transmission
3.123.2 Oroites tricks Maiandrios, messenger of Polykrates, into thinking he has great wealth		no	yes		
3.128.2–5 Bagaios, body-guards, and killing of Oroites	τάδε ἐμηχανήσατο, σοφίῃ καὶ μὴ βίῃ 3.127.2	yes	yes	object, writing	transmission

3.130.1–2 Dareios and Demokedes		no	yes		
3.153.1–158.2 Zopyros mutilates himself	δόλον . . . ἐξέφαινε 3.158.2	yes	yes	object (body)	transmission
4.134.3 Dareios' scheme (following Gobryas) to leave Scythia secretly		no	yes		
4.139.2 Histiaios tricks Scythians into thinking Ionians are destroying bridge over Istros.		no	yes		
4.146.4 Wives of Minyai exchanging clothes with husbands to get them out of jail	δόλον 4.146.3	yes	yes	object (clothing)	transmission
4.154.3 Etearkhos uses open-ended oath on Themision	ἀπατῇ 4.154.4	yes	yes	oath	transmission
4.154.4 Themision's counter-manipulation		yes	yes	oath	reception
4.201.1–3 Manipulation of oath by Amasis the Persian	δόλῳ 4.201.1	yes	yes	oath	transmission
5.12.1–13.3 Two Paionian brothers aim for tyranny, device of sister		no	no		
5.20.1–5 Alexander dresses men as women, who kill Persians at banquet		yes	yes	clothing	transmission

Trick	*Trickster Vocabulary*	*Manipulation of signs?*	*Successful?*	*Sign Type*	*Stage of Signification Process*
5.24.1–25.1 Dareios tricks Histiaios into leaving Miletos and coming to Sardis and Susa		no	yes		
5.35.3 Histiaios and the tattooed head of the messenger		yes	yes	object (body)	transmission
5.49.1–50.3 Aristagoras tries to deceive Kleomenes with map	σοφός, διαβάλλων 5.50.2	yes	no	object	transmission
5.63.1 Corruption of Pythia, Alkmaionidai and Kleisthenes (cf. 5.66.1)	μηχανή 6.123.1	yes	yes	oracle	transmission
5.106.3–107 Histiaios tricks Dareios	διέβαλλε 5.107	no	yes		
6.62.1–2 Ariston's manipulation of oath	μηχανᾶται δὴ τοιάδε 6.62.1 τῇς ἀπάτης τῇ παραγωγῇ 6.62.2	yes	yes	oath	transmission
6.65.3 Leotykhides swears falsely in public oath		no	yes		
6.66.1–3 Kleomenes and Kobon corrupt Pythia		yes	yes	oracle	transmission
6.77.3 Argives detect and make use of Spartan signals		yes	yes	military signal	reception

6.78.1–2 Kleomenes' counter-manipulation and change of code		yes	yes	military signal	transmission
6.79.1–2 Kleomenes tricks Argives into coming out of hiding		no	yes		
6.125.3–5 Alkmeon and gold dust		no	yes		
6.115, 6.121–124 Flashing shield shown at Marathon to Persian fleet as sign to sail to Athens		no	no	military signal	
7.6.3 Onomakritos inserts false oracles into collection of Musaios		yes	no	oracle	transmission
7.6.4 Onomakritos at Susa recites oracles selectively		yes	yes	oracle	transmission
7.15.3 Artabanos wears Xerxes' clothing in order that the same dream appear to him		yes	yes	object (clothing)	transmission
7.239.3 Demaratos and the wax tablet	μηχανᾶται τοιάδε 7.239.3	yes	yes	object	transmission
8.5.1–3 Themistokles tricks Eurybiades and Adeimantos into staying, keeps remainer of money for himself		no	yes		
8.22.1–3 Themistokles uses inscription to invite Ionians to desert		yes	yes	writing	transmission

Trick	*Trickster Vocabulary*	*Manipulation of signs?*	*Successful?*	*Sign Type*	*Stage of Signification Process*
8.24.1–25.2 Xerxes' ruse to conceal true number of dead		no	no		
8.27.3 Tellias uses chalk on Phocians for mutual identification	σοφίζεται . . . τοιόνδε 8.27.3	yes	yes	object (body)	transmission
8.28 Phocians devise trap for Thessalian cavalry		no	yes		
8.75.1–3 Themistokles' secret message to Xerxes		no	yes		
8.87.2–4 Artemisia sinks an allied ship to fool Greek pursuer and Xerxes		no	yes		
8.109.1–5 Themistokles talks Athenians out of immediate pursuit of Persians to Hellespont	διέβαλλε 8.110.1	no	yes		
8.137.5 Perdikkas and the circle of sun		yes	yes	gesture	reception
9.33.4–5 Teisamenos gets Spartans to make him and brother citizens		no	yes		
9.34.1–2 Melampous gets the Argives to give him and brother part of kingdom		no	yes		

9.94.1–3 People of Apollonia cheat Euenios out of full compensation		no	yes		
9.98.2–4 Leotykhidas imitates Themistokles (8.22.1–3) re Ionians		no	yes		
9.110.2–112 Amestris' manipulation of traditional Persian birthday promise		yes	yes	oath	transmission
9.116.2–3 Artayktes uses ambiguous words: pays lip service to truth	διεβάλετο 9.116.2	yes	yes	ainetic speech	transmission
9.120.2–4 Artayktes interprets portent: attempts to secure own release		yes	no	portent	reception

Bibliography

Aly, W. 1969. *Volksmärchen, Sage und Novelle bei Herodot und seinen Zeitgenossen.* Göttingen.

Armayor, O. K. 1978. "Herodotus' Persian Vocabulary." *Ancient World* 1:147–156.

Asheri, D. 1989. *Erodoto. Le Storie. Libro I. La Lidia e la Persia.* Milan.

——. 1990. *Erodoto. Le Storie. Libro III. La Persia.* Milan.

Asheri, D., Lloyd, A. B., Corcella, A., Murray, O., Moreno, A. 2007. *A Commentary on Herodotus. Books 1–4.* Oxford.

Audring, G. 1981. "*Proastion*: Zur Funktion der stadtnahen Landzone archaischer Poleis." *Klio* 63:215–231.

Austin, J. L. 1962. *How to Do Things with Words.* New York.

Austin, N. 1972. "Name Magic in the *Odyssey*." *Classical Antiquity* 5:1–19.

Bakker, E. 2002. "The Making of History: Herodotus' *historiês apodexis*." In: Bakker et al. 2002:3–32.

Bakker, E., De Jong, I., Van Wees, H. (eds.). 2002. *Brill's Companion to Herodotus.* Leiden.

Baragwanath, E. 2008. *Motivation and Narrative in Herodotus.* Oxford.

Barth, H. 1964. "Einwirkungen der vorsokratischen Philosophie auf die Herausbildung der historiographischen Methoden Herodots." In: H.-J. Diesner (ed.), *Neue Beiträge zur Geschichte der Alten Welt*, 2.173–183. Berlin.

Beck, I. 1971. *Die Ringkomposition bei Herodot und ihre Bedeutung für die Beweis-technik.* Hildesheim and New York.

Benardete, S. 1969. *Herodotean Inquiries.* The Hague.

Bencsik, A. 1994. *Schelmentum und Macht: Studien zum Typus σοφὸς ἀνήρ bei Herodot.* Bonn.

Benveniste, E. 1969. *Le vocabulaire des institutions indo-européennes.* Paris.

Bichler, R. 1985. "Die 'Reichsträume' bei Herodot: Eine Studie zu Herodots schöpferischer Leistung und ihre quellenkritische Konsequenz." *Chiron* 15:125–147.

Bierl, A. 2009. *Ritual and Performativity: The Chorus of Old Comedy*. Tr. A. Hollmann. Hellenic Studies 20. Washington, D.C.

Björk, G. 1964. "ONAR IDEIN: De la perception du rêve chez les anciens." *Eranos* 44:306–314.

Bloch, R. 1963. *Les prodiges dans l'antiquité classique*. Paris.

Boedeker, D. 1988. "Protesilaos and the End of Herodotus' *Histories*." *Classical Antiquity* 7:30–48.

——. 2002. "Epic Heritage and Mythical Patterns in Herodotus." In: Bakker et al. 2002:97–116.

Bottéro, J. 1982. "L'Oniromancie en Mésopotamie ancienne." *Ktema* 7:5–18.

Bouché-Leclerq 1879–1882. *Histoire de la divination dans l'antiquité*. Paris.

Bowden, H. 2003. "Oracles for Sale." In: Derow and Parker 2003:256–274.

——. 2005. *Classical Athens and the Delphic Oracle*. Cambridge.

Brandt, H. 1998. "Pythia, Apollon und die älteren griechischen Tyrannen." *Chiron* 28:193–212.

Braund, D. 1998. "Herodotus on the Problematics of Reciprocity." In: C. Gill, N. Postlethwaite, and R. Seaford (eds.), *Reciprocity in Ancient Greece*, 159–180. Oxford.

Breed, B. 1999. "Odysseus Back Home and Back from the Dead." In: M. Carlisle and O. Levaniouk (eds.), *Nine Essays on Homer*, 137–161. Lanham, Md.

Bremmer, J. 1996. "The Status and Symbolic Capital of the Seer." In: R. Hägg (ed.), *The Role of Religion in the Early Greek Polis*, 97–109. Stockholm.

Burkert, W. 1979. *Structure and History in Greek Mythology and Ritual*. Berkeley.

——. 1985a. "Herodot über die Namen der Götter: Polytheismus als historisches Problem." *Museum Helveticum* 42:121–132.

——. 1985b. *Greek Religion*. Cambridge, Mass.

——. 1990. "Herodot als Historiker fremder Religionen." In: G. Nenci (ed.), *Hérodote et les peuples non grecs*, 1–32. Geneva.

——. 1992. *The Orientalizing Revolution: Near Eastern Influence on Greek Culture in the Early Archaic Age*. Tr. M. Pinder and W. Burkert. Cambridge, Mass.,

——. 1996. *Creation of the Sacred: Tracks of Biology in Early Religions*. Cambridge, Mass.

Cairns, D. L. 1996. "'Off with Her ΑΙΔΩΣ': Herodotus 1.8.3–4." *Classical Quarterly* 46: 78–83.

Calame, C. 2003. *Myth and History in Ancient Greece: The Symbolic Creation of a Colony*. Tr. D. Berman. Princeton.

Camerer, L. 1965. *Praktische Klugheit bei Herodot: Untersuchungen zu den Begriffen μηχανή, τέχνη, σοφίη*. Tübingen.

Cameron, H. D. 1970. "The Power of Words in the *Seven Against Thebes*." *Transactions of the American Philological Association* 101:95–118.

Carpenter, R. 1956. "A Trans-Saharan Caravan Route in Herodotus." *American Journal of Archaeology* 60:231–242.

Casevitz, M. 1982. "Les mots du rêve en grec ancien." *Ktema* 7:67–73.

Ceccarelli, P. 1993. "La fable des poissons de Cyrus (Hérodote, I, 141): Son origine et sa fonction dans l'économie des Histoires d'Hérodote." *Métis* 8:29–57.

Chamberlain, D. 1999. "On Atomics Onomastic and Metarrhythmic Translations in Herodotus." *Arethusa* 32:263–312.

Chiasson, C. 1979. *The Question of Tragic Influence on Herodotus*. Diss. Yale.

———. 1986. "The Herodotean Solon." *Greek, Roman, and Byzantine Studies* 27:249–262.

Chuvin, P. 1991. *Mythologie et géographie dionysiaques*. Clermont-Ferrand.

Colakis, M. 1986. "The Laughter of the Suitors in *Odyssey* 20." *Classical World* 79: 137–141.

Colvin, S. 1999. *Dialect in Aristophanes and the Politics of Language in Ancient Greek*. Oxford.

Cook, J. M. 1983. *The Persian Empire*. London.

Corcella, A. 1984. *Erodoto e l'analogia*. Palermo.

———. 1993. *Erodoto. Le Storie. Libro IV. La Scizia e la Libia*. Milan.

Crahay, R. 1956. *La littérature oraculaire chez Hérodote*. Paris.

Darbo-Peschanski, C. 1987. *Le discours du particulier: Essai sur l'enquête hérodotéenne*. Paris.

Del Corno, D. 1966. "Contributi papirologici allo studio dell'onirocritica." *Atti dell' XI Congresso Internazionale di Papirologia*, 109–117. Milan.

Delplace, C. 1980. *Le griffon de l'archaisme à l'époque impériale: Étude iconographique et essai d'interprétation symbolique*. Bruxelles.

Denniston, J. D. 1996. *The Greek Particles*. Indianapolis.

Derow, P. and Parker, R. (eds.) 2003. *Herodotus and His World: Essays from a Conference in Memory of George Forrest*. Oxford.

Detienne, M. and Vernant, J.-P. 1978. *Cunning Intelligence in Greek Culture and Society*. Tr. J. Lloyd. Chicago.

Devereux, G. 1976. *Dreams in Greek Tragedy: An Ethno-psycho-analytical Study*. Berkeley.

——. 1995. *Cléomène le roi fou: Étude d'histoire ethnopsychanalytique*. Paris.

Dewald, C. 1985. "Practical Knowledge and the Historian's Role in Herodotus and Thucydides." In: *The Greek Historians: Literature and History. Papers Presented to A. E. Raubitschek*, 47–63. Saratoga.

——. 1987. "Narrative Surface and Authorial Voice in Herodotus' *Histories*." *Arethusa* 20:147–170.

——. 1993. "Significant Objects in Herodotus." In: R. Rosen and J. Farrell (eds.), *Nomodeiktes: Greek Studies in Honor of Martin Ostwald*, 55–70. Ann Arbor.

——. 1997. "Wanton Kings, Pickled Heroes, and Gnomic Founding Fathers: Strategies of Meaning at the End of Herodotus' *Histories*." In: D. Roberts, F. Dunn, and D. Fowler (eds.), *Classical Closure: Reading the End in Greek and Latin Literature*, 62–82. Princeton.

——. 2002. "'I Didn't Give My Own Genealogy': Herodotus and the Authorial Persona." In Bakker et al. 2002:267–289.

Dewald, C. and Marincola, J. 1987. "A Selective Introduction to Herodotean Studies." *Arethusa* 20:9–40.

——. (eds.). 2006. *The Cambridge Companion to Herodotus*. Cambridge.

Diels, H. 1897. *Parmenides Lehrgedicht: Griechisch und Deutsch*. Berlin.

Dierichs, A. 1981. *Das Bild des Greifen in der frühgriechischen Flächenkunst*. Münster.

Dillery, J. 2005. "Chresmologues and Manteis: Independent Diviners and the Problem of Authority." In Johnston and Struck 2005:167–231.

Dodds, E. R. 1951. *The Greeks and the Irrational*. Berkeley.

Dougherty, C. 1992. "When Rain Falls from the Clear Blue Sky: Riddles and Colonization Oracles." *Classical Antiquity* 11:28–44.

Dumézil, G. 1976. *Mythe et epopée II. Types épiques indo-européens: Un héros, un sorcier, un roi*. Paris.

——. 1978. *Romans de Scythie et d'alentour*. Paris.

——. 1984. "L'Intronisation de Darius." *Acta Iranica* 23:143–149.

Edmunds, L. 1997. "The Seal of Theognis." In: L. Edmunds and R. Wallace (eds.), *Poet, Public, and Performance in Ancient Greece*, 29–48. Baltimore.

Egermann, F. 1968. "Arete und tragische Bewusstheit bei Sophokles und Herodot." In: W. Marg (ed.), *Herodot: Eine Auswahl aus der neueren Forschung*, 249–255. Munich.

Erbse, H. 1991. "Fiktion und Wahrheit im Werke Herodots." *Nachrichten der Akademie der Wissenschaften in Göttingen. Philologisch-historische Klasse* 4:131–150.

Evans, J. A. S. 1991. *Herodotus, Explorer of the Past: Three Essays*. Princeton.

Faraone, C. 1993. "Molten Wax, Spilt Wine, and Mutilated Animals: Sympathetic

Magic in Near Eastern and Early Greek Oath Ceremonies." *Journal of Hellenic Studies* 113:60–80.

Ferrari, G. 1997. "Figures in the Text: Metaphors and Riddles in the *Agamemnon*." *Classical Philology* 92:1–45.

Finlayson, R. 1995. "Women's Language of Respect: *isihlonipho sabafazi*." In: R. Mesthrie (ed.), *Language and Social History: Studies in South African Socio-linguistics*, 140–153. Cape Town.

Flower, M. A. 2008a. "The Iamidae: A Mantic Family and Its Public Image." In: B. Dignas and K. Trampedach (eds.), *Practitioners of the Divine: Greek Priests and Religious Officials from Homer to Heliodorus*, 187–206. Cambridge, Mass.

——. 2008b. *The Seer in Ancient Greece*. Berkeley.

Fohl, H. 1913. *Tragische Kunst bei Herodot*. Diss. Rostock.

Fontenrose, J. 1978. *The Delphic Oracle*. Berkeley.

Fornara, C. 1990. "Human History and the Constraint of Fate in Herodotus." In: J. W. Allison (ed.), *Conflict, Antithesis, and the Ancient Historian*, 25–45. Columbus.

Fowler, R. L. 1996. "Herodotus and His Contemporaries." *Journal of Hellenic Studies* 116:62–87.

Frisch, P. 1968. *Die Träume bei Herodot*. Meisenheim am Glan.

Garland, R. 1990. "Priests and Power in Classical Athens." In: M. Beard and J. North (eds.), *Pagan Priests: Religion and Power in the Ancient World*, 75–91. Ithaca.

Georges, P. 1994. *Barbarian Asia and the Greek Experience*. Baltimore.

Gera, D. L. 2003. *Ancient Greek Ideas of Speech, Language, and Civilization*. Oxford.

Gould, J. 1990. *Herodotus*. London.

Graf, F. 1996. *Gottesnähe und Schadenzauber: Die Magie in der griechisch-römischen Antike*. Munich.

Gray, V. 1996. "Herodotus and the Images of Tyranny: The Tyrants of Corinth." *American Journal of Philology* 117:361–389.

——. 2002. "Short Stories in Herodotus' *Histories*." In: Bakker et al. 2002:291–317.

Griffiths, A. 2001. "Kissing Cousins: Some Curious Cases of Adjacent Material in Herodotus." In: Luraghi 2001:161–178.

Groningen, van B. A. 1949. *Herodotus' Historiën*. Leiden.

Habicht, C. 1985. *Pausanias' Guide to Ancient Greece*. Berkeley.

Hall, E. 1989. *Inventing the Barbarian: Greek Self-Definition through Tragedy*. Oxford.

Halliday, W. R. 1913. *Greek Divination*. London.

Harrison, T. 2000. *Divinity and History: The Religion of Herodotus*. Oxford.

Hartog, F. 1988. *The Mirror of Herodotus*. Berkeley.

———. 1999. "'Myth into Logos': The Case of Croesus; or, the Historian at Work." In: R. Buxton (ed.), *From Myth to Reason? Studies in the Development of Greek Thought*, 183–196. Oxford.

Heesterman, J. C. 1957. *The Ancient Indian Royal Consecration. The Rājasūya Described According to the Yajus Texts and Annoted.* The Hague.

Heintz, F. 1998. "The Archaeological Context of Circus Curses." *Journal of Roman Archaeology* 11:337–342.

Henrichs, A. 1976. "Despoina Kybele: Ein Beitrag zur religiösen Namenkunde." *Harvard Studies in Classical Philology* 80:253–286.

———. 1981. "Human Sacrifice in Greek Religion: Three Case Studies." In: J. Rudhardt and O. Reverdin (eds.), *Le sacrifice dans l'antiquité* (Entretiens sur l'Antiquité Classique 27), 195–235. Geneva.

———. 1993. "The Tomb of Aias and the Prospect of Hero Cult in Sophokles." *Classical Antiquity* 12:165–180.

———. 1994. "Der rasende Gott: Zur Psychologie des Dionysos und des Dionysischen in Mythos und Literatur." *Antike und Abendland* 40:31–58.

Herrmann, P. 1993. "Inschriften von Sardeis." *Chiron* 23:233–266.

Hirsch, S. W. 1985. "Cyrus' Parable of the Fish: Sea Power in the Early Relations of Greece and Persia." *Classical Journal* 81:222–229.

Hohti, P. 1977. "ΣΥΜΒΑΛΛΕΣΘΑΙ: A Note on Conjectures in Herodotus." *Arctos* 11: 5–14.

Hollmann, A. 2000. "*Epos* as Authoritative Speech in Herodotus' *Histories*." *Harvard Studies in Classical Philology* 100:207–225.

How, W. and Wells, J. 1928. *A Commentary on Herodotus.* Oxford.

Huber, L. 1965. *Religiöse und politische Beweggründe des Handelns in der Geschichtsschreibung des Herodot.* Diss. Tübingen.

Immerwahr, H. 1954. "Historical Action in Herodotus." *Transactions of the American Philological Association* 85:16–45.

———. 1960. "'Ergon': History as a Monument in Herodotus and Thucydides." *American Journal of Philology* 81:261–290.

———. 1966. *Form and Thought in Herodotus.* Cleveland.

Jacobson, H. 1975. "The Oath of the Delian League." *Philologus* 119:256–258.

Jakobson, R. 1960. "Linguistics and Poetics." In: T. Sebeok (ed.), *Style in Language*, 350–377. Cambridge, Mass.

———. 1962. *Selected Writings.* Vol. I. The Hague.

Jakobson, R. and Halle, M. 1971. *Fundamentals of Language.* 2nd ed. The Hague.

Jameson, M. 1991. "Sacrifice before Battle." In: V. Hanson (ed.), *Hoplites: The Classical Greek Battle Experience*, 197–227. London.

Johnston, S. I. and Struck, P. (eds.). 2005. *Mantikê: Studies in Ancient Divination.* Leiden.

Jones, C. P. 1987. "Stigma: Tattooing and Branding in Graeco-Roman Antiquity." *Journal of Roman Studies* 77:139–155.

Kahn, C. 1979. *The Art and Thought of Heraclitus. An Edition of the Fragments with Translation and Commentary.* Cambridge.

Keaveney, A. 1996. "Persian Behaviour and Misbehaviour: Some Herodotean Examples." *Athenaeum* 84:23–48.

Kessels, A. H. M. 1978. *Studies on the Dream in Greek Literature.* Utrecht.

Kett, P. 1966. *Prosopographie der historischen griechischen Manteis bis auf die Zeit Alexanders des Grossen.* Erlangen.

Kirchberg, J. 1965. *Die Funktion der Orakel im Werke Herodots.* Göttingen.

Kirk, G. S. and Raven, J. E. 1963. *The Presocratic Philosophers.* Cambridge.

Klees, H. 1965. *Die Eigenart des griechischen Glaubens an Orakel und Seher. Ein Vergleich zwischen griechischer und nichtgriechischer Mantik bei Herodot.* Stuttgart.

Knippschild, S. 2002. *"Drum bietet zum Bunde die Hände": Rechtssymbolische Akte in zwischenstaatlichen Beziehungen im orientalischen und griechisch-römischen Altertum.* Stuttgart.

Köhnken, A. 1988. "Der dritte Traum des Xerxes bei Herodot." *Hermes* 116:24–40.

Koshelenko, G. A., Kruglikova, I. T. and Dolgorukov, V. S. (eds.). 1984. *Antichnye gosudarstva Severnogo Prichernomor'ia.* Moscow.

Kraay, C. 1976. *Archaic and Classical Greek Coins.* Berkeley.

Kühn, J.-H. and Fleischer, U. 1989. *Index Hippocraticus.* Göttingen.

Kuhrt, A. 1988. "The Giving of Earth and Water." In: A. Kuhrt and H. Sancissi-Weerdenburg (eds.), *Achaemenid History*, III: *Method and Theory*, 87–99. Leiden.

Kurke, L. 1995. "Herodotus and the Language of Metals." *Helios* 22:36–64.

———. 1999. *Coins, Bodies, Games, and Gold: The Politics of Meaning in Archaic Greece.* Princeton.

———. 2009. "'Counterfeit Oracles' and 'Legal Tender': The Politics of Oracular Consultation in Herodotus." *Classical World* 102:417–438.

Lallot, J. 1974. "*Xymbola kranai*: Réflexions sur la fonction du *sumbolon* dans l'*Agamemnon* d'Eschyle." *Cahiers internationaux de symbolisme* 26:39–48.

Lateiner, D. 1977. "No Laughing Matter: A Literary Tactic in Herodotus." *Transactions of the American Philological Association* 107:173–182.

———. 1987. "Non-Verbal Communication in Herodotus." *Arethusa* 20:83–119.

———. 1989. *The Historical Method of Herodotus.* Toronto.

———. 1990. "Deceptions and Delusions in Herodotus." *Classical Antiquity* 9:230–246.

Lavelle, B. M. 1991. "The Compleat Angler: Observations on the Rise of Peisistratos in Herodotus (1.59–64)." *Classical Quarterly* 41:317–324.

Legrand, Ph.-E. 1932–1954. *Hérodote, Histoires*. Paris.

Levaniouk, O. 2007. "The Toys of Dionysos." *Harvard Studies in Classical Philology* 103:165–202.

———. 2011. *Eve of the Festival: Making Myth in Odyssey 19*. Hellenic Studies 46. Washington, D.C.

Levine, D. 1982/3. "Homeric Laughter and the Unsmiling Suitors." *Classical Journal* 78:97–104.

Lévy, E. 1982. "Le rêve homérique." *Ktema* 7:23–41.

———. 1997. "Devins et oracles chez Hérodote." In: J.-G. Heintz (ed.), *Oracles et prophéties dans l'antiquité*, 345–365. Paris.

Linforth, I. M. 1924. "Herodotus' Avowal of Silence in His Account of Egypt." *University of California Studies in Classical Philology* 7.9:269–292.

Lloyd, A. B. 1989. *Erodoto. Le Storie. Libro II. L'Egitto*. Milan.

Lloyd, G. E. R. 1966. *Polarity and Analogy: Two Types of Argumentation in Early Greek Thought*. Cambridge.

———. 1979. *Magic Reason and Experience: Studies in the Origin and Development of Greek Science*. Cambridge.

———. 1992. *Polarity and Analogy: Two Types of Argumentation in Early Greek Thought*. Bristol.

Lloyd-Jones, H. 1983. *The Justice of Zeus*. Berkeley.

Loraux, N. 1993. *The Children of Athena: Athenian Ideas about Citizenship and the Division between the Sexes*. Tr. C. Levine. Princeton.

Luraghi, N. (ed.). 2001. *The Historian's Craft in the Age of Herodotus*. Oxford.

———. 2009. "The Importance of Being λόγιος." *Classical World* 102:439–456.

Macan, R. W. 1895. *Herodotus. The Fourth, Fifth, and Sixth Books*. London.

———. 1908. *Herodotus. The Seventh, Eighth, and Ninth Books*. London.

Malkin, I. 1987. *Religion and Colonization in Ancient Greece*. Leiden.

———. 1989. "Delphoi and the Founding of Social Order in Archaic Greece." *Métis* 4: 129–153.

———. 2003. "'Tradition' in Herodotus: The Foundation of Cyrene." In: Derow and Parker 2003:153–170.

Manetti, G. 1993. *Theories of the Sign in Classical Antiquity*. Tr. C. Richardson. Bloomington.

Marincola, J. 1987. "Herodotean Narrative and the Narrator's Presence." *Arethusa* 20:121–138.

Masaracchia, A. 1990. *Erodoto. La battaglia di Salamina. Libro VIII delle Storie.* Milan.

Maul, S. 2003. "Omina und Orakel. A. Mesopotamien." In: *Reallexikon der Assyriologie und Vorderasiatischen Archäologie*, 10.45–88.

Maurizio, L. 1995. "Anthropology and Spirit Possession: A Reconsideration of the Pythia's Role at Delphi." *Journal of Hellenic Studies* 115:69–86.

——. 1997. "Delphic Oracles as Oral Performances: Authenticity and Historical Evidence." *Classical Antiquity* 16:316–334.

Meuli, K. 1975. *Gesammelte Schriften.* Ed. T. Gelzer. Basel.

Mikalson, J. 2002. "Religion in Herodotus." In: Bakker et al. 2002:187–198.

——. 2003. *Herodotus and Religion in the Persian Wars.* Chapel Hill.

Müller, C. W. 1965. *Gleiches zum Gleichem: Ein Prinzip frühgriechischen Denkens.* Wiesbaden.

Müller, D. 1981. "Herodot—Vater des Empirismus?" In: G. Kurtz, D. Müller, W. Nicolai (eds.), *Gnomosyne. Menschliches Denken und Handeln in der frühgriechischen Literatur. Festschrift W. Marg*, 299–318. Munich.

Munson, R. 2001a. *Telling Wonders: Ethnographic and Political Discourse in the Work of Herodotus.* Ann Arbor.

——. 2001b. "*Ananke* in Herodotus." *Journal of Hellenic Studies* 121:30–50.

——. 2005. *Black Doves Speak: Herodotus and the Languages of Barbarians.* Hellenic Studies 9. Washington, D.C.

Müri, W. 1976. *Griechische Studien: Ausgewählte wort- und sachgeschichtliche Forschungen zur Antike.* Basel.

Nagy, G. 1979. *The Best of the Achaeans.* Baltimore.

——. 1983. "*Sêma* and *Noêsis*: Some Illustrations." *Arethusa* 16:35–55.

——. 1987. "Herodotus the *Logios*." *Arethusa* 20:175–184.

——. 1990a. *Greek Mythology and Poetics.* Ithaca.

——. 1990b. *Pindar's Homer: The Lyric Possession of the Epic Past.* Baltimore.

——. 1996. *Poetry as Performance.* Cambridge.

——. 2001. "The Sign of the Hero: A Prologue to the *Heroikos* of Philostratus." In: J. K. Berenson Maclean and E. B. Aitken (eds.), *Flavius Philostratus, Heroikos*, xv–xxxv. Atlanta.

Nenci, G. 1994. *Erodoto. Le Storie. Libro V. La rivolta della Ionia.* Milan.

Noegel, S. 2007. *Nocturnal Ciphers: The Allusive Language of Dreams in the Ancient Near East.* New Haven.

Nöth, W. 1990. *Handbook of Semiotics.* Indianapolis.

Oppenheim, A. L. 1956. *The Interpretation of Dreams in the Ancient Near East.* Philadelphia.

——. 1974. "A Babylonian Diviner's Manual." *Journal of Near Eastern Studies* 33: 197–220.

Page, D. L. 1951. "Simonidea." *Journal of Hellenic Studies* 71:133–142.

Palmer, L. 1980. *The Greek Language.* Atlantic Highlands, N.J.

Panitz, H. 1935. *Mythos und Orakel bei Herodot.* Diss. Greifswald.

Parke, H. and Wormell, D. 1956. *The Delphic Oracle.* Oxford.

Parker, R. 1983. *Miasma: Pollution and Purification in Early Greek Religion.* Oxford.

——. 1985. "Greek States and Greek Oracles." In: P. Cartledge and F. Harvey (eds.), *Crux: Essays Presented to G. E. M. de Ste Croix*, 298–326. Oxford.

Pease, A. S. 1920–1923. *M. Tulli Ciceronis de Divinatione.* 2 vols. Urbana.

Pelling, C. 1996. "The Urine and the Vine: Astyages' Dreams at Herodotus 1.107–8." *Classical Quarterly* 46:68–77.

Pellizer, E. 1993. "Periandro di Corinto e il forno freddo." In: *Tradizione e innovazione nella cultura greca da Omero all'età ellenistica. Scritti in onore di Bruno Gentili*, II.801–11. Roma.

Peradotto, J. 1969. "Cledonomancy in the *Oresteia*." *American Journal of Philology* 90: 1–21.

——. 1990. *Man in the Middle Voice: Name and Narration in the Odyssey.* Princeton.

Piérart, M. 2003. "The Common Oracle of the Milesians and the Argives (Hdt. 6.19 and 77)." In: Derow and Parker 2003:275–296.

Pohlenz, M. 1973. *Herodot: Der erste Geschichtsschreiber des Abendlandes.* Stuttgart.

Pötscher, W. 1958. "Götter und Gottheit bei Herodot." *Wiener Studien* 71:5–29.

Powell, J. E. 1937. "Puns in Herodotus." *Classical Review* 51:103–105.

Pratt, L. 1993. *Lying and Poetry from Homer to Pindar: Falsehood and Deception in Archaic Greek Poetics.* Ann Arbor.

Prier, R. 1978. "*Sema* and the Symbolic Nature of Pre-Socratic Thought." *Quaderni urbinati di cultura classica* 29:91–100.

Pritchett, W. K. 1971–1979. *The Greek State at War.* 5 vols. Berkeley.

Privitera, G. A. 1965. *Laso di Ermione.* Rome.

Pucci, P. 1996. *Enigma Segreto Oracolo.* Pisa.

Raaflaub, K. 2002. "Philosophy, Science, Politics: Herodotus and the Intellectual Trends of His Time." In Bakker et al. 2002:149–186.

Reinhardt, K. 1966. *Vermächtnis der Antike.* Göttingen.

Richards, I. A. 1979. *Principles of Literary Criticism*. New York.

Richardson, N. J. 1974. *The Homeric Hymn to Demeter.* Oxford.

Romm, J. 1994. *The Ends of the Earth in Ancient Thought: Geography, Exploration, and Fiction*. Princeton.

Rosenberger, V. 1995. "Der Ring des Polykrates im Lichte der Zauberpapyri." *Zeitschrift für Papyrologie und Epigraphik* 108:69–71.

Saïd, S. 2002. "Herodotus and Tragedy." In: Bakker et al. 2002:117–147.

Saussure, de F. 1983. *Course in General Linguistics*. C. Bally and A. Sechehaye (eds.), tr. R. Harris. London.

Schmitt, R. 1967. "Medisches und persisches Sprachgut bei Herodot." *Zeitschrift der Deutschen Morgenländischen Gesellschaft* 117:119–145.

Scholes, R. 1982. *Semiotics and Interpretation*. New Haven.

Schütrumpf, E. 1989. "Traditional Elements in the Concept of *hamartia* in Aristotle's *Poetics*." *Harvard Studies in Classical Philology* 92:137–156.

Scullion, S. 2006. "Herodotus and Greek Religion." In: Dewald and Marincola 2006: 192–208.

Sebeok, T. and Brady, E. 1979. "The Two Sons of Croesus: A Myth about Communication in Herodotus." In T. Sebeok (ed.), *The Sign and Its Masters*, 168–179, 288–290. Austin.

Shapiro, H. A. 1990. "Oracle-Mongers in Peisistratid Athens." *Kernos* 3:335–345.

Snell, B. 1973. "Gyges und Kroisos als Tragödien-Figuren." *Zeitschrift für Papyrologie und Epigraphik* 12:197–205.

Sokolowski, F. 1969. *Lois sacrées des cités grecques*. Paris.

Solmsen, F. 1982. "Two Crucial Decisions in Herodotus." In *Kleine Schriften* III, 76–109. Hildesheim.

Stahl, H. P. 1968. "Herodots Gyges-Tragödie." *Hermes* 96:385–400.

Stein, H. 1889–1896. *Herodotos erklärt von Heinrich Stein*. Berlin.

Stein, P. 1909. *ΤΕΡΑΣ*. Diss. Marburg.

Steiner, D. 1994. *The Tyrant's Writ*. Princeton.

Steinhauser, K. 1911. *Der Prodigienglaube und das Prodigienwesen der Griechen*. Diss. Tübingen.

Stockinger, H. 1959. *Die Vorzeichen im homerischen Epos: Ihre Typik und ihre Bedeutung*. Diss. Munich.

Struck, P. 2004. *Birth of the Symbol: Ancient Readers at the Limits of Their Texts*. Princeton.

———. 2005. "Divination and Literary Criticism?" In Johnston and Struck 2005: 147–165.

Svenbro, J. 1993. *Phrasikleia: An Anthropology of Reading in Ancient Greece*. Tr. J. Lloyd. Ithaca.

Thomas, R. 2000. *Herodotus in Context: Ethnography, Science, and the Art of Persuasion.* Cambridge.

van der Veen, J. E. 1996. *The Significant and the Insignificant: Five Studies in Herodotus' View of History.* Amsterdam.

van Dijk, G.-J. 1997. ΑΙΝΟΙ, ΛΟΓΟΙ, ΜΥΘΟΙ: *Fables in Archaic, Classical, and Hellenistic Greek Literature.* Leiden.

van Lieshout, R. G. A 1970. "A Dream on a καιρός of History." *Mnemosyne* 23:225–249.

——. 1980. *Greeks on Dreams.* Utrecht.

Verdenius, W. J. 1962. "ΑΙΝΟΣ." *Mnemosyne* 15:389.

Vernant, J.-P. 1974. "Paroles et signes muets." *Divination et rationalité*, 9–25. Paris.

——. 1990. *Myth and Tragedy in Ancient Greece.* Tr. J. Lloyd. New York.

Vernant, J.-P. and Vidal Naquet, P. 1990. *Myth and Tragedy in Ancient Greece.* Tr. J. Lloyd. New York.

Versnel, H. S. 1977. "Polycrates and His Ring: Two Neglected Aspects." *Studi storico-religiosi* I, 17–46.

Vinagre, M. 1996. "Die griechische Terminologie der Traumdeutung." *Mnemosyne* 49:257–282.

West, S. 1988a. *A Commentary on Homer's Odyssey. Vol. I: Introduction and Books i-viii.* Ed. A. Heubeck, S. West, J. B. Hainsworth. Oxford.

——. 1988b. "The Scythian Ultimatum (Herodotus iv 131, 132)." *Journal of Hellenic Studies* 108:207–211.

——. 2003. "Croesus' Second Reprieve and Other Tales of the Persian Court." *Classical Quarterly* 53:416–437.

Winkler, J. 1990. *The Constraints of Desire: The Anthropology of Sex and Gender in Ancient Greece.* New York.

Zeitlin, F. 1982. *Under the Sign of the Shield: Semiotics and Aeschylus' Seven Against Thebes.* Rome.

Index Locorum

Index of Greek Words

Subject Index